What's COOKING?

What's Cooking?

**MORE THAN TWO THOUSAND RECIPES
TO VARY YOUR EVERYDAY COOKING**

TORMONT

Design and Production

Communiplex Marketing Inc.

Project Director

Rolande Dussault

Project and Cuisine Coordinator

Chef Yvan Bélisle

Photography

Michel Bodson

Stylist

Murielle Bodson

Food Preparation

Chef Michel Simonnet

Nutrition and Health

Claire Robillard, P.Dt.

Contributing Editors

Jane Brierley
Marie-Carole Daigle
Angela Rahaniotis

Computer Editor

Martine Lamarche

Legal deposit: 2nd quarter 1990

Bibliothèque nationale du Québec

National Library of Canada

Published by
Tormont Publications Inc.
338 St Antoine St. East
Montreal, Canada H2Y 1A3
Tel: (514) 954-1441
Fax: (514) 954-1443

ISBN 2-921171-34-1
Printed in the USA

FOREWORD

What's Cooking? is an innovative cookbook designed especially for the everyday cook.

The widescale changes in our modern style of living have profoundly altered our eating and cooking habits. With the accelerated pace of life, we are often hard-pressed merely to find the time to sit down and share a pleasant moment with family and friends.

This cookbook is your passport to planning and preparing appetizing and nourishing meals with confidence and ease, enabling you to create a hospitable and enjoyable atmosphere at your table.

What's Cooking? provides not only recipes, but helpful hints and advice on cooking techniques that make the most of everything you prepare. With nearly 2,000 recipes and variations to choose from, you'll never be stuck for an answer when people ask, "What's cooking?"

We hope this book will help you rediscover some of our best culinary traditions, accented with a modern touch, and inspire you to practice the art of cooking every day.

Bon appetit!

WHAT'S COOKING?

People who cook day in and day out find themselves running short of ideas. Yet each day the same question arises. Most of you are familiar with the problem. Busy schedules often make it impossible to be in the kitchen for hours at a stretch. Mealtime looms and the fridge is full of good things, but somehow on closer inspection they seem unlikely to go together—a few vegetables, some leftovers, a little cheese. What can you do about it?

You'd like to serve meals that are not only well-balanced, but pleasing to the eye and good to eat.

What's Cooking? is overflowing with ideas that will stimulate your culinary creativity and tempt you to try new food combinations. The recipes provide a course in practical cooking techniques, along with dozens of variations and time-saving hints, all brought together in this book with just one thing in mind: to help you respond quickly and easily to the eternal question, "What's cooking?"

You'll soon realize that with a little imagination it's often possible to perform miracles!

WHAT'S IN IT FOR YOU?

Preparing and sharing food with family and friends can be a source of pleasure and fulfillment for all concerned. The trick is to find the key to imaginative, tasty cooking based on simple procedures that can be easily varied.

This book is based on the theory that people enjoy food that looks appetizing, smells enticing, and, last but not least, tastes delicious. We want readers to take a second look at familiar foods and learn about new or unusual dishes.

With this in mind, we've illustrated our recipes with over eight hundred full-color photographs showing attractively prepared and served dishes.

In the first part of the book, we discuss the art of blending food flavors and textures with seasonings and condiments, how to cook and keep food, and what you should know about the nutritional elements involved.

You can use *What's Cooking?* as a handy reference guide for planning wholesome menus and appealing snacks or short-order treats for unexpected guests.

CONTENTS

86

Beef

126

Veal

148

Lamb

168

Pork

200

Game

210

Fish

246

Vegetables

312

Salads

340

Pasta

354

Cereals

366

Breads

378

Dairy Products

394

Eggs

408

Tofu, Nuts and Seeds

420

Soups

442

Sauces

460

Desserts

504

Glossary

505

Index

THE ART OF COOKING

"There's no accounting for taste," runs the old adage. However that may be, people enjoy discussing the pleasures of the table and what makes food taste good, whether it's a tender pie crust, a succulent roast, a fragrant soup, or a plate of fresh-baked cookies. The art of cooking depends not only on our skill in the kitchen, but on our knowledge of ingredients and techniques.

EATING AND HEALTH

Food: What's in it for you?

All the foods we eat supply us with energy, expressed in terms of calories or kilojoules. Energy needs differ with each individual, depending on height, age, weight, sex, bone structure and the intensity of physical activity, either in sports or manual labor.

If we store more energy than we need, our body mass increases. Conversely, if we eat less than our body needs, our stored fat is used up and we lose weight.

Food contains glucids (sugars), proteins, lipids (fats), vitamins, minerals, dietary fibers and water. However, only the glucids, proteins and lipids produce energy.

Glucids

Glucids are also called sugars or carbohydrates. They represent the main source of energy for the human body. You'll find them mainly in fruits and fruit juices, vegetables, milk, yogurt, bread, cereals, rice, pasta, potatoes and legumes (broad beans, etc.). Other major sources of glucids are white and brown sugars, honey, molasses, syrups, jams, candies, and other sugar treats. However, this second group contains virtually no vitamins, minerals or dietary fibers, and is therefore very low in nutritional value.

Proteins

Proteins help us build, repair, and renew body tissue. They form antibodies, elements in the blood that help us fight infection. Meat, poultry, fish and eggs are the main sources of protein. Milk and dairy products, as well as nuts, seeds, and legumes also supply protein.

Lipids

We're more familiar with the term "fats" than lipids. Despite their high calorie quotient, lipids help us absorb essential substances for good health, such as vitamins A, D, E and K. Consuming lipids gives us a feeling of having eaten well (satiety), and helps maintain our body temperature.

Cholesterol is a component of lipids, and our bodies need it to function properly. Among other things, cholesterol plays a part in manufacturing Vitamin D and certain hormones. It also acts as a building block for cellular membranes. However, high levels of blood cholesterol can, in the long run, cause hardening of the arteries and cardiovascular diseases.

Here are a few recommendations designed to help lessen the danger of developing cardiovascular problems.

- Achieve and maintain an ideal weight for health.
- Stop smoking.
- Exercise regularly.
- Increase your intake of dietary fibers, particularly those found in legumes, barley, oats and fruit.
- Cut down your total intake of fats.

Where do we find fats?

Fats are found in oils, butter, margarine, vegetable fat and meat. Watch out for disguised sources of fat, such as nuts, sauces, certain cheeses, delicatessen meats, pies, cakes and pastries.

Vitamins and Minerals

Vitamins and minerals are necessary for good health. We have to get a sufficient amount of them in our food, since our bodies can't manufacture them, for the most part. Actually, they are all present in food, although in varying quantities. Let's look at how some of them work.

Vitamin A

- Aids night vision.
- Keeps skin and mucous membranes healthy.
- Helps normal development of bones and teeth.

Vitamin B (Thiamin, Riboflavin and Niacin)

- Helps the body use energy contained in food.
- Encourages normal growth and appetite.
- Helps the nervous system function properly.

Vitamin C

- Helps heal lesions and maintains healthy gums.
- Keeps the walls of blood vessels in good condition.

Vitamin D

- Helps the body use calcium and phosphorus to build and maintain healthy bones and teeth.

Calcium

- Helps build and maintain healthy bones and teeth.
- Helps normal coagulation of blood and normal functioning of the nervous system.

Iron

- Helps build red corpuscles needed for carrying oxygen.

Combinations That Promote Health

Calcium and Vitamin D

Vitamin D helps the body absorb calcium. For this reason, milk is an ideal food, because it contains both Vitamin D and calcium.

Iron and Vitamin C

Vitamin C helps the absorption of iron. If you are serving iron-rich liver, for example, include in the same meal a food rich in Vitamin C (orange, grapefruit, kiwi, cantaloup, strawberries, tomato juice or broccoli).

Dietary Fibers

Dietary fibers are vegetable components that aren't digested by the body. They help us feel full after a meal, and prevent or correct constipation. The fibers in such foods as legumes, barley and fruit are known to help decrease blood cholesterol levels. There are a number of other sources of fiber, including vegetables, breads, and whole-grain cereals.

Water

The human body is 65% water. This water acts as a means of transportation for nutritive elements, and helps the body eliminate waste matter. Water also acts as a body temperature regulator.

All foods contain a certain percentage of water. As a general rule, the higher this percentage, the less energy (i.e., fewer calories) the food provides.

Alcohol

Alcoholic drinks supply the body with a great deal of energy, despite their low nutritional value. Alcohol is also recognized for its ability to stimulate the appetite as well as reduce the speed of reflex actions or the ability to concentrate, particularly on an empty stomach. Drinks before a meal are a good example of this phenomenon. Alcohol abuse can damage the nervous system, cause ulcers, or lead to cirrhosis of the liver, a chronic liver disease. In the long run, alcohol abuse can lead to substituting alcohol for more nutritious food, and result in social and economic problems.

Table 1

Percentage of Water and Energy Value of Certain Foods

Food	Quantity	Percentage Water	Calories	Kilojoules
Sugar	100 g	0.5	385	1611
All-purpose White Flour	100 g	12	364	1523
Creamed Cottage Cheese	100 g	79	103	433
Celery	100 g	94.7	16	65
Iceberg Lettuce	100 g	95.9	13	53

Table 2

Components of Some Alcoholic Drinks

Drinks	Quantity	Glucids (Grams)	Alcohol (Grams)	Energy Value (Calories)	(Kilojoules)
Red Wine or Dry White Wine (12 % alcohol)	3 ½ oz (100 mL)	0	9	63	260
Spirits (gin, rum, vodka, whisky)	1 ½ oz (45 mL)	0	15	105	440
Regular Beer	12 oz (340 mL)	10 to 13	15	150	630
Light Beer	12 oz (340 mL)	8	11	110	460

Table 3

Energy Value of Food Components

Food Components	Calories per g	Kilojoules per g
Glucids	4	17
Proteins	4	17
Lipids	9	37

Table 4

Main Nutrients in Food Groups

Nutrients	Milk and Milk Products	Breads and Cereals	Fruits and Vegetables	Meat, Fish Poultry and Substitutes
Glucids	✓	✓	✓	
Proteins	✓			✓
Lipids	✓			✓
Vitamin A	✓		✓	✓ (organs)
Vitamin B	✓	✓		✓
Vitamin C			✓	
Vitamin D	✓			
Iron		✓	✓	✓
Calcium	✓			
Water	✓	✓	✓	✓

A Question of Weight?

Many people are dissatisfied with their present weight and would like to become thinner. It's a preoccupation especially common among women, and the reason is not hard to understand. Advertising is constantly pitching the image of the gracefully slender young woman. But losing weight for the purpose of looking like a model is not always very realistic. Some women even adopt dietary habits that are quite dangerous for their health.

How Much Should You Weigh?

According to the new concept of "healthy weight," each person has his or her optimum weight range. To find out whether your present weight falls within this range, calculate your BMI (Body Mass Index) according to the charts on the right and on the opposite page. This index applies to men and women between the ages of 20 and 60. It can apply to the under-20 group as well, as long as body growth is complete (from 18 up). The BMI doesn't apply to children, adolescents, pregnant women, or people over 65.

Calculating your BMI makes it possible to determine the risk of developing health problems associated with obesity or excessive thinness. If your BMI is outside the healthy weight range, you should consult a physician and dietician/nutritionist to help change certain eating and living habits. If, on the other hand, your BMI is within the healthy weight range, everything is fine.

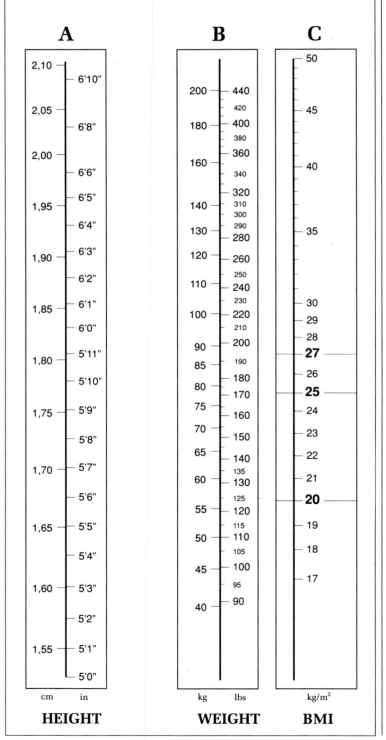

Body Mass Index

How to find your BMI—it's easy
1. Mark an X at your height on line A.
2. Mark an X at your weight on line B.
3. Take a ruler and join the two X's.
4. To find your BMI, extend the line to line C.

Diet Foods

Many people wrongly believe that diet food means slimming food. Eating diet food doesn't necessarily lead to weight loss, however, since the energy component in the particular food may not be reduced.

By definition, a diet food is one in which a single or several components, such as sugars, fats, salt, or calories, have been altered. In some countries, manufacturers are obliged by law to label diet products under specific headings, for example:

Reduced Sugar Foods

These are reduced in glucids (sugars) but not in calories.

Examples: Biscuits, candies and chocolate

Sugarless Foods

These contain a negligible quantity of sugar and a maximum of one calorie per 3 ½ oz (100 mL).

Examples: Sugarless soft drinks

Reduced Calorie Foods

Food in this category supplies a maximum of half the normal calories.

Example: Reduced calorie puddings

Low Calorie Foods

These supply a maximum of 15 calories per serving as listed on the label.

Examples: Low calorie jams and jellies

Low Sodium Foods

This category must not contain more than half the normal sodium content.

Examples: Low sodium peanut butter, soups, tomato juice

Low Fat Foods

This heading includes food with reduced cholesterol levels.

Example: Egg Beaters

These few explanations will help you understand that diet foods aren't simply slimming foods. What's more, they aren't essential for losing weight.

Range of Acceptable Weight

(Based on Body Mass Index)

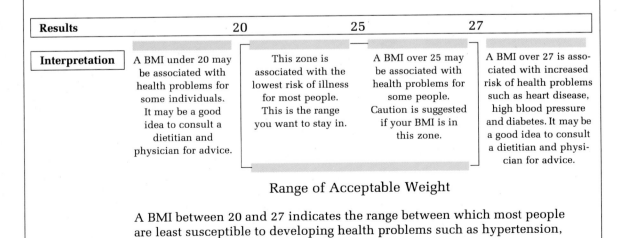

Results		20	25	27
Interpretation	A BMI under 20 may be associated with health problems for some individuals. It may be a good idea to consult a dietitian and physician for advice.	This zone is associated with the lowest risk of illness for most people. This is the range you want to stay in.	A BMI over 25 may be associated with health problems for some people. Caution is suggested if your BMI is in this zone.	A BMI over 27 is associated with increased risk of health problems such as heart disease, high blood pressure and diabetes. It may be a good idea to consult a dietitian and physician for advice.

Range of Acceptable Weight

A BMI between 20 and 27 indicates the range between which most people are least susceptible to developing health problems such as hypertension, diabetes, or cardiovascular diseases.

What About Light Foods?

The term "light" is not subject to the same regulations as "diet" in describing foods. Manufacturers are merely obliged to state how the product has been lightened—whether in texture, taste, fats, calories and so on. It's worth noting that if only the taste is light, the product's energy value is not reduced.

Read the labels. This is the only way to find out the nutritional value and to compare different products. You should be aware that sometimes it's better to buy the regular product than a light version.

How to Balance Menus

To guarantee good nutrition, you must eat foods from the following groups every day.

Milk and Milk Products

- Children under 11, 2 to 3 servings
- Teenagers, 3 to 4 servings
- Pregnant and nursing women, 3 to 4 servings
- Adults, 2 servings

Examples of 1 serving:

- 1 cup (250 mL) milk
- ¾ cup (180 mL) yogurt
- 1 ½ oz (45 g) Cheddar or soft cheese

Breads and Cereals

- 3 to 5 servings of whole or enriched grains

Examples of 1 serving:

- 1 slice of bread
- ½ cup (125 mL) cooked cereal
- ¾ cup (180 mL) ready-to-eat cereal
- ½ to ¾ cup (125 to 180 mL) cooked rice or pasta
- 1 muffin or roll

Fruits and Vegetables

- 4 to 5 servings (including at least 2 servings of vegetables)

Examples of 1 serving:

- ½ cup (125 mL) vegetables or fruits (fresh, frozen, or canned)
- ½ cup (125 mL) juice (fresh, frozen or canned)
- 1 medium potato, carrot, tomato, peach, apple, orange or banana

Meat, Fish, Poultry or Substitute

- 2 servings

Examples of 1 serving:

- 2 to 3 oz (60 to 90 g) cooked lean meat, fish, poultry or liver
- 1 cup (250 mL) cooked legumes
- 2 oz (60g) Cheddar cheese
- 2 eggs

Recommended foods supply between 100 and 1400 calories (between 4000 and 6000 kilojoules).

We suggest choosing foods that are low in fat, sugar and salt.

Buying Healthy Food And Budgeting For It

- Plan your menus in relation to weekly specials.
- Draw up your shopping list at home, and stick to it once you're in the store.
- Read product labels. Buy the food, not a brand name or a game inside a pretty package.
- Buy large packages rather than small if you have the space to store them and expect to use up the contents within a short time.
- Buy fresh fruits and vegetables in season, or use frozen or canned if they aren't available.
- Keep impulse buying to a minimum by avoiding impromptu visits to the supermarket between regular marketing days.
- Don't do your grocery shopping when you're hungry.

Reading Labels

All food products containing more than one component (soups, biscuits, cereals, and so on) must list the ingredients. However, the packaging of 100% pure, unsweetened orange juice, for example, will merely describe the single product.

Manufacturers must list ingredients in order of quantity, starting with the highest amount.

There are various ways of describing ingredients. For example, words describing sugar content include honey, malt syrup, corn syrup, and molasses. You should also look for words ending in OSE, as these generally describe sugar components. Examples include glucose, dextrose, fructose, lactose, maltose, saccharose, and levulose, among others.

It is worth noting that all these forms of sugar are energy foods with 4 calories or 17 kilojoules per 0.035 oz (1 g).

People who want to avoid salt should look for the word SODIUM on labels.

Helpful Slimming Hints

- Whole milk can be replaced with skimmed or partially skimmed milk.

- Try replacing mayonnaise with plain yogurt in dips and salad dressings.

- Choose cheeses made with skimmed or partially skimmed milk, and therefore with a reduced calorie content.

- Go easy on deep-fried or sauce-covered foods.

- Chill stocks and sauces. The fat content rises to the surface and can be easily removed.

- Contrary to what most people believe, cooking with wine doesn't mean adding surplus calories to your food. Recipes usually call for dry wine. When boiled, the alcohol evaporates, leaving only the low-calorie wine.

Food Myths

Grapefruit makes fats dissolve.

False. No food can do this, even if it is acidic. In any case, how can a food containing glucids (sugars) help in losing weight? The only way to lose weight is to reduce consumption of calories to less than your energy requirements, so that the body will be forced to burn up its fat reserves.

Bread, potatoes and pasta must be cut out of the diet of anyone wanting to lose weight.

False. It's more often the abuse of these foods and their garnishes—butter, margarine, jams, cream sauces, and sour cream—that turn them into high calorie foods.

In any case, you shouldn't forget that bread, potatoes, and pasta are important sources of vitamins and minerals.

A banana can replace a steak.

False. A fruit made basically of glucids can't replace a source of proteins and fats.

Gelatin hardens your nails.

False. Gelatin is a protein which is digested in the same way as proteins from other sources. Therefore it doesn't directly affect anything so specific as fingernails.

Cheese causes constipation.

False. Constipation is more likely to be the result of a lack of dietary fibers, water, and physical exercise.

Butter and margarine supply exactly the same number of calories.

True. However, there is a major difference between the two. Butter contains cholesterol, whereas margarine contains none.

BLENDING FLAVORS

What's Cooking? is not just a recipe book. It's a guide to the techniques and psychology of cooking. In fact, this book opens the door to a whole new philosophy of blending flavors.

Many of us tend to stick with the flavors we know —familiar but limited. Yet supermarkets and natural food stores are overflowing with all kinds of spices, herbs, fruits, vegetables, and even edible flowers.

We're stimulated not only by the look of all these good things, but by the irresistible aromas that waft by our nostrils. The question is, how are we going to use them?

Have you ever thought about the possibility of gradually introducing these new ingredients into your everyday cooking? This book will encourage you to enlarge your range of familiar tastes and to explore new blends and flavors in the meals you prepare every day for family and friends.

Odor Memory

You may be surprised to learn that by developing your odor memory, you can remember how foods taste by simply smelling them. Try rubbing an herb between thumb and forefinger. Breathe in the aroma, then taste the herb. Do this several times, concentrating on what you're doing. This is actually an exercise in olfactory memory. With practice, you'll soon be able to remember the taste of an aromatic herb.

Learn to recognize the texture and feel of food, and to take pleasure in imagining dishes or even entire menus, by blending flavors, textures, odors and shapes.

Complementary Foods

What makes a recipe turn out well, and why do some foods go together better than others?

To help you understand and become familiar with ingredients, we've drawn up a table (pages 26 and 27) showing the major food families according to intensity of flavor, from the mildest to the strongest.

Read through this table and try to imagine the odor and texture of each ingredient. Try putting some of them together, keeping in mind the following principles.

Blending Foods

• Liven up a mild meat or fish with a more robust sauce. Soften the taste of a strong vegetable with a delicate sauce.

For example, enhance the delicate flavor of chicken with a tarragon sauce.

• Don't hesitate to experiment with the proportions of spices and herbs to suit yourself, or to increase the quantity of spices to give an ethnic dish a more authentic flavor.

• Pork, a meat with a medium-strong flavor, goes very well with mandarin oranges, which have a slightly acidic quality, and a pinch of rosemary (a strong flavor) or lots of parsley (a mild flavor).

• Delicate fish will be improved by a dash of mustard, a little sorrel (faintly bitter), or the subtle flavor of a mushroom topping.

• A purée of carrots will be improved by the pronounced flavor of a pinch of savory, grated nutmeg, or a generous addition of diced zucchini.

Blending Herbs and Spices

• Spices and herbs enhance the smell and taste of food.

• It is important to learn what proportions work best.

• Mild spices and herbs can be blended successfully, since each flavor will have a chance to come through, even though all are very subtle. Be careful not to mask a mild spice with a stronger one, and learn how to balance different flavor concentrations.

Flavor Concentration

• When you use two spices or herbs of unequal strength, you can increase or decrease the proportions so that the taste of each will be equally strong or "concentrated."

For example, $^1/_2$ tsp (2 mL) of tarragon in a sauce requires twice that amount of chives (1 tsp or 5 mL) to get equal flavor concentration.

• Change the proportions in accordance with the main ingredients of the dish or garnish you are preparing.

For example, a sauce requires a greater concentration of flavor than a soup. Parsley sauce needs twice as much parsley (an herb with a low flavor concentration) as parsley soup. A sauce needs $^1/_4$ tsp (1 mL) of strong-tasting rosemary compared to a pinch for soup.

Once you understand the nature of different foods and seasonings, you'll find it easy to use up leftovers, as well as develop dishes that are appetizing, well-balanced and—above all—varied. Practice brings the confidence to experiment creatively.

Here are a few examples of unusual combinations that have met with considerable success. Try to identify their flavor concentration and to imagine the result.

Meat

• pork and mandarin oranges
• veal and kiwi
• chicken and Brie cheese
• lamb and pine nuts
• beef and grapes

Fish

• fish and mustard
• fish and pears
• fish and sorrel
• fish and celery seed
• fish and cucumber

Vegetables

• purée of turnips and apples
• broccoli and blue cheese
• avocado and coriander
• spinach and grapefruit
• carrots and honey

Salads

• brown rice and pomegranate
• watercress and pistachio nuts
• endives and wild garlic
• curly lettuce and fennel
• macaroni and smoked salmon

Spices and Aromatic Herbs

• $^1/_4$ tarragon, $^1/_2$ basil, $^1/_4$ garlic
• $^1/_3$ oregano, $^1/_3$ coriander, $^1/_3$ sage
• $^1/_2$ fennel, $^1/_4$ ginger, $^1/_4$ nutmeg
• $^1/_4$ chives, $^1/_2$ chervil, $^1/_4$ parsley

Variations and Handy Ideas

If you hesitate to experiment or feel more comfortable following a recipe, you'll find lots of encouragement in the many additional ideas and variations listed in *What's Cooking?* Make a point of looking at these as well as the introductions to each recipe. You'll soon find that, with some small touch, it's possible to transform the look and taste of numerous dishes. You'll also learn plenty of handy ideas and techniques that will make cooking easier and give you better results.

	NEUTRAL	NEUTRAL TO MILD	MILD	MILD TO MEDIUM	
Spices and Fines Herbes			Paprika Parsley • *Use freely*		
Vegetables	Iceberg lettuce • *Very flat taste*	Artichoke Avocado Cucumber Eggplant Squash Zucchini		Carrot Mushroom Parsnip Potato Boston lettuce Curly lettuce Romaine lettuce • *Fairly flat taste*	
Meat			Veal	Fish Chicken and Turkey	

MEDIUM	MEDIUM TO STRONG	STRONG	STRONG TO VERY STRONG	VERY STRONG
Basil Chervil Chives Dill Marjoram Oregano Sage • *Use for intensity of flavor* (sweet) Cinnamon Citronella Mint Nutmeg Pink peppercorns Sugar • *Use in small to medium quantities. Can lessen bitter or acid taste of certain foods*		Aniseed Bay leaf Coriander Cumin Fennel Juniper berries Rosemary Saffron Savory Tarragon Thyme Turmeric • *Use small quantities of these aromatic condiments, as they may mask other flavors*	Cayenne pepper Cloves Garlic Ginger Ground or crushed chilies Horseradish White, Black or Green pepper • *Use in small quantities as these condiments can completely mask other flavors and develop a bitter taste of their own*	
Turnip Lamb's lettuce (Corn salad) Red curly lettuce *at amer* • *Slightly bitter*	Asparagus Beet Broccoli Brussels sprouts Cauliflower Celery Corn (Cob) Fennel Fiddlehead greens Leek Snow peas Sweet pepper Tomato Yellow or Green beans • *Flavor concentration medium to strong depending on freshness and season*			Garlic Horseradish Hot pepper Onion Radish Shallot • *Very distinctive and slightly bitter taste, highly concentrated, often used to liven up food* Chicory Curled endive Endive Radicchio Watercress • *Bitter to very bitter* Sorrel Spinach • *Distinctive flavor*
Beef Pork		Lamb	Game • *Distinctive for each species*	

A PERSONAL TOUCH

Herbs and spices are the basis of the seasonings and condiments that complement and enhance our food in the kitchen or at the table.

Seasonings may be savory or sweet, but these are not the only criteria in choosing and blending herbs and spices. Seasonings are used to develop, balance, enhance or play down the taste of our food. What's more, they can make food look delicious, from the green of sprinkled parsley or a fiery dash of paprika to the soft rose of pink peppercorns.

The world of seasonings and condiments is enormously rich and varied. Most belong to the vegetable kingdom, and are classified into six main families: spices, herbs and seeds; acid condiments; bitter condiments; sweet condiments; fatty condiments; and mixed condiments.

Spices are grown all over the world, and can truly change the taste of a food. The subtle aroma of herbs, whether fresh or dried, develops a distinctive but delicate flavor in food.

Seeds, which often figure in recipes from distant lands, actually add flavor to a dish, as well as texture. The four families of condiments, if used with discretion, can liven up the most bland foods.

Get to know all the seasonings and condiments, and learn their flavors by heart. You'll then be able to add a personal touch to your recipes and transform them into dozens of new dishes.

Spices, Herbs, and Seeds

Every kitchen cupboard contains cloves, cinnamon, various salts, paprika, and chili powder. But how many unfamiliar seasonings surprise us with their delicate aroma and taste!

Paprika		Curry	
Fennel	Mint	Tarragon	Chervil
Pink pepper	Black pepper	White pepper	Green pepper
Chive		Sorrel	
Cloves	Salt	Saffron	Nutmeg
Rosemary	Savory	Thyme	Sage
Cinnamon		Bay leaves	
Basil		Parsley	

Herbs, or "fines herbes" as they are sometimes called, offer us an imposing array of aromas and flavors. All have distinctive tastes that, whether alone or combined, stimulate our taste buds and sense of smell, and increase our pleasure in eating.

Western cooking often neglects the interesting qualities of seeds. Once you have become familiar with their use, however, you'll no doubt be a keen fan.

Acid Condiments

The family of acid condiments basically consists of various vinegars (plain or aromatic), citrus juices (lemon, lime, grapefruit), and wines.

Bitter Condiments

Bitter condiments fall into three categories: vegetable seasonings (garlic, shallot, onion and leek); condiments in the proper sense (mustard, horseradish, and radishes); and bitter or aromatic condiments (lemon or orange peel, cocoa, coffee, peppers, ginger).

Sweet Condiments

Sweet condiments naturally include sugar in various forms (white and brown sugar, icing sugar, molasses, caramel), as well as various syrups, honeys, and fruit preparations that go with certain dishes (ketchup, chutney, applesauce, cranberry jelly).

Fatty Condiments

This family has several categories, and includes all oils, butters, margarines, and animal fats.

Commercial Condiments

For people who have really very little time to cook, there are many commercial condiments that can prove very practical. These include angostura bitters, and various types of sauces such as Worcestershire, soy, tamari, hoisin, and oyster sauce.

PREPARATION TECHNIQUES

Give Your Table a Gourmet Atmosphere

What makes the difference between a great chef and the run-of-the-mill cook? Very often it's attention to detail which distinguishes the accomplished chef. Steamed potatoes that are nicely rounded, a filet mignon decorated with a fancy-cut tomato, a dip with vegetables cut in a variety of shapes—these little touches in well-prepared food add immeasurably to the pleasure of serving and eating a meal.

You don't need expensive kitchen equipment or endless hours of work to accomplish the same thing. If you learn the ABC's of cutting fruit and vegetables, you'll find your dishes taking on a new lease on life. Cut fruit and vegetables in squares, circles, slices, wedges, or fancy sections, and make them stand out on the plate.

Rectangular Cuts

The various rectangular cuts can alter the time required for cooking.

Sticks: pieces ½ inch wide (1 cm) and between 1 ½ to 3 inches (3 to 6 cm) long.

Jardinière: a stick cut in half lengthwise between 1 ½ to 3 inches (3 to 6 cm) long, and ¼ inch (0,5 cm) wide.

Paysanne: a jardinière cut in sections, between ½ to 1 inch (1 to 2,5 cm) in length and ¼ inch (0,5 cm) wide.

Julienne: slivers about 2 to 4 inches (5 to 10 cm) long and about as thick as a piece of cooked spaghetti.

For greater variety, rectangles can be given a diamond shape or cut slightly on the bias.

Shaped Vegetables

To shape a vegetable, use an end, or cut the vegetable into sections 2 inches (5 cm) long and 1 inch (2,5 cm) thick. With a sharp knife, round the piece and pare away the ends to a slight point.

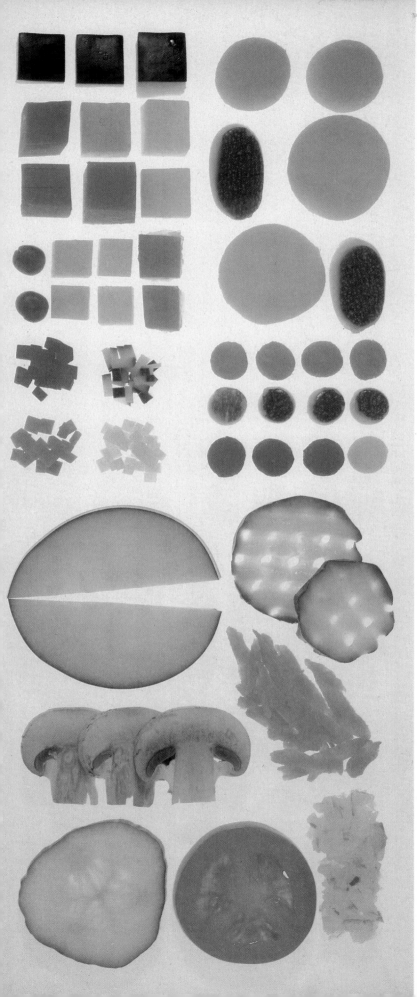

Square Cut

Diced: small cubes of $^{1}/_{8}$ to $^{1}/_{2}$ inch (2 mm to 1 cm), although the larger dimension is the more usual.

Macédoine: vegetables diced in cubes of $^{1}/_{4}$ to $^{1}/_{2}$ inch (0,5 to 1 cm). This can be done by cutting sticks of jardinières into even sections.

Brunoise: tiny diced vegetables, done by cutting julienned ingredients into even sections.

Slices and Wedges

Slice: a horizontal or cross cut, as with a cucumber.

Wedge: a round vegetable or fruit cut into quarters or sometimes eighths, or the natural vertical division (of an orange, for example).

Balls

Balls: small, rounded pieces of different diameters. Use a "Parisian spoon" to shape them. Vegetables such as carrots, parsnips, and turnips are easily cut in this way, as are firm-fleshed fruits such as apples, melons, or cantaloups. Depending on their size, they are called parisienne (about $^{3}/_{4}$ inch or 2 cm), noisette (about $^{5}/_{8}$ inch or 1,5 cm), pearl (about $^{3}/_{8}$ inch or 1 cm), or olive (an oval about $^{3}/_{8}$ x $^{3}/_{4}$ inch or 1 x 2 cm).

Other Cuts

The food processor and chopper make it possible to cut food in a number of ways: finely or thickly sliced, chopped (into very small pieces), grated or shredded, or wavy cuts.

COOKING TECHNIQUES

Each food reacts differently to different cooking methods. You may boil a stew with impunity, but you can't do it to a beefsteak! Learn the appropriate cooking method for each kind of food, and you'll be as adept as any chef. What's more, once you understand the principles involved, you'll be able to vary the taste and appearance of dishes.

Braising

Braising consists of first searing the meat on all sides to form a crust. Once this is done, take the meat out of the casserole, pour off the fat, and deglaze by pouring enough liquid into the casserole to reach halfway up the meat. Put the meat back, cover, and simmer slowly. Be careful not to let the liquid boil or simmer too energetically. A gentle steam will envelop the meat. Turn meat frequently so that all sides take a turn in the cooking liquid. Oven cooking makes for even braising, although you can do it on top of the stove if you have a casserole with a thick bottom.

Pressure Cooking

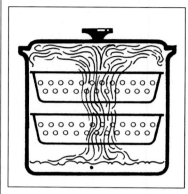

This is done in a special pot equipped with a pressure valve. The pot is hermetically sealed. The method saves time and, because only a small amount of liquid is used, keeps the water-soluble vitamins from being leached out of the foods.

"Bain-marie"

This method is used mostly for cooking delicate sauces. In France, the method is termed "bain-marie," and consists of a small saucepan placed or held over water in a larger container. Very often this can be done by simply using a double boiler. The purpose is to keep foods away from direct heat, especially those containing eggs or cream. Place a ramekin, mold, saucepan, etc., in a larger receptacle that is half filled with very hot (not boiling) water. While this method may take a little longer, it doesn't require as much watching, and there is far less risk of burning.

Blanching

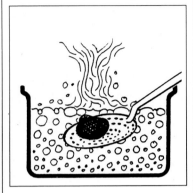

To blanch an ingredient, you must put it into boiling, lightly salted water for a period of 30 seconds to 4 minutes, and then transfer it to icy cold water in order to halt the cooking. Blanching makes it possible to begin cooking an ingredient, and to resume cooking later. It is mostly used in preparing vegetables for freezing. Blanching prevents discoloration.

Steaming

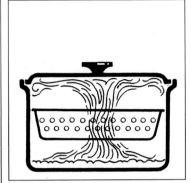

Steaming is done in a form of double boiler that has the top half perforated with large holes, so that the food can be steamed rather than boiled. The cover prevents the steam from escaping. For small quantities of vegetables you can use a daisy wheel steamer that fits into almost any saucepan. You can flavor the cooking water with spices or aromatic herbs and/or vegetables, wilted celery leaves, parsley stalks, or similar ingredients. Keep an eye on the level of liquid throughout cooking. If it is too high, the food will simply be boiled; if it is too low you'll burn the saucepan and give the food a burnt taste.

Boiling

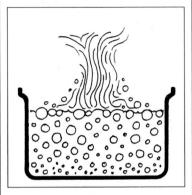

Water is the sole source of heat here. Meat that is to be cooked should be added after the water has been brought to a rolling boil, in order to close the pores and seal precious juices inside. On the other hand, bones or meat used for stock should be added when the water is cold. As the water comes to a boil, the flavor and goodness are drawn out of the ingredients. Boiling is equally useful in cooking vegetables, eggs, and fish.

Deep Frying

A food dropped into oil or fat at a temperature of 200 to 500 °F (100 to 260 °C) will cook evenly on all surfaces. Foods with a soft consistency, such as croquettes or Parmesan fondues, must be cooked at a high heat in order to form a crust rapidly and keep their shape. Foods such as potatoes, on the other hand, are cooked in two successive sessions: the first to sear them and seal in the goodness and flavor, the second to cook the inside. The hotter the oil, the less is absorbed by the food. It's therefore best to keep the cooking temperature as high as possible, although you should check first to find the combustion point of the oil or fat you're using.

Glazing and au gratin

A dish cooked in a sauce, or with a sauce ladled over it, can be further cooked in the oven to give the surface a brown or golden color. You can speed up the process by dotting the surface with knobs of butter, a few drops of oil, fresh breadcrumbs, sliced or grated cheese, or even several of these ingredients at once. Foods that are already in a sauce will become completely colored in cooking. Some dishes that are already partially cooked can simply be run briefly under the broiler. If the food browns before the cooking is finished, cover it with aluminum foil until done.

Poaching

Most food can be poached. This method uses water just below the boiling point. The cooking liquid can be flavored with spices or aromatic herbs. A stock can be used instead. Add a few drops of vinegar to the water before cooking eggs. This speeds up the coagulation of the egg white.

Flambéing

Food is usually poached before being flambéed. This method consists of pouring a small amount of alcohol (such as Cognac, Grand Marnier, etc.) onto the food in a frying pan or a long-handled flambéing pan, and lighting it. The alcohol evaporates, but the food is left with a distinctive flavor.

Grilling and Broiling

Food such as chops or beef and fish steaks are basted in oil, butter, or some other condiment, and cooked over a high heat source such as charcoal, on a hot rack or grill (also oiled or greased in order to sear the food and keep it from sticking). The meat must be turned over once only, otherwise the grilling process won't be successful. In order to give the meat the attractive crisscross pattern characteristic of grilled food, give it a half turn (on the same side) as it cooks on the rack. Similar foods can be broiled in the oven. The heat source is above the meat in this case. See the next section (Barbecuing) for details. Marinated meat should be patted dry before broiling, otherwise it will boil in the marinade instead of being seared under the broiler.

Barbecuing

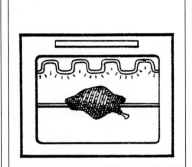

Barbecuing or roasting on a spit in the oven cooks the food uniformly. You can use the lower element only, or heat the broiler as well. If you're using both elements, watch the cooking closely and baste the meat frequently. It will brown rapidly. If it is as brown as you want it before the cooking is done, turn off the broiler and finish cooking with the lower element only.

Oven Roasting

The best way to cook a large piece of meat is to subject it to the dry heat of an oven. Heat the oven to a very high temperature. Meanwhile, heat an oiled roasting pan, place the meat in it, and put it in the oven to sear. Turn the heat down after a quarter of the cooking time has passed. You can also sear the meat on all sides in a large stove-top casserole before putting it in the oven. If you want the meat well done, baste it once or twice with its juices during cooking. If steam forms in the oven during cooking, open the door an inch or two, briefly, now and then.

Marinating

Marinating can be both a preparation for cooking, and a cooking method in itself. The marinade is usually made up of an acidic ingredient (such as vinegar, wine, or a citrus juice), a fatty ingredient (oil), and aromatic ingredients (spices, herbs, vegetables, or alcohol). Raw foods such as thin slices of fish, seafood, or meat, can be cooked simply by being left in the marinade for a few hours. Larger pieces will be tenderized and flavored by the marinade. These should be drained and patted dry before being cooked at a high heat.

Microwaving

Microwaving is a very rapid cooking method. The waves of electronic energy produced by the oven activate the molecules of water in the food, and the friction of their movement produces enough heat to cook it.

PRESERVING TECHNIQUES

Food is at its freshest immediately after it is harvested, slaughtered, or taken from the sea. The quality of freshness is very important to the taste and nutritional value of food. To retain it, we must keep two key aspects in mind: hygiene and preservation.

Food processing plants are subjected to strict hygiene regulations. The same is not true of your home. A few rules of your own, however, will prevent the spread of bacteria:

- Always wash your hands in hot water between each stage of food preparation.
- Use clean utensils and containers for each operation. For example, don't taste your sauce with the same spoon used for stirring.
- Always disinfect your cutting board after using it for raw food (a polyethylene board is preferable to wood for this reason).
- Cover cuts and small wounds with a waterproof bandage.
- Never smoke near your work areas.

There are various ways of preserving the freshness of food. In earlier times, people looked for ways of keeping food longer so that it could be stored for use when fresh produce wasn't available. Nowadays, the various preservation techniques that have been developed are aimed at giving us a year-round supply of the foods we need in the best condition possible.

There are a number of procedures, either natural or industrial, that make it possible to preserve food. The so-called "natural" methods use certain additives such as sugar (jams and jellies), salt (as in delicatessen or charcuterie meats), vinegar (as in marinades), alcohol (for fruit), oils (for fish), and clarified fats (pâtés).

Industrial methods treat foods for varying lengths of time with certain preservation procedures. Think for example of dehydration—or more simply, drying—whereby vegetables, herbs and even certain kinds of fish can be preserved. Canning and bottling consists of sterilizing both container and food, and sealing the latter in a vacuum. Smoking is a centuries' old method of preservation, which in our day is usually confined to meat, poultry, seafood and fish.

There is no doubt that the best method for preserving food is to freeze it. This consists of rapidly lowering the temperature of food to −5 °F (−19 °C) or less, thus preserving nutritive value, color, and taste. Most modern refrigerators have a freezer compartment that makes it possible to freeze things at home. To do this effectively, you have to keep a few useful rules in mind:

- Try as best you can to create a vacuum packing (with no air).
- Use heavy-duty aluminum foil for food that you are planning to keep for three weeks or less.
- For food that you want to keep for longer periods, use special freezer plastic bags, or a bag that can be hermetically sealed.
- Don't use ordinary plastic wrap. It stretches and then loses its sealing capacity once it becomes cold.

In freezer plants the method known as deep freezing is now generally used. Food is flash-frozen to temperatures of −18 to −40 °F (−30 to −40 °C). This makes it possible to preserve nutritive qualities even better than by ordinary freezing.

The simplest method of preserving food, and the most common in North America, is still refrigeration. By merely keeping food cold, we can slow down bacterial activity. Ideally, a refrigerator should be under 42 °F (6 °C) and over 30 °F (−1 °C). Although it is such an easy method, you can improve its effectiveness with a few additional precautions:

- Cool food down (half covered) before putting it in the refrigerator.
- Always put food in plastic containers that can be hermetically sealed, or be careful to cover food tightly with aluminum foil (the dull surface on the inside), waxed paper, or plastic wrap.

Freezing

Freezing is practical, but it isn't the total answer to preserving food. Some foods do not store well at temperatures below freezing.

Lettuce
Thawed lettuce will be too soft and taste flat.

Tomatoes, sweet and hot peppers
These foods lose their crisp texture, although they can be used in cooking.

Eggs
An uncooked egg will swell and burst. A cooked egg will become hard and rubbery. However, you can freeze beaten eggs.

Spicy foods
Seasonings of all kinds undergo change when frozen, either becoming stronger or weaker. It's preferable to adjust seasoning after thawing and heating a dish, rather than before freezing it.

Refrigeration

For how long? That's the crucial question. Smelling the food isn't a sure way of telling whether it's still edible or not. Often, food that is in fact rotten looks perfectly healthy. Here are a few simple rules to follow:

Meat
• Large pieces

Take the meat out of its original packaging and seal it hermetically (but not too tightly), and change the wrapping and plate every day. It will keep two or three days.

• Sliced meat such as chops, steaks, or escalopes

If possible, put a sheet of waxed paper or butcher's paper between each slice. Follow the same procedure as for large pieces of meat. It will keep two or three days.

• Ground meat

This will keep a day or two at the most.

• Processed meat such as sausages, bacon, delicatessen meats.

These will keep five or six days in their original packaging.
Once a package is opened, wrap the food carefully in plastic wrap. It will keep two or three days.

• Cooked meat

Cooled and wrapped in plastic wrap, it will keep two or three days.

Poultry
Poultry is often contaminated by varying amounts of salmonella. To avoid growth of this bacteria, you must carefully wash everything that has touched the raw meat. Apart from this, keeping poultry doesn't require any special techniques.
It will keep for two or three days on a plate loosely wrapped in plastic wrap (change plate and wrapping every day). It will keep for the same length of time when cooked, cooled and covered.

Fish
• Raw fish

Rinse it under icy water and pat it dry. It will keep one or two days on a plate wrapped in plastic wrap. Change the wrapping after the first day.

• Cooked fish

Cool and cover with plastic wrap. It will keep two or three days.

• Smoked fish

This will keep for three to five days in its original wrapping or in a plastic wrap.

Cheese
Wrapped in two thicknesses of plastic wrap, it will keep two to three weeks.

Eggs
Eggs are sensitive to refrigerator odors and changes in temperature. Keep them in their original packaging, for a maximum of two weeks.

Lettuce
Washed and well drained, lettuce should be kept in a plastic bag loosely closed, so that you create a sort of greenhouse humidity that is ideal for keeping this product. Lettuce will keep up to two weeks.

Vegetables (the blossom, leaf, or fruit section)
These will keep five days in the refrigerator, unwashed, in a hermetically sealed container.

Vegetables (root)
These will keep two weeks, washed and well dried.

Hard fruit (apples, pears, citrus fruit)
These will keep for two weeks in a plastic bag.

Soft fruit (strawberries, raspberries, blueberries)
These will keep two or three days if spread on a tray and covered with a dishcloth.

CHICKEN

Chicken, turkey, goose, duck, Cornish game hen —all these barnyard fowl, raised for their meat, belong to the poultry family.

Poultry has long been a mainstay of our daily meals, from the fat capon that made Grandma glow with pride to the delicate quail that has become fashionable in recent years.

Chicken, however, is the member of the poultry family that has remained a perennial favorite on our tables. Hot or cold, roasted or fried, whole or in pieces, served with a sauce or in a casserole, chicken is a true jack-of-all-trades in the kitchen.

Chicken freezes well and can be easily unfrozen—a real blessing when last-minute guests turn up on your doorstep. Thaw it in the refrigerator if time allows, or in the microwave if you're in a hurry.

Chicken is popular as a lean meat, although people concerned about their health or weight are careful to remove the skin, since it has a high fat content.

How to Truss a Chicken

- Slip a fairly long piece of string under the chicken.

- Bring each end of the string up and between the thighs and breast.

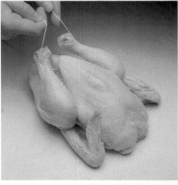

- Crisscross the string under the drumsticks.

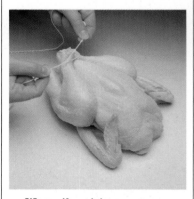

- Wrap the string once around the drumsticks and crisscross it once more.

- Turn chicken over, breast down.

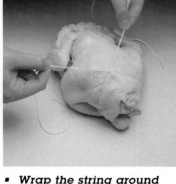

- Wrap the string around the tail end.

- Tighten the string and tie a knot.

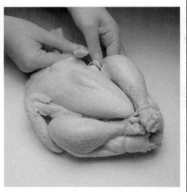

- Slip wing tips under the string between the thighs and breast.

HOW TO CUT UP A CHICKEN

- Slit the chicken down the middle of the breast.

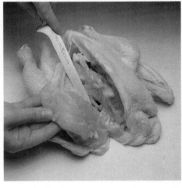

- Keeping the knife pressed against the carcass, gently slide the blade downward and detach the breast.

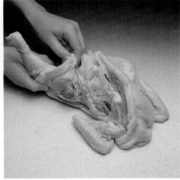

- Bend back the thigh and break the upper joint.

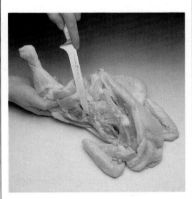

- Insert the blade into the joint and remove the leg.

- Cut each leg in two, slicing through the fatty vein above the middle joint.

- This is the result.

- Remove the wings and cut off the tips.

- Here's the cut up chicken.

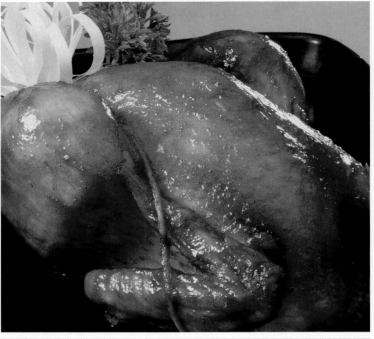

Honey and Orange Glazed Chicken

This chicken looks wonderfully festive and makes a good dinner party dish. Serve it whole, garnished with mandarin orange segments, either fresh or canned.

	4 servings
1	whole chicken, 4 ½ lbs (2 kg)
2 tbsp	(30 mL) oil or butter
	salt and pepper
	pinch of thyme
1 ¼ cups	(310 mL) orange juice
2 tbsp	(30 mL) grated orange peel
1 tsp	(5 mL) savory
1 tbsp	(15 mL) chicken consommé
⅓ cup	(80 mL) honey
2 tsp	(10 mL) lemon juice

■ Preheat oven to 350 °F (175 °C).

■ Truss chicken. Baste with butter or oil and season with salt, pepper, and thyme.

■ Place in a roasting pan and cook until golden, about 45 minutes.

■ Meanwhile, in a large bowl, combine the other ingredients.

■ Pour mixture over the golden chicken and cook 1 hour longer, basting often.

■ At the end of cooking process, boil the cooking juices until thick and baste the chicken with this sauce.

Barbecued Chicken

We're all familiar with whole barbecued chicken. But this barbecue sauce can be used as a delicious baste for chicken breasts and legs, small pork roasts or chops, or even ground meat!

	4 to 6 servings
1	chicken, 4 to 6 lbs (1,8 to 2,7 kg)
¼ cup	(60 mL) butter
	salt and pepper
2 cups	(500 mL) commercial barbecue sauce
1 cup	(250 mL) water
2 tbsp	(30 ml) oil
1	onion, grated
2 tbsp	(30 mL) cornstarch
1 cup	(250 mL) ketchup
5 tbsp	(75 mL) brown sugar
5 tbsp	(75 mL) vinegar
	salt and pepper
½ tsp	(2 mL) Worcestershire sauce

■ Preheat oven to 350 °F (175 °C).

■ Baste chicken with butter, season with salt and pepper and place in a covered casserole.

■ Add barbecue sauce. Add 1 cup (250 mL) of water and cover.

■ Cook approximately 1 ½ hours, basting frequently.

■ In a large skillet, heat oil and sauté onions. Add cornstarch and stir.

■ Add other ingredients and simmer for 10 minutes.

■ Pour sauce over chicken and serve.

Salt-crusted Cornish Game Hen

Appearances notwithstanding, this recipe is not overly salty. If you prefer duck, simply increase the cooking time to 3 hours.

4 servings	
4	Cornish game hens
1	onion, quartered
½ tsp	(2 mL) thyme
4	garlic cloves, un-peeled
2 ¼ lbs	(1 kg) coarse salt

■ Preheat oven to 425 °F (220 °C).

■ Place an onion quarter, a garlic clove, and a pinch of thyme inside each bird. Truss.

■ Spread a layer of coarse salt in the bottom of a baking dish or a roasting pan. Place the Cornish hens on the layer of salt and cover them with salt, pressing with your hand to make the salt stick.

■ Cook for 1 hour. Remove from oven and crack salt crust with a ladle. Wipe off excess salt with a pastry brush. Serve.

Cornish Game Hen with Herbs

Poultry meat has a light enough texture to bring out the aroma and taste of fine herbs. Use fresh herbs in season, doubling the quantity given in the recipe.

4 servings	
4	Cornish game hens
2	slices lemon
¼ tsp	(1 mL) savory
1	onion, sliced
1	carrot, diced
½ cup	(125 mL) celery leaves
	salt and pepper
14 oz	(398 mL) canned consommé
2 tbsp	(30 mL) fresh parsley, chopped
1 tsp	(5 mL) tarragon
1 cup	(250 mL) plain yogurt

■ Preheat oven to 375 °F (190 °C).

■ Clean and dry hens and rub skin and cavity with lemon slices.

■ Place onion segments, diced carrot and celery leaves inside each cavity, sprinkle with savory and season with salt and pepper.

■ Truss hens, place in a casserole dish and cover. Cook for approximately 40 minutes.

■ When cooked, remove the hens and keep warm. Pour off the fat and add consommé to the remaining juice. Let liquid reduce to three quarters.

■ Fold plain yogurt and fine herbs into liquid, adjust seasoning. Serve.

CHICKEN BREASTS

Chicken Breasts Poached in Basque Broth

For an innovative touch, use leek instead of green and red peppers.

4 servings

1 tbsp	(15 mL) butter	
1	onion, finely chopped	
1	green bell pepper, finely chopped	
1	sweet red pepper, finely chopped	
1	garlic clove, minced	
2 cups	(500 mL) chicken stock or consommé	
4	boned chicken breasts, 6 oz (170 g) each	
	pinch of thyme	
1	bay leaf	
	salt and pepper	
2 tsp	(10 mL) chopped parsley	

■ In a medium-size saucepan or stove-top casserole dish, melt butter, add onion and peppers, cover and simmer, without browning, over low heat. Add garlic and stir. Add chicken stock. Place the chicken breasts in the saucepan and bring to a boil.

■ Add thyme and bay leaf, and season with salt and pepper. Cover and cook over low heat for about 20 minutes.

■ When cooked, arrange chicken breasts on a serving dish. Top each portion with peppers and onions. Ladle chicken stock over the chicken, sprinkle with parsley and serve.

Chicken Breasts Mascarade

Breaded chicken that isn't fried—a culinary masquerade that will please weightwatchers!

4 servings

Breading

6	slices bacon, cooked and chopped	
¼ cup	(60 mL) onion, chopped	
1 tbsp	(15 mL) chopped parsley	
2 tbsp	(30 mL) breadcrumbs	
½ tsp	(2 mL) basil	
	salt and pepper	
4	chicken breasts, 6 oz (170 g) each	
	sauce of your choice	

■ Place daisy steamer in saucepan containing ½ inch (1,25 cm) water. Bring to a boil.

■ Meanwhile, in a bowl, combine all breading ingredients.

■ Skin chicken breasts, coat with a thin layer of breading and garnish with any one of the 8 garnishing choices on the opposite page. Steam coated, garnished breasts for 20 minutes.

■ Arrange on a serving dish. Coat with the sauce of your choice.

Eight Irresistible Garnishes for Chicken Mascarade

Left

Grapes, Cranberries and Miniature Corn

- Arrange garnishes over breaded chicken breasts and cook.

- Leave grapes in tiny clusters to prevent them from falling off the chicken.

Julienned Carrots, Turnips and Zucchini with Watercress

- Arrange a mixture of julienned carrots, turnips and zucchini over breaded chicken breasts. Season with salt and pepper and cook.

- When done, garnish with a bouquet of watercress and raw, thinly sliced onion rings.

Fruit Medley

- Place 1 apricot half, 1 pear segment (sprinkled with lemon juice) and 1 lime slice over breaded chicken breasts. Sprinkle with curry powder and cook.

- When done, garnish with the fruit of your choice.

Shrimp and Asparagus

- Decorate breaded chicken breasts with a few shrimp and asparagus tips. Season with salt and pepper, top with a pat of butter and cook.

- When done, garnish with lemon wedge and celery leaves.

Right

Cucumber and Pepper

- Cover the breaded chicken breasts with finely sliced cucumber and chopped sweet pepper. Season with salt and pepper and cook.

- When done, garnish with chopped parsley or chives and mandarin segments.

Mushroom, Egg, and Tomato

- Decorate each breaded chicken breast with a few finely sliced mushrooms, lightly sautéed in butter, 2 slices of hard-boiled egg and 1 tomato slice. Season and cook.

- When done, garnish with fresh tarragon leaves.

Green Garnish

- Steam 4 lettuce leaves for 30 seconds.

- Place 1 slice of cooked ham and 1 slice of cheese on each breaded chicken breast.

- Wrap each combination in a lettuce leaf and cook.

Tuna, Bacon, and Chives

- Mix together equal amounts of cooked bacon bits and flaked tuna. Cover each breaded chicken breast with this mixture, sprinkle with chopped chives and cook.

- When done, garnish each chicken breast with peeled grapefruit segments, (be sure to remove the white fiber).

Pepper and Parsley Chicken Breasts

You can prepare these peppered chicken breasts and the accompanying parsley butter a day ahead of time, and cook them just before the family arrives.

4 servings

Parsley Butter

2 tbsp	(30 mL) butter
1 tbsp	(15 mL) parsley
1 tsp	(5 mL) lemon juice
1/2 tsp	(2 mL) beef consommé

4	boned chicken breasts, 6 oz (170 g) each
4 tsp	(20 mL) black peppercorns, crushed
2 tsp	(10 mL) coriander seeds, crushed
1 tbsp	(15 mL) butter
2 tsp	(10 mL) oil
	salt and pepper

■ Prepare the parsley butter at least 1 hour ahead of time.

■ Let the butter soften in a small bowl, add all the ingredients, then mix. Follow the instructions on page 384 for preparing round pats of butter.

■ Skin the chicken breasts and sprinkle them lightly with crushed peppercorns and coriander.

■ Heat the oil and melt the butter in a skillet, add the chicken breasts, and cook over low heat.

■ Arrange the chicken breasts on a serving dish, top them with a pat of parsley butter, and serve.

Lightly pound meat and marinate for 2 hours in peach juice. Drain marinade. Using thin strips of waxed paper, cover alternate sections of chicken breasts and sprinkle exposed sections with paprika. Reverse operation and sprinkle other sections with curry powder and cook. Garnish with peaches sautéed in butter.

Follow the recipe for Pepper and Parsley Chicken Breasts and replace parsley butter with a mixture of grated Parmesan cheese and chopped parsley to be added toward the end of the cooking process. Serve on a bed of tomato-flavored noodles.

Stuffed Chicken Breasts Cordon Bleu

This is a classic chicken dish. Try Emmenthal or Gruyère if you prefer these cheeses, and keep your Cheddar for another time.

4 servings

4	boned chicken breasts, 6 oz (170 g) each
4	slices ham
3 ½ oz	(100 g) grated Cheddar cheese
3 tbsp	(45 mL) flour
2	eggs, beaten
	salt and pepper
½ cup	(125 mL) breadcrumbs
2 tbsp	(30 mL) butter
2 tsp	(10 mL) oil
	commercial cream of mushroom sauce

■ Preheat oven to 325 °F (160 °C).

■ Skin chicken breasts, slit and spread butterfly-style. Place a slice of ham in each breast. Sprinkle with grated Cheddar, and press firmly to close.

■ Dredge each stuffed breast with flour and dip into beaten eggs. Season with salt and pepper, then coat with breadcrumbs.

■ In an ovenproof skillet, heat oil, melt butter and gently sear chicken breasts on both sides until golden. Finish cooking in oven approximately 25 minutes.

■ Pour cream of mushroom sauce over top and serve.

* Illustrated recipe on the left side

Spinach-stuffed Chicken Breasts

For this recipe, we recommend the tube-stuffing method described on the previous page.

4 servings

4	boned chicken breasts, 6 oz (170 g) each
½ cup	(125 mL) cooked spinach, drained
1	egg
	salt and pepper
¾ cup	(180 mL) tomato sauce

■ Preheat oven to 400 °F (205 °C).

■ Skin chicken breasts, cut away filet mignon from the underside of chicken breast and draw out the tendons.

■ In a blender, finely chop filets mignons of chicken with spinach. Add the egg and season with salt and pepper.

■ Slit the breast top-center style, butterfly-style or tube-style, and fill the cavity with stuffing.

■ Pour tomato sauce in a baking dish and add stuffed chicken breasts. Cover dish with aluminum foil.

■ Cook in oven approximately 40 minutes.

■ Carve stuffed chicken breasts into thin slices and arrange fan-like on a serving dish.

* Illustrated recipe on the right side

CHICKEN BREAST STRIPS

Poultry breast sliced in strips can be served in dozens of original and mouth-watering combinations, eight of which you will find on the opposite page. Chicken strips cook in no time—something you'll appreciate when you're in a hurry.

Chicken Breast Strips with Mushrooms

You've run out of cream? Simply use evaporated milk.

4 servings	
5 tsp	(25 mL) butter
1 ⅓ cup	(330 mL) mushrooms, sliced
¼ tsp	(1 mL) thyme
1 tsp	(5 mL) lemon juice
4 tsp	(20 mL) vegetable oil
1 lb	(450 g) white chicken meat, skinned, cut into strips
	salt and pepper
1 cup	(250 mL) 35% cream
10 oz	(284 mL) canned cream of mushroom soup
4 tsp	(20 mL) parsley

■ In a skillet, melt butter and sauté mushrooms until golden. Add thyme and lemon juice, stir and set aside.

■ In a separate skillet, heat oil and sauté chicken strips, season with salt and pepper, and remove excess fat from skillet when chicken strips are cooked.

■ Fold 35% cream into cream of mushroom soup and let mixture boil for 1 minute over medium heat. Adjust seasoning, sprinkle with parsley and serve.

SHRIMP, TOMATOES, GARLIC AND BASIL

- Sauté chicken with 1 cup (250 mL) shrimp until liquid has evaporated. Add 1 chopped garlic clove, 2 diced tomatoes and ¼ tsp (1 mL) basil. Cook for a few minutes.

CLAMS AND CUCUMBERS

- Sauté 1 cup (250 mL) julienned cucumbers, and set aside. Sauté chicken. Add 8 oz (237 mL) drained clams and cucumbers to chicken. Add ½ cup (125 mL) cream and a little clam juice and cook until sauce thickens to taste.

CURRY AND FRIED BANANAS

- Sprinkle chicken with 1 tbsp (15 mL) curry powder and sauté in butter. Cut banana into thick slices, dip into beaten egg and fry. Sprinkle mixture with 2 tbsp (30 mL) roasted coconut.

CHEDDAR AU GRATIN

- Mix 2 egg yolks with ½ cup (125 mL) grated Cheddar and pour over chicken and mushrooms. Sprinkle with a little paprika and broil for 1 minute.

PEACHES, PINEAPPLE, AND ALMONDS

- Sauté chicken with ⅓ cup (80 mL) almonds. Add ½ cup (125 mL) peach segments and same amount of pineapple chunks with a bit of juice.

CREAM OF TOMATO AND TORTELLINI

- Sauté chicken in butter. Add 1 ½ cups (375 mL) cooked tortellini and 8 oz (237 mL) cream of tomato soup to mixture.

BEER AND ONIONS

- Sauté chicken in butter. Add ¾ cup (180 mL) beer and thicken with cornstarch. Garnish with onion rings dipped in flour and fried.

RED GRAPES

- Sauté chicken in butter. Add 2 tbsp (30 mL) white wine and ½ cup (125 mL) red grapes. Reduce the liquid a little then add ⅓ cup (80 mL) 35% cream.

Cubed chicken

Beer-flavored Chicken Breasts

You'll be pleasantly surprised by the flavor...

4 servings

3 tbsp	(45 mL) butter
1 cup	(250 mL) carrots, diced
³/₄ cup	(180 mL) celery, diced
1 cup	(250 mL) onions, diced
2	sprigs of fresh rosemary
¹/₂ tsp	(2 mL) salt
¹/₂ tsp	(2 mL) freshly ground pepper
1 ¹/₂ lbs	(675 g) chicken breasts, diced
12 oz	(341 mL) beer
2 tbsp	(30 mL) chicken consommé
3 tbsp	(45 mL) sour cream
2 tbsp	(30 mL) butter
2 cups	(500 mL) mushrooms

■ Preheat oven to 350 °F (175 °C).

■ In an oven-proof casserole, melt butter, add vegetables, and cook for 5 minutes. Sprinkle diced chicken breasts with rosemary, salt and pepper and place in casserole. Arrange vegetables around diced chicken breasts. Pour consommé and beer over mixture, let boil, cover and cook in oven for 1 hour.

■ Remove casserole from oven, divide chicken into 4 servings and keep warm in oven.

■ Bring vegetables and cooking juices to a boil and pour sour cream into mixture.

■ In a skillet, melt 2 tbsp (30 mL) butter, sauté mushrooms then add them to sauce. Pour sauce over chicken breasts.

Chicken Pie

Why not try green beans in this dish?

4 servings

Velouté Sauce

¹/₄ cup	(60 mL) butter
¹/₄ cup	(60 mL) flour
1 cup	(250 mL) milk
1 ¹/₂ cups	(375 mL) chicken consommé
	salt and pepper
2 ¹/₂ cups	(625 mL) chicken breasts, cooked and diced
2 cups	(500 mL) carrots, cooked and diced
14 oz	(284 mL) canned green peas
	pastry for 2 pie crusts

■ Preheat oven to 400 °F (205 °C).

■ In a sauce pan, melt butter, blend in flour, pour milk slowly into mixture and stir constantly.

■ Add chicken consommé, season with salt and pepper and bring to a boil.

■ Reduce heat and let simmer for 5 minutes.

■ Line a pie plate with 1 crust, add diced chicken, vegetables and sauce and top with second crust.

■ Bake in oven for 40 minutes or until crust is golden.

Chicken Kebabs

String a few cherry tomatoes onto the skewers and serve on a bed of steamed rice or with golden fried potatoes and a lightly tossed green salad. What a nice way to bring back summer warmth and the memory of succulent outdoor meals!

4 servings

Marinade

½ cup	(125 mL)	oil
¼ cup	(60 mL)	soy sauce
¼ cup	(60 mL)	honey
2 tbsp	(30 mL)	lemon juice
1 tsp	(5 mL)	grated lemon peel
1 tsp	(5 mL)	minced garlic
		chopped parsley

1 ½ lbs	(675 g)	chicken breasts, cubed
8		canned or cooked small potatoes
8		mushroom caps
16		sweet red pepper wedges
16		green bell pepper wedges
16		onion wedges

■ In a large bowl, combine all marinade ingredients, add cubed chicken breasts and let marinate for 4 to 6 hours, stirring from time to time.

■ Slide cubed chicken onto skewers, alternating with vegetables.

■ Place skewers on a microwave-safe platter and cook chicken kebabs in microwave at MEDIUM-HIGH for 10 to 12 minutes. Let stand 5 minutes.

■ Garnish each chicken kebab with parsley and chives.

VARIATIONS

- Cook kebabs 7 to 8 minutes over charcoal. Turn halfway through cooking process.
- Replace chicken with turkey, rabbit, pork or beef.
- Cook potatoes in tomato juice sweetened to taste.
- Alternate half-slices of lemon and orange on skewers.

CHICKEN ESCALOPES

Chicken escalopes are a delicacy that is sometimes difficult to find. Be sure you can buy them before planning a menu, or prepare them yourself as described here.

How to shape a chicken escalope

- *Slice the boned breast of chicken in half, lengthwise.*

- *Place the meat between 2 sheets of wax paper and pound lightly with the flat side of a large knife or with a meat mallet.*

Have you often wondered what to do with leftover egg whites? Why not cook them and toss them with a mixed salad?

Chicken Escalopes with Zucchini

4 servings	
¹/₄ cup	(60 mL) butter
2	zucchinis, sliced in rounds
	salt and pepper
¹/₄ tsp	(1 mL) thyme
4	chicken escalopes, ¹/₄ lb (115 g) each
	seasoned flour
2	egg yolks, beaten
6 tbsp	(90 mL) breadcrumbs
2 tsp	(10 mL) lemon juice
4 tsp	(20 mL) water
2 tbsp	(30 mL) grated Parmesan cheese

■ In a skillet, heat 2 tbsp (30 mL) butter, sauté zucchini slices, season with salt and pepper, sprinkle with thyme and keep warm in oven.

■ Dredge chicken escalopes with seasoned flour, dip into beaten egg yolks and coat with breadcrumbs.

■ In a separate skillet, heat 2 tbsp (30 mL) butter and cook chicken escalopes over low heat. Remove from skillet, place in a serving dish in the oven to keep warm.

■ Using the same skillet, pour in lemon juice and water, stir gently then pour liquid over escalopes.

■ Place the chicken escalopes on a bed of zucchini, sprinkle with grated Parmesan and serve.

Chicken Walnut Escalopes

Buy chopped walnuts rather than whole. They cost less and save time.

4 servings

Breading

½ cup	(125 mL) corn flakes
2 tsp	(10 mL) parsley
¾ tsp	(3 mL) lemon-flavored pepper
2 tbsp	(30 mL) finely chopped walnuts
4	chicken escalopes, ¼ lb (115 g) each
2	egg yolks, beaten

■ In a bowl, combine all breading ingredients and toss gently.

■ Dip chicken escalopes in egg yolks and dredge with breading.

■ In a microwave-safe dish, arrange the escalopes and cook at MEDIUM for 2 minutes.

■ Turn escalopes over, then cook another 2 minutes.

■ Let stand 5 minutes before serving.

Rolled Chicken Escalopes

For festive occasions, serve this dish with honey-coated, julien-ned carrots on a bed of wild rice.

4 servings

Seasoned butter

1 tbsp	(15 mL) butter
	pinch of chives
	pinch of garlic powder
	pinch of ground black pepper

Breading

½ cup	(125 mL) corn flakes
1 tbsp	(15 mL) grated Parmesan cheese
1 tsp	(5 mL) parsley
1 tsp	(5 mL) paprika
2	egg yolks, beaten
8	chicken escalopes, 2 oz (60 g) each

■ Preheat oven to 350 °F (175 °C).

■ In a small bowl, combine butter, chives, garlic powder, and pepper, and whip until mixture is well blended.

■ In a large bowl, mix corn flakes with grated Parmesan, parsley and paprika.

■ Place a pat of seasoned butter on each chicken escalope. Roll, dip into egg yolks, dredge with breading and secure each with a toothpick.

■ Cook in oven for 20 to 25 minutes.

CHICKEN WINGS

Forgotten, frowned upon, or even thrown away, chicken wings usually end up in the soup pot. But properly prepared, they are surprisingly good and give any meal a party atmosphere.

Chicken wings are immensely popular for entertaining, and also easy on the budget.

How to prepare chicken wings

- **Only use this part of the chicken wing (not the tip).**

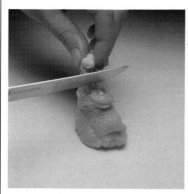

- **Pare the meat away from the bone.**
- **Pull back all the skin and meat.**

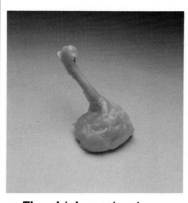

- **The chicken wing is ready to cook.**

Fried Chicken Wings

You won't need a sauce for these crispy, perfectly seasoned chicken wings. A creamy coleslaw adds a complementary touch.

4 servings		
2 tbsp	(30 mL) vegetable oil	

Seasoned Flour

1 cup	(250 mL) flour	
½ tsp	(2 mL) paprika	
¼ tsp	(1 mL) garlic salt	
¾ tsp	(3 mL) ginger	
½ tsp	(2 mL) basil	
½ tsp	(2 mL) curry powder	
¼ tsp	(1 mL) thyme	
½ tsp	(2 mL) coriander, crushed	
	salt and pepper	
20	chicken wings	
3	eggs, beaten	
2 tbsp	(30 mL) milk	
2 cups	(500 mL) breadcrumbs	

- In a deep-fryer, heat oil to 375 °–400 °F (190 °–205 °C).

- In a large bowl, combine all seasoned flour ingredients. Dredge chicken wings with this mixture.

- In a separate bowl, whip milk and eggs. Dip chicken wings in the liquid then coat with breadcrumbs.

- Preheat oven to 350 °F (175 °C).

- Fry chicken wings in deep-fryer for 4 minutes.

- Finish cooking process in oven for 10 to 15 minutes.

Chicken Wings Tai-Pan

The ideal dish for those who want to spend the summer out of the kitchen. There are no cooking utensils to wash, except for a measuring cup and marinade bowl, and the chicken is eaten as a finger-food.

4 servings		

Marinade

4 tsp	(20 mL) ginger	
2 tbsp	(30 mL) soy sauce	
1	sweet red pepper, puréed	
¼ cup	(60 mL) lemon juice	
1 tsp	(5 mL) Tabasco sauce	
¼ tsp	(1 mL) thyme	
1 tsp	(5 mL) mint	
½ cup	(125 mL) olive oil	
1 tbsp	(15 mL) wine vinegar	
2 lbs	(900 g) chicken wings	
	salt and pepper	

- In a large bowl, combine all marinade ingredients. Add chicken wings, cover and marinate overnight.

- Light barbecue.

- Drain chicken wings and cook over barbecue, turning them often. Baste with marinade during cooking.

- Season with salt and pepper just before serving.

Honey-flavored Chicken Wings

No child can resist the tempting aroma of honey-coated chicken wings. Neither can an adult, for that matter. Just remember to have plenty of table napkins handy!

4 servings

2 tbsp	(30 mL) oil
	salt and pepper
2 lbs	(900 g) chicken wings
1	garlic clove, crushed
2 tbsp	(30 mL) soy sauce
¼ cup	(60 mL) commercial brown gravy
⅓ cup	(80 mL) honey
4 tsp	(20 mL) tomato paste
2 tbsp	(30 mL) carrots, julienned
1 tsp	(5 mL) chopped parsley

■ In a large skillet, heat oil.

■ Season chicken wings with salt and pepper and cook over low heat for 15 minutes, turning 4 or 5 times during cooking process.

■ Remove chicken wings from skillet and pour off cooking fat.

■ Add garlic to skillet, stir for 20 seconds then add other ingredients.

■ Return chicken wings to skillet with sauce, cover and cook over medium heat for 5 minutes. Garnish with julienned carrots and chopped parsley, and serve.

Chicken Wings Milanese

Garnish your serving dish with a few chopped hard-boiled eggs.

4 servings

2 tbsp	(30 mL) vegetable oil
2 lbs	(900 g) chicken wings
½ tsp	(2 mL) thyme
1	onion, finely chopped
¾ cup	(180 mL) carrots, diced
2	garlic cloves, minced
19 oz	(540 mL) canned tomatoes
2 cups	(500 mL) commercial brown gravy
2 tbsp	(30 mL) chopped parsley

■ In a large skillet, heat oil and cook chicken wings over medium heat for about 5 minutes. Turn a few times during cooking and season with salt, pepper and thyme.

■ Add onion and carrots and cook for 3 minutes, stirring constantly, then add garlic and cook 30 seconds longer.

■ Stir in the tomatoes and cook over medium heat for 10 minutes.

■ Prepare gravy according to package directions, pour into skillet and cover. Cook 10 minutes longer.

■ Place chicken wings and vegetables on a serving dish, coat with sauce and sprinkle with parsley.

CHICKEN LEGS

Chicken legs come in two parts: the top part or thigh and the lower section or drumstick. Which is better tasting? No two people can agree.

Roasted Chicken Legs

A simple recipe that goes a long way. Follow our suggestions or let your imagination run free to give your meals a personal touch.

4 servings	
6	whole chicken legs
3 tbsp	(45 mL) butter
	salt and pepper
	pinch of thyme
½ cup	(125 mL) hot water

■ Preheat oven to 350 °F (175 °C).

■ Place a pat of butter on each chicken leg, and season with salt, pepper, and thyme.

■ Place chicken legs in a large casserole dish and cook in oven for 20 to 25 minutes or until tender.

■ During cooking process, baste with hot water combined with a small amount of melted butter, and turn from time to time.

ALMOND-FRIED CHICKEN LEGS

• Bread chicken legs with flour, egg and sliced almonds and fry.

• Wrap in aluminum foil and finish cooking in oven.

PARSLEY CHICKEN LEGS

• Preheat oven to 400 °F (205 °C).

• Chop 6 garlic cloves, add 3 tbsp (45 mL) parsley, a handful of breadcrumbs and a few drops of oil.

• Dredge chicken legs with this mixture. Cook in oven, uncovered, for 30 minutes or until chicken legs are nicely golden. Cover, and cook in oven 10 minutes longer.

GLAZED FRUIT CHICKEN LEGS

• Roast chicken legs and let stand to cool.

• Garnish with cherries, mandarin segments, peach wedges and a few green grapes.

• Coat with a fine layer of gelatin. Refrigerate.

Braised Chicken Legs with Rotini

You needn't feel guilty about leftover pasta when serving it with this appetizing braised chicken dish.

4 servings		
2 tbsp	(30 mL)	oil
6		whole chicken legs
		salt and pepper
1		onion, sliced
1		bay leaf
1 tsp	(5 mL)	marjoram
5 ½ oz	(156 mL)	tomato paste
1 cup	(250 mL)	water
2 cups	(500 mL)	rotini pasta, cooked

■ In a large skillet, heat oil, melt butter and cook chicken legs until golden. Season with salt and pepper.

■ Add onion, bay leaf, and marjoram.

■ In a bowl, dilute tomato paste in water. Pour over chicken legs, cover skillet and let simmer for 20 minutes.

■ Add cooked rotini to mixture, let simmer for 10 minutes and serve.

* Illustrated recipe

Caribbean-style Chicken Legs

4 servings		
6		whole chicken legs
2 cups	(500 mL)	boiling water
1 tbsp	(15 mL)	chili powder
2 tsp	(10 mL)	salt
¼ tsp	(1 mL)	pepper
¼ tsp	(1 mL)	cinnamon
¼ cup	(60 mL)	onion, chopped
¼ cup	(60 mL)	butter
¼ cup	(60 mL)	oil
19 oz	(540 mL)	canned pineapple, with juice
1 cup	(250 mL)	seedless green grapes
2		bananas, sliced lengthwise
1		avocado
2 tbsp	(30 mL)	cornstarch
¼ cup	(60 mL)	cold water

■ Preheat oven to 375 °F (190 °C).

■ Wash chicken legs and place in a large cast iron casserole. Add water, chili powder, salt, pepper, cinnamon, and onion.

■ Close casserole tightly and simmer mixture for 30 minutes until meat is tender.

■ When cooked, remove chicken legs, drain on paper towel, pour cooking juice through sieve and set aside.

■ Using the same casserole, heat oil, melt butter, brown chicken legs and set aside.

■ Drain pineapple, keeping the juice.

■ Add the pineapple juice and enough boiling water to the cooking juice to make 4 cups (1 L) and pour liquid over chicken.

■ Place pineapple chunks over chicken legs, cook 10 minutes in oven, and baste often.

■ Arrange chicken legs covered with pineapple chunks in serving dish. Garnish with grapes, sliced bananas, and avocado wedges. Set aside.

■ In a small bowl, dissolve cornstarch in cold water, pour into cooking juice and sweeten to taste. Coat chicken legs with sauce.

Chicken Tropicana

Sweet-and-sour sauce is a popular condiment that originally came to us from the Orient. It provides a tangy contrast to our traditional menus.

4 servings

1	4 lb (1,80 kg) chicken, cut up
1	egg, beaten
1/2 cup	(125 mL) flour
1/3 cup	(80 mL) olive oil
19 oz	(540 mL) canned pineapple, sliced
	water
1/3 cup	(80 mL) honey
2 tbsp	(30 mL) cornstarch
	pineapple syrup
3/4 cup	(180 mL) wine vinegar
1 tbsp	(15 mL) soy sauce
1/4 tsp	(1 mL) ground ginger
1	cube concentrated chicken stock
1/4 tsp	(1 mL) garlic powder
1	green bell pepper, cut into thin strips
1	fresh pineapple (optional)

■ Preheat oven to 375 °F (190 °C).

■ Wash chicken, pat dry and carve into pieces.

■ In a bowl, combine beaten egg and flour, and dip chicken pieces into batter.

■ In a large skillet, heat oil and cook chicken pieces until golden.

■ Place chicken pieces in shallow roasting pan and set aside.

■ Drain pineapple, pour syrup into measuring cup and add enough water for 1 1/4 cups (300 mL) of liquid.

■ In a saucepan, combine honey, cornstarch, pineapple juice, vinegar, soy sauce, ginger, garlic, and concentrated chicken stock and bring to boil, stirring constantly. Let mixture boil for 2 minutes then pour sauce over chicken.

■ Cook in oven, uncovered, for 30 minutes. Add pineapple slices and green bell pepper strips to mixture. Cook 30 minutes longer or until chicken is tender.

■ Serve in pineapple crowns or directly in the plate.

How to make a pineapple crown

▪ *Slice off crown and stem of pineapple; cut fruit into thick slices.*

▪ *Scoop out flesh without damaging the pineapple shell.*

Chicken with Olives and Mushrooms

If you find the olives too salty, simply soak them in cool water for 30 minutes before cooking.

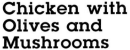

4 servings	
2 tbsp	(30 mL) butter
1/2 lb	(225 g) mushrooms, sliced
	salt and pepper
2 tbsp	(30 mL) chopped parsley
2 tbsp	(30 mL) oil
8	pieces of chicken
2 tbsp	(30 mL) onion, chopped
2 tbsp	(30 mL) tomato paste
1 cup	(250 mL) commercial chicken stock
1/2 cup	(125 mL) pitted olives

■ In a large skillet, melt butter.

■ Sauté mushrooms until cooking juices have completely evaporated. Season with salt and pepper, sprinkle with parsley and set aside.

■ In a casserole, heat oil, cook chicken pieces until golden, and season with salt and pepper.

■ Add onion and tomato paste and cook 2 minutes longer, stirring constantly.

■ Add chicken stock and olives and let mixture simmer for 1 hour, over low heat.

■ Arrange chicken around the mushrooms on the serving dish, and spoon over the cooking juice.

Mustard Chicken

This recipe calls for hot mustard, but you might try the mild variety for a change. It imparts a slightly sweet taste to the chicken meat.

4 servings	
8	pieces of chicken
1 tbsp	(15 mL) Dijon mustard
1 tbsp	(15 mL) oil
1 tsp	(5 mL) butter
1/3 cup	(80 mL) milk
	salt and pepper
3/4 cup	(180 mL) 35% cream

■ Skin chicken pieces and coat generously with mustard.

■ In a large skillet, heat oil, melt butter and cook chicken pieces until golden. Degrease skillet then pour milk into skillet, season to taste.

■ Reduce heat to the lowest setting and cook chicken until meat detaches easily at the touch of the fork.

■ Stir in the cream, heat for a few minutes and serve.

BONED CHICKEN LEGS

Boning a chicken leg is easier than it seems. Simply follow these step-by-step instructions.

How to bone chicken legs

- **Pull back the skin by inserting fingers between the skin and flesh and pulling it back to tip of the drumstick.**

- **With a sharp knife, cut through the bone just above the drumstick.**

- **Slice meat off bone and remove tendons.**

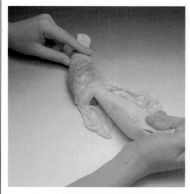

- **Mince meat and prepare stuffing. With a pastry bag with nozzle attachment, stuff chicken skin; make sure to push stuffing deep into skin pocket.**

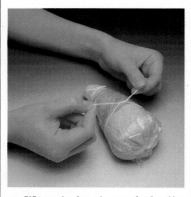

- **Fold excess skin and tuck it under the leg.**

- **Wrap in heat-proof plastic and tie.**

- **Stuffed chicken leg is ready to cook.**

Herb-and-Ham Stuffed Chicken Legs (Basic Recipe)

4 servings	
4	chicken legs, boned

Stuffing

1	onion
¼ lb	(115 g) sliced ham
	salt and pepper
1	egg
2 tbsp	(30 mL) evaporated milk
	boiling water
4 tsp	(20 mL) parsley
1 tsp	(5 mL) chives
6 tbsp	(90 mL) breadcrumbs
14 oz	(398 mL) canned cream of celery soup
14 oz	(398 mL) canned tomato sauce
¼ tsp	(1 mL) tarragon

- Preheat oven to 375 °F (190 °C).
- Finely chop onion, ham, and chicken leg meat. Season with salt and pepper, fold in egg and evaporated milk.
- Pipe stuffing into chicken legs. Wrap in heat-proof plastic, seal ends tightly and cook in boiling water for 20 minutes.
- Meanwhile, combine parsley, chives and breadcrumbs in a bowl.
- Remove stuffed chicken legs from plastic wrap. Place in a baking dish containing cream of celery soup, sprinkle generously with herbs and breadcrumb mixture and cook in oven for 15 minutes.
- Slice stuffed chicken legs into medallions, coat with tomato sauce, sprinkle with tarragon and serve.

Six Stuffing Combinations for Chicken Legs

Shrimp Stuffing

- Replace ham with shrimp. Add 1 tbsp (15 mL) tomato paste to basic recipe.

Cheese Stuffing

- Replace ham with 6 tbsp (90 mL) grated Cheddar cheese.

Vegetable Medley Stuffing

- Replace ham with diced carrots, celery, turnip, and sweet red peppers. Boil vegetables in lightly salted water, drain, and add to stuffing mixture.

Spinach Stuffing

- Replace ham with 6 tbsp (90 mL) drained and chopped spinach.

Caper and Olive Stuffing

- Replace ham with ⅓ cup (80 mL) stuffed olives along with 1 oz (25 g) capers. Replace cream of celery soup with cream of tomato soup.

Mushroom Stuffing

- Replace ham with 6 tbsp (90 mL) chopped mushrooms, previously sautéed with bacon bits.

From left to right, chicken legs stuffed with:
Shrimp ▪ Vegetable Medley ▪ Spinach ▪ Herb-and-ham (p. 62) ▪ Capers and Olives ▪ Mushrooms

CHOPPED CHICKEN

Chicken Merry-go-round in Pita Bread

An ideal recipe for out-door meals or a family picnic. Remember to refrigerate or keep on ice in the hamper until ready to use.

4 servings

4	pita breads
1 lb	(450 g) cooked, chopped chicken
¼ cup	(60 mL) mayonnaise
2	ripe avocados, diced
¼ cup	(60 mL) tomatoes, diced
2 tsp	(10 mL) lemon juice
1 tbsp	(15 mL) parsley
1 tbsp	(15 mL) onion, chopped
¼ tsp	(1 mL) Tabasco Sauce
	salt and pepper

■ Combine all ingredients in a food processor, season to taste, and stuff pita breads with mixture.

■ Slice ½ avocado into pieces, place on top of the stuffing, and garnish with lemon wedges, along with tiny parsley bouquets.

■ *Put the ingredients into a food processor.*

■ *Coarse chop the ingredients for maximum of 15 seconds.*

■ *Garnish the pita breads.*

■ *You'll need these ingredients.*

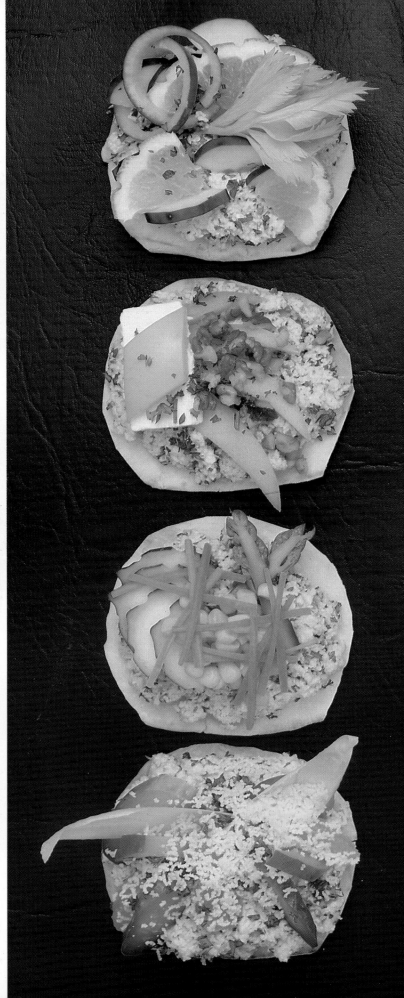

Eight Special Stuffings for Pita Bread

Left Column

- Add ¼ cup (60 mL) thinly sliced cucumber, ¼ cup (60 mL) chopped red onion, 2 tsp (10 mL) mint , 4 orange wedges, and celery leaves.

- Add 1 mango and 1 apple, each cut into wedges, 3 tbsp (45 mL) walnuts, and ¼ lb (115 g) feta cheese.

- Combine ¼ cup (60 mL) mixed julienned vegetables with ¼ cup (60 mL) corn niblets, 1 sliced zucchini, and ¼ cup cooked rice.

- Slice or chop 2 hard-boiled eggs, and mix with ¼ cup (60 mL) shredded lettuce, 3 tbsp (45 mL) pickles, and 2 endives separated into leaves, each leaf garnished with orange wedges.

Right Column

- Combine 2 tomatoes, cut in wedges, small parsley sprigs, chives, ¼ cup (60 mL) red cabbage, 2 apples cut in pieces, and ¼ cup (60 mL) cottage cheese.

- Combine ¼ cup (60 mL) mayonnaise with 1 puréed avocado, 4 chopped green onions, ¼ cup (60 mL) sweet red pepper, ¼ cup (60 mL) cottage cheese and ¼ cup (60 mL) chopped fresh fines herbes.

- Fill pita bread with a mixture of ¼ cup (60 mL) mayonnaise, ½ cup (125 mL) celery, ¼ cup (60 mL) radishes, 1 cup (250 mL) chopped or flaked chicken, and ¼ cup (60 mL) chopped red onion.

- Mix together ¼ cup (60 mL) vegetable medley, ¼ cup (60 mL) Gruyère cheese, 2 tomatoes, and ¼ cup (60 mL) finely shredded lettuce.

Chicken Cutlets "Pojarsky"

This version of the versatile croquette is especially good when the chicken is put through a fine meat-grinder instead of being chopped by hand.

---

4 servings

Chicken Cutlets

1 lb	(450 g) uncooked chicken, chopped
1	onion, chopped
2 tbsp	(30 mL) chopped parsley
6 tbsp	(90 mL) milk
³/₄ cup	(180 mL) breadcrumbs
2	eggs
2	garlic cloves, minced
	salt and pepper
2	eggs, beaten
2 cups	(500 mL) breadcrumbs
¹/₄ cup	(60 mL) butter

■ Preheat oven to 375 °F (190 °C).

■ In a large bowl, combine all chicken cutlet ingredients and add breadcrumbs to thicken batter.

■ Shape cutlets according to illustrated step-by-step instructions. Refrigerate for a few hours.

■ Dip each cutlet into eggs and coat with breadcrumbs.

■ In a skillet, melt butter and cook chicken cutlets over very low heat for 3 minutes on each side until golden.

■ Cook in oven 30 minutes longer. Serve with a cream of mushroom sauce.

■ *Roll mixture into a 4 oz (115 g) patty.*

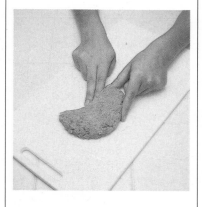

■ *Shape patty into a small cutlet.*

Chopped Chicken Loaf with Mushrooms

Keep this recipe handy when looking for ways to serve leftover poultry. Simply freeze any leftovers until you have enough to prepare this tasty loaf.

4 servings

2 tbsp	(30 mL) butter
1 cup	(250 mL) mushrooms, quartered
1 tsp	(5 mL) salt
1/2 tsp	(2 mL) pepper
2 1/4 lbs	(1 kg) chopped chicken
1/4 cup	(60 mL) mayonnaise
3 tbsp	(45 mL) green bell pepper, minced
1	onion, grated
2	eggs
1/4 cup	(60 mL) breadcrumbs
1 cup	(250 mL) canned cream of mushroom soup, undiluted

■ Preheat oven to 350 °F (175 °C).

■ In a skillet, melt butter and sauté mushrooms, season with salt and pepper and set aside.

■ In a large bowl, mix together all other ingredients, then spread half the mixture in a loaf pan.

■ Cover mixture with sautéed mushrooms.

■ Spread other half of mixture over mushrooms and bake in oven for 1 hour. Serve.

Chicken Crêpes

People will think you've spent hours in the kitchen preparing this gourmet dish. What's the secret? Make plenty of crêpes beforehand, wrap them individually or in handy packs, and freeze them.

4 servings

2 tbsp	(30 mL) butter
1	onion, chopped
1 cup	(250 mL) celery, diced
1/2	green bell pepper or sweet red pepper, diced
2 cups	(500 mL) chicken, cooked, chopped
	salt and pepper
	poultry seasoning
1 1/2 cups	(375 mL) béchamel sauce
8	cooked crêpes
1/2 tsp	(2 mL) paprika

■ Preheat oven to 400 °F (205 °C).

■ In a skillet, melt butter and sauté onion, celery, diced pepper, and chopped chicken. Season with salt, pepper, and poultry seasoning, then blend in 1/2 cup (125 mL) béchamel sauce.

■ Spoon filling over crêpes, roll and place in baking dish. Heat in oven for approximately 20 minutes until golden.

■ Remove from oven. Pour over the rest of the béchamel sauce, and sprinkle with paprika.

* Illustrated recipe

Chicken and Cheese Baguette

Slender sticks of hot French bread stuffed with chicken and cheese make an ideal snack for relaxed evenings around the television set. Keep it warm in aluminum wrap so that family and friends can help themselves.

4 servings	
1	baguette
1/4 cup	(60 mL) milk
3 tbsp	(45 mL) soft butter
1 1/2 cups	(375 mL) chicken, cooked, chopped
3 tbsp	(45 mL) onion, chopped
1 tsp	(5 mL) garlic, chopped
3	eggs
1/4 cup	(60 mL) grated cheese
1/4 tsp	(1 mL) thyme
	salt and pepper

■ Preheat oven to 350 °F (175 °C).

■ Slice baguette in two, lengthwise, scoop out a shallow trough on each half. Soak the scooped-out bread in milk, and set aside.

■ Butter the baguette halves and broil lightly.

■ In a bowl, combine all other ingredients, along with the soaked bread.

■ Stuff baguette halves with this mixture, close halves, wrap in aluminum foil and cook in oven for 35 minutes.

■ Slice into serving portions and serve hot or cold.

VARIATIONS

• **Combine a small amount of béchamel sauce with 1/2 cup (125 mL) cooked, drained spinach and add to stuffing mixture.**

• **Place hard-boiled egg slices along open-faced Cheddar baguette, close and cook in oven. Slice into serving portions, sprinkle with grated Parmesan cheese and serve.**

• **Arrange cooked carrot sticks and cooked leek white rings on the open-faced baguette, close and cook.**

GIBLETS

Chicken Livers with Mushrooms

Served as an hors d'oeuvre on small pieces of toast, this recipe yields 6 to 8 servings. Keep the chicken livers tender by not overcooking them.

4 servings

8	slices of bacon
1 lb	(450 g) chicken livers, halved
½ lb	(225 g) mushrooms, sliced
1 tsp	(5 mL) salt
¼ tsp	(1 mL) pepper
½ tsp	(2 mL) marjoram
1 tbsp	(15 mL) flour
1 cup	(250 mL) 35% cream
1 tbsp	(15 mL) fines herbes

■ In a hot cast iron skillet, fry bacon until crisp, drain and set aside.

■ Pour out bacon fat, leaving only about 2 tbsp (30 mL) in skillet.

■ Add chicken livers and mushrooms, season with salt, pepper, and marjoram and cook over medium heat for 3 to 4 minutes.

■ Add flour to mixture, stir gently and cook 30 seconds longer.

■ Add cream and cook over low heat until mixture thickens.

■ Add bacon and serve on toast, garnished with fines herbes such as parsley, chives, tarragon and chervil.

The appetizing tomato sauce in this recipe helps tone down the taste of chicken livers for those who aren't fond of them.

4 servings

1 tbsp	(15 mL) olive oil
10	chicken hearts
10	chicken gizzards
10	chicken livers
	salt and pepper
2	garlic cloves, finely sliced
½ tsp	(2 mL) oregano
28 oz	(796 mL) canned ground tomatoes
2 tbsp	(30 mL) chopped parsley
2 tbsp	(30 mL) grated Parmesan cheese
	steamed rice

■ In a cast iron skillet, heat oil over high heat.

■ Sauté giblets, reduce heat to medium, season with salt and pepper. Stir giblets to cook evenly. Let simmer for 5 to 8 minutes.

■ Add garlic and oregano.

■ Pour ground tomatoes and their juice over giblets and let simmer for 30 minutes or until juice has completely evaporated.

■ Sprinkle with parsley and Parmesan, then adjust seasoning.

■ Serve on a bed of rice, steamed in chicken stock.

* Illustrated recipe

69

CHICKEN STOCK

There is no substitute for the wholesome taste of home-made stock. Commercial products, however good, simply can't measure up.

Chicken stock is economical and easy to prepare. Our recipe provides enough to serve four people and freeze the rest for a later meal.

Basic Chicken Stock

If you freeze the stock, let it cool first, then skim off the excess fat before freezing.

4 servings	
1	chicken carcass
1 cup	(250 mL) leftover stuffing
8 cups	(2 L) water
1	onion, halved
1	carrot, sliced
4	celery stalks, with leaves, cut into chunks
2	garlic cloves, unpeeled, crushed
1	small turnip, peeled
1	tomato
5	parsley sprigs
¼ tsp	(1 mL) thyme
½ tsp	(2 mL) pepper
1	bay leaf
1 tsp	(5 mL) coarse salt

■ Combine all the ingredients in a large pot and bring to a boil. Reduce heat and cook for 2 hours. Skim off the froth during cooking so that the stock is nice and clear.

■ Pour the stock through a sieve, and degrease when cooled.

■ Garnish to taste. (Consult the list on the following page for variations.)

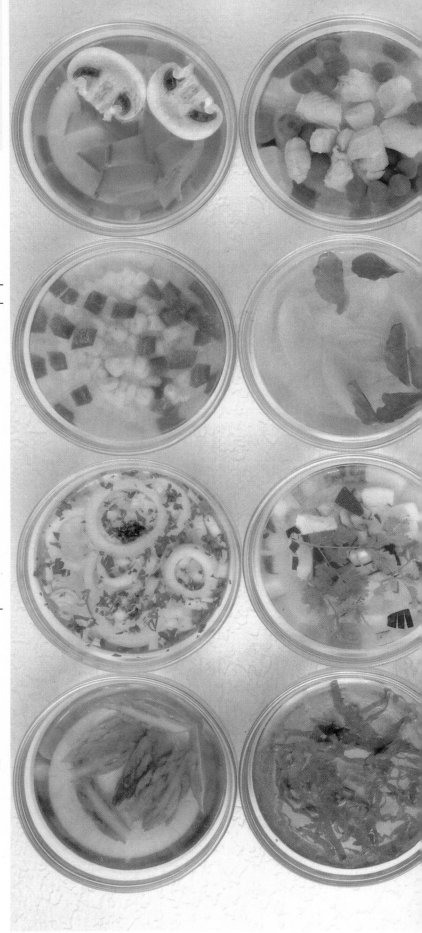

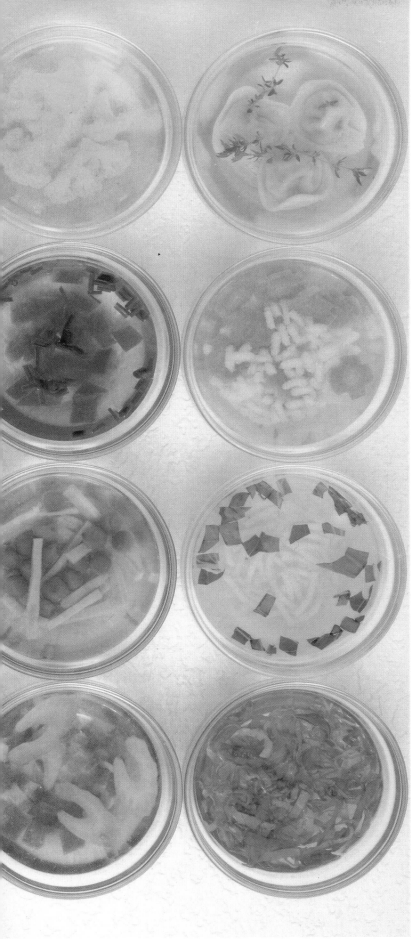

Sixteen Innovative Ways To Flavor Stock

First Column

Snow Peas and Mushrooms

- Add both ingredients to the stock during cooking.

Corn Niblets, Sweet Red Peppers and Rice

- Cook these ingredients in the stock for 15 minutes.

Broccoli, Onion Rings, and Parsley

- Cook all 3 ingredients in the stock for 5 minutes.

Fresh Asparagus Spears

- Cook asparagus spears in the stock for 7 minutes.

Second Column

Chicken and Peas

- Add both ingredients to the stock.

Leek, Turnip and Watercress

- Heat these ingredients in the stock.

Radishes, Hard-boiled Egg Rings, and Chervil

- Heat these ingredients in the stock.

Bacon and Spinach

- Fry bacon then add to fresh spinach, and cook in the stock.

Third Column

Curry-flavored Cauliflower Flowerets

- Cook cauliflower in the stock, and sprinkle with curry powder.

Diced Tomatoes and Chives

- Add these ingredients directly to the stock.

Ham and Green Peas

- Warm both ingredients in the stock.

Bacon, Celery and Tomatoes

- Sauté bacon bits along with sliced tomatoes and celery, then add to the stock.

Fourth Column

Tortellini and Thyme

- Cook both ingredients in the stock for 15 minutes.

Sliced Carrots and Rice

- Cook both ingredients in the stock for 15 minutes.

Pesto

- In a small bowl, combine a chopped garlic clove, a large pinch of basil and a few drops of olive oil, heat for 30 seconds in a small saucepan. Add to the stock with a handful of noodles.

Shredded Lettuce Leaves

- Drop a fair amount of shredded lettuce leaves into the stock.

Tradition has it that the Mayflower settlers ate wild turkey at the first Thanksgiving dinner in America. A century earlier, the Spaniards found turkeys already domesticated by the Aztecs in Mexico. "Turkey" is, of course, a misnomer for what must have seemed an exotic bird to New World adventurers.

The now familiar barnyard bird took a long time to find its way into European cuisine. While it figures as a traditional holiday roast in most North American households, we tend to ignore it for the rest of the year. Yet turkey is a relatively cheap meat that lends itself to a variety of recipes—two very good reasons for taking a second look at this versatile bird.

Most of us aren't aware of whether we're buying a turkey-hen or the male of the species. There is a difference, however. The meat of the male tends to be drier, and it should be larded with thin strips of bacon or pork fat to keep it moist while roasting.

TURKEY

Stuffed Turkey

There's nothing more festive than a steaming turkey, roasted to a turn, awaiting the hospitable host's carving knife. Although it is a traditional Thanksgiving and Christmas meat, roast turkey can be served at any time of year with a variety of novel stuffings. Venture into the new world of variations suggested on the opposite page. Family and friends won't want to wait a year for a repeat performance.

10 to 12 servings	
¼ cup	(60 mL) butter
3	onions, chopped
1 lb	(450 g) pork meat, diced
1 lb	(450 g) beef, diced
2 cups	(500 mL) uncooked rice (fast-cooking)
2 cups	(500 mL) celery, chopped
1 tbsp	(15 mL) fines herbes
1	turkey, 10 to 12 lbs (4,5 to 5,4 kg)
6	slices bacon
3	onions, sliced
6	slices solid pork fat
	salt and pepper
1 tbsp	(15 mL) fines herbes
2 tsp	(10 mL) paprika

■ Preheat oven to 325 °F (160 °C).

■ In a large skillet, melt butter and sauté onions.

■ Add diced meat, rice, celery and 1 tbsp (15 mL) fines herbes, and cook for 15 to 20 minutes.

■ Stuff turkey with this mixture.

■ Line a roasting pan with aluminum foil and pork fat slices, then put in the turkey.

■ Place sliced onions and 6 bacon slices on top of turkey, season with salt and pepper, sprinkle with 1 tbsp (15 mL) fines herbes and paprika.

■ Cook in oven 20 to 30 minutes per pound (per 450 g).

Eight Original Stuffings

You'll enhance the flavor of the stuffing by chopping or thinly slicing the vegetables. Start with the basic recipe shown on page 74, and incorporate these imaginative combinations.

First Column

Nut Stuffing
- Walnuts, grated coconut, almonds, wild rice, and white rice.

Fruit Stuffing
- Cranberries, red currants rice, prunes, kiwi.

Garden-fresh Stuffing
- Leek, white onions, potatoes, celery, carrots.

Second Column

Meat Stuffing
- Cooked tortellini, green peas, carrots, ground beef.

Pickle Stuffing
- Bacon, pearl onions, pickles, parsley, garlic, hard-boiled eggs.

Third Column

Cheese Stuffing
- Cheddar and Parmesan cheese, milk-soaked bread, red onions, shallots.

Tomato Stuffing
- Tomatoes, bacon, ham, potatoes, fines herbes.

Persillade
- Chopped parsley and garlic, pine nuts, turnip, sweet red peppers.

TURKEY BREASTS

Turkey Escalopes with Cream

The escalopes will have a slightly nutty flavor if you dredge them in a mixture of $^2/_3$ bread-crumbs and $^1/_3$ walnuts, or a half-and-half blend of walnuts and peanuts.

4 servings

4	turkey escalopes
	seasoned flour
1	egg, beaten
1 cup	(250 mL) bread-crumbs
$^1/_4$ cup	(60 mL) butter
1 $^1/_4$ cups	(310 mL) mush-rooms
	salt and pepper
1 tsp	(5 mL) lemon juice
1 cup	(250 mL) 35% cream

■ Dredge escalopes with seasoned flour, dip in beaten egg, and coat with breadcrumbs.

■ In a large skillet, melt butter and cook escalopes over low heat for 3 minutes on each side.

■ Remove escalopes from skillet and keep warm in oven.

■ Using the same skillet, sauté mushrooms for a few minutes, season with salt and pepper, sprinkle with lemon juice and stir gently.

■ Stir in cream and cook until mixture is thick and smooth. Adjust seasoning and serve piping hot.

Clean the mushrooms thoroughly, using as little water as possible, and slice off the tough part of the stem. A fine rather than a coarse liver pâté will give the filling a smoother consistency.

The crust should be either puff pastry or pâte brisée, otherwise known as short pastry, as these stand up well to moist fillings. For short pastry, use $^1/_2$ cup of butter, 2 cups of sifted flour, $^1/_2$ teaspoon of salt, and about $^1/_2$ cup of water to get the equivalent of a 9-inch pie shell.

4 servings

4	bacon slices, minced
1 $^1/_2$ cups	(375 mL) mush-rooms, chopped
	salt and pepper
2	slices of pâté de foie
2 tbsp	(30 mL) butter
1	turkey breast, skinned and bone
1	crust, short pastry or puff pastry
3	ham slices
1	egg yolk
1 cup	(250 mL) commer-cial brown gravy
	leftover stuffing (optional)

■ Preheat oven to 350 °F (175 °C).

■ In a skillet, melt bacon, sauté mushrooms gently until liquid has completely evaporated, season with salt and pepper, and set aside.

■ Add pâté de foie, stir, chop pâté, then refrigerate.

■ Roll out pastry dough into a rectangle.

■ In a skillet, melt butter, sear turkey meat until golden, and set aside to cool.

■ Place turkey breast on top of pastry dough, coat with bacon and mushroom mix-ture and place ham slices on top.

■ Moisten pastry edges, seal, and baste with egg yolk.

■ Bake for 40 minutes.

■ Pour gravy over turkey breast Wellington and serve.

* Illustrated recipe

Glazed Turkey Breasts

An appetizing dish topped with delicate lemon slices and a sweet-and-sour glaze. Vary the fresh look and taste of the citrus fruit by using half lemon, half lime, and garnishing each serving with mandarin orange segments.

4 servings

1 tbsp	(15 mL) oil
1 tbsp	(15 mL) butter
2	turkey breasts, boned, skinned
1	onion, chopped
6	lemons, thinly sliced
1/3 cup	(80 mL) ketchup
1/3 cup	(80 mL) water
3 tbsp	(45 mL) brown sugar

■ Preheat oven to 350 °F (175 °C).

■ In a skillet, heat oil, melt butter, sear turkey breasts until golden, place in a baking dish, and set aside.

■ Using the same skillet, sauté onion and spread over turkey breasts, cover with lemon slices.

■ In a small bowl, combine ketchup, water, and brown sugar, and pour mixture over garnished turkey breasts. Cook in oven for 45 minutes.

Turkey with Vegetables Au Gratin

A last-minute run under the grill gives the grated Cheddar topping an attractive golden-brown color. Use pale yellow Cheddar rather than orange for a pleasant contrast with the vegetables. There's no difference in taste.

4 servings

1/4 cup	(60 mL) butter
1	turkey breast, 2 1/4 lbs (1 kg)
1 cup	(250 mL) broccoli flowerets
1 cup	(250 mL) cauliflower flowerets
1	green bell pepper, sliced
10 oz	(284 mL) canned baby carrots
10 oz	(284 mL) canned miniature corn
1 1/2 cups	(375 mL) brown gravy
8 oz	(225 g) grated Cheddar cheese

■ Preheat oven to 450 °F (230 °C).

■ In a skillet, melt butter and sauté turkey breast gently until fully cooked.

■ In a daisy steamer, cook broccoli, cauliflower, and green bell pepper for approximately 10 minutes.

■ Arrange cooked turkey breast in the middle of a baking pan, and place vegetables around the meat. Coat with gravy and sprinkle with grated cheese. Run under the grill until the cheese is lightly browned.

* Illustrated recipe

ROLLED TURKEY BREASTS

Roast, rolled turkey breast, with a fragrant fruit or vegetable stuffing, stays tender and moist in the oven if you take the trouble to baste it frequently.

Avoid the risk of burns from hot oven racks by using a glass baster with a rubber syringe—a handy utensil devised for just this purpose.

Rolled Turkey Breast

If you like the lively color of paprika, sprinkle it generously over the turkey roll when the meat is done. Paprika not only enhances the look, but adds a healthy dose of vitamin C for your family or guests.

4 servings

1	turkey breast
1 tsp	(5 mL) lemon juice
	salt and pepper
	pinch of paprika
3 tbsp	(45 mL) softened butter
³/₄ cup	(180 mL) fruit juice or juice of vegetables from stuffing
2 tbsp	(30 mL) sugar

■ Preheat oven to 425 °F (220 °C).

■ Slit the turkey breast to make a stuffing pocket.

■ In a bowl, combine fruit or vegetables suggested on the following page, and sprinkle with lemon juice.

■ Spoon stuffing into the pocket.

■ Roll and tie the turkey breast, season with salt and pepper and sprinkle with paprika.

■ Smear the roll with butter and cook in oven for 10 minutes.

■ Reduce oven temperature to 350 °F (175 °C), add juices and sugar, and cook turkey for another hour, basting frequently.

Four Fruit Stuffings
Four Vegetable Stuffings

Pineapple and Raisins

- Mix together 1 cup (250 mL) pineapple chunks, ¼ cup (60 mL) raisins and 1 cup (250 mL) pineapple juice.

Peaches and Apricots

- Combine ¾ cup (180 mL) canned peaches with ¾ cup (180 mL) canned apricots, ½ cup (125 mL) diced honeydew melon and ¾ cup (180 mL) orange juice blended with ¼ cup (60 mL) canned peaches.

Apples and Mandarin Oranges

- Mix together 1 diced apple, ½ cup (125 mL) green grapes, ½ cup (125 mL) canned mandarins and 1 cup (250 mL) apple juice.

Carrots and Zucchini

- Combine ¾ cup (180 mL) julienned carrots, with ¾ cup (180 mL) julienned zucchini and 1 cup (250 mL) chicken stock blended with ¼ cup (60 mL) tomato juice.

Eggplant, Celery and Tomatoes

- Mix together ¼ cup (60 mL) diced eggplant, ½ cup (125 mL) diced celery, ¼ cup (60 mL) diced tomatoes, and 1 cup (250 mL) tomato juice.

Leek and Sweet Red Peppers

- Combine ½ cup (125 mL) chopped leek, ½ cup (125 mL) diced sweet red peppers, and 1 cup (250 mL) vegetable juice.

Cranberries and Rhubarb

- Combine ¾ cup (180 mL) cranberries with ¾ cup (180 mL) rhubarb, ½ cup (125 mL) diced cantaloup and 1 cup (250 mL) cranberry juice.

Asparagus and Mushrooms

- Blend ½ cup (125 mL) canned asparagus with 1 cup (250 mL) blanched mushrooms and 1 cup (250 mL) chicken stock.

TURKEY LEGS

Turkey legs have the double advantage of being conveniently sized and relatively inexpensive. They are usually sold vacuum-packed and frozen, and can be kept in the freezer to be thawed out individually when you need one or more. They freeze well and retain their flavor. A single leg will provide a hearty meal for two people.

■ **Make sure the meat is well browned on both sides. Onions and garlic should be cooked until golden. Add tomato juice.**

■ **Add citrus juice and seasonings after 4 minutes of cooking.**

This recipe calls for fresh turkey legs sliced through the bone in one-inch portions. Ask your butcher to do this for you.

4 servings	
4 tsp	(20 mL) vegetable oil
2 lbs	(900 g) turkey leg cut "osso boco"
	salt and pepper
	pinch of thyme
1	onion, chopped
2	garlic cloves, finely sliced
¼ cup	(60 mL) flour
¾ cup	(180 mL) tomato juice
6 tbsp	(90 mL) orange juice
1 tsp	(5 mL) lemon juice
2 cups	(500 mL) chicken stock
1	bay leaf
2	pinches of cayenne pepper

■ Preheat oven to 350 °F (175 °C).

■ In a skillet, heat oil and cook meat until golden, season with salt and pepper, and sprinkle with thyme.

■ Add onion and cook until golden.

■ Add garlic, and cook for 1 minute.

■ Sprinkle mixture with flour, stir and cook for 3 to 4 minutes.

■ Add liquids and bay leaf to mixture, sprinkle with cayenne pepper and cook over low heat for 10 minutes.

■ Return to oven and cook 60 minutes longer.

* Illustrated recipe

Turkey Leg Casserole

This complete main dish cooks in less than 30 minutes in the microwave, giving you time for a pleasant interlude before the meal.

4 servings

2	whole turkey legs
1	small package instant onion soup mix
¼ cup	(60 mL) brown sugar
¼ cup	(60 mL) chili sauce
10 oz	(284 mL) canned cream of mushroom soup
½ cup	(125 mL) water
4	potatoes, finely sliced
1	onion, finely chopped
3	celery stalks, sliced

■ In a large microwave casserole, combine all ingredients, cover and cook for 10 minutes at HIGH.

■ Reduce microwave temperature to MEDIUM-HIGH and cook 20 minutes longer. Stir once during cooking process, let stand, still covered, for 5 minutes before serving.

Braised Turkey Legs

Pasta shells (gnocchi), bows, and spirals (rotini) are just a few of the various pasta you can use when preparing this recipe. For added color, serve whole wheat pasta.

4 servings

2 tbsp	(30 mL) oil
2	whole turkey legs
	salt and pepper
1	onion, sliced
1	bay leaf
½ tsp	(2 mL) marjoram
8 oz	(237 mL) tomato paste
1 cup	(250 mL) water
½ tsp	(2 mL) salt
1 cup	(250 mL) cooked macaroni

■ In a large skillet, heat oil, and cook turkey legs on both sides until golden.

■ Degrease skillet, then season with salt and pepper.

■ Add onion, bay leaf, and marjoram, and set aside.

■ In a bowl, dilute tomato paste in water and pour into skillet. Season with salt, cover and let simmer for 30 minutes.

■ Add cooked macaroni and cook 10 minutes longer.

Rum-flavored Turkey Legs

While the turkey leg is in the oven, wash and peel about 10 medium-sized carrots. Place them in the oven in a covered baking dish filled with 1/2 cup of water, 30 minutes before the meat is ready. Uncover for the last 15 minutes.

4 servings

1/4 cup	(60 mL) orange juice
1/4 cup	(60 mL) rum
1/4 cup	(60 mL) melted butter
1/2 tsp	(2 mL) grated orange peel
1/2 tsp	(2 mL) salt
1/8 tsp	(0,5 mL) pepper
1/8 tsp	(0,5 mL) ground ginger
1	garlic clove, minced
2	whole turkey legs

■ Preheat oven to 350 °F (175 °C).

■ In a bowl, combine all ingredients except turkey legs.

■ Baste turkey legs generously with mixture.

■ In a shallow baking dish, arrange turkey legs skin side up.

■ Place baking dish in oven, ladle with leftover basting mixture from time to time, and cook for an hour or until meat is golden and tender.

Turkey Legs with Bouquet of Herbs

If you have no home-made chicken stock on hand, use a commercial chicken or vegetable bouillon. These products are very salty, however, and you should only use 1/4 tsp salt in this case.

4 servings

2 tbsp	(30 mL) oil
2	whole turkey legs
1/2 tsp	(2 mL) salt
1/2 tsp	(2 mL) pepper
1/4 tsp	(1 mL) chervil
1/4 tsp	(1 mL) basil
1/4 tsp	(1 mL) tarragon
1 tsp	(5 mL) parsley
1	garlic clove, finely sliced
2	French (dry) shallots, finely sliced
2 cups	(500 mL) chicken stock

■ Preheat oven to 350 °F (175 °C).

■ In a large skillet, heat oil and cook turkey legs on all sides until golden.

■ Add seasonings and stock and bring to a boil.

■ Place turkey legs in a casserole, pour in the stock and cook in oven for 45 minutes. Baste often.

* Illustrated recipe

Turkey Legs with Almonds

Make your own breadcrumbs from left-over or stale bread. Dry it out and put it through the blender.

4 servings

Seasoned Breadcrumbs

½ cup	(125 mL) chopped almonds
½ cup	(125 mL) breadcrumbs
2 tbsp	(30 mL) chopped parsley
½ tsp	(2 mL) salt
¼ tsp	(1 mL) pepper
1	egg, lightly beaten
½ cup	(125 mL) milk
¼ cup	(60 mL) flour
2	whole turkey legs
¼ cup	(60 mL) flour
	juice of 2 lemons
8	lemon slices
2 tbsp	(30 mL) slivered almonds

■ Preheat oven to 350 °F (175 °C).

■ Combine first 5 ingredients in a bowl and set aside.

■ In a separate bowl, beat egg and milk. Set aside.

■ Dredge turkey legs with flour, dip into milk and egg mixture and coat with breadcrumb mixture.

■ Place breaded turkey legs in a greased baking dish and cook for 1 hour or until cooking juices come out clear when meat is pricked.

■ Sprinkle with lemon juice 4 times during cooking.

■ Garnish with lemon slices, slivered almonds and serve.

Turkey Legs with Prunes

Put this attractive dish on a serving platter and bring it to the table for carving. If you have no mint, use tarragon instead.

4 servings

2	whole turkey legs
2 cups	(500 mL) prune juice
	salt and pepper
2 tbsp	(30 mL) oil
1 cup	(250 mL) chicken stock
24	pitted prunes
8	fresh mint leaves
1 tsp	(5 mL) pink peppercorns

■ Preheat oven to 350 °F (175 °C).

■ Soak turkey legs in prune juice for 15 minutes.

■ Drain and keep juice.

■ In a skillet, heat oil, sear turkey legs, season with salt and pepper and cook in oven for 45 minutes.

■ Meanwhile, in a saucepan, combine the chicken stock and prune juice and bring to a boil. Set aside.

■ Fifteen minutes into cooking process, baste turkey with half the cooking juices. Repeat 15 minutes later.

■ When done, carve turkey legs, coat with cooking juices, and garnish with prunes, mint leaves and pink peppercorns.

* Illustrated recipe

Turkey Breast Strips in Broccoli Cream

Although you may usually prefer to cut off broccoli stalks, there's no need to throw them away. Peel and freeze them for later use. You can substitute them for the broccoli flowerets in this recipe.

4 servings

1 ¼ cups	(310 mL) chicken stock
6 tbsp	(90 mL) onion, chopped
1	garlic clove, chopped
1 ¼ cups	(310 mL) broccoli flowerets
½ cup	(125 mL) 35% cream
3 tbsp	(45 mL) butter
1 lb	(450 g) turkey breast strips
	salt and pepper

■ In a saucepan, bring chicken stock to a boil, add onion, garlic, broccoli, and cream and let mixture simmer for 10 minutes.

■ Pass mixture through a vegetable mill. If necessary, cook a few minutes longer to desired thickness.

■ In a skillet, melt butter, sauté turkey strips and season with salt and pepper.

■ Degrease the skillet then pour broccoli cream over the meat and cook for 2 minutes over low heat.

■ Remove from heat, adjust seasoning and serve.

Diced Turkey Fricassee with Leek

Be sure to cook the leek gently, so that it becomes somewhat transparent but doesn't brown. The attractive green and white of the leek contrasts pleasantly with the tomato garnish.

4 servings

1 tbsp	(15 mL) oil
2 tbsp	(30 mL) butter
1 lb	(450 g) white turkey meat, diced
	salt and pepper
1 cup	(250 mL) leek, finely sliced
4 tsp	(20 mL) flour
½ cup	(125 mL) chicken stock
½ tsp	(2 mL) tarragon
6 tbsp	(90 mL) tomatoes, diced
1	sprig of fresh tarragon

■ In a skillet, heat oil and melt butter.

■ Brown the turkey and season with salt and pepper.

■ Add leek and cook, without browning, over medium heat for 5 minutes. Sprinkle with flour and stir gently for 30 seconds.

■ Add chicken stock and tarragon, cook for a few minutes until the sauce is the desired thickness and adjust seasoning to taste.

■ Pour mixture into serving dish. Decorate with diced tomatoes, and garnish with fresh tarragon.

* Illustrated recipe

Turkey Shells

An appetizing dish that you can also prepare with leftover chicken.

4 servings

2 tbsp	(30 mL) butter
¼ cup	(60 mL) flour
2 cups	(500 mL) milk
2 tbsp	(30 mL) sherry
1 tsp	(5 mL) onion, grated
¼ tsp	(1 mL) basil
¼ tsp	(1 mL) celery seeds
	pinch of cayenne pepper
4 cups	(1 L) cooked turkey, cut into pieces
	salt and pepper
¼ cup	(60 mL) Parmesan cheese
¼ cup	(60 mL) Emmenthal cheese
6	slices of bread

■ Preheat oven to 400 °F (205 °C).

■ In the top part of a double-boiler, melt butter, add flour, slowly pour in milk, stirring all the while, and cook until sauce thickens.

■ Add sherry, onion, basil, celery seeds, cayenne pepper and turkey pieces, season with salt and pepper, and cook 15 minutes longer.

■ Add Parmesan and Emmenthal, stir to melt cheeses, then set aside.

■ Remove bread crust, flatten white part with a rolling pin and coat with butter. Place bread in muffin molds to form shells.

■ Bake in oven for a few minutes until golden.

■ Fill with turkey mixture and serve.

* Illustrated recipe

Turkey Leg Pie

When you're ready to place the turkey pie in the oven, baste the crust with a lightly beaten egg white, using a pastry brush. The pie will come out nicely golden.

4 servings

2 tbsp	(30 mL) oil
2	carrots, diced
1	potato, diced
1	broccoli, cut into flowerets
1	celery stalk, diced
2	onions, finely sliced
14 oz	(398 mL) mushroom pieces
2 cups	(500 mL) chicken stock
2	turkey legs, cooked, boned
1 cup	(250 mL) white turkey meat, cooked, diced
1 tbsp	(15 mL) cornstarch
2	pie crusts

■ Preheat oven to 350 °F (175 °C).

■ In a large skillet, heat oil and sauté vegetables.

■ Add chicken stock and simmer for approximately 20 minutes.

■ Add turkey meat to mixture and set aside.

■ In a bowl, dissolve cornstarch in small amount of chicken stock and add to vegetable mixture to thicken.

■ Line pie plate with a pie crust, fill with turkey mixture and cover with second pie crust. Seal edges.

■ Cook in oven for 30 minutes or until crust is golden.

For most people, "meat" means "red meat", and beef in particular. Our tables have been traditionally laden with an assortment of roasts, stews, steaks, meatballs and other dishes that use beef as the basic ingredient.

Beef lost some of its popularity several years ago because of its high fat content. Now the pendulum has swung back, and beef is again an item on well-balanced menus. Beef producers have done considerable research in an effort to offer health-conscious cooks the leanest meat possible.

BEEF

HOW TO PREPARE TOURNEDOS

HOW TO CUT UP BEEF

- *Open the piece into a butterfly-shaped medallion.*

- *Slice filet into a piece weighing 6 oz (180 g).*

- *Slice it almost through on the flat side.*

- *Cut a slice of lard or a slice of bacon the same width as the medallion.*
- *Wrap it around the meat.*
- *Secure the fat to the meat with a toothpick.*

How to cut beef strips

- *Preferably choose a cut of beef containing little or no fatty marbling.*
- *Cut a ½ inch (1 cm) thick slice.*

- *Cut this same slice into strips of equal thickness. For smaller strips, simply cut each strip in half.*

How to dice beef

- *Cut a slice of beef 1 inch (2,5 cm) thick.*
- *Slice this piece into even-sized strips.*
- *Cut the strips into cubes.*

HOW TO STUFF A FILET MIGNON

- Slice a 5 oz (150 g) piece of filet mignon.
- Lie it flat and make an incision in the side.

- Using the tip of the knife, deepen the cavity without cutting it through.

- Using a spoon or a pastry bag with nozzle attachment, fill the cavity with stuffing.

- Spread stuffing evenly throughout the cavity.
- Close with a toothpick.

HOW TO PREPARE A STEAK

- Lie steak flat.
- Remove excess fat from sides and tip.

- Carve small notches every inch (2,5 cm) or so on the fatty side to prevent steak from curling up.

- Lie the rib steak flat when coating with pepper or other ingredients so that it will adhere well to the meat.
- Spread pepper evenly over the entire surface.
- Press with your fingers so that the pepper will penetrate the meat surface.

HOW TO BRAISE DICED BEEF

HOW TO MAKE GRILL MARKS ON BEEF

- Brown beef cubes on all sides in hot oil or butter.

- Add vegetables and cook until golden.

- Sprinkle with flour.

- Deglaze and pour liquid over mixture.

- Cook in the oven at 400 °F (205 °C) for 15 minutes or until tender.

- Place meat diagonally across hot grill surface.

- During cooking, give the meat a one-quarter turn.

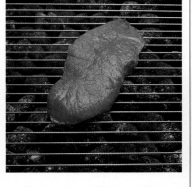

- The result is a criss-cross pattern on the meat surface.

HOW TO FRY STEAK

- *Sear steak in hot oil or butter*

- *For medium-cooked steak, turn steak over when droplets of blood appear on meat surface.*

- *Season and deglaze.*

FOUR STEPS TO COOKING STEAK

Cooking a steak can often be a hit or miss affair. Considering all the elements that can affect its success—the type of stove, the skillet, the thickness of the meat—you clearly need a certain amount of skill. Nevertheless, there are a few simple guidelines that you can follow to achieve satisfying results.

Choose an 8 oz (225 g), 1 inch (2,5 cm) thick steak, to be cooked over high heat.

Very rare or almost raw: Sear the steak for about 1 minute on each side. The meat will be browned on the outside, cooked just beneath the surface, and very red in the centre.

Rare: Sear the steak for about 2 minutes on each side. Again, the meat will be browned on the outside, cooked just beneath the surface, and red or even bleeding in the centre.

Medium: Cook the steak for about 3 or 4 minutes on each side. The meat will be well-browned on the surface and pink in the centre.

Well done: Cook the steak for about 5 minutes on each side. The meat will be uniformly cooked through. We don't recommend this, however, as the flavor is largely lost.

VERY RARE OR ALMOST RAW

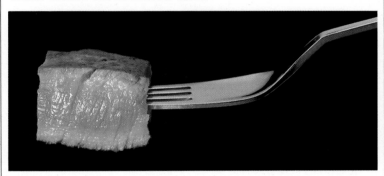

RARE

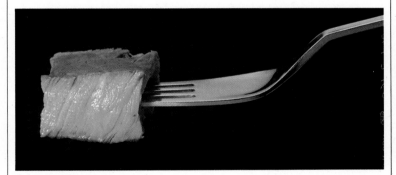

MEDIUM

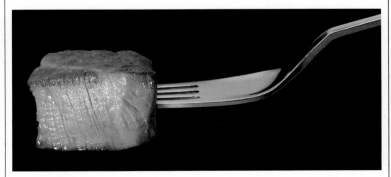

WELL DONE

Beefsteak

History tells us that British soldiers brought beefsteak to Europe shortly after the Battle of Waterloo. Since that time, this modest cut of beef and its many variations have been the source of countless gastronomical delights.

Whether rare or medium, smothered in pepper sauce or simply fried with a side order of fries, steak is a mealtime favorite.

Minute Pepper Steak

For special occasions, use rib or T-bone steaks when preparing this recipe.

4 servings

2 tsp	(10 mL)	black pepper, freshly ground
4		½ inch (1,25 cm) thick steaks, inside round or sirloin
2 tbsp	(30 mL)	butter
1 tbsp	(15 mL)	Worcestershire sauce
1 tsp	(5 mL)	lemon juice
½ tsp	(2 mL)	celery salt
½		garlic clove, minced
3 tbsp	(45 mL)	water

■ Spread ground pepper on waxed paper and press steaks onto it, making sure pepper adheres well to meat.

■ Combine all other ingredients in a bowl.

■ In a skillet, melt butter, sear steaks on one side, turn and baste cooked surface with sauce.

■ When steaks are well seared on both sides, pour the rest of the sauce into the skillet and cook to desired taste.

■ Garnish steaks with sauce and serve.

■ If you need more sauce, remove steaks and pour ½ cup (125 mL) water or beef broth into hot skillet. Allow liquid to reduce by half.

Eight Interesting Variations for Pepper Steak

- When turning steak, add 2 finely sliced garlic cloves to skillet, and cook until golden.

- Sauté 4 thinly sliced French (dry) shallots in skillet and add them to the steaks when turning.

- When turning steak, add 1 cup (250 mL) mushroom pieces and cook alongside meat.

- Sauté half a very finely sliced leek in a skillet and add to steak when turning.

- Add ¼ cup (60 mL) diced tomatoes to skillet just before pouring sauce over meat. Replace lemon juice with 1 tbsp (15 mL) tomato juice.

- When turning steak, add ¼ cup (60 mL) various-colored diced peppers to skillet.

- Mix green or pink peppercorns with ground black peppercorns.

- If you want a thicker sauce, add 2 tbsp (30 mL) 35% cream to basic sauce mixture.

93

Steak with Seasoned Mushrooms

Pressed for time? Why not open a can of mushrooms? Enhance this dish with oyster mushrooms or even exotic Chinese mushrooms.

4 servings

½ cup	(125 mL) melted butter
4	1 ½ inch (4 cm) thick T-bone steaks
1 cup	(250 mL) fresh mushrooms, sliced
¼ cup	(60 mL) steak sauce
	salt and pepper

- Preheat the broiler at least 10 minutes before cooking time.

- In a small saucepan, melt butter over low heat.

- Meanwhile, place steaks on broiling pan and coat with one-third melted butter.

- Broil steaks at least 4 inches (10 cm) from the grill.

- Turn steaks after 5 minutes, coat with another third melted butter and broil 5 minutes longer.

- Remove steaks and coat with last third melted butter.

- Spread sliced mushrooms over steaks, add the steak sauce and season with salt and pepper.

- Broil basted steaks and mushrooms 3 minutes longer for medium-cooked meat.

- Adjust cooking time according to your preference for doneness.

Replace steak sauce with mustard.

Replace steak sauce with ketchup.

Barbecued Rib Steak with Cheese

This recipe will be just as tasty whether you prepare it with round steak or sirloin steak. Give it a personal touch by garnishing with your favorite cheese, such as Cheddar, Mozzarella or even Roquefort.

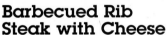

4 servings	
4	rib steaks, 8 oz (225 g) each
1 tsp	(5 mL) steak spices
4 tsp	(20 mL) peanut oil
1/2 tsp	(2 mL) Worcestershire sauce
1 tsp	(5 mL) grated Parmesan cheese
6 oz	(170 g) sliced Gruyère or Emmenthal cheese

■ Heat barbecue 20 minutes before cooking time.

■ Cut small notches in fatty edge of steaks every 2 inches (5 cm). This will prevent steak ends from curling up.

■ In a small bowl, mix all ingredients except cheeses.

■ Baste steaks generously with mixture and cook on barbecue to desired taste. Baste with sauce mixture from time to time and turn once only.

■ Three minutes before the cooking is finished, sprinkle steaks with Parmesan, cover with sliced Gruyère or Emmenthal and let the cheese melt before serving.

Flank End Steak with Fried Parsley

Flank end steak should be very rare to medium-rare only, otherwise it will lose its tenderness. Italian parsley makes an attractive variation.

4 servings	
4	flank end steaks, 6 oz (170 g) each
1 tbsp	(15 mL) peanut oil
1 tsp	(5 mL) butter salt and pepper
1 cup	(250 mL) peanut oil
1 cup	(250 mL) sprigs of dried parsley

■ In a large skillet, heat oil to smoking, fry flank end steaks on both sides, add butter and season with salt and pepper.

■ Remove steaks from skillet and let stand for 3 minutes before serving.

■ Meanwhile, in a small heavy saucepan, heat oil until bubbles form on surface when you insert a wooden spoon.

■ Drop sprigs of parsley into hot oil, fry for 20 seconds then remove and sprinkle over steaks.

■ If you like a sauce, deglaze steak skillet with 1/2 cup (125 mL) water or an equal amount of beef stock.

■ Serve with a tomato-flavored butter.

FILETS

Filet mignon is the greatest of beef delicacies, and its tender meat really does seem to melt in the mouth. Connoisseurs of fine cooking consider it the pinnacle of gourmet eating.

This is a very simple recipe that lends itself to numerous variations. Instead of the parsley called for in the seasoned butter, you can add tarragon, chives, or even a few sesame seeds. The tomato paste can be replaced by horseradish.

A few drops of sesame oil added to the cooking oil will enhance the flavor.

4 servings	
½ cup	(125 mL) unsalted butter
2 tbsp	(30 mL) horseradish in vinegar
2 tsp	(10 mL) chopped parsley
	a few drops of Worcestershire sauce
4	filets mignons, 4 oz (115 g) each
2 tbsp	(30 mL) peanut oil
	salt and pepper

■ In a bowl, soften butter, then blend in horseradish, parsley and Worcestershire sauce.

■ Shape seasoned butter into 4 small pats and refrigerate for 20 minutes.

■ Meanwhile cut a cavity along the thick side of each filet mignon.

■ In a large skillet, heat oil to smoking, sear filets mignons, season to taste when turning.

■ Remove filets mignons from skillet and place a pat of butter in each cavity.

■ Allow butter to melt for 1 minute and serve.

96

Microwave Beef in Puff Pastry

Using a few modern-day shortcuts, you can whip up this classic dish in no time flat, thanks to the microwave oven. Pâté de campagne can be just as tasty as the finer-textured pâté de foie gras. You can add canned vegetables—sliced carrots or asparagus spears—before closing the pastry.

4 servings

4	frozen puff pastry shells
4	filets mignons, each 1 inch (2,5 cm) thick
4 oz	(115 g) pâté de foie gras
	salt and pepper
2 tbsp	(30 mL) melted butter
2 tsp	(10 mL) soy sauce
1	egg yolk

■ Thaw puff pastry shells. With rolling pin, flatten and shape each into a rectangle, sprinkle a small amount of flour on pastry shell to avoid it sticking to rolling pin.

■ Put 1 oz (30 g) pâté de foie in the middle of each pastry shell; place filets mignons on the pâté and season with salt and pepper.

■ Wrap each filet mignon in its pastry and brush with melted butter.

■ Combine soy sauce, egg yolk, and the remaining butter, and brush the crust with the mixture.

■ Place garnished filets mignons on a microwave-safe dish. Cook at MEDIUM-HIGH for 3 to 4 minutes. Rotate dish one-half turn halfway through cooking.

• *Put pâté onto pastry and place filet mignon on top.*

• *Wrap each filet mignon in its pastry, then brush with the egg.*

Tournedos

Beef aficionados will love tender filet mignon served tournedos-style.

You can enhance the classic tournedos flavor with any number of sauces that harmonize with the rest of your menu. The eight shown on the opposite page provide a good range of flavors and textures.

4 servings

4	4 oz (115 g) tournedos
2 tbsp	(30 mL) peanut oil
	salt and pepper

■ Preheat oven to 350 °F (175 °C).

■ In a skillet, heat oil and cook tournedos steaks for 3 minutes on each side. When turning, roll each steak on its side to sear edges. Season with salt and pepper.

■ Place tournedos steaks in oven and cook briefly to desired doneness.

■ Using the same skillet, prepare your favorite sauce.

Tournedos with Spinach

Worried that vegetables take too long to cook? With this recipe, they'll be ready in 30 seconds!

4 servings

4	filets mignons
4	strips of bacon or pork fat
1 lb	(450 g) fresh spinach, stems removed, or frozen spinach, thawed
2 tsp	(10 mL) olive oil
2 tsp	(10 mL) peanut oil or sunflower oil
	salt and pepper
2 tsp	(10 mL) onion, chopped
1/4 cup	(60 mL) green olives, chopped
1/4 cup	(60 mL) white vermouth

■ Preheat oven to 350 °F (175 °C).

■ Blanch a few spinach leaves in boiling, salted water and let stand to cool, then pat dry.

■ Fold spinach leaves to same width as bacon or pork fat strips.

■ Wrap blanched spinach leaves around filet mignon, wrap bacon strips around spinach leaves, and tie string around bacon strips, making sure spinach is covered.

■ In a skillet, heat oil mixture and sear tournedos 4 minutes each side, then roll each tournedos on its sides to fry bacon evenly.

■ Remove tournedos from skillet and season with salt and pepper. Reduce heat to low.

■ Place tournedos on an ovenproof plate and keep warm in oven.

■ Using the same skillet, cook onions, olives and remaining spinach, stirring constantly.

■ After 30 seconds, pour vermouth over mixture, then remove skillet from heat.

■ Remove tournedos from oven.

■ Remove string, arrange tournedos on a serving dish, garnish with vegetables and serve.

* Illustrated recipe

Sauces, clockwise from the top:
Tomato ▪ Shallot ▪ Brie ▪ Two-pepper ▪
Mustard ▪ Pearl Onion ▪ Almond ▪
Tarragon

8 Gourmet Sauces

Shallot Sauce

- Sauté 3 finely sliced French (dry) shallots until transparent but not browned.

- Deglaze skillet with 1 tbsp (15 mL) wine vinegar and reduce liquid almost completely.

- Pour ¼ cup (60 mL) beef stock over mixture and reduce mixture by half.

- Add 1 tsp (5mL) kneaded butter (beurre manié, made by rubbing together equal parts of flour and butter, and rolling into small balls for use in thickening sauces). Stir well and simmer for 2 minutes.

Tarragon Sauce

Follow same technique as for shallot sauce. Simply replace shallots with 1 tsp (5 mL) chopped onion and ¼ tsp (1 mL) chopped garlic.

- When deglazing skillet, add ½ tsp (2 mL) chopped tarragon.

Grilled Almond Sauce

- Sauté 2 tbsp (30 mL) slivered almonds in 2 tsp (10 mL) butter until golden and set aside.

- Using the same skillet, heat ¼ cup (60 mL) butter until foamy, add juice of ½ lemon along with sautéed almonds and garnish with chopped parsley.

Pearl Onion Sauce

- Follow same technique as for shallot sauce, replacing shallots with 12 pearl onions, sliced in half along with 1 tsp (5 mL) finely chopped onion.

Two-pepper Sauce

- Follow same technique as for shallot sauce, replacing shallots with 1 tsp (5 mL) chopped onion and ¼ tsp (1 mL) chopped garlic.

- When deglazing skillet, add ¼ tsp (1 mL) each of ground black peppercorns and green peppercorns.

Mustard Sauce

- Sauté 1 tsp (5 mL) finely chopped onion until transparent but not browned.

- Add ½ cup (125 mL) beef stock to onions and reduce mixture by half.

- Reduce heat and blend in 2 tbsp (30 mL) Dijon mustard.

- Add 1 tbsp (15 mL) 35% cream, cook for 2 minutes without boiling.

Creamed Brie Sauce

- Follow same technique as for mustard sauce, replacing mustard with 3 tbsp (45 mL) Brie cheese (slice off crust) and increasing cream to ¼ cup (60 mL).

Tomato Sauce

- Sauté 1 tsp (5 mL) minced onions until transparent but not browned.

- Add ½ cup (125 mL) beef stock to onions then reduce mixture by half.

- Reduce heat and add 2 tbsp (30 mL) tomato paste.

- Add 1 tbsp (15 mL) 35% cream and cook for 2 minutes without boiling.

HOW TO STUFF AND COOK ROAST BEEF

We all remember the traditional Sunday roast beef with its pleasant aroma wafting through the house long before dinnertime. There's no reason why this fine tradition should be forgotten. Preparing a tender, moist roast is one of the simplest cooking techniques.

How to stuff roast beef

- Make a lateral cut without opening the ends.

- Open the cavity.

- Spread strong mustard in the cavity.

- Fill with stuffing of your choice.

- With a trussing needle, close cavity.

- If you prefer, tie with string as shown.

How to cook roast beef

- Preheat oven to 400 °F (205 °C).

- In hot oil, sear roast on all sides until brown.

- Season when meat is well browned.

- Place in a roasting pan.

- Cook for 15 to 20 minutes per pound (per 450 g) depending on desired doneness.

- For tasty pan juice, add finely-chopped vegetables and beef stock.

Roast Beef au Jus

No fuss, no muss. Roast beef is simple to prepare and uses very few utensils. The seasoned flour called for in this recipe can be prepared in quantity and kept in a tightly-closed jar for your next roast. Just dredge it, pop it in the oven, et voila!

8 servings

Seasoned flour

2 cups	(500 mL)	flour
2 tbsp	(30 mL)	salt
1 tbsp	(15 mL)	celery salt
1 tbsp	(15 mL)	pepper
2 tbsp	(30 mL)	dry mustard
¼ cup	(60 mL)	paprika
2 tbsp	(30 mL)	garlic powder
1 tsp	(5 mL)	ginger
½ tsp	(2 mL)	thyme
½ tsp	(2 mL)	basil
½ tsp	(2 mL)	oregano
1	4.4 lb sirloin roast (2 kg), with bone or boneless	
1 cup	(250 mL)	beef stock

■ In a bowl, combine all seasoned flour ingredients, and keep in a tightly closed jar for future use.

■ Preheat oven to 450 °F (230 °C).

■ Dredge roast beef with seasoned flour and place in roasting pan with a rack.

■ Sear roast beef in oven for 20 minutes then reduce oven temperature to 400 °F (205 °C).

■ Cook roast beef 10 minutes per pound (per 450 g), for rare meat, 15 minutes per pound (per 450 g) for medium-cooked meat, and 20 minutes per pound (per 450 g) for well-done meat.

■ Twenty minutes before the meat is done, baste with beef stock.

■ You can use another tender cut, if you prefer. Get your butcher to prepare it. Remember that large roasts have more flavor.

Roast Beef Stuffed with Wild Garlic

Wild garlic is a very recent culinary discovery. Its flavor is somewhat milder than that of regular garlic. It actually looks more like a shallot, with a slightly yellow bulb. When in season, you can find it in any open-air market. Throughout the rest of the year, it is sold in tiny glass jars in your local supermarket.

8 servings

1	3 to 4 lb (1,5 to 2 kg) roast beef, rolled, boneless
¼ cup	(60 mL) hot prepared mustard
3 tbsp	(45 mL) parsley, chopped
2 tbsp	(30 mL) minced wild garlic
	salt and pepper
3 tbsp	(45 mL) peanut oil
2 cups	(500 mL) beef stock
1 cup	(250 mL) water

■ Preheat oven to 400 °F (205 °C).

■ Prepare roast beef for stuffing by removing string and slitting the meat lengthwise to form a deep stuffing pocket.

■ Spread cavity generously with hot mustard, sprinkle with parsley, add wild garlic and season with salt and pepper.

■ Retie roast. Don't let the stuffing seep through, as it might burn during cooking.

■ In an oven-proof skillet, heat oil and sear roast on all sides.

■ Put skillet and roast in the oven and cook 15 minutes per pound (per 450 g).

■ When the roast is done, transfer it to a serving dish.

■ Over medium heat, deglaze skillet with beef stock and water.

■ Reduce liquid by half and serve sauce with roast beef.

VARIATIONS

• **Replace hot mustard with 2 tbsp (30 mL) tomato paste and 2 tbsp (30 mL) chili sauce.**

• **Replace parsley with basil.**

• **Replace wild garlic with regular garlic.**

102

Roast Beef with Wine

Red wine and beef complement one another in cooking. The fragrant bouquet of the former blends well with the flavor of the latter.

You don't need to pick the finest vintage for cooking. Avoid using cheap wines as they often have a high chemical content.

8 servings

1 tbsp	(15 mL) butter
¼ cup	(60 mL) carrots, finely chopped
¼ cup	(60 mL) onions, finely chopped
¼ cup	(60 mL) leek, finely chopped
¼ cup	(60 mL) celery, finely chopped
½ cup	(125 mL) dry red wine
1 tbsp	(15 mL) flour
3 cups	(750 mL) beef stock
1 tbsp	(15 mL) corn oil
1	2 to 3 lb (900 g to 1,4 kg) roast beef, rolled, boneless
	salt and pepper

Bouquet garni prepared with:

1	pinch of thyme
1	bay leaf
2	pinches of ground pepper
2	pinches of parsley

■ In a heavy skillet, melt butter and cook carrots, onions, leek and celery then add flour, stirring constantly for 1 minute.

■ Deglaze skillet with wine and reduce liquid by half.

■ Add beef stock and reduce by one-third, then set aside.

■ In a thick-bottomed casserole, barely larger than the meat, heat oil, sear meat on all sides and season with salt and pepper.

■ Pour in sauce and simmer for 1 hour, partially covered.

■ Fifteen minutes before end of cooking process, add bouquet garni.

■ Put the roast on a warm serving dish, cover with aluminum foil, and let stand for 10 minutes. Slice.

■ If you want a thicker sauce, run vegetables and sauce through blender, but remember to remove bay leaf first.

TIME-SAVERS

• **Cook vegetables in the casserole with the meat.**

• **Replace the sauce recipe with a commercial sauce mix.**

SPARERIBS

Beef Ribs with Mustard

Aromatic "old-fashion-ed" prepared mustard, with coarsely-ground seeds, is the keynote of this dish. For a spicier flavor, replace the water with tomato juice and ¹/₂ tsp (2mL) sugar.

4 servings

2 lbs	(900 g) beef ribs
3 tbsp	(45 mL) flour
1 tbsp	(15 mL) dry mustard
2 tbsp	(30 mL) oil
1	bay leaf
	pinch of thyme
	salt and pepper
1 cup	(250 mL) hot water
¹/₂ cup	(125 mL) red wine
2 tbsp	(30 mL) "old-fash-ioned" prepared mustard

■ Dredge each beef rib with mixture of flour and dry mustard.

■ In a heavy skillet, heat oil and cook beef ribs a few at a time.

■ Place beef ribs in a stove-top casserole dish and season with bay leaf, thyme, salt and pepper.

■ Pour hot water, wine and "old-fashioned" mustard over beef rib mixture and simmer for 1 hour over low heat, half covered, stirring from time to time.

* Illustrated recipe

Sweet-and-Sour Garlic-flavored Beef Ribs

Tamari sauce contains less sodium than soy sauce. Try it, you might find it more to your taste.

4 servings

¹/₂ cup	(125 mL) ketchup
¹/₂ cup	(125 mL) brown sugar
2 tbsp	(30 mL) vinegar
¹/₂ cup	(125 mL) water
2	garlic cloves
2 tbsp	(30 mL) soy sauce
2 tbsp	(30 mL) cayenne pepper
¹/₂ tsp	(2 mL) cumin
1 tbsp	(15 mL) oil
	salt and pepper
2 lbs	(900 g) beef ribs

■ Preheat oven to 350 °F (175 °C).

■ In a saucepan, combine the first 8 ingredients.

■ Meanwhile, in a skillet, heat oil, sauté beef ribs and season with salt and pepper.

■ Place beef ribs in a baking dish, coat ribs with sauce and cook for 1¹/₄ hours, stirring often.

Beef Ribs with Barbecue Sauce

Serve these ribs with brown rice and mixed vegetables, or try baked potatoes and a green salad for a simple, well-balanced meal.

4 servings

Marinade

½ cup	(125 mL) ketchup	
1 cup	(250 mL) water	
1 tbsp	(15 mL) sugar	
1 tsp	(5 mL) salt	
20	black peppercorns	
	pinch of savory	
4	garlic cloves, chopped fine	
2	onions, thinly sliced	
3 tbsp	(45 mL) soy sauce	
2 lbs	(900 g) beef ribs, cross cut	

■ In a bowl, combine all marinade ingredients.

■ In a large microwave-safe dish, pour marinade over beef ribs, and refrigerate for 24 hours, stirring 2 or 3 times during marinating process.

■ Remove beef ribs from dish and set aside.

■ Boil marinade in microwave at HIGH for 5 minutes.

■ Add beef ribs and cook at MEDIUM for 30 minutes.

■ Stir once, then cook at MEDIUM for 30 minutes more or until ribs are tender to taste.

* Illustrated recipe (upper half)

Beef Ribs with Honey Sauce

If you have no pressure-cooker, this dish will be just as tasty when cooked in the oven at 325 °F (160 °C).

4 servings

3 tbsp	(45 mL) oil	
2 lbs	(900 g) beef ribs, cross cut	
1 cup	(250 mL) water	
2	onions, finely sliced	
	salt and pepper	

Honey Sauce

½ cup	(125 mL) honey	
2 tbsp	(30 mL) soy sauce	
¼ cup	(60 mL) sweet-and-sour sauce	
½ cup	(125 mL) water	
½ cup	(125 mL) chili sauce	
2	garlic cloves, finely chopped	

■ In a pressure-cooker, heat oil and cook beef ribs several at a time for a few minutes.

■ In a skillet, sauté the onions gently, then add them to beef ribs and season with salt and pepper.

■ Pour water over beef rib mixture, seal pressure-cooker cover, set pressure regulator and cook for 25 minutes. Turn off heat and let pressure reduce.

■ In a bowl, combine honey sauce ingredients, pour over beef ribs and let mixture simmer for 10 minutes.

* Illustrated recipe (bottom half)

Cubed beef

Pressed for time? Reduce your cooking time by half and prepare this dish in the pressure-cooker in less than 45 minutes.

4 servings	
1 tbsp	(15 mL) corn oil
½ cup	(125 mL) carrots, diced
24	pearl onions
½ cup	(125 mL) celery, sliced
2 tbsp	(30 mL) flour
1 lb	(450 g) beef cubes

Seasoning

1 tbsp	(15 mL) puréed tomatoes
¼ tsp	(1 mL) thyme
¼ tsp	(1 mL) pepper
¼ tsp	(1 mL) salt
2	garlic cloves, finely chopped
1	bay leaf
2 cups	(500 mL) beef stock
¼ cup	(60 mL) dry red wine
½ lb	(250 g) fresh mushrooms, sliced

■ In a stove-top casserole, heat oil and sauté carrots with onions and celery.

■ Dredge beef cubes with flour, add to vegetables and sear on all sides.

■ Add seasoning ingredients.

■ Pour beef stock and wine over meat to cover. Add a small amount of water if there is not enough liquid, and let mixture simmer for 1 ½ hours, covered.

■ Twenty minutes before cooking ends, add mushrooms.

Diced Beef with Tomatoes

Beef becomes wonderfully tender when simmered for an hour, as in this recipe for diced beef. Its juices add a delicious flavor to the accompanying tomato sauce. To make the most of the sauce, serve this dish with rice or potatoes.

4 servings	
1 tbsp	(15 mL) oil
1 tbsp	(15 mL) butter
1 lb	(450 g) beef cubes
14 oz	(398 mL) canned tomato soup
14 oz	(398 mL) canned tomatoes
¾ cup	(180 mL) celery, chopped
14 oz	(398 mL) canned mushrooms
½ tsp	(2 mL) ginger
3 tbsp	(45 mL) Worcestershire sauce
2 tbsp	(30 mL) brown sugar
3 tbsp	(45 mL) vinegar
	garlic salt, to taste
	salt and pepper

■ Preheat oven to 350 °F (175 °C).

■ In a large skillet, heat oil, melt butter and sear beef cubes. Put the seared meat in a casserole dish and keep warm in oven.

■ Degrease skillet, add all other ingredients and bring to a boil.

■ Pour mixture over beef cubes, then cook in oven for 1 hour.

■ Transfer to a hot serving dish.

* Illustrated recipe

Polynesian Beef Kebabs

Get out of the kitchen on hot summer days and cook this recipe over the barbecue.

4 servings

Marinade

14 oz	(398 mL)	canned pineapple chunks
1/4 cup	(60 mL)	brown sugar
1/4 cup	(60 mL)	vinegar
1 tbsp	(15 mL)	soy sauce
1 lb	(450 g)	beef cubes
16		fresh mushrooms
16		pieces green bell pepper
16		cherry tomatoes
2 tbsp	(30 mL)	cornstarch
2 tbsp	(30 mL)	cold water

■ Preheat oven to 350 °F (175 °C).

■ In a large bowl, combine all marinade ingredients, pour marinade over beef cubes and refrigerate to marinate for 6 to 8 hours.

■ Remove beef cubes and pineapple chunks, and set marinade aside.

■ Slide beef cubes on the skewers, alternating with mushrooms, pineapple chunks and peppers, then place a cherry tomato at each end of skewer.

■ Cook kebabs in oven.

■ Dissolve cornstarch in cold water. In small saucepan, heat marinade, add cornstarch mixture, and stir gently for a few minutes until mixture begins to thicken. Pour over kebabs.

* Illustrated recipe

Filet Mignon Sauté

Beef sautés are a popular family dish in France, where this dish originated. Its robust flavor will satisfy the hearty eaters at your table.

4 servings

1 tbsp	(15 mL)	oil
1 tbsp	(15 mL)	butter
1 lb	(450 g)	filet mignon, cut into large cubes
12		pearl onions, blanched
12		mushroom caps
		salt and pepper
		pinch of thyme
1/4 cup	(60 mL)	white wine
1/2 cup	(125 mL)	beef stock
1 tsp	(5 mL)	kneaded butter (half butter, half flour)
		pinch of finely chopped parsley

■ In a cast iron skillet, heat oil, melt butter and sear filet mignon cubes.

■ Add onions and mushrooms, season with salt and pepper and sprinkle with thyme.

■ Deglaze skillet with white wine, then reduce liquid by half.

■ Add beef stock and kneaded butter and stir until sauce is smooth.

■ Sprinkle with parsley and serve.

107

Beef strips

Beef Stroganoff

Watching your weight? Simply replace sour cream with plain yogurt.

8 servings

2 lbs	(900 g) filet of beef
3 tbsp	(45 mL) flour
½ tsp	(2 mL) salt
¼ tsp	(1 mL) pepper
3 tbsp	(45 mL) vegetable shortening
3	onions, thinly sliced
½ cup	(125 mL) tomato juice
10 oz	(284 mL) canned beef consommé
½ tsp	(2 mL) sugar
½ cup	(125 mL) sour cream
½ lb	(250 g) mushrooms, sliced
3 tbsp	(45 mL) Burgundy wine (optional)

■ Cut filet of beef into thin strips, dredge beef strips with flour, salt and pepper, or with seasoned flour.

■ In a skillet, melt vegetable shortening and sauté beef strips with onions.

■ Add tomato juice, beef consommé and sugar.

■ Reduce heat and let mixture simmer until beef is tender.

■ Blend in sour cream, mushrooms, and wine and heat but do not boil.

Beef Sukiyaki

Wash spinach leaves thoroughly. The easiest way is to fill the kitchen sink with cold water and swish the spinach leaves in it.

4 servings

3 tbsp	(45 mL) vegetable oil
1	medium-size onion, sliced
4	large mushrooms, sliced
1 lb	(450 g) beef cut in strips
½ lb	(225 g) fresh spinach
1 cup	(250 mL) celery, sliced diagonally
4	shallots
¼ cup	(60 mL) soy sauce
2 tbsp	(30 mL) sugar
10 oz	(284 mL) canned beef consommé

■ In a heavy skillet, heat oil and sauté onion.

■ Add mushrooms and beef strips and cook for 2 minutes.

■ Add spinach and cook for 1 minute.

■ Add celery and cook for 1 minute.

■ Cut shallots lengthwise into strips, then add to mixture.

■ Blend soy sauce into mixture, and cook for 1 minute.

■ Pour beef consommé into mixture, add sugar, and let simmer for 2 minutes, then serve.

* Illustrated recipe

Beef Strips with Peppers

Prepare this recipe with your leftover roast beef.

4 servings

2 tbsp	(30 mL) vegetable oil
2 lbs	(900 g) beef, cut into ½ inch (1,25 cm) wide strips
1	onion, diced
¼ cup	(60 mL) soy sauce
¼ cup	(60 mL) sugar
	salt and pepper
¼ tsp	(1 mL) ginger
2	sweet peppers, cut into strips
4	tomatoes, cut into wedges
¼ cup	(60 mL) water
1 cup	(250 mL) bean sprouts (optional)

■ In a skillet, heat oil and sauté beef strips.

■ Add onions, soy sauce, sugar, salt, pepper, ginger, sweet peppers, tomato wedges, and water, then cook for 15 minutes.

■ Add bean sprouts, if desired, at the very end, or in sweet pepper shells (blanched), as in our photograph.

* Illustrated recipe

Beef with Mushrooms

This one-casserole dinner is inexpensive and nourishing. You can replace the round beef strips with medium-lean hamburger.

4 servings

1 tbsp	(15 mL) butter or margarine
1 lb	(450 g) round steak, cut into thin strips
	salt and pepper
4	potatoes, diced
4	carrots, cut into small sticks
10 oz	(284 mL) canned cream of mushroom soup
1 cup	(250 mL) water

■ In a large skillet, melt butter and sauté steak strips.

■ Place strips in microwave-safe dish, add potatoes, stir gently, and cover with carrot sticks.

■ Combine cream of mushroom soup and water, pour over carrots and season.

■ Cook in microwave at HIGH for 10 minutes.

■ Check for doneness, stir, and cook 10 minutes longer.

Marinated BEEF

Serving marinated dishes requires simple planning. Marinate one day, serve the next. Marinating softens meat fibers, and you can choose cheaper cuts when preparing these types of dishes.

Beer-flavored Beef

Serve this marinated beef with a side dish of sauerkraut and you'll have the makings of a Bavarian feast. Wash it down with a light ale.

4 servings

Marinade

8 oz	(237 mL)	beer
¼ cup	(60 mL)	oil
2 tbsp	(30 mL)	cider vinegar
1		onion, thinly sliced
2		garlic cloves, finely chopped
1		bay leaf
¼ tsp	(1 mL)	thyme
½ tsp	(2 mL)	salt
½ tsp	(2 mL)	pepper
1 tbsp	(15 mL)	oil
4		¾ inch (2 cm) thick blade, round or cross-rib steaks
4		slices bacon, cut into small pieces
2		onions, thinly sliced
		chopped parsley

■ In a large bowl, combine all marinade ingredients.

■ Using a fork, prick the meat several times.

■ Put steaks on a plate, coat with marinade, cover and refrigerate for 8 hours or overnight.

■ Drain steaks and pat dry, then set marinade aside.

■ In a skillet, heat oil to smoking, sear steaks, turn meat and add bacon bits and onions.

■ Meanwhile, reduce marinade over high heat by one-third.

■ Pour marinade sauce over steaks and garnish with parsley.

Flank Steak

Grilled flank steak needs no oil or butter. Weight-watchers can therefore treat themselves to the fragrant red wine sauce in this recipe with a clear conscience.

4 servings

Marinade

³/₄ cup	(180 mL) dry red wine
1	garlic clove, minced
¹/₂ tsp	(2 mL) oregano
¹/₂ tsp	(2 mL) salt
¹/₄ tsp	(1 mL) pepper
4	flank steaks or inside round steaks, 1 inch (2,5 cm) thick
1 tbsp	(15 mL) cornstarch
2 tbsp	(30 mL) cold water

■ Preheat oven broiler.

■ In a large bowl, combine all marinade ingredients.

■ Using a fork, prick the meat several times.

■ Put steaks on a plate, coat with marinade, cover and refrigerate to marinate 18 to 24 hours. Turn meat 2 or 3 times during marinating.

■ Drain steaks and set marinade aside.

■ Broil steaks 5 or 6 minutes on each side for medium-rare meat.

■ Meanwhile, blend corn-starch and water, add to marinade, and heat, stirring, until the sauce thickens to a translucent ruby color.

■ Set the steaks on a warm serving platter, pour on the wine sauce, and serve.

HELPFUL HINTS

• If you set the steaks to marinate in an air-tight container, you can simply flip it over a few times to turn the meat in the marinade.

• The sauce will be richer if you add 3 tbsp (45mL) 35% cream.

VERSATILE HAMBURGER

Hamburger is a wonderfully versatile form of beef. A cook has no truer friend in a tight situation. Ground beef can be easily frozen in small portions for convenient use.

Meatballs, meat loaves, stuffings—hamburger can be served in sundry ways that will surprise and satisfy a hungry family.

Supermarkets stock hamburger with varying fat content, usually described as lean, semi-lean, and regular. The semi-lean variety is preferable for most dishes. The regular makes dishes greasy, and the lean, lacking in fat, tends to toughen with cooking.

Basic Recipe for Meatballs

A basic recipe is never boring when accompanied by tasty, innovative garnishes. We offer you 25 to start with ...

4 servings

1 lb	(450 g) ground beef
1	egg
1 tbsp	(15 mL) onions, chopped
¼ tsp	(1 mL) garlic, chopped
	salt and pepper
½ tsp	(2 mL) Worcestershire sauce
1 tbsp	(15 mL) oil

■ Combine the first six ingredients and shape into meatballs. For a nearly raw to rare-cooked meatball, shape 4 meatballs per pound (450 g), and for a medium-rare to well-done meatball, shape 5 meatballs per pound (450 g).

■ Sear meatballs in oil over high heat, then reduce heat halfway through cooking process. Allow 1 minute cooking time on each side for raw meatballs, 1 ½ minutes for rare, 2 minutes for medium, and 3 minutes for well-done meatballs.

114

25 Little Treats

First Column

Red and green grapes with radishes

Tomato sauce and chives

Dijon mustard and "old-fashioned" mustard

Sliced mushrooms and parsley

Olives and cheese

Second Column

Marinated, whole oyster mushrooms with sesame seeds

Red and green cabbage, finely chopped and marinated

Bean sprouts and red onions

Kiwi and tarragon

Horseradish and sliced ginger root

Third Column

Sliced beets and coriander

Braised leek

Diced eggplant

Oranges and pink peppercorns

Sliced red and white onions

Fourth Column

Cantaloup and tarragon

Anchovies and capers

Peppers, two or three colors

Green onions

Pickles and pearl onions

Fifth Column

Tomatoes and basil

Steak sauce and chervil

Celery and saffron

Red and white radishes with rosemary

Sliced zucchini and cauliflower flowerets

Add your own choice of grated cheese to any one of the above combinations.

Vegetable-stuffed Hamburger

Try this vegetable-stuffed hamburger minus the bun for a nourishing new treat for young and old.

4 servings	
1 lb	(450 g) ground beef
1	egg
¼ tsp	(1 mL) Worcestershire sauce
	salt and pepper
½ cup	(125 mL) onion, chopped
½ cup	(125 mL) green bell pepper, chopped
½ cup	(125 mL) celery, chopped

First Method

■ Combine ground beef, egg and Worcestershire sauce in a large bowl and season with salt and pepper. Stir in chopped vegetables.

■ Cook over high heat then reduce heat halfway through.

Second Method

■ Combine ground beef, egg, Worcestershire sauce and salt and pepper in a bowl. Shape meat into thin patties.

■ Arrange chopped vegetables between two patties and seal edges tightly.

■ Sear patties over high heat then reduce heat halfway through cooking.

* Illustrated recipe

Hamburger with Onions

Just the right blend of ingredients, even those most commonly found in any kitchen, can turn a dull hamburger into a mouth-watering delight.

4 servings	
1 lb	(450 g) ground beef
1	egg
½ tsp	(2 mL) Worcestershire sauce
	salt and pepper
1	small package instant onion soup mix
1	garlic clove, finely chopped

■ Combine ground beef, egg and Worcestershire sauce in a bowl with onion soup mix and garlic, and season with salt and pepper.

■ Sear hamburgers over high heat, then reduce heat halfway through cooking.

Super Steak Tartare

Steak Tartare is definitely an acquired taste, but well worth trying.

Be sure to use the freshest and finest quality beef, extra lean. Ask your butcher to grind it for you while you wait.

---
4 servings
---

10 oz	(284 g) very lean, freshly-ground hamburger
2	egg yolks
1 tbsp	(15 mL) onion, chopped
½ tsp	(2 mL) capers, chopped
2	anchovies, chopped
1 tsp	(5 mL) sour pickles, chopped
¼ tsp	(1 mL) salt
¼ tsp	(1 mL) ground black pepper
4	drops of Tabasco sauce
1 tsp	(5 mL) Worcestershire sauce

- Combine all ingredients and shape into patties.
- Serve with french fries and mayonnaise.

Beef Wheels

This intriguing and delectable way of serving hamburger is a sure-fire conversation piece. Surprisingly, the ingredients and preparation are perfectly simple.

---
4 servings
---

2 tbsp	(30 mL) oil
1 lb	(450 g) lean ground beef
1	onion, thinly sliced
¼ cup	(60 mL) ketchup
¼ tsp	(1 mL) garlic salt
¼ tsp	(1 mL) pepper
¾ cup	(180 mL) canned cream of mushroom soup

Pastry

2 ½ cups	(560 mL) flour
2 tbsp	(30 mL) baking powder
½ tsp	(2 mL) salt
1 tsp	(5 mL) curry powder
½ cup	(80 mL) vegetable shortening
⅓ cup	(80 mL) milk

- Preheat oven to 400 °F (205 °C).
- In a skillet, heat oil and sauté ground beef with onion. Pour off excess fat.
- Add ketchup, garlic salt, pepper, and cream of mushroom soup and let stand to cool.
- In a large bowl, combine pastry ingredients, knead and roll pastry into a 12-inch (30 cm) square.
- Spoon meat mixture onto pastry square, roll and press with fingers to seal. Slice into 8 pieces, 1 ½ inches (4 cm) thick.
- In a well-greased, round baking dish, arrange 7 wheels in a circle and place one in the middle.
- Cook in oven for 20 to 25 minutes and serve hot, coated with brown gravy or mushroom sauce.

Stuffed Rolls

A caterer might decorate these stuffed rolls with olives, pickles or red and green sweet pepper strips. Why not try it yourself?

24 rolls

3 tbsp	(45 mL) oil
1	large onion, finely chopped
3 lbs	(1,4 kg) ground beef
10 oz	(284 mL) canned chicken gumbo soup
½ cup	(125 mL) chili sauce or ketchup
2 tsp	(10 mL) mustard
	salt and pepper
24	salad rolls

■ Preheat oven to 350 °F (175 °C).

■ In a skillet, heat oil, fry onions, then add ground beef and fry until meat is fully cooked.

■ Add other ingredients, stir, let mixture simmer over low heat for 1 hour or until nearly all the liquid has evaporated, then let stand to cool.

■ Slit rolls in half, lengthwise, and spoon small amount of mixture into each, then wrap in aluminum foil.

■ Warm stuffed loaves for 20 minutes in oven before serving.

Spinach Tart

Give this spinach tart extra zest by seasoning it with Italian spices.

Add a 2-cup (500 mL) layer of cooked rice between the spinach and the meat for a more nourishing dish.

4 servings

8 oz	(225 g) puff pastry, thawed
1 tbsp	(15 mL) oil
1 lb	(450 g) lean ground beef
1	onion, chopped
½ cup	(125 mL) mushrooms, sliced
1	garlic clove, chopped
	chopped parsley, to taste
1 tsp	(5 mL) butter
8 oz	(237 mL) package fresh spinach

■ Preheat oven to 425 °F (220 °C).

■ Line a 10-inch (25 cm) pie plate with half the pastry.

■ In a skillet, heat oil and cook meat, then set aside.

■ Using the same skillet, cook onions, mushrooms and garlic, add meat, sprinkle with parsley and set aside.

■ In a separate skillet, heat 1 tsp (5 mL) oil and gently sauté spinach.

■ Spoon meat mixture onto puff pastry, cover with a layer of spinach and top mixture with second pastry shell.

■ Bake in oven for 20 minutes, then reduce oven heat to 350 °F (175 °C) and bake 15 minutes longer.

Stuffed Peppers

Enhance the already delightful look and taste of stuffed peppers by topping each one with a half-slice of bacon before cooking.

4 servings

1 tbsp	(15 mL) oil
1 lb	(450 g) ground beef
½ cup	(180 mL) cooked rice
1	onion, chopped
1	garlic clove, finely chopped
2 cups	(500 mL) tomatoes, cut into pieces
2 tbsp	(30 mL) Worcestershire sauce
	salt and pepper
1 cup	(250 mL) grated mild Cheddar cheese
4 to 6	sweet peppers

■ Preheat oven to 350 °F (175 °C).

■ In a skillet, heat oil and cook ground beef.

■ Add rice, onion, garlic, tomatoes, Worcestershire sauce, salt and pepper, and let mixture simmer for 10 minutes.

■ Stir in 3/4 cup (180 mL) grated Cheddar.

■ Lie the peppers on their sides, slice off one-third, scoop out pulp from the remainder, and sprinkle inside with salt.

■ Fill peppers with meat mixture and cook for 25 minutes in oven.

■ Three minutes before the end of cooking, add rest of cheese and run under the broiler for a few minutes.

* *Illustrated recipe*

Stuffed Zucchini

Keep the scooped-out zucchini. Dice and freeze it for later use in a hearty soup.

4 servings

2 tbsp	(30 mL) oil
1 lb	(450 g) ground beef
1	large onion, finely sliced
1	carrot, grated
1	green bell pepper, finely sliced
2 or 3	fresh tomatoes, sliced
	pinch of fresh parsley
	pinch of chives
1	shallot, finely chopped
	pepper
2	medium-size unpeeled zucchini, halved lengthwise
1	garlic clove, finely chopped
10 oz	(284 mL) canned cream of tomato soup
2 or 3	fresh tomatoes, sliced
½ cup	(125 mL) grated Mozzarella cheese

■ In a skillet, heat 1 tbsp (15 mL) oil, sauté ground beef, remove from heat, and set aside.

■ Using the same skillet, heat the remaining oil, sauté onion, carrot, and pepper, and reduce heat. Add meat, cream of tomato soup, tomatoes and seasonings, and simmer for a few minutes then set aside.

■ Slice zucchini lengthwise and scoop out half the pulp, spoon meat mixture into cavity, and spread grated or sliced Mozzarella over stuffing.

■ Broil stuffed zucchini halves a few minutes to melt cheese. Serve.

* *Illustrated recipe*

Upside Down Meat Pie

Enhance the nutritional value of this wholesome meal by adding a few spoonfuls of wheat germ to the meat mixture.

4 servings

2 tbsp	(30 mL) butter
1	onion, finely chopped
2 cups	(500 mL) ground beef
10 oz	(284 mL) canned tomato soup
	salt and pepper

Pastry

1 ½ cups	(375 mL) flour
1 tbsp	(15 mL) baking powder
	pinch of salt
1 tsp	(5 mL) paprika
1 tsp	(5 mL) celery salt
¼ cup	(60 mL) butter
1 cup	(250 mL) milk

■ Preheat oven to 450 °F (230°C).

■ In a skillet, melt butter, sauté onion then add ground beef and sauté for a few minutes.

■ Fold tomato soup into meat mixture and heat to boiling, let simmer about 20 minutes, then remove from heat and set aside.

■ In a large bowl, combine pastry ingredients until mixture is smooth and roll out pastry.

■ Pour meat and tomato soup mixture into a pie plate and top with pastry crust.

■ Cook in oven for 20 minutes.

■ Turn out onto serving dish.

VARIATIONS

• **Cover beef and tomato soup mixture with sliced cheese or smoked ham.**

• **Place a few leaves of fresh, blanched spinach between meat and pastry.**

120

Easy Meat Loaf

You'll get a lighter, more economical meat loaf by replacing the whole milk with recon- stituted powdered milk.

8 servings

1 ½ cups	(375 mL) bread, diced
1 cup	(250 mL) milk
2 lbs	(900 g) ground beef
½ cup	(125 mL) celery, chopped
½ cup	(125 mL) carrots, grated
1	onion, chopped
1	egg
1 tbsp	(15 mL) prepared horseradish
2 tsp	(10 mL) salt
¼ tsp	(1 mL) pepper

■ Preheat oven to 375 °F (190 °C).

■ In a large bowl, combine bread and milk and let stand for 5 minutes, then add all other ingredients.

■ Fold mixture into a loaf pan. Cut 8 thin, serving- portion lines across top of loaf.

■ Bake in oven for 1 hour.

* Illustrated recipe

Old-fashioned Meat Loaf

Fiber-rich oatmeal adds an old-fashioned but nutritious element to this simple recipe.

8 servings

2 lbs	(900 g) ground beef
¼ cup	(60 mL) rolled oats
2 tsp	(10 mL) salt
¼ tsp	(1 mL) pepper
	pinch of savory
½ cup	(125 mL) onion, chopped
1	egg, beaten
¼ cup	(60 mL) milk
2 tsp	(10 mL) Worcestershire sauce

■ Preheat oven to 375 °F (190 °C).

■ In a large bowl, mix together ground beef, rolled oats, onion, and seasonings.

■ In a separate bowl, com- bine beaten egg, milk, and Worcestershire sauce, then fold into first mixture.

■ Pour mixture into a 9 in x 5 in (22 cm x 12 cm) loaf pan and bake in oven for 1 hour. Serve with sauce of your choice.

Beef and Bacon Meatballs

If you buy a commercial brand of beef stock, make sure you reduce the amount of salt in the recipe. Vary the recipe by replacing tomato juice with vegetable juice.

4 servings

1 ½ lbs	(675 g) ground beef
½ cup	(125 mL) rolled oats
1	onion, chopped
	salt and pepper
¼ tsp	(1 mL) powdered mustard
½	bacon slice per meatball
1 tbsp	(15 mL) butter
1 cup	(250 mL) tomato juice, beef or chicken stock

■ Preheat oven to 350 °F (175 °C).

■ In a large bowl, mix together ground beef, rolled oats, chopped onion, powdered mustard, salt, and pepper and shape into meatballs.

■ Wrap each meatball in a half-slice of bacon and secure with a toothpick.

■ In skillet, melt butter and brown meatballs.

■ Degrease skillet, then pour tomato juice, beef or chicken stock over meatballs.

■ Place mixture in a baking dish and cook in oven for 45 minutes.

■ Add small amounts of stock to mixture during cooking process as needed.

Pacific Island Meatballs

Sweet red pepper adds a touch of color to this recipe, although this ingredient can be expensive out of season.

4 servings

1 ½ lbs	(675 g) ground beef
1	finely chopped garlic clove
2 tbsp	(30 mL) oil
2 tbsp	(30 mL) cornstarch
½ cup	(125 mL) brown sugar
1 tsp	(5 mL) salt
1 tbsp	(15 mL) soy sauce
⅓ cup	(80 mL) white vinegar
1 cup	(250 mL) beef stock
1 ⅓ cups	(330 mL) boiling water
1 ⅓ cups	(330 mL) instant rice
1 cup	(250 mL) green bell pepper, sliced

■ Shape ground beef into 24 small meatballs.

■ In a skillet, heat oil, sauté garlic and brown meatballs.

■ In a bowl, mix together cornstarch, brown sugar, salt, soy sauce, vinegar and beef stock and heat mixture until thick, then keep warm.

■ In a saucepan, pour boiling water over rice and green bell pepper, then cover and let mixture simmer for 10 minutes or until rice is tender.

■ Arrange meatballs on a serving dish with rice.

Meatballs in Jiffy Sauce

If you prefer, replace rice with partially cooked pasta.

4 servings

1 ½ lbs	(675 g) ground beef
2 tbsp	(30 mL) oil
1	medium-size onion, chopped
10 oz	(284 mL) canned sliced mushrooms
2 tbsp	(30 mL) flour
	chopped parsley
	salt and pepper
2 tsp	(10 mL) Worcestershire sauce
10 oz	(284 mL) canned cream of mushroom soup
1 ½ cups	(375 mL) beef stock
1 ½ cups	(375 mL) instant rice

■ Shape ground beef into small meatballs.

■ In a skillet, heat oil and brown meatballs.

■ Add onions and mushrooms and sauté over low heat, then add flour, parsley, salt, and pepper.

■ In a bowl, combine Worcestershire sauce and cream of mushroom soup, and pour over meatballs, then bring to a boil.

■ In a separate bowl, mix together beef stock and instant rice.

■ Using the same skillet, arrange meatballs around the edge then pour rice mixture in the middle and bring to a boil, cover and let simmer for 5 minutes before serving.

Beef with Cheese

These appetizing meatballs melt in your mouth. Use your favorite cheese, or finish up leftovers.

4 servings

1 lb	(450 g) ground beef
1	onion, finely chopped
12	Mozzarella or Cheddar cubes, ¾ inch (2 cm) square
1 cup	(250 mL) instant rice, uncooked
10 oz	(284 mL) canned tomato soup
10 oz	(284 mL) canned tomato juice

■ Preheat oven to 350 °F (175 °C).

■ Combine ground beef and onion, season to taste and shape into 12 meatballs.

■ Insert a cheese cube inside each meatball, then roll meatballs in rice.

■ Place meatballs in a baking dish, coat meatballs with half the tomato soup and half the tomato juice and cover with rest of rice.

■ Cook in oven for 45 minutes, then add other half of tomato juice, if necessary.

Beef Tacos

For a truly Mexican-style meal, place small ramekins of grated cheese, sour cream, and spicy taco sauce in the center of the table.

4 servings

2 tbsp	(30 mL)	butter
1 lb	(450 g)	ground beef
1		medium-size onion, finely chopped
1		garlic clove, minced
8 oz	(237 mL)	canned tomato sauce
2 tsp	(10 mL)	chili powder
½ tsp	(2 mL)	salt
4		6 or 7-inch (15 or 17 cm) taco shells
4		lettuce leaves, finely shredded

■ In a skillet, melt butter and sauté ground beef, onion and garlic.

■ Fold in tomato sauce, chili powder and salt, then cook for approximately 3 minutes.

■ Put a taco shell between 2 moistened paper towels, then repeat operation for all tacos.

■ Heat paper-covered tacos for 30 seconds in microwave at HIGH.

■ Remove the paper, line tacos with shredded lettuce, and add the meat mixture. Serve.

Chili Con Carne

The true Latin-American dish is "chili peppers with meat"— probably too hot for most northern palates. If you like that south-of-the-border taste, increase the chili powder.

4 servings

2 tsp	(10 mL)	oil
1 tsp	(5 mL)	butter
1 lb	(450 g)	ground beef
2		medium-size onions, finely chopped
½ cup	(125 mL)	celery, chopped
10 oz	(284 mL)	canned tomatoes
10 oz	(284 mL)	canned red kidney beans
		salt and pepper
1 tbsp	(15 mL)	prepared mustard
2 tsp	(10 mL)	chili powder
1 tsp	(5 mL)	paprika
1 tsp	(5 mL)	garlic salt

■ In a large skillet, heat oil, melt butter and cook ground beef, onions and celery over low heat.

■ Add other ingredients.

■ Simmer over low heat from 25 to 30 minutes.

■ Serve piping hot.

124

Beef and Sausage Medley

This dish looks quite different if you arrange the sausages in a circle on a baking dish. Prepare the sauce separately, and ladle it over the sausages before baking.

4 servings

12	smoked beef sausages
8 oz	(125 g) ground beef
1	onion, chopped
1	green bell pepper, chopped
2	celery stalks, chopped
1 tbsp	(15 mL) vinegar
10 oz	(284 mL) canned mushrooms
10 oz	(284 mL) canned cream of tomato soup
½ cup	(125 mL) chili sauce
½ cup	(125 mL) ketchup
1 tbsp	(15 mL) brown sugar

- Preheat oven to 350 °F (175 °C).

- Cut sausages into ½ inch (1,25 cm) thick pieces.

- In a bowl, combine the chopped vegetables, and add other ingredients.

- Pour mixture into an ovenproof casserole and cook in oven from 20 to 30 minutes.

- Serve on a bed of rice.

Baby Beef Liver

Such iron-rich food deserves to become a regular on any family's weekly menu.

4 servings

1 lb	(450 g) baby beef liver, sliced
½ cup	(125 mL) milk

Seasoned flour

1 cup	(250 mL) flour
	salt and pepper
½ tsp	(2 mL) marjoram
½ tsp	(2 mL) thyme
½ tsp	(2 mL) basil
1 tsp	(5 mL) parsley
1 tbsp	(15 mL) oil
1 tbsp	(15 mL) butter
1 cup	(250 mL) onion, minced
¼ tsp	(1 mL) Worcestershire sauce
	pinch of garlic salt

- Soak liver slices in milk for 15 minutes and drain.

- Mix together all seasoned flour ingredients and dredge liver.

- In a skillet, melt butter and cook liver slices until middle is lightly pink.

- Meanwhile, in a separate skillet, heat oil and sauté onions, then season with Worcestershire sauce and garlic salt.

- Arrange liver on a serving dish, coat with sauce and serve.

Veal is the best meat for capturing delicate flavors.

Milk-fed veal, a traditionally popular delicacy, is slowly being overtaken by the grain-fed variety. Both have much to recommend them.

The pale pink color of milk-fed veal and its mild taste offer culinary advantages. The animal has not had time to put on weight, however, and the meat tends to be dry.

Grain-fed veal comes from a more mature animal that has been weaned and fed on a grain diet. With a few months' extra growth, this animal gives more substantial meat that is less lean and therefore more tender than its milk-fed cousin.

VEAL

VEAL ESCALOPES

This slender piece of veal has been a source of inspiration to many chefs. There are dozens of so-called traditional ways of preparing it. Italian recipes head the list—*saltimbocca*, *scaloppine*, *piccata*—and every Italian family has its own versions.

Since escalopes tend to be a bit dry, they are often cooked in sauce. When breaded, as with *Wiener Schnitzel* or veal *milanaise*, they are absolutely delicious.

Preparing veal escalopes

- *Choose veal slices weighing no more than 3 to 5 oz (90 to 150 g) each.*
- *Place veal slices between two sheets of waxed paper or brown butcher's paper.*

- *With the aid of a meat mallet, flatten the veal slices. If you don't have a meat mallet, use the bottom of a bottle, a small casserole or the flat side of a large knife.*

- *If you do not use a meat mallet, lightly flatten veal slices and make fine indentation marks on the meat surface to facilitate further flattening.*

Rolled Veal Paupiéttes

This flavorful recipe is guaranteed to impress family and friends.

4 servings	
1 tbsp	(15 mL) butter
1	onion, finely chopped
2 cups	(500 mL) soft part of bread, pressed
1	egg, lightly beaten
1/2 cup	(125 mL) cooked, leftover ground veal (optional)
	salt and pepper
	pinch of herbs, to taste
4	veal escalopes, 4 oz (115 g) each
1/4 cup	(60 mL) flour
2	slices bacon
10 oz	(284 mL) canned tomatoes

- In a skillet, melt butter and sauté onion, then add soft part of bread, remove from heat and let stand to cool.

- Fold egg into mixture, season with salt, pepper, and herbs, and add cooked, leftover ground veal.

- Season veal escalopes with salt and pepper. Spread mixture over each, then roll and tie, and dredge lightly with flour.

- In a skillet, melt bacon, add veal paupiettes and brown. Reduce heat.

- Add tomatoes, cover and simmer over low heat for 30 minutes. Serve.

Veal Scallopini Italiano

For an authentic Italian look, garnish this dish with black or green olives.

4 servings

½ tsp	(2 mL)	salt
¼ tsp	(1 mL)	pepper
1 tbsp	(15 mL)	flour
4		veal scallopini, 4 oz (115 g) each
¼ cup	(60 mL)	butter
¼ cup	(60 mL)	white wine
½ tsp	(2 mL)	parsley
½ tsp	(2 mL)	oregano
½ tsp	(2 mL)	basil
½ cup	(125 mL)	tomato sauce

■ In a large bowl, combine first 3 ingredients and dredge scallopini with this mixture.

■ In a large heated skillet, melt butter and sauté veal scallopini at least 4 minutes each side. Put the meat on a serving dish and keep warm.

■ Deglaze skillet with white wine, add herbs and tomato sauce then let mixture simmer, uncovered, for 10 minutes.

■ Pour seasoned sauce over veal scallopini. Serve.

* Illustrated recipe

Veal Escalopes with Cheddar

The mild pan sauce suggested here can be replaced with a spicy tomato sauce that will blend well with the distinctive flavor of Cheddar cheese.

4 servings

4		veal escalopes, 6 oz (170 g) each
		salt and pepper
2 tbsp	(30 mL)	flour
1		egg, lightly beaten
½ cup	(125 mL)	breadcrumbs
⅓ cup	(80 mL)	mild grated Cheddar cheese
1 tbsp	(15 mL)	butter
1 tbsp	(15 mL)	oil
2 cups	(500 mL)	mushrooms
½ cup	(125 mL)	beef stock
1		parsley sprig, chopped

■ Preheat oven to 300 °F (150 °C).

■ Pound escalopes with meat mallet then season with salt and pepper.

■ Pour flour into one bowl, beaten egg into a second, and breadcrumbs and grated Cheddar into a third.

■ Dip veal escalopes, one by one, in flour, in beaten egg, and finally in breadcrumbs and grated Cheddar mixture.

■ In a large skillet, melt butter, heat oil and cook the veal. Remove the meat and keep warm in a serving dish.

■ Using the same skillet, sauté mushrooms, then remove from heat and keep warm in serving dish.

■ Pour beef stock into skillet and bring to a boil then simmer 2 to 3 minutes and adjust seasoning.

■ Remove veal from oven, top with mushrooms, sauce and parsley. Serve.

VEAL NOISETTES

Veal noisettes are small pieces of lightly pounded veal weighing approximately 2 oz to 3 oz (50 g to 75 g) each. You should count on 2 to 3 noisettes per serving.

Sautéed Veal Noisettes with Mushrooms

You can vary the sauce by adding a spoonful of tomato paste to the stock before reducing it.

4 servings	
8	veal noisettes, 2 oz (60 g) each
3 tbsp	(45 mL) flour
2 tsp	(10 mL) vegetable oil
1 tbsp	(15 mL) butter
	salt and pepper
1 ½ cups	(375 mL) fresh mushrooms
¼ cup	(60 mL) white wine
¼ cup	(60 mL) beef or veal stock
¼ cup	(60 mL) 35% cream
1 tsp	(5 mL) chopped parsley

■ Preheat oven to 300 °F (150 °C).

■ Dredge the meat with flour.

■ In a large skillet, heat oil, melt butter and sear the meat over high heat. Reduce heat and cook until center of meat turns pink, then season with salt and pepper.

■ Add mushrooms and let simmer over low heat.

■ Remove veal noisettes from skillet, transfer to an oven-proof serving dish and keep warm.

■ Deglaze skillet with white wine, stir gently and reduce liquid almost completely.

■ Pour veal or beef stock into mixture, boil for a few minutes. Reduce sauce by half, then adjust seasoning.

■ Blend cream into sauce and pour mixture over veal noisettes. Garnish with parsley and serve.

Veal Noisettes with Sesame Seeds

Don't grind the sesame seeds in a blender, as you'll loose the pleasantly crunchy texture. Crush them lightly, if at all, before adding them to the breadcrumbs.

4 servings

1 tbsp	(15 mL) flour
8	veal noisettes, 2 oz (60 g) each
1	egg, lightly beaten
2 tbsp	(30 mL) breadcrumbs
1 tbsp	(15 mL) ground sesame seeds
1 tbsp	(15 mL) butter
2 tsp	(10 mL) peanut oil
4	drops sesame oil
	salt and pepper
¼ cup	(60 mL) beef stock
	juice of ½ lemon

■ Preheat oven to 300 °F (150 °C).

■ Dredge veal noisettes with flour, then dip into egg and roll in mixture of breadcrumbs and sesame seeds.

■ In a large skillet, heat oils and melt butter. Sear the meat on both sides. Season with salt and pepper and keep warm in serving dish.

■ In the same skillet, heat beef stock and lemon juice, and stir gently.

■ Remove veal noisettes from oven, cover with sauce and serve.

VARIATIONS

• **Replace chopped sesame seeds with nuts.**

• **Sprinkle veal noisettes with your favorite fruit juice, then add lemon juice and garnish with small wedges of fresh fruit as shown here.**

131

Veal MEDALLIONS

Medallions may be round or oval. They are slightly thicker than noisettes and weigh between 4 and 6 oz (120 and 180 g) each. They are usually served sautéed or pan-fried.

Meat-stuffed Veal Medallions

Make sure to finely chop the bacon and the ham for the stuffing. This brings out the flavor.

4 servings

Stuffing

½ cup	(125 mL) bacon pieces
½ cup	(125 mL) chopped cooked ham
½ cup	(125 mL) chicken stock
	salt and pepper
4	veal medallions, 1 in (2,5 cm) thick each
2 tbsp	(30 mL) steak sauce
2 tbsp	(30 mL) melted butter
1 tsp	(5 mL) oil

■ Preheat oven to broil.

■ In a heated skillet, fry bacon and ham at high heat and stir gently.

■ Degrease skillet, add small amount of chicken stock and let mixture simmer for 4 minutes. Add rest of chicken stock and let boil for 1 minute. Season with salt and pepper.

■ Cut a cavity in the side of each veal medallion. Fill with stuffing and close with toothpicks. Baste stuffed veal medallions with steak sauce and melted butter.

■ Place stuffed veal medallions on lightly oiled broiling pan. Broil 6 inches (15 cm) from heat source, approximately 4 minutes on each side.

■ Baste medallions occasionally with liquid from broiling pan.

STUFFING VARIATIONS

• In a skillet, melt 1 tsp (5 mL) butter, add 1 ½ cups (375 mL) cleaned spinach, with stems removed, stir until spinach begins to wilt and season with salt and pepper.

• Stuff with canned vegetables such as carrots, wax beans or corn niblets.

• Stuff with puréed fruit, then garnish with mint leaves.

Three-pepper Veal Medallions

Whole black, green, and pink peppercorns are pretty and piquant, blending particularly well with the mild taste of veal. Add small shrimp to your platter to give family and friends a special treat.

4 servings

1	shrimp-flavored oriental noodle mix
1	three-pepper sauce mix
4	veal medallions, 4 oz (115 g) each
1/4 cup	(60 mL) commercial steak sauce
2 tbsp	(30 mL) melted butter
	salt and pepper

■ Prepare noodles and sauce according to package directions, and keep warm.

■ Make small cross-wise cuts on both sides of the meat, and baste with steak sauce.

■ In a large skillet, melt butter and sear the meat on both sides. Reduce heat, season with salt and pepper, and cook 3 to 4 minutes.

■ Place the meat on a bed of oriental noodles and pour three-pepper sauce over it. Garnish with small shrimp and serve.

Veal Medallions with Asparagus and Herbs

A dash of wine, a dot of cream... all you need is the subtle flavor of herbs to complete a delightful recipe. Keep it a secret!

4 servings

1/4 cup	(60 mL) white wine
	pinch of marjoram
	pinch of thyme
	pinch of oregano
	pinch of basil
1	cream of asparagus soup mix
8	veal medallions, 2 oz (60 g) each
	salt and pepper
3 tbsp	(45 mL) flour
2 tbsp	(30 mL) butter
2 tbsp	(30 mL) 35% cream

■ Preheat oven to 300 °F (150 °C).

■ In a skillet, heat white wine and herbs over medium heat, then reduce liquid to three-quarters. Keep warm.

■ Prepare cream of asparagus soup mix according to package directions.

■ Season meat with salt and pepper and dredge with flour.

■ In a separate skillet, melt butter and sear the meat on both sides, then remove from stove and keep warm.

■ Deglaze skillet with wine, add cream of asparagus soup and stir gently.

■ Blend in the cream, then adjust seasoning.

■ Arrange the meat on a serving dish, ladle the sauce over it, and serve.

VEAL CHOPS

Veal chops are standard fare in France, but for some reason aren't popular here, although they're readily available and simple to prepare. They make excellent meat for broiling or barbecuing. Chops weigh from 8 to 10 oz (240 g to 340 g) each. They can be used in most pork chop recipes, although a littler larger.

Capers are the buds of the Mediterranean plant, "Capparis spinosa", pickled in vinegar or brine. The slightly bitter taste is used to liven up sauces.

4 servings	
Marinade	
1	bottle, 12 oz (341 mL) Porter or brown ale
¼ cup	(60 mL) vegetable oil
2 tbsp	(30 mL) soy sauce
4	veal chops
	salt and pepper
¼ cup	(60 mL) capers in vinegar
2 tbsp	(30 mL) kneaded butter (beurre manié)

- In a bowl, mix all marinade ingredients.

- Marinate veal chops for 2 hours prior to cooking time.

- Light barbecue and grease barbecue grill.

- Drain veal chops and pat dry. Barbecue for 4 minutes on each side. Rotate ¼ turn after two minutes to make attractive crisscross marks. Season with salt and pepper.

- Meanwhile, in a small saucepan, heat half the marinade over low heat, add the kneaded butter and stir for 3 minutes with wire whisk.

- Pour sauce into serving dish, place veal chops in the sauce and garnish with capers.

Veal Chops with Onions

Add a touch of color with red onions.

4 servings		
1 tbsp	(15 mL) oil	
2 tbsp	(30 mL) butter	
4	veal chops	
1	small garlic clove, finely chopped	
1	onion, finely sliced	
	salt and pepper	
¼ cup	(60 mL) white wine	
⅓ cup	(80 mL) 15% cream	

■ Preheat oven to 300 °F (150 °C).

■ In a thick skillet, melt butter, heat oil and brown veal chops for 6 minutes on each side. Add garlic and onion, cook without browning and season with salt and pepper, then remove chops from skillet and keep warm.

■ Deglaze skillet with white wine over high heat, then reduce liquid by half. Add cream, cook 2 to 3 minutes, stirring constantly. Coat veal chops with sauce and serve immediately.

VARIATIONS

• **Replace onions with strips of green bell peppers and sweet red peppers.**

• **Replace white wine with ½ cup (125 mL) beef stock and/or replace cream with 1 tbsp (15 mL) sour cream.**

Easy Veal Chops

The veal chops will be even tastier if you use fresh thyme. You need only use 1 teaspoon. Cut up any leftover thyme sprigs and refrigerate them in oil.

4 servings		
1 tbsp	(15 mL) Worcestershire sauce	
1 tsp	(5 mL) vegetable oil	
1 tsp	(1 mL) thyme	
4	veal chops	
	salt and pepper	
4	bacon slices, each cut into 4 pieces	

■ Preheat oven to broil.

■ In a small bowl, pour first 3 ingredients.

■ Baste veal chops with mixture, then place in broiling pan, 6 inches (15 cm) from heat source. Broil at least 2 minutes on each side, and season with salt and pepper.

■ Arrange bacon on top of meat and broil for 6 minutes, occasionally basting with marinade.

Veal roasts

Loin Roast of Veal

This is surely one of the more popular recipes you will want to try. The beauty of it is that it's very easy to prepare. You have all the ingredients in your kitchen.

6 to 10 servings		
2 tbsp	(30 mL) butter	
2 tbsp	(30 mL) vegetable shortening	
	salt and pepper	
1	onion, finely sliced	
1 tsp	(5 mL) marjoram	
1 tsp	(5 mL) savory	
2 tsp	(10 mL) dry mustard	
1	loin roast of veal, 3 to 5 lbs (1,4 to 2,3 kg)	

■ Preheat oven to 425 °F (220 °C)

■ In a bowl, mix butter and vegetable shortening, and season with salt and pepper.

■ Add onion, season with marjoram, savory and dry mustard.

■ Coat veal with this mixture.

■ Cook roast in oven, uncovered, 15 minutes per pound, and baste 3 or 4 times during cooking process.

■ Garnish with asparagus and serve.

The slightly spicy lemon sauce has a tangy taste you'll enjoy. When they are in season, try using mandarin oranges or clementines to decorate the roast.

6 servings		
3 tbsp	(45 mL) vegetable oil	
1	veal shoulder, 3 lbs (1,4 kg), boned and rolled	
3	onions, chopped	
	juice of 2 lemons	
	julienned peel of 1 lemon	
2 cups	(500 mL) chicken stock	
	pinch of chervil, to taste	
	pinch of thyme, to taste	
1	bay leaf	
	salt and pepper	
¼ cup	(60 mL) kneaded butter (beurre manié)	
½ cup	(125 mL) 15% cream	

■ Preheat oven to 220 °C (425 °F).

■ In a stove-to-oven casserole dish, heat oil and brown veal shoulder on all sides.

■ Add onions, juice of 1 lemon, julienned lemon peel, chicken stock, and seasonings and stir gently. Cover and cook in oven for 1 ¼ hours.

■ Meanwhile, prepare kneaded butter and stir gently to blend well.

■ At the end of cooking time, remove roast from the casserole dish, turn off the oven and keep roast warm in serving dish.

■ On stove, add kneaded butter to cooking sauce, add juice of the other lemon and stir sauce until smooth.

■ Add cream, cook over low heat without boiling. Adjust seasoning.

■ Transfer veal roast to serving dish, coat with sauce and serve.

* Illustrated recipe

VARIATIONS

• Garnish roast of veal with a variety of citrus fruits.

• Replace juice and julienned lemon peel with tomato juice and julienned tomatoes.

Three-salt Tender Veal

Potatoes, carrots and other vegetables will capture all the flavor of the meat.

6 servings

2 tbsp	(30 mL) butter
1	veal roast, 3 lbs (1,4 kg)
1 cup	(250 mL) water
	pinch of salt
	pinch of garlic salt
	pinch of onion salt
1 cup	(250 mL) beef stock
1 cup	(250 mL) potatoes, diced
1 cup	(250 mL) carrots, diced
1 cup	(250 mL) Chinese cabbage, cut into strips

■ In a pressure cooker, melt butter and brown roast on all sides.

■ Pour water over roast, sprinkle with 3 salts, then seal cover of pressure cooker and cook for 1 hour over medium heat.

■ Open pressure cooker and pour beef stock over roasted veal. Add potatoes, carrots, and cabbage, then seal cover once again and cook 15 minutes longer.

■ Adjust seasoning. Serve hot.

VARIATIONS

• **Replace garlic salt with fines herbes.**

• **Add a variety of vegetables to roasted veal such as broccoli, wax or green beans, cabbage, onions, mushrooms and celery.**

Stuffed Roast of Veal

Bring the stuffed roast of veal to the table and carve it while it's still nice and hot. The delicious aroma of apple stuffing is sure to whet your family's appetite.

6 to 10 servings

3 tbsp	(45 mL) butter

Apple Stuffing

2 cups	(500 mL) soft part of bread, diced
1	onion, finely chopped
3	celery stalks, diced
2	apples, diced
½ tsp	(2 mL) chopped parsley
¼ tsp	(1 mL) marjoram
¼ tsp	(1 mL) thyme
1	veal roast, 3 to 5 lbs (1,4 to 2,3 kg), boned

■ Preheat oven to 400 °F (205 C°)

■ In a large skillet, melt butter, mix all stuffing ingredients, cook gently for 10 minutes and let stand to cool.

■ Stuff veal roast cavity with apple stuffing, close cavity and secure with a skewer or tie with string.

■ Roast veal in uncovered roasting pan, about 20 minutes per pound.

VARIATION

• **Use this apple stuffing for other meats.**

CUBED VEAL

Cream of Mushroom Veal

For those who don't like mushrooms, make the sauce with cream of asparagus soup, cream of tomato, or even cream of cauliflower or broccoli.

4 servings

1 lb	(450 g) cubed veal
2 tbsp	(30 mL) vegetable oil
¼ cup	(60 mL) celery, sliced
¼ cup	(60 mL) onion, sliced
¼ cup	(60 mL) carrots, diced
1	garlic clove, finely sliced
¼ cup	(60 mL) sherry, or port, or red wine
5 oz	(142 mL) canned cream of mushroom soup
½ cup	(125 mL) water
	salt and pepper
¼ cup	(60 mL) sour cream
½ tsp	(2 mL) chopped parsley

■ In a large skillet, heat oil to smoking and sear veal cubes. Add celery, onions, carrots, and garlic and sauté vegetables, then remove excess oil.

■ Deglaze skillet with sherry, port, or red wine and reduce liquid by half, then add cream of mushroom soup and water. Season with salt and pepper and bring to a boil.

■ Reduce heat to medium, cover and let simmer for 40 minutes. Remove from heat, add sour cream and stir gently.

■ Spoon veal stew onto a serving dish, sprinkle with parsley and serve.

This recipe freezes and reheats well. If you've mastered the freezer-to-microwave technique, you'll find it a very convenient dish.

4 servings

1 lb	(450 g) cubed veal
1	onion, sliced
1 tbsp	(15 mL) oil
1 cup	(250 mL) leeks, cut into rounds
½ cup	(125 mL) carrots, cut into sections
½ cup	(125 mL) green bell peppers or sweet red peppers, cut into strips
4 cups	(1 L) hot beef stock
¼ cup	(60 mL) rice
¾ cup	(180 mL) fresh green peas or frozen green peas
¾ cup	(180 mL) cauliflower flowerets
½ cup	(125 mL) potatoes, diced
½ cup	(125 mL) turnip, diced
	salt and pepper
	chopped parsley
	pinch of tarragon

■ Preheat oven to 375 °F (190 °C).

■ In a stove-to-oven casserole dish, heat oil. Cook veal cubes and onion until golden. Add leeks, carrots, and peppers and pour hot beef stock over mixture. Cover and cook for 40 minutes in oven.

■ At the end of cooking process, add rice, green peas, cauliflower, potatoes and turnips and season with salt and pepper. Sprinkle with parsley and tarragon.

■ Cover, return to oven and cook 15 minutes longer.

* Illustrated recipe

Apple Cider Veal Stew

Try an innovative approach... cider! This might be the perfect opportunity to impress your guests on a brisk autumn evening.

4 to 6 servings

3 tbsp	(45 mL) flour
1 tsp	(5 mL) salt
1/4 tsp	(1 mL) pepper
1/4 tsp	(1 mL) thyme
1 lb	(450 g) cubed veal
2 tbsp	(30 mL) vegetable oil
1 cup	(250 mL) apple cider
1/4 cup	(60 mL) water
1 tbsp	(15 mL) vinegar
2	carrots, diced
2	potatoes, diced
1	onion, sliced
1	celery stalk, sliced
1	apple, peeled, and diced

■ In a large bowl, combine flour, salt, pepper and thyme.

■ Dredge veal cubes with flour.

■ In an enamelled cast iron casserole, heat oil to smoking, and sear veal cubes. Pour off the fat.

■ Pour apple cider, water, and vinegar over veal cubes, bring to a boil, stirring from time to time.

■ Reduce heat to medium, cover and cook for 30 minutes or until meat is tender.

■ Add vegetables and apple to simmering stew, cook 15 minutes longer or until vegetables are tender.

Veal Cubes in Barbecue Sauce

Browned veal cubes simmer gently in a mustard-tomato sauce to produce this mildly spicy dish.

4 servings

Barbecue Sauce

2 tsp	(10 mL) oil
1/2 cup	(125 mL) onions, chopped
1/2 cup	(125 mL) celery, diagonally sliced
1	garlic clove, finely chopped
1 tbsp	(15 mL) brown sugar
1 tbsp	(15 mL) mild mustard
5 oz	(142 mL) canned tomato soup
1/2 cup	(125 mL) water
1 tsp	(5 mL) white vinegar
1/4 tsp	(1 mL) each, mixed thyme and rosemary
	pinch of chili powder
	salt and pepper
1 lb	(450 g) cubed veal
1 tbsp	(15 mL) oil

■ Preheat oven to 375 °F (190 °C).

■ In a large skillet, heat oil and cook onions, celery and garlic without browning.

■ Add brown sugar, mustard, tomato soup, water and vinegar, and stir gently, then add spices. Let mixture simmer for 10 minutes, then remove from stove and set aside.

■ In a separate skillet, heat oil to smoking and sear veal cubes.

■ Place meat in an ovenproof dish, coat with prepared barbecue sauce and cook, partially covered, for about 20 minutes.

Veal strips

Veal strips are an excellent ingredient for economical, one-casserole meals. Vegetables and sauce are generally simmered with the meat, and served with a complement of potatoes, rice, pasta, or on top of puff pastry shells.

Any chasseur recipe worthy of the name contains the traditional blend of mushrooms, onions, tomatoes and wine.

- Preheat oven to 300 °F (150 °C).

- Dredge veal strips with flour.

- In a skillet, heat oil, sear veal strips, then keep warm on a serving dish.

- Using the same skillet, melt butter and cook onions, leek and mushrooms without browning.

- Add veal strips; sauté over high heat.

- Deglaze with red wine and reduce liquid by half. Pour tomatoes and beef stock into mixture, season with salt and pepper and bring to a boil. Reduce heat and let simmer for 25 minutes over low heat.

- Sprinkle with parsley. Serve.

VARIATIONS

- **Add green vegetables such as green peas, broccoli flowerets, and halved Brussels sprouts. Pour a small amount of cream over mixture.**

- **Replace beef stock with 1 cup (250 mL) tomato juice.**

4 servings	
2 tbsp	(30 mL) flour
1 lb	(450 g) veal strips
1 tbsp	(15 mL) vegetable oil
1 tbsp	(15 mL) butter
1/4 cup	(60 mL) onions, chopped
1/4 cup	(60 mL) leek, finely sliced
1/4 cup	(125 mL) mushrooms, finely sliced
1/4 cup	(60 mL) red wine
1/2 cup	(125 mL) ground tomatoes
1 1/2 cups	(375 mL) beef stock
1 tbsp	(15 mL) chopped parsley
	salt and pepper

140

Veal Strips and Snow Peas

Snow peas resemble plump green string beans. They cook quickly, and are often lightly sautéed. In this recipe, they are simmered in a béchamel sauce.

4 servings

1 lb	(450 g) veal strips
1 tbsp	(15 mL) vegetable oil
1	garlic clove, finely chopped
¼ cup	(60 mL) onions, chopped
¼ cup	(60 mL) white wine
½ cup	(125 mL) béchamel sauce
½ cup	(125 mL) chicken stock
¼ cup	(60 mL) snow peas, diagonally sliced
	salt and pepper
¼ cup	(60 mL) 15% cream

■ Preheat oven to 300 °F (150 °C).

■ In a skillet, heat oil to smoking, sear veal strips, remove from skillet and keep warm on serving dish.

■ Using the same skillet, cook garlic and onions without browning. Pour off the fat, deglaze with white wine and reduce liquid by half.

■ Add béchamel sauce and chicken stock, stir gently, add snow peas and season with salt and pepper. Let mixture simmer for 20 minutes then remove from stove and add cream.

■ Place veal strips on a serving dish, coat with sauce and serve.

VARIATIONS

- When adding garlic and onions, include ½ cup (125 mL) diced potatoes and ¼ cup (60 mL) diced carrots to mixture.

- Replace chicken stock with beef stock.

- Sprinkle ½ cup (125 mL) grated cheese over veal strips and broil to melt cheese

- Serve finely sliced veal strip dish in patty shells or in an au gratin dish, as illustrated.

GROUND VEAL

Veal Meatballs in Spicy Sauce

Ground veal has less fat than ground pork. Its flavor is more delicate than that of ground beef. For a change of pace, try substituting ground veal in some of your ground beef recipes.

8 servings

2 tbsp	(30 mL) butter
2 ¼ lbs	(1 kg) ground veal
¼ cup	(60 mL) breadcrumbs
1	garlic clove, finely chopped
2 tsp	(10 mL) prepared mustard
⅛ tsp	(0,5 mL) white pepper

Spicy Sauce

5 ½ oz	(156 mL) tomato paste
¾ cup	(180 mL) water
½ cup	(125 mL) wine vinegar
¼ cup	(60 mL) lemon juice
2 tbsp	(30 mL) Worcestershire sauce
½ cup	(125 mL) brown sugar, well packed
1 tsp	(5 mL) dry mustard
1 tsp	(5 mL) salt
¼ tsp	(1 mL) chili powder

■ Put butter into a 7 inch x 13 inch (17 cm x 34 cm) microwave-safe dish and cook for 1 minute at MEDIUM or until butter is softened, then remove and set aside.

■ In a large bowl, combine all ingredients (except spicy sauce ingredients), add ground veal and shape into 18, 1 inch (2,5 cm) meatballs.

■ Place meatballs in dish on top of softened butter, cover with sheet of waxed paper.

■ Cook for 8 minutes at MEDIUM, then drain.

■ Meanwhile, in a bowl, mix all spicy sauce ingredients, pour over meatballs and cover.

■ Cook 8 to 12 minutes at MEDIUM or until meatballs are well done.

■ Let stand, covered, for 5 minutes, then serve.

Veal Croquettes

Children love these croquettes shaped into chops. Served with spinach and corn niblets, they make a colorful and nourishing meal.

4 servings

Croquettes

1 lb	(450 g) ground veal
	salt and pepper
	pinch of curry
¼ cup	(60 mL) soft part of bread
¼ cup	(60 mL) ketchup
½ tsp	(2 mL) chili powder
1 tbsp	(15 mL) vegetable oil
1 tbsp	(15 mL) butter
1 cup	(250 mL) cooked rice

■ In a large bowl, mix croquette ingredients and shape into small chops.

■ In a skillet, heat oil, melt butter and cook croquettes. Remove when cooked and keep warm.

■ Using the same skillet, sauté rice in oil and add salt to taste.

■ Place chops on a serving dish on little mounds of rice.

VARIATIONS

• **You may wish to replace veal with ground beef or a combination of veal and beef.**

• **This recipe is delicious when coated with a tomato sauce.**

Stuffed Cabbage

If you prefer to serve this dish in individual portions, break the cabbage into leaves. Blanch the leaves, stuff them with the meat mixture, then roll them and secure each one with a toothpick.

8 servings

1	medium-size cabbage
2 tbsp	(30 mL) butter
1	medium-size onion, chopped
2 cups	(500 mL) ground veal, cooked
1 cup	(250 mL) cooked rice
	salt and pepper
	pinch of celery salt
	pinch of savory

■ Chop off top portion of cabbage and scoop out the middle.

■ In a skillet, melt butter and sauté onion.

■ Add ground veal, cooked rice, celery salt, and savory. Stir well and season with salt and pepper.

■ Fill cabbage cavity with this mixture, replace top of cabbage, then place stuffed cabbage in cheesecloth, tie with string and set aside.

■ In a large saucepan, pour water up to 3 ½ inches (9 cm) from top, boil water and season with salt.

■ Place wrapped stuffed cabbage in boiling water, reduce heat and poach stuffed cabbage for 35 minutes over low heat.

■ Remove stuffed cabbage from water and drain on paper towel.

■ Serve with a tomato sauce.

VARIATIONS

- Add fresh mushrooms and grated Parmesan cheese to ground veal mixture.

- Poach stuffed cabbage in beef stock, with a small amount of vegetable juice.

- Instead of cabbage, stuff green bell peppers or tomatoes, as illustrated.

143

OSSO BUCO

Classic Osso Buco

Osso buco makes excellent use of the leg of veal with its nutritious marrow bones. The leg is sliced horizontally to make convenient portions. The meat is braised in stock, then flavored with onion and tomato.

4 servings

3 tbsp	(45 mL) oil
2 lbs	(900 g) veal shanks, cut "osso buco"
2 tbsp	(30 mL) onions, chopped
4 cups	(1 L) beef stock
1 tbsp	(15 mL) tomato paste
1	bay leaf
	pinch of thyme
2 tsp	(10 mL) parsley
	salt and pepper
2 tbsp	(30 mL) kneaded butter (beurre manié)

■ In a heavy saucepan, heat oil and sear veal, add chopped onions and stir.

■ Add tomato paste and beef stock. Season with bay leaf, thyme, parsley, salt and pepper, then simmer for about 1 hour.

■ Place veal in a serving dish and keep warm. Blend sauce with kneaded butter, adjust seasoning, pour over meat and serve.

The veal shank or shin is cut horizontally into thick, wheel-like slices known as "rouelles" in France and "osso buco" in Italy.

4 servings

2 lbs	(900 g) veal shanks, cut "osso bucco"
3 tbsp	(45 mL) oil
1 tbsp	(15 mL) onions, chopped
1	garlic clove, finely chopped
1 tbsp	(15 mL) tomato paste
2 tbsp	(30 mL) flour
2 cups	(500 mL) beef stock
2 cups	(500 mL) chicken stock
1	bay leaf
	pinch of rosemary
1/4 tsp	(1 mL) ground black pepper
1/4 tsp	(1 mL) nutmeg
2 tsp	(10 mL) parsley
	salt
4	endives, halved
1/2 cup	(125 mL) mushrooms, thinly sliced

■ In a heavy saucepan, heat oil and sear meat. Add onions and garlic, and stir.

■ Add tomato paste and flour.

■ Add beef and chicken stock, then season with bay leaf, rosemary, pepper, nutmeg, parsley and salt. Let mixture simmer for about 1 hour.

■ Halfway through cooking process, add endives. Add mushrooms 15 minutes before end of cooking time, adjust seasoning and serve.

* Illustrated recipe

HOW TO PREPARE AND COOK VEAL KIDNEYS

- Remove transparent skin covering kidneys. Place them upside down on a flat surface and slice off fatty portions with a pointed knife.

- After most of the fatty tissue is removed, the kidneys should look like those shown here. You may now stuff and tie them or simply cook as is.

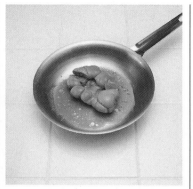

- Sear one side of veal kidneys in smoking-hot oil.

- Turn over and cook in oven set at 400 °F (205 °C) for about 5 minutes.

- Meanwhile, using another skillet, cook chopped onions and garlic in oil or unsalted butter until transparent. Add beef stock and reduce liquid by half.

- Stir in "old-fashioned" prepared mustard.

- Take veal shanks out of the oven and coat them with sauce.

Marinated Liver and Kidneys

Make sure you pat both liver and kidneys dry before dredging them with flour. Sauté them in smoking-hot oil.

4 servings		

Marinade

³/₄ cup	(180 mL)	tomato juice
3 tbsp	(45 mL)	lemon juice
3 tbsp	(45 mL)	oil
3 tbsp	(45 mL)	onions, chopped
2		crushed bay leaves
1 lb	(450 g)	veal liver and kidneys

■ In a bowl, combine tomato juice, lemon juice, oil, onions and crushed bay leaf. Pour over veal kidneys and liver. Cover and refrigerate for at least 12 hours.

■ Pat liver and kidneys dry with paper towel, dredge with flour and set aside.

■ Heat oil to smoking in a thick skillet and sear liver and kidneys.

Veal Liver à l'Orange

Veal liver is the tastiest liver of all. Its pale pink meat remains tender and juicy after cooking.

4 servings

4 tsp	(20 mL) mild mustard
4	slices veal liver
3 tbsp	(45 mL) flour
2 tbsp	(30 mL) oil
	salt
	juice of 3 oranges
1	seedless orange, thinly sliced
3 tbsp	(45 mL) butter
3 tbsp	(45 mL) Curaçao

■ Preheat oven to 300 °F (150 °C).

■ Coat both sides of veal liver with mild mustard and dredge with flour.

■ In a skillet, heat oil to smoking, sear liver slices for 3 minutes on each side and salt to taste.

■ Place veal liver in an oven-proof serving dish and keep warm.

■ Squeeze orange juice into the same skillet, add butter and Curaçao and let mixture boil for 3 minutes.

■ Coat liver with sauce, and garnish with thin slices of orange.

Veal Liver Romano

Yogurt is the perfect ingredient to make a creamy, but light sauce.

4 servings

2 tbsp	(30 mL) peanut oil
½ cup	(125 mL) onions, chopped
2	garlic cloves, finely chopped
⅓ cup	(80 mL) dry white wine
⅓ cup	(80 mL) tomato juice
2 tbsp	(30 mL) flour
½ tsp	(2 mL) powdered mustard
1 lb	(450 g) veal liver, sliced
	salt and pepper
½ cup	(125 mL) low fat plain yogurt
3 tbsp	(45 mL) grated Romano cheese
	chopped fresh parsley

■ Preheat oven to 300 °F (150 °C).

■ In a skillet, heat 1 tbsp (15 mL) oil, sauté onions and garlic but do not brown. Degrease the skillet. Add wine and tomato juice and let simmer for 4 minutes, then keep warm in serving dish.

■ Dredge veal liver with mixture of flour and powdered mustard.

■ In a separate skillet, heat remaining oil, sear liver and season with salt and pepper. Place in oven to keep warm.

■ In a bowl, stir remaining flour and yogurt to a creamy texture, pour into tomato sauce and cook 3 to 4 minutes over low heat.

■ Place veal liver in sauce mixture and cook for 5 minutes.

■ Sprinkle with Romano cheese and garnish with chopped parsley.

Veal Kidneys with Candied French Shallots

The delicate French (dry) shallot should not be confused with the more pungent green onion that most people call shallots.

4 servings

1 lb	(450 g) veal kidneys, trimmed
2 tbsp	(30 mL) peanut oil
1 tsp	(5 mL) vegetable oil
1 tbsp	(15 mL) butter
¼ cup	(60 mL) French (dry) shallots, finely sliced
1 tbsp	(15 mL) port or red wine
½ tsp	(2 mL) honey
1 tbsp	(15 mL) wine vinegar or blackcurrant vinegar
½ cup	(125 mL) beef stock
	salt and pepper

■ Preheat oven to 350 °F (175 °C).

■ In a cast iron skillet, sear veal kidneys on 3 sides in smoking peanut oil.

■ Turn and cook in oven, in skillet, for 5 minutes.

■ In a separate skillet, heat vegetable oil and melt butter, then cook shallots until transparent. Pour port, honey and vinegar over mixture and reduce mixture almost completely.

■ Add beef stock, season with salt and pepper, and let mixture reduce by ⅓ then remove from heat.

■ Remove kidneys from oven and let stand 2 to 3 minutes.

■ Slice into ½ inch (1 cm) thick pieces, place in a serving dish and pour the sauce mixture over the meat.

Veal Kidneys with Old-fashioned Mustard

The mild, aromatic flavor and coarsely chopped seeds of "old-fashioned" mustard (moutarde de Meaux) make it an ideal ingredient for mustard sauce.

4 servings

2 tbsp	(30 mL) peanut oil
1 lb	(450 g) whole veal kidneys, trimmed
1 tbsp	(15 mL) butter
1	garlic clove, minced
1 tbsp	(15 mL) onion, chopped
3 tbsp	(45 mL) wine vinegar
½ cup	(125 mL) beef stock
4 tsp	(20 mL) "old-fashioned" prepared mustard
1 tsp	(5 mL) chopped parsley
	salt and pepper

■ Preheat oven to 350 °F (175 °C).

■ In a cast iron skillet, sear veal kidneys on 3 sides in smoking peanut oil.

■ Turn and place skillet in oven for 5 minutes.

■ In a separate skillet, melt butter and cook garlic and onion.

■ Deglaze skillet with wine vinegar and reduce liquid by half.

■ Add beef stock, reduce by ⅓ and remove from heat.

■ Add mustard and stir gently.

■ Remove skillet from oven, pour sauce over kidneys, season with salt and pepper and sprinkle with chopped parsley.

Springtime and lamb seem to go together naturally and, it's not surprising to find roast lamb as a traditional Easter dish in many countries.

For a variety of reasons, fresh lamb isn't a standard item on supermarket meat counters in North America. Frozen New Zealand lamb is usually available, cut into legs, shoulders, or chops, and even made into sausages.

Butchers can usually get good, fresh local lamb in season. The animal matures faster in our colder, northern areas than in New Zealand because it is fed on grain rather than grazing in pastures. Our lamb is slaughtered at an earlier age and is therefore more lean and tender.

LAMB

LAMB MEDALLIONS

Medallions are small round or oval pieces of meat cut from a larger, boned portion. They need only light cooking, and remain tender as a result. Their convenient size makes them ideal for arranging attractive serving platters.

Field-grown watercress is sold in bunches in the vegetable or salad sections of most supermarkets. Specialty fruit and vegetable shops may stock the more delicate watercress grown in beds of running water.

4 servings

4	lamb loins, boned
2 tbsp	(30 mL) butter
	salt and pepper
	pinch of thyme
1	bunch of watercress
2	tomatoes, finely diced
1	garlic clove, finely sliced
½ cup	(125 mL) tomato juice
1 tsp	(5 mL) lemon juice

■ Preheat oven to 275 °F (130 °C).

■ Slice each loin of lamb into 4 medallions and pound lightly with meat mallet.

■ In a skillet, melt butter and cook medallions for 2 minutes on each side, then season with salt, pepper, and thyme. Remove medallions from skillet and keep warm. Using the same cooking butter, add watercress, tomatoes and garlic, simmer for 30 seconds, stirring gently. Add tomato juice and lemon juice and cook for 1 minute longer.

■ Adjust seasoning; coat medallions with sauce and garnish with small watercress bouquet.

VARIATIONS

• Replace watercress with either shredded spinach, lettuce or cabbage.

• Replace tomato juice with the following zucchini purée: melt 2 tbsp (30 mL) butter then mix together and cook 1 sliced zucchini and a small amount of garlic and purée in blender.

• Replace watercress and diced tomato with julienned cucumber steeped in butter and a few mint leaves.

Lamb Medallions Bergère

The delicious aroma of garlic blends wonderfully with the taste of lamb.

4 servings

3 tbsp	(45 mL) butter
1	sweet red pepper, finely sliced
1	green bell pepper, finely sliced
1	onion, chopped
	salt and pepper
4	garlic cloves, minced
½ cup	(125 mL) milk
4	loins of lamb, boned
	thyme and rosemary, to taste

■ In a skillet, melt 1 tbsp (15 mL) butter and cook half the peppers (red and green) with onion. Season with salt and pepper, stir and cook over low heat for 7 minutes.

■ Add garlic, then pour milk over mixture, stir and cook over low heat for 10 minutes. Blend to desired smoothness in blender, then set aside.

■ Blanch other half of peppers in lightly salted boiling water for 3 minutes, drain, then set aside.

■ Slice loin of lamb into 4 medallions and pound lightly with meat mallet.

■ In a skillet, melt remaining butter, cook lamb medallions and season with salt, pepper, thyme, and rosemary.

■ Place lamb medallions in a serving dish and keep warm.

■ In cooking fat, sauté blanched peppers for 1 minute, spread over medallions and coat with sauce.

VARIATIONS

- Replace peppers with French (dry) shallots. Arrange mixture on a bed of butter-fried croûtons, as shown here.

- Replace milk with either beef stock or consommé. Garnish bottom of serving dish with a ring of cucumber slices, blanched in lightly salted boiling water for 2 minutes.

- Replace sliced peppers with diced peppers and arrange in layers, then garnish with celery pieces, lightly coated with flour and pan-fried.

LAMB FILETS

Lamb Filets Provençale

Garnish the serving platter with green and black olives to give this recipe a truly Provençale look.

4 servings

2 tsp	(10 mL) olive oil
2 tbsp	(30 mL) butter
12	lamb tenderloin filets
	salt and pepper
	pinch of thyme
	pinch of rosemary
20	pearl onions
1 tsp	(5 mL) sugar
6	garlic cloves, finely sliced
2 tbsp	(30 mL) parsley
1	tomato, diced
½ cup	(125 mL) stock
2 tsp	(10 mL) lemon juice
¼ cup	(60 mL) fine breadcrumbs

■ Preheat oven to broil.

■ In a skillet, heat oil, melt butter and brown lamb, then season with salt, pepper, thyme, and rosemary. Remove from heat and keep warm.

■ Sauté pearl onions and sugar in the same cooking fat over medium heat until golden, then add garlic, parsley, and tomato and cook for 1 minute longer.

■ Add stock and lemon juice and cook until liquid is reduced to three-fourths.

■ Place lamb filets in an oven-proof serving dish, coat with sauce, sprinkle with breadcrumbs then broil until golden.

Add eggplant (seeded, peeled, and diced) to turn this dish into a ratatouille niçoise.

Some cooks like to add diced potatoes as a variant.

4 servings

2 tbsp	(30 mL) butter
12	lamb tenderloin filets
	salt and pepper
1	zucchini, diced
¼ cup	(60 mL) onions, chopped
1	sweet red pepper, diced
1	small carrot, diced
1	tomato, diced
3	garlic cloves, minced
	pinch of thyme
1	bay leaf
¾ cup	(180 mL) tomato juice
4 tsp	(20 mL) chopped parsley

■ In a skillet, melt butter and sauté lamb.

■ Remove meat from skillet and season with salt and pepper.

■ Add vegetables, garlic, thyme, and bay leaf to cooking fat, season with salt and pepper and cook until liquid evaporates completely.

■ Add tomato juice and cook over moderate heat for 5 minutes.

■ When cooked, warm lamb filets in ratatouille for 1 minute.

■ Place lamb in serving dish, top with ratatouille and sprinkle with parsley.

* Illustrated recipe

LAMB STEAKS

Marinated Leg of Lamb Steaks

You might try replacing powdered ginger with ¹/₂ teaspoon grated fresh ginger.

4 servings

4	garlic cloves, finely sliced
4	slices leg of lamb

Marinade

3 tbsp	(45 mL) olive oil
5	mint leaves, thinly sliced
¹/₂ cup	(125 mL) dry white wine
	pinch of thyme
	pinch of ginger
	salt and pepper
1 tsp	(5 mL) freshly ground black pepper

■ Preheat oven to broil.

■ Stick sliced garlic slivers into meat.

■ In a bowl, combine all marinade ingredients, add meat and marinate for at least 6 hours. Turn from time to time.

■ Place meat in a baking dish and broil for at least 6 minutes on each side.

■ Baste lightly with marinade before serving.

This cut is a leg chop, marrow-bone in, treated as a marinated steak. You'll find the marinade lends a delicate aroma to the meat.

When buying olive oil, remember that the best kind is "cold-pressed."

4 servings

Marinade

2 tbsp	(30 mL) olive oil
16	French (dry) shallots, finely sliced
1 tsp	(5 mL) tarragon
2 tsp	(10 mL) basil
1 tsp	(5 mL) chopped parsley
	pinch of thyme
	salt and pepper
4	steaks of leg of lamb
2 tbsp	(30 mL) butter

■ Eight hours before cooking time, combine all marinade ingredients in a small bowl.

■ Place meat in marinade, cover and refrigerate.

■ In a skillet, melt butter and cook meat 4 to 6 minutes on each side.

■ Baste lightly with marinade just before serving.

* Illustrated recipe

LEG OF LAMB

Leg of lamb is, in fact, the lamb's hind quarter. It tastes best when roasted. Its fatty outer layer only needs a light coating of oil or butter to prevent it from drying up during cooking.

How to bone and stuff a leg of lamb

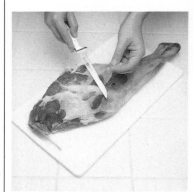

- *Cut off the outer fat, leaving only a thin layer.*

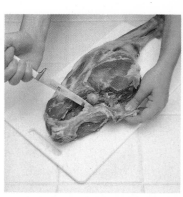

- *Turn the leg over and cut around the bone with a pointed knife.*

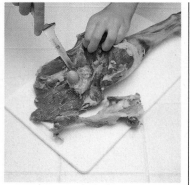

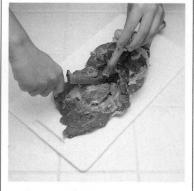

- *Once the first bone is removed, cut around the head of the second bone.*

- *Gradually detach the bone, using the knife tip, without tearing the meat.*

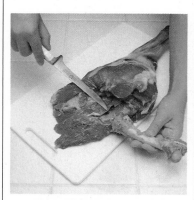

- *Remove the second bone.*

- *Stuff the cavity.*

- *Fold and tie.*

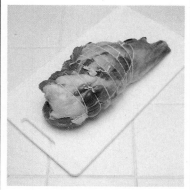

- *Chop off the lower shin. The leg of lamb is ready for cooking.*

Savory Leg of Lamb Stuffings

Chicken and Mushroom Stuffing

- In a bowl, mix together 1 lb (450 g) chopped chicken, 1 chopped onion, 1 cup (250 mL) mushroom pieces, 3 finely chopped garlic cloves, 2 eggs and ¼ cup (60 mL) chopped parsley.

- Season with salt and pepper.

- Stuff leg of lamb cavity with this mixture and tie.

Herb Stuffing

- Baste inside of leg of lamb with 3 tbsp (45 mL) Dijon mustard.

- Mix together 1 tsp (5 mL) tarragon, 1 tsp (5 mL) basil, 1 tsp (5 mL) parsley, 1 tsp (5 mL) mint and 4 chopped garlic cloves. Add 1 egg and season with salt and pepper.

- Stuff leg of lamb with this mixture and tie.

Mint and Fruit Stuffing

- Combine ¼ cup (60 mL) canned diced pears, ¼ cup (60 mL) canned diced peaches and ½ cup (125 mL) frozen raspberries and drain well, then add 1 tbsp (15 mL) chopped mint.

- Stuff leg of lamb cavity with this mixture and tie.

Stuffed Leg of Lamb

It's always better to thaw leg of lamb in the refrigerator.

8 servings

1 lb	(450 g) ground veal
1	onion, chopped
½ cup	(125 mL) fine breadcrumbs
¼ cup	(60 mL) milk
4	garlic cloves, finely sliced
⅓ cup	(80 mL) chopped parsley
2	eggs
4 ½ lb	(2 kg) boned leg of lamb
¼ cup	(60 mL) butter
	salt and pepper
	pinch of thyme
1 cup	(250 mL) beef con-sommé

■ Preheat oven to 450 °F (230 °C).

■ In a bowl, combine ground veal, onion, bread-crumbs, milk, garlic, parsley and eggs. Stuff leg of lamb with mixture and tie to close.

■ Baste with butter, brown in oven for 10 minutes, then reduce oven temperature to 350 °F (175 °C).

■ Season with salt, pepper, and thyme and pour beef consommé over meat.

■ Cook 60 minutes, basting often.

■ Remove leg of lamb from oven, carve into thin slices and keep warm.

■ Let cooking liquid reduce and pour over the meat.

■ Serve with roasted pota-toes and a variety of vege-tables.

Rolled Leg of Lamb Boulangère

The potatoes will absorb the sweet juices liberated during cooking.

8 servings

4 ½ lb	(2 kg) leg of lamb
	salt and pepper
	pinch of thyme
2 tbsp	(30 mL) oil
2 tbsp	(30 mL) butter
2 cups	(500 mL) onions, sliced
3 cups	(750 mL) potatoes, sliced
2 cups	(500 mL) chicken stock or consommé
½ cup	(125 mL) chopped parsley

■ Preheat oven to 425 °F (220 °C).

■ Bone and tie leg of lamb and season with salt, pepper and thyme.

■ In an oven-proof casserole, heat oil, melt butter and sear leg of lamb.

■ Reduce oven heat to 350 °F (175 °C) and cook for approximately 30 minutes.

■ Add onions and potatoes, then pour stock over mixture, adjust seasoning, bring to a boil and cook for another 30 minutes.

■ When cooked, carve leg of lamb into thin slices. Sprinkle parsley over potatoes and adjust seasoning.

Garlic-flavored Leg of Lamb

A whole leg of lamb is more difficult to carve than a boned leg, but it's much tastier.

8 servings

4 ½ lb	(2 kg) leg of lamb, with bone
4 tsp	(20 mL) Dijon mustard
4 tsp	(20 mL) tomato paste
	salt and pepper
	pinch of thyme
	pinch of rosemary
6	garlic cloves, blanchd for 5 minutes
24	pearl onions
1 tbsp	(15 mL) sugar
4 tsp	(20 mL) lemon juice
1 cup	(250 mL) consommé

■ Preheat oven to 450 °F (230 °C).

■ Baste leg of lamb with Dijon mustard and tomato paste, season with salt, pepper, thyme, and rosemary and bake until golden.

■ Reduce oven heat to 350 °F (175 °F) and cook 60 minutes longer. After 30 minutes, add garlic, onions, sugar, and lemon juice.

■ After 45 minutes, pour consommé over leg of lamb, then baste and finish cooking.

■ Remove leg of lamb from oven, carve into thin slices and keep warm.

■ Reduce cooking juices, and pour over the meat.

Mushroom-stuffed Lamb Rolls

Don't forget to remove toothpicks just before bringing this dish to the table.

4 servings

1 tbsp	(15 mL) prepared mustard
8	slices roast of lamb, cooked
3 tbsp	(45 mL) butter
1	small onion, sliced
1 cup	(250 mL) canned mushrooms
1 cup	(250 mL) canned tomato soup
	salt and pepper
4 tsp	(20 mL) chopped parsley
½ tsp	(2 mL) fines herbes

■ Coat each roasted lamb slice with prepared mustard.

■ In a skillet, melt butter, sauté onions and mushrooms and season with salt and pepper. Divide mixture evenly onto each lamb slice.

■ Roll each slice and secure with toothpicks.

■ Pour tomato soup into a stove-top casserole. Add the meat, sprinkle with parsley and fines herbes, then let mixture simmer over medium heat 5 to 10 minutes.

VARIATIONS

- **Replace tomato soup with a cream of asparagus soup and replace mushrooms with canned asparagus tips.**

- **Replace tomato soup with a cream of mushroom soup.**

157

LOIN OF LAMB

Boning a loin of lamb

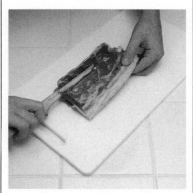

- *Insert the knife blade between meat and bone. Cut along the edge of the bone under the loin.*

- *Remove the loin.*

- *Trim off the fat and tendon.*

Stuffing a loin of lamb

- *Insert the knife blade into one end of the trimmed loin.*

- *Repeat for the other end and widen the opening to form a cavity.*

- *With a pastry bag and nozzle, pipe stuffing into cavity.*

- *Press to spread stuffing evenly inside cavity.*

Making loin of lamb rolls

- *Slit the loin lengthwise, and spread open.*

- *Pipe in the stuffing of your choice.*

- *Roll and tie securely.*

Lamb Rolls with Hazelnuts

You'll find hazelnuts (or filberts) with the cake and pastry ingredients in your grocery store. They're usually sold by the bag.

4 servings

4	loins of lamb, boned
¼ cup	(60 mL) butter
1	onion, chopped
30	chopped hazelnuts
1	carrot, julienned
	salt and pepper
1	garlic clove, finely chopped
	pinch of thyme
	green peppercorn sauce
2 tbsp	(30 mL) chopped parsley

■ Preheat oven to 375 °F (190 °C).

■ Open the boned loins of lamb.

■ In a skillet, melt half the butter, cook onion, hazelnuts, carrot and garlic; season with salt, pepper, and thyme and cook for 3 minutes.

■ Spread the meat with the stuffing, roll and tie.

■ Using the same skillet, melt remaining butter and brown the meat.

■ Cook in oven for approximately 15 minutes then let stand for 5 minutes before carving.

■ Place loins in a serving dish, coat with green peppercorn sauce, sprinkle with parsley and serve.

VARIATION

• Serve the lamb with cucumbers garnished with fines herbes and mint, as shown here.

RACK OF LAMB

Preparing a rack of lamb

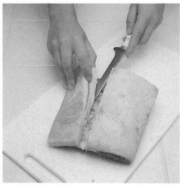

- *Cut through the skin halfway up the rack. Remove fat from bones.*

- *Remove fat between each rib and scrape each one carefully until smooth.*

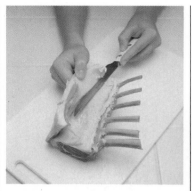

- *Remove a thick layer of fat from the meat.*

- *Remove ligament along the loin. The rack is ready for cooking.*

Before cooking, cut each section of the rack part way through, and you'll have less trouble carving it at the table.

4 servings		
¼ lb	(115 g)	uncooked white chicken meat, chopped
1 tbsp	(15 mL)	basil, chopped
1 tbsp	(15 mL)	chopped parsley
1		garlic clove, finely chopped
1		egg
2 tbsp	(30 mL)	35% cream
2 tbsp	(30 mL)	butter
2		racks of lamb, trimmed
		salt and pepper
		pinch of thyme
		garlic and tomato sauce

- Preheat oven to 425 °F (220 °C).

- In a small bowl, combine chicken, basil, parsley, and garlic and add egg.

- Pour cream in gradually, stir, then season with salt and pepper.

- With a thin knife, hollow out a cavity in each rack of lamb by cutting into both ends of the meat.

- With a pastry bag with nozzle attachment, pipe stuffing into cavity.

- In a stove-to-oven casserole dish, melt butter, sear racks of lamb over high heat, then season with salt, pepper, and thyme and bake for 20 minutes.

- Serve with garlic and tomato sauce.

Rack of Lamb with Potatoes

Lardons are small chunks of smoked, lean bacon that are added to certain dishes to enhance the flavor.

4 servings

2 tbsp	(30 mL) butter
2	prepared racks of lamb
	salt and pepper
	pinch of thyme
¼ lb	(115 g) lardons
20	pearl onions
8 oz	(227 mL) canned mushrooms
4	medium-sized potatoes, sliced
1	garlic clove, finely sliced
2 tbsp	(30 mL) chopped parsley

■ Preheat oven to 350 °F (175 °C).

■ In a stove-top casserole, melt butter and sear racks of lamb, then season with salt, pepper and thyme and add lardons along with vegetables.

■ Cook uncovered in oven for approximately 30 minutes; baste from time to time with cooking juices.

■ Remove from oven, arrange meat in a serving dish and keep warm in oven.

■ Degrease cooking juices, add garlic and parsley, stir and pour over lamb. Serve.

Rack of Lamb Persillade

The seasoning known as "persillade" is a blend of chopped parsley and herbs such as rosemary, thyme and bay leaf, mixed with oil. Sometimes fine, dried breadcrumbs are added.

4 servings

2 tbsp	(30 mL) butter
2	racks of lamb, trimmed
	salt and pepper
	thyme and rosemary
1	crushed bay leaf
¼ cup	(60 mL) fine breadcrumbs
2 tsp	(10 mL) olive oil
2 tbsp	(30 mL) chopped parsley
2	garlic cloves, finely sliced
½ cup	(125 mL) water

■ Preheat oven to 450 °F (230 °C).

■ In a skillet, melt butter and cook racks of lamb over high heat until golden.

■ In a small bowl, combine all the spices and season racks of lamb with mixture.

■ Cook racks of lamb in oven for approximately 15 minutes; halfway through cooking process, turn racks of lamb.

■ Meanwhile, in another bowl, combine breadcrumbs, oil, parsley, and garlic.

■ When cooked, baste fatty side of racks of lamb with breadcrumb mixture and return to oven to brown topping, then place in a serving dish and keep warm.

■ Degrease cooking juices, add water, stir and reduce mixture by half, then pour over sliced racks of lamb.

* Illustrated recipe

VARIATIONS

• Add 2 tbsp (30 mL) grated Parmesan cheese to breadcrumb mixture to give racks of lamb an Italian touch.

• Prepare racks of lamb in the same manner as Leg of Lamb Boulangère (see recipe on page 156).

• Before cooking racks of lamb, baste with a mixture of one part mustard and two parts tomato paste.

• Replace olive oil with chopped bacon bits. When cooked, sprinkle grated Cheddar chese over racks of lamb, then brown lightly under the broiler.

LAMB CHOPS

Spicy Lamb Chops

Vary the amount of curry powder for a more or less spicy dish, according to your family's preferences.

4 servings

12	lamb chops
3 tbsp	(45 mL) vegetable oil
2 tsp	(10 mL) curry powder
1	medium-size onion, chopped
½ cup	(125 mL) beef stock or water
¼ tsp	(1 mL) ginger
¼ tsp	(1 mL) dry mustard
½ tsp	(2 mL) salt
¼ cup	(60 mL) 15% cream

■ Trim excess fat off lamb chops.

■ In a skillet, heat oil and cook onion with curry powder, but do not brown.

■ Add lamb chops and cook until golden.

■ Pour beef stock or water over mixture, season with salt, cover and let simmer over low heat 20 to 25 minutes until meat is tender and juicy.

■ In a saucepan, heat cream, then pour slowly over lamb chops, stir but do not boil.

■ Place meat in a serving dish and serve.

Saffron is by far the most expensive spice on the market. The best you can buy is sold in filaments—the pollen-bearing, dried stigma that are extracted from the autumn crocus or saffron flower. It lends a lovely golden color to any dish.

4 servings

12	lamb chops
4 tsp	(20 mL) soy sauce
3 tbsp	(45 mL) vinegar
1 tbsp	(15 mL) Worcestershire sauce
1 tbsp	(15 mL) tomato paste
⅓ cup	(80 mL) butter
3 cups	(750 mL) water
	salt
	pinch of saffron
1	large carrot, peeled, thinly sliced
1 ½ cups	(375 mL) long-grained rice
1 cup	(250 mL) mushrooms, sliced
1 cup	(250 mL) cooked green peas
	chopped parsley

■ Pat lamb chops dry with paper towel.

■ In a bowl, combine soy sauce, vinegar, Worcestershire sauce, and tomato paste.

■ Baste one side of lamb chops with mixture and let stand for 30 minutes, then turn lamb chops, baste other side and let stand for 30 minutes.

■ In a skillet, melt a small amount of butter, fry lamb chops for 10 to 15 minutes and turn during cooking process. Baste with remaining soy sauce mixture.

■ In a large saucepan, bring water to a boil, season with salt, add saffron and sliced carrot and pour rice into water. Cook 15 to 20 minutes, drain and rinse under cold water. Set aside.

■ In the same saucepan, melt remaining butter, cook mushrooms, add green peas and cooked rice and heat well.

■ Turn the rice mixture out onto a heated serving dish, arrange lamb chops on top, and garnish with chopped parsley.

* Illustrated recipe

Breaded Lamb Chops

Be sure to cook the lamb chops over low heat, otherwise the breading will brown before the meat is done.

4 servings

Garlic Butter

¼ cup	(60 mL) butter
4	garlic cloves, finely sliced
1 tsp	(5 mL) lemon juice
1 tbsp	(15 mL) chopped parsley
12	lamb chops
1 cup	(250 mL) seasoned flour
2	eggs, beaten
1 cup	(250 mL) fine breadcrumbs
2 tbsp	(30 mL) vegetable oil
4 tsp	(20 mL) chopped parsley

■ In a bowl, combine all ingredients for garlic butter and set aside.

■ Dredge lamb chops first with seasoned flour, then dip into beaten eggs and finally into breadcrumbs.

■ In a skillet, heat oil and cook lamb chops over low heat for 6 minutes on each side.

■ Place in serving dish, baste with melted garlic butter and sprinkle with parsley.

Lamb Chops with Mint Sauce

You've never fully appreciated the exquisite flavor of lamb until you've tasted it with a delicious mint sauce.

4 servings

Mint Sauce

¼ cup	(60 mL) water
1 tbsp	(15 mL) brown sugar
¼ cup	(60 mL) fresh mint leaves, finely chopped
	salt and pepper
¼ cup	(60 mL) cider vinegar
¼ cup	(60 mL) vegetable oil
12	lamb chops
2 tbsp	(30 mL) vegetable oil

■ Pour water into a saucepan, add brown sugar and stir, then bring to boil and set aside.

■ In a bowl, combine mint leaves with salt and pepper, then pour water and brown sugar mixture over mint leaves, add cider vinegar and vegetable oil and let liquid steep for 30 minutes.

■ Baste lamb chops with mint sauce.

■ In a skillet, heat oil and cook lamb chops over medium heat for 10 minutes on each side. Baste often with mint sauce during cooking process.

■ Season with salt just before serving.

CUBED LAMB

Carbonnade of Lamb with Beer

Carbonnade is a Flemish specialty. It is usually made with strips of beef cooked in beer. Our lamb recipe offers a delicious variation.

4 servings

2	potatoes, diced
¼ cup	(60 mL) butter
1 tbsp	(15 mL) onion, finely sliced
¼ cup	(60 mL) flour
12 oz	(341 mL) brown beer
2 cups	(500 mL) cooked lamb, cubed
	salt and pepper
1 tsp	(5 mL) chopped parsley

- Cook potatoes in microwave oven, then let stand to cool.

- In a saucepan, melt butter, cook onion, add flour and stir.

- Pour beer over onion mixture, stirring constantly, and let mixture simmer over low heat 2 to 3 minutes.

- Add lamb cubes and potatoes, and season with salt and pepper.

- Let mixture simmer until it has completely absorbed liquid, then sprinkle with parsley.

You're probably familiar with moussaka, a hearty Greek dish in which lamb and eggplant blend nicely. We've created an interesting adaptation to make your life a little simpler.

4 servings

1 lb	(450 g) cubed lamb
14 oz	(398 mL) stewed tomatoes, chopped
6 oz	(170 mL) tomato paste
½ tsp	(2 mL) ground ginger
¼ tsp	(1 mL) ground cinnamon
4	stalks of chives, chopped
2 tbsp	(30 mL) fresh parsley
	salt and pepper
4 to 8	eggplant slices
¼ cup	(60 mL) melted butter
½ cup	(125 mL) sour cream

- Preheat oven to broil.

- In an 8-cup microwave-safe bowl, mix together cubed lamb, tomatoes, tomato paste, ginger, cinnamon, chives, and parsley, and season with salt and pepper.

- Cover bowl with a sheet of waxed paper and cook in microwave at MEDIUM for 8 to 9 minutes.

- Remove from microwave, stir and cover. Return to microwave and cook at MEDIUM for 5 to 6 minutes or until sauce thickens and lamb is tender to taste. Remove from microwave and let stand.

- Baste eggplant slices with melted butter, place in oven-proof dish and broil both sides until golden (about 2 minutes on each side).

- Place grilled eggplant slices on a heated serving dish; pour lamb mixture over eggplant and garnish with sour cream.

* Illustrated recipe

Lamb Fricassee

A few mushrooms, a cream sauce, and you've got a delicious casserole made from leftover lamb.

4 servings	
8 oz	(227 mL) canned cream of mushroom soup
½ cup	(125 mL) milk or 15% cream
8 oz	(227 mL) canned mushroom pieces
2 cups	(500 mL) cooked lamb, cubed
2 tbsp	(30 mL) chopped parsley

■ In a saucepan, thin down cream of mushroom soup with milk or cream.

■ Add mushroom pieces and lamb cubes and heat mixture without boiling for 6 or 7 minutes.

■ Sprinkle with chopped parsley and serve.

Marinated Lamb Kebab

This is an authentic shish-kebab recipe for those who love Mediterranean food.

4 servings	
Marinade	
1	onion
¼ cup	(60 mL) oil
2 tbsp	(30 mL) lemon juice
1	bay leaf
¼ tsp	(1 mL) thyme
	salt and pepper
1 ½ lbs	(675 g) shoulder of lamb, trimmed and cubed
2	onions, cut into 4 wedges
8	cherry tomatoes
2	green bell peppers, diced
16	whole mushrooms
2	pineapple slices, cut into 8 pieces
8	bacon slices, halved, rolled

■ In a bowl, combine all marinade ingredients, add lamb cubes and refrigerate for 2 to 3 hours to marinate. Stir from time to time.

■ Preheat oven to broil.

■ Slip lamb cubes onto skewers, alternating with vegetables, pineapple pieces, and rolled bacon.

■ Broil, turn and baste with marinade during broiling.

■ Serve on a bed of rice.

GROUND LAMB

Lamb Croustade

Crusty bread, hollowed out and stuffed with spicy ground lamb, is delightfully appetizing to the eye—an important element in the enjoyment of food.

4 servings

2 tbsp	(30 mL) butter
1 lb	(450 g) ground lamb
1	onion, chopped
½ cup	(125 mL) rice
1 ½ cups	(375 mL) hot beef stock
¼ cup	(60 mL) chopped parsley
	salt and pepper
½ tsp	(2 mL) sage
¼ tsp	(1 mL) dry mustard
	pinch of cinnamon
1	loaf of crusty bread
	tomato sauce

■ Preheat oven to 325 °F (160 °C).

■ In a stove-top casserole, melt butter and brown the lamb lightly, then add onion and rice.

■ Add beef stock, parsley, salt, pepper, sage, mustard, and cinnamon and bring to a boil. Let mixture simmer for 20 minutes or until liquid is completely absorbed.

■ Cut a ¾ inch (2 cm) slice off one end of crusty bread, remove soft part of bread, leaving a ½ inch (1,25 cm) layer under the crust.

■ Fill cavity with lamb mixture and replace end slice.

■ Wrap stuffed crusty bread in thick aluminum foil and bake for 20 to 30 minutes.

■ Cut into thick slices and coat with tomato sauce.

Try something exotic for a change and replace humdrum ketchup and relish with a mango or pineapple chutney.

4 to 6 servings

1 lb	(450 g) ground lamb
1 tsp	(5 mL) curry
½ tsp	(2 mL) onion salt
½ tsp	(2 mL) salt
¼ tsp	(1 mL) pepper
1	egg
¾ cup	(180 mL) fine breadcrumbs

■ Preheat oven to 350 °F (175 °C).

■ In a large bowl, combine all ingredients and shape into round, flat patties.

■ Place patties in an oven-proof dish in oven, on middle rack; cook on each side for 5 minutes.

■ Serve on toasted buns, topped with garnish of your choice.

* Illustrated recipe

Lamb-stuffed Pickle Rolls

Use fresh white or whole-wheat breadcrumbs.

6 servings

1 ½ lbs	(675 g) ground lamb
1 cup	(250 mL) fresh, soft part of bread
1	egg, lightly beaten
1 cup	(250 mL) tomato sauce or cream of tomato soup
1 tsp	(5 mL) dry mustard
	salt and pepper
2	large dill pickles
1 tbsp	(15 mL) oil
1 tsp	(5 mL) butter
8 oz	(227 mL) cream of celery soup
¼ cup	(60 mL) dill pickle juice
1 tbsp	(15 mL) chopped parsley

■ Preheat oven to 350 °F (175 °C).

■ In a bowl, combine ground lamb, bread, egg, tomato sauce, mustard, salt, and pepper.

■ Slice dill pickles lengthwise into thin slivers; wrap each pickle around ground lamb mixture and shape into rolls.

■ In a skillet, heat oil, melt butter and cook lamb rolls then place in ovenproof dish.

■ In a separate bowl, combine cream of celery soup, dill pickle juice, and parsley and pour over lamb rolls, then bake for approximately 25 minutes.

Lamb Cabbage Rolls

Serve these stuffed cabbage rolls on a colorful bed of saffron rice with diced green peppers and carrots.

4 servings

8	cabbage leaves
1 lb	(450 g) ground lamb
1	onion, finely sliced
	salt and pepper
½ tsp	(2 mL) thyme
3 tbsp	(45 mL) rice

Sauce

2 tbsp	(30 mL) butter
2 tbsp	(30 mL) flour
2 tbsp	(30 mL) tomatoes, diced
1 cup	(250 mL) tomato juice
	salt and pepper
1	bay leaf

■ Blanch cabbage leaves in lightly salted boiling water for 5 minutes, drain and let stand to cool.

■ In a bowl, combine ground lamb, onion, salt, pepper, thyme, and rice.

■ Spread 1 tbsp (15 mL) of mixture onto each cabbage leaf, roll and set aside.

■ In a saucepan, melt butter, add flour and heat for a few minutes.

■ Add tomatoes and tomato juice, season with salt and pepper and bring to a boil.

■ Place cabbage rolls in sauce with bay leaf; cover, simmer for 1 hour.

167

"Tout est bon dans le cochon," say the French, and with good reason. From pork jowls to pig's knuckles, the hog has always been an excellent food source. It is economical to raise on the farm and to buy in the supermarket. Pork butchers have developed more than three dozen cuts, including the organs, that can be used in numerous recipes.

Pork juices are fairly sweet, and the browned meat produces a slightly caramelized effect that makes a rich brown pan juice and delicious sauces. The meat itself adapts well to a range of sweet or savory condiments to produce such dishes as fragrant garlic-stuffed pork roast, barbecued chops, kebabs, succulent glazed ham and pineapple, sweet and sour spareribs, tasty pork crackling, and countless casseroles.

PORK

PORK RACK

With or without the bone, pork is well suited to roasting or braising.

Pork rack tastes better when roasted with the bone in, but you can ask your butcher to bone and roll the meat if you prefer.

Pricking a pork rack

• **With a sharp pointed knife, make small incisions in the meat.**

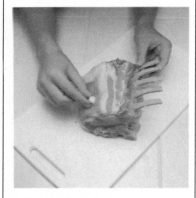

• **Place half a garlic clove in each incision.**

Potatoes, carrots and turnip are a favorite trio in Flemish cuisine. You might like to add a few rounds of steamed sausage and some cabbage leaves to this appetizing dish.

8 servings	
4 ½ lb	(2 kg) pork rack
1	garlic clove, thinly sliced
2 tbsp	(30 mL) vegetable oil salt and pepper
2	medium-size onions, cut into wedges
½ cup	(125 mL) beer
½ cup	(125 mL) potatoes, diced
½ cup	(125 mL) diced carrots
½ cup	(125 mL) turnip, diced
1 tbsp	(15 mL) kneaded butter (beurre manié) (optional)

■ Make small cuts in the pork and insert garlic.

■ In a skillet, heat oil and sear pork on all sides, then season with salt and pepper.

■ Add onions and beer, cover and cook over low heat for about 45 minutes or until loin of pork is almost tender. If necessary, add liquid during cooking process.

■ Add vegetables, cover and cook for 15 minutes or until meat and vegetables are done, then add kneaded butter to make a smooth sauce.

Cranberry-glazed Pork Rack

You can buy whole cranberries out of season in the frozen food section of most supermarkets.

4 servings

4 ½ lbs	(2 kg) loin of pork, with bone
⅓ cup	(80 mL) brown sugar
⅓ cup	(80 mL) molasses
¼ cup	(60 mL) vinegar
½ cup	(125 mL) water
¼ tsp	(1 mL) ground cloves
¼ tsp	(1 mL) ground cinnamon
2 cups	(500 mL) cranberries

■ Preheat oven to 425 °F (220 °C).

■ Place loin of pork in an oven-proof dish, fatty side up and sear in oven.

■ Reduce oven temperature to 350 °F (180 °C) and cook for 15 minutes per pound.

■ In a saucepan, combine brown sugar, molasses, vinegar, water and spices, bring to a boil. Add cranberries, let simmer for 15 minutes then pour through sieve for a smooth sauce.

■ Baste loin of pork with sauce. Increase oven temperature to 425 °F (220 °C), cook for 15 minutes and baste from time to time.

■ Remove from oven and let stand for 10 minutes, then carve.

VARIATIONS

Glazed with Walnuts

• **Prepare recipe following same procedure as Cranberry-glazed Pork Rack, omitting cranberries.**

• **When coating roast with sauce, sprinkle loin of pork with ¼ cup (60 mL) chopped walnuts.**

Cinderella Pork Chops

Children love these lightly orange-flavored pork chops. The orange garnish and translucent brown sauce give them a mouth-watering appearance.

4 servings

2 tbsp	(30 mL) oil
8	½ inch (1,25 cm) thick pork chops
¼ tsp	(1 mL) pepper
1	small package instant onion soup mix
8	orange slices, peeled
1 cup	(250 mL) orange juice

■ In a skillet, heat oil, cook pork chops and season with pepper.

■ Sprinkle onion soup mix over pork chops, place orange slice on each, pour orange juice over mixture and bring to a boil. Cover and simmer for 30 minutes or until pork chops are very tender.

Honey-flavored Pork Chops

If the honey has crystallized in the jar, take off the cover and warm it in the microwave for a few minutes. Check every 30 seconds to see whether the crystals have dissolved.

4 to 6 servings

8	¾ inch (2 cm) thick pork chops
	garlic salt and pepper
1 tbsp	(15 mL) oil
1 tbsp	(15 mL) butter
¼ cup	(60 mL) liquid honey
¼ cup	(60 mL) white wine or cider

■ Preheat oven to 350 °F (175 °C).

■ Remove excess fat from pork chops; season with garlic salt and pepper.

■ In a skillet, heat oil and melt butter; cook pork chops for a few minutes; transfer to oven-proof dish; add 2 tbsp (30 mL) liquid honey to mixture; cover with aluminum foil; bake 20 minutes.

■ Baste with rest of honey; cover; cook 15 minutes longer.

■ Add white wine or cider; cook, uncovered, 10 minutes.

Pork Chop Dinner

You can replace half the carrots in this recipe with rutabagas.

4 servings

3 tbsp	(45 mL) butter
2	medium-size onions, cut into 6 pieces
6	potatoes, cut into 8 pieces
6	medium-size carrots, sliced
	salt and pepper
8	½ inch (1,25 cm) thick pork chops
1	package pork chop breading
	parsley

■ Preheat oven to 425 °F (220 °C).

■ In a skillet, melt butter, sauté vegetables and season with salt and pepper.

■ Place vegetables in oven-proof dish, cover with aluminum foil and bake for 15 minutes.

■ Meanwhile, trim excess fat from pork chops, and coat with breading according to package directions.

■ In same skillet, sear breaded pork chops on one side only, for 1 minute.

■ Place cooked side over vegetables and cook, uncovered in oven, until tender to taste, then sprinkle with parsley.

Pork Chops with Mushroom Sauce

For a pretty effect, slice potatoes with the wavy edge of the vegetable cutter.

4 servings

	salt and pepper
8	pork chops ½ inch (1,25 cm) thick each
2 tbsp	(30 mL) butter
4	potatoes, thinly sliced
10 oz	(284 mL) canned cream of mushroom soup
8	knobs of butter
	breadcrumbs

■ Preheat oven to 350 °F (175 °C).

■ Season each pork chop with salt and pepper.

■ In a skillet, melt butter and sear pork chops.

■ Place in oven-proof dish, add potatoes and cream of mushroom soup, and place knobs of butter over mixture. Sprinkle with breadcrumbs and bake for 30 minutes.

STUFFED PORK CHOPS

Stuffed pork chops are easy on the budget and have a delightfully savory taste. A single stuffed pork chop will satisfy most appetites.

Butterfly Pork Chops

When time is of the essence, simply garnish butterfly pork chops with cheese. On the other hand, if you're feeling creative, put your talent to the test with one of following delightful stuffing combinations.

4 servings	
4	pork chops, 1 inch (2,5 cm) thick each
	salt and pepper
1 tbsp	(15 mL) Worcestershire sauce
1 tbsp	(15 mL) peanut oil
1	slice of cheese or stuffing of your choice

■ Preheat oven to 350 °F (175 °C).

■ Trim excess fat off pork chops. Slice each one lengthwise up to bone to form a cavity. Season cavity with salt and pepper; baste both sides of pork chop with Worcestershire sauce.

■ In a skillet, heat peanut oil and sear pork chops over high heat, 2 minutes each side.

■ Garnish cavity with stuffing and bake for 15 to 20 minutes.

Eight Variations for Butterfly Pork Chops

Tomato and Parmesan Stuffing

- Mix together 2 large seeded, diced tomatoes, 1 tbsp (15 mL) tomato purée or ketchup along with 4 tsp (20 mL) Parmesan cheese, and a pinch of basil, salt and pepper.

Baby Shrimp Stuffing

- In a blender, mix ½ cup (125 mL) baby shrimp and 1 tsp (5 mL) shallots, with 1 tbsp (15 mL) chili sauce, salt and pepper.

- Garnish each chop with 4 or 5 whole baby shrimp.

  N.B.: Add 1 tsp (5mL) horseradish without vinegar to enhance the stuffing.

Persillade

- In a blender, chop 1 cup (250 mL) parsley with ½ tsp (2 mL) garlic, season with salt and pepper. Add 1 tsp (5 mL) olive oil and stir gently.

  N.B.: Add 1 tsp (5 mL) relish for a sweet flavor.

Ham Mousse Stuffing

- In a blender, mix together 1 tbsp (15 mL) prepared mustard, ½ cup (125 mL) cooked ham and ¼ tsp (1 mL) garlic. Season with salt and pepper.

Roquefort

- Blend together ¼ cup (60 mL) Roquefort cheese or crumbled blue cheese with 1 tbsp (15 mL) softened butter. Season with salt and pepper.

  N.B.: You might like to combine a milder cheese with the Roquefort for a more subtle taste.

Sweet Pepper and Spinach

- In a skillet, melt 1 tbsp (15 mL) butter and sauté ¼ cup (60 mL) diced peppers (either green bell, sweet red, and/or yellow). Pour in 1 tbsp (15 mL) white wine, then add 1 ½ cups (375 mL) fresh spinach leaves and stir gently until leaves begin to wilt. Season with salt and pepper.

Brussels Sprouts and Bacon

- Blanch ½ cup (125 mL) Brussels sprouts for 4 minutes and drain, then slice in half.

- In a skillet, lightly sauté 4 bacon slices, cut into pieces, add Brussels sprouts and sauté for a few minutes. Adjust seasoning.

Pâté de Foie with Cognac and Tarragon

- With a fork, mash ½ cup (125 mL) pâté de foie. Add 1 tsp (5 mL) cognac, brandy or another liqueur to the pâté and add a pinch of chopped tarragon. Season with salt and pepper.

SPARERIBS

Pineapple Spareribs

These days, spareribs have gained such popularity that some restaurants serve them as a specialty. Learn to prepare them yourself. Your family will think they're eating out!

4 servings

½ cup	(125 mL) pineapple juice
½ cup	(125 mL) corn syrup
2 tbsp	(30 mL) soy sauce
½ tsp	(2 mL) salt
3 lbs	(1,4 kg) small pork spareribs

■ Preheat oven to 400 °F (205 °C).

■ In a deep bowl, combine first 4 ingredients, add spareribs and marinate for approximately 1 hour, turning from time to time.

■ Bake for 1 hour or until meat is tender. Turn over a few times during cooking process and baste with marinade.

Spareribs Teriyaki

Serve these spareribs with the sticky rice found in oriental grocery stores.

4 servings

3 lbs	(1,4 kg) spareribs
¼ cup	(60 mL) soy sauce
½ cup	(125 mL) onion, sliced
2 tbsp	(30 mL) brown sugar, well packed
1	finely sliced garlic clove
1 tsp	(5 mL) ground ginger
½ tsp	(2 mL) salt
1 tbsp	(15 mL) sherry
3 cups	(750 mL) apricot juice or orange juice
5 tsp	(25 mL) cornstarch
2 tbsp	(30 mL) water

■ Preheat oven to 400 °F (205 °C).

■ Slice spareribs in half through the middle and separate into 3-inch (7,5 cm) pieces, then place in a three-quart (4 L) stove-top casserole.

■ In a bowl, combine soy sauce, onion, brown sugar, garlic, ginger, salt, sherry, and juice. Pour mixture over spareribs, cover and cook for 1 hour, turning spareribs every 20 minutes. Meanwhile, dissolve cornstarch in water and set aside.

■ Place spareribs in a serving dish and keep warm. Skim excess fat off sauce and add dissolved cornstarch. Stir over high heat for 5 to 6 minutes or until sauce thickens, then pour over spareribs.

Barbecued Spareribs

Replace ketchup with chili sauce.

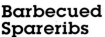

4 servings	
3 lbs	(1,4 kg) spareribs
3 tbsp	(45 mL) bacon fat or oil
1	garlic clove
3	onions, finely sliced
1 cup	(250 mL) ketchup
½ cup	(125 mL) cider vinegar
1 tsp	(5 mL) curry powder
1 tsp	(5 mL) paprika
¼ tsp	(1 mL) chili powder (optional)
3 tbsp	(45 mL) brown sugar
½ tsp	(2 mL) salt
	pinch of pepper
½ tsp	(2 mL) dry mustard

■ Preheat oven to 400 °F (205 °C).

■ Carve ribs into bite-size pieces.

■ In a skillet, melt bacon fat or heat oil, cook garlic until golden, remove garlic and set aside. Sauté spareribs.

■ In an oven-proof dish, combine spareribs, garlic and onions.

■ In a bowl, mix together all other ingredients and pour over spareribs, cover and bake for 1 hour or until meat is tender to taste.

Marinated Spareribs

Don't hesitate to marinate spareribs for a long time, since they will be that much tastier.

4 servings	
3 lbs	(1,4 kg) spareribs
¼ cup	(60 mL) tomato paste
¼ cup	(60 mL) soy sauce
2	large onions, finely sliced
¼ cup	(60 mL) tomato soup
2 cups	(500 mL) chicken stock
¼ tsp	(1 mL) salt
¼ tsp	(1 mL) pepper

■ Preheat oven to 400 °F (205 °C).

■ In a large bowl, combine all ingredients; marinate for 12 hours.

■ Pour mixture into an oven-proof dish and bake for 1 hour. Serve.

PORK ESCALOPES

Vodka and Pepper Pork Escalopes

The simple sauce that accompanies this dish gives it a distinctive flavor. You might even want to try it with steak.

4 servings

4	pork escalopes
¼ tsp	(1 mL) salt
2 tbsp	(30 mL) black peppercorns, crushed
1 tbsp	(15 mL) butter
½ cup	(125 mL) mushrooms, finely sliced
3 tbsp	(45 mL) vodka
⅓ cup	(80 mL) 35% cream

■ Preheat oven to 300 °F (150 °C).

■ Season pork with salt and coat with black crushed peppercorns.

■ In a skillet, melt butter, sear pork on both sides, place in a serving dish and keep warm.

■ Using the same skillet, sauté mushrooms for approximately 3 minutes. Deglaze skillet with vodka, add cream, cook over low heat, and stir until mixture is smooth, without boiling.

■ Pour sauce over pork escalopes. Serve.

Make sure you cook these thin slices of pork very lightly.

4 servings

½ cup	(125 mL) plain yogurt
2 tsp	(10 mL) Dijon prepared mustard
1 tbsp	(15 mL) flour
1 tsp	(5 mL) sugar
1 lb	(450 g) pork (filet, loin or nut), cut into ¾ inch (2 cm) thick slices
	salt and pepper
1 tbsp	(15 mL) butter
½ cup	(125 mL) vegetable stock
3	shallots, finely sliced

■ Preheat oven to 275 °F (130 °C).

■ In a bowl, combine yogurt, mustard, flour and sugar and set aside.

■ Place pork slices between 2 sheets of plastic wrap, pound meat to ¼ inch (0,5 cm) thickness, then season with salt and pepper.

■ In a skillet, melt butter. Cook pork over medium heat until lightly browned, place on serving dish, and keep warm.

■ Using the same skillet, add vegetable stock, and yogurt mixture and beat with a wire whisk until sauce thickens. Pour sauce over pork escalopes and garnish with finely sliced shallots.

* Illustrated recipe

Spicy Pork Escalopes

You'll find that pork blends well with the sweet flavor of fruit. When in season, why not decorate this dish with fresh raspberries.

4 servings

¹/₄ cup	(60 mL) flour
4	pork escalopes, ³/₈ inch (1 cm) thick each
2 tbsp	(30 mL) oil
	salt and pepper
³/₄ tsp	(3 mL) dry mustard
¹/₂ tsp	(2 mL) cloves
	pinch of allspice
¹/₂ tsp	(2 mL) cinnamon
¹/₄ cup	(60 mL) vinegar
3	large onions, cut into ¹/₂ inch (1,25 cm) thick pieces
1 tsp	(5 mL) cornstarch
1 cup	(250 mL) hot water
¹/₄ cup	(60 mL) raspberry jam

■ Preheat oven to 350 °F (175°C).

■ Dredge pork escalopes with flour. In a skillet, heat oil and sear escalopes on both sides, then place in an oven-proof dish.

■ In a bowl, combine salt, pepper, mustard, spices, and vinegar and pour over pork escalopes. Place onion slices over mixture, then bake for approximately 45 minutes.

■ Meanwhile, dissolve cornstarch in ¹/₂ cup (125 mL) hot water.

■ Place pork escalopes with onions in a serving dish. Skim cooking juice, add dissolved cornstarch, stir, then add raspberry jam as well as rest of hot water. Coat escalopes with sauce and serve.

Pork Escalopes with Prunes

Replace red currant jelly with apricot jelly.

4 servings

20	pitted prunes
¹/₂ cup	(125 mL) white wine
3 tbsp	(45 mL) flour
4	pork escalopes
1 tbsp	(15 mL) butter
	salt and pepper
1 tbsp	(15 mL) red currant jelly
1 cup	(250 mL) 15% cream

■ In a bowl, soak prunes in wine overnight.

■ Preheat oven to 275 °F (130 °C).

■ Dredge pork with flour.

■ In a skillet, melt butter, sear pork over high heat and season with salt and pepper, then cook for 5 to 6 minutes. Remove meat from skillet and keep warm.

■ In a saucepan, bring wine and prunes to a boil and simmer over low heat for approximately 30 minutes, then drain prunes and set aside.

■ Reduce liquid by half, add red currant jelly, lower the heat, then pour cream over mixture and cook over medium heat for 3 minutes, stirring without letting the sauce boil.

■ Pour sauce over pork. Garnish with prunes. Serve.

PORK NOISETTES

Pork Noisettes Waldorf

Waldorf salad, made with apple chunks and walnut halves, is the inspiration for this recipe. Bring a touch of Normandy cuisine to this pork dish with a two spoonfuls of Calvados blended into thick, fresh cream.

4 servings	
1 lb	(450 g) pork filet
1 tbsp	(15 mL) peanut oil
1 tbsp	(15 mL) butter
4	French (dry) shallots, finely sliced
1	apple, peeled and sliced
¼ cup	(60 mL) walnut halves
2 tbsp	(30 mL) Cognac or Calvados
	salt and pepper
⅓ cup	(80 mL) 35% cream

■ Preheat oven to 275 °F (130 °C).

■ Cut pork filet into ½ inch (1 cm) thick, oval slices (noisettes).

■ In a skillet, heat oil, melt butter and sauté pork noisettes, then place in a serving dish and keep warm.

■ Using the same skillet, sauté shallots, apple and walnut halves, deglaze with Cognac or Calvados, then season with salt and pepper. Add cream, cook over low heat and stir until mixture is smooth, without letting the sauce boil.

■ Pour sauce over pork noisettes and serve.

Replace apricots with small fresh peaches when they're in season. Peel and slice them in wedges.

4 servings	
1 ½ lb	(675 g) loin of pork
2	garlic cloves, finely sliced
	salt and pepper
3 tbsp	(45 mL) butter
1 tbsp	(15 mL) flour
½ cup	(125 mL) milk
⅓ cup	(80 mL) sour cream
2 tbsp	(30 mL) apricot jam
1 tbsp	(15 mL) Cognac (optional)
2	apricots, sliced

■ Slice the loin of pork into small noisettes, ½ inch (1 cm) thick.

■ In a bowl, combine garlic, salt and pepper and coat pork noisettes with mixture.

■ In a skillet, melt half the butter and sauté pork noisettes. Remove from heat and let stand.

■ Using the same skillet, melt rest of butter, add flour and mix well, then pour milk into mixture and cook slowly, stirring constantly until it thickens. Add pork noisettes, cover and simmer for 10 minutes.

■ Add sour cream, apricot jam, and Cognac, and heat until boiling. Remove immediately.

■ Place pork noisettes in serving dish, coat with sauce and garnish with apricot slices.

* Illustrated recipe

Pork Noisettes Mascarade

Remember that coated or breaded meat must always cook over low heat, otherwise the outer layer will cook too fast. If this happens, finish the cooking in the oven (or give the noisettes 2 minutes in the microwave).

4 servings

8	2 oz (30 g) pork noisettes
	breading or mascarade of your choice
1 tbsp	(15 mL) oil
1 tbsp	(15 mL) butter
	salt and pepper

■ Coat pork noisettes with the breading or "mascarade" of your choice and press firmly to make it adhere well to meat.

■ In a skillet, heat oil and melt butter. Cook noisettes over low heat, then season with salt and pepper.

VARIATIONS

Leaf Mascarade

• Blanch 4 large romaine, endive lettuce leaves or Chinese cabbage leaves for 2 to 3 minutes in boiling salted water, then drain and pat dry.

• In a skillet, heat oil, melt butter and sauté pork noisettes. Season with salt and pepper when ³/₄ done.

• Remove from skillet, wrap pork noisettes in lettuce or cabbage leaves and sauté on each side for 30 seconds.

• Baste with tomato sauce or ketchup. Add the herbs or spices of your choice before wrapping the noisettes in the leaves.

Sesame Seeds

• Crush 2 tbsp (30 mL) sesame seeds to powder, then add 2 tbsp (30 mL) whole sesame seeds.

• Replace sesame seeds with poppy seeds, celery seeds, fennel or dill seeds.

Flour and Paprika

• Mix 2 tbsp (30 mL) mild paprika with 2 tbsp (30 mL) flour.

• Dip pork noisettes in 1 beaten egg, then coat with paprika and flour mixture.

PORK TENDERLOINS

Pork Tenderloins with Vermouth

If you're counting calories, use plain yogurt instead of sour cream.

4 servings

4	small pork tenderloins
1 tbsp	(15 mL) oil
1 tbsp	(15 mL) butter
1	large, finely sliced garlic clove
	black pepper, coarsely chopped
1/4 cup	(60 mL) dry white vermouth
1/4 cup	(60 mL) chicken stock
2 tsp	(10 mL) cornstarch
1 tbsp	(15 mL) white vermouth
1/2 cup	(125 mL) sour cream

■ Preheat oven to 350 °F (175 °C).

■ In a skillet, heat oil, melt butter and sear pork tenderloins over high heat, then place in a casserole dish. Add garlic, pepper, 1/4 cup (60 mL) vermouth and chicken stock, cover and bake for 30 minutes. Remove pork tenderloins from casserole and keep warm.

■ In a bowl, dissolve cornstarch in 1 tbsp (15 mL) vermouth and set aside.

■ Pour cooking juice through sieve, skim off excess fat, then add dissolved cornstarch, stir and cook until smooth.

■ Continue to stir while adding sour cream. Heat through and serve with pork tenderloins.

Whenever you bring stuffed meat to the table, family and friends will think it's a special occasion. You won't actually spend more time than usual in the kitchen.

4 servings

2	pork tenderloins, 3/4 lb (350 g) each
1	lemon, halved
2 tbsp	(30 mL) butter
1	onion, finely chopped
1 cup	(250 mL) breadcrumbs, well packed
1 tsp	(5 mL) sage leaves, crumbled
1/2	lemon peel, grated
1/2 tsp	(2 mL) salt
1/4 tsp	(1 mL) pepper
	flour
1	egg
2	bacon slices, chopped
1 tbsp	(15 mL) kneaded butter (beurre manié)
1 1/2 cups	(375 mL) beef stock

■ Preheat oven to 350 °F (175 °C).

■ Split each tenderloin lengthwise, without separating completely, then spread open and rub lemon over meat. Set aside.

■ In a skillet, melt butter and sauté, but do not brown, onions over medium heat.

■ Remove from heat. Add breadcrumbs, sage, lemon peel, salt, and pepper. Stir, then add egg.

■ Spoon stuffing onto a pork tenderloin, cover with the other, tie with string and coat lightly with flour.

■ In a stove-top casserole, melt chopped bacon. Cook pork tenderloins on both sides until golden, cover, then bake for 40 minutes.

■ Remove tenderloins from casserole, place in a serving dish and keep warm.

■ Add 1 tbsp (15 mL) kneaded butter to cooking juice and stir, then pour beef stock over mixture and reduce liquid to half or until the sauce reaches desired smoothness. Pour sauce into a gravy boat and serve with stuffed pork tenderloins.

* Illustrated recipe

Pork Tenderloins with Raisins

Start soaking the raisins in the morning. You can drain them quickly when you're ready to begin cooking.

4 servings

½ cup	(125 mL) raisins
2 cups	(500 mL) hot water
3 tbsp	(45 mL) flour
1 lb	(450 g) pork tenderloins
2 tbsp	(30 mL) oil
	salt and pepper
1 tbsp	(15 mL) butter
3	French (dry) shallots, chopped
½ cup	(125 mL) red wine
1 cup	(250 mL) beef stock
¼ cup	(60 mL) 15% cream
1 tbsp	(15 mL) chopped parsley

■ Preheat oven to 350 °F (175 °C).

■ Let raisins plump up in hot water for 1 hour, then drain and set aside.

■ Dredge pork tenderloins with flour.

■ In a skillet, heat oil and sear flour-coated pork tenderloins over high heat, season with salt and pepper, remove from heat and cook in the oven for 10 minutes.

■ In a separate skillet, melt butter, then sauté shallots and drained raisins. Deglaze with red wine and reduce liquid by half.

■ Pour beef stock into skillet, bring to a boil, then add pork tenderloins and let mixture simmer for 4 minutes.

■ Add cream, reduce heat to low and sprinkle with chopped parsley.

■ Remove pork tenderloins from skillet, slice and serve on a platter in its sauce. Garnish with raisins and serve.

Pork Tenderloins with Leeks

Make sure to wash leeks thoroughly.

4 servings

6 tbsp	(90 mL) butter
2	leek whites, finely sliced
½ cup	(125 mL) onions, finely sliced
3 tbsp	(45 mL) celery, finely sliced
1 ½ cups	(375 mL) breadcrumbs
½ tsp	(2 mL) fresh savory
¼ tsp	(1 mL) salt
¼ tsp	(1 mL) pepper
1 ½ lbs	(675 g) pork tenderloins
2	garlic cloves, finely sliced
¼ cup	(60 mL) Cognac
2 cups	(500 mL) beef stock
	salt and pepper
2 tbsp	(30 mL) flour
1 cup	(250 mL) mushrooms, sliced

■ Preheat oven to 350 °F (175 °C).

■ In an oven-proof skillet, melt 2 tbsp (30 mL) butter, sauté but do not brown the leeks, half the onions and celery, then remove from heat, add breadcrumbs and seasoning, and let stand to cool.

■ Slice pork tenderloins lengthwise without separating, pound delicately with meat mallet to flatten.

■ Spoon cooled stuffing onto the pork tenderloins, fold and secure with skewer or toothpick.

■ Using the same skillet, melt 2 tbsp (30 mL) butter and sauté rest of onions with garlic and pork tenderloins. Pour Cognac and beef stock over mixture, then season with salt and pepper.

■ Cook, uncovered, in oven, for 30 to 40 minutes and baste often with sauce while cooking.

■ Slice the meat and serve in its sauce on a platter.

PORK ROASTS

Boning a loin of pork

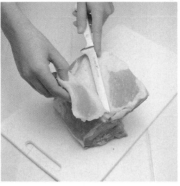

- *Slice away excess fat on tip of bones.*

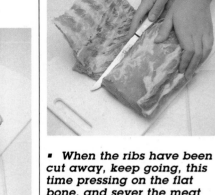

- *Slide the knife between the meat and the bones, pressing the blade against the bone.*

- *When the ribs have been cut away, keep going, this time pressing on the flat bone, and sever the meat completely.*

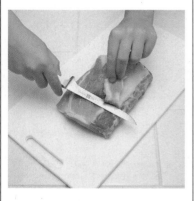

- *Remove fat and ligaments to give the roast an attractive look.*

- *The roast is ready for cooking.*

Stuffing and rolling a pork roast

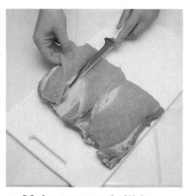

- *Slit the meat along its length without cutting completely through.*

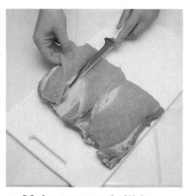

- *Make a second slit to "unfold" the roast completely, somewhat like a wallet.*

- *Spread meat open and spoon on the stuffing.*

- *Roll, tie with string or secure with a skewer.*

Easy Pork Roast

About 20 minutes before the meat is cooked, put vegetables (such as partially boiled whole potatoes and carrots, with frozen green peas) in the casserole.

4 to 6 servings

2 tbsp	(30 mL) vegetable oil
3 lb	(1,4 kg) pork roast
	salt and pepper
2 cups	(500 mL) commercial barbecue sauce
1 cup	(250 mL) water
¼ cup	(60 mL) red wine
1 tbsp	(15 mL) Dijon mustard
	pinch of rosemary
	pinch of thyme
	pinch of nutmeg
1 tbsp	(15 mL) chopped parsley
1	bay leaf

■ In a skillet, heat oil and sear pork roast on all sides, then season with salt and pepper.

■ Place roast in a medium-size cast iron casserole and set aside.

■ In a bowl, combine all other ingredients, pour over roast pork and bring to a boil. Reduce heat and let mixture simmer, partially covered, for approximately 1 hour and 15 minutes.

■ Remove roast pork from casserole, let stand for 10 minutes, then carve.

Roast Pork with Pineapple

Pork with a Hawaiian touch!

4 to 6 servings

3 tbsp	(45 mL) peanut oil
3 lb	(1,4 kg) pork roast
8 oz	(227 mL) pineapple chunks
1 ¼ cups	(300 mL) water
2 tbsp	(30 mL) molasses
1 tsp	(5 mL) dry mustard
	salt and pepper
2 tbsp	(30 mL) cornstarch
1 cup	(250 mL) chicken stock
1 tbsp	(15 mL) wine vinegar

■ Preheat oven to 425 °F (220 °C).

■ In an oven-proof skillet, heat oil and sear pork roast on all sides then place in oven-proof serving dish.

■ Drain pineapple and reserve juice.

■ In a bowl, mix pineapple juice with water, add molasses, mustard, salt and pepper, then pour liquid over pork. Cover and bake for approximately 1 hour, basting every 15 minutes. Remove cover during last 15 minutes of cooking.

■ Place roast pork in a serving dish and keep warm.

■ In a bowl, dissolve cornstarch in chicken stock and set aside. Skim excess fat off cooking juice, add vinegar and dissolved cornstarch and bring to a boil, stirring constantly, then add pineapple chunks. Adjust seasoning and pour sauce over pork slices.

* Illustrated recipe

Pork blends well with numerous aromatic herbs. Basil, mint, sage—these and other herbs give a distinctive taste to slowly-cooked meat.

Stuffed Roast Pork

You can create a minor sensation when introducing your family to a variety of stuffings for roast pork. Follow a few simple variations we've suggested, use your imagination and try to create your own delectable stuffed pork dishes.

4 to 6 servings

3 lb	(1,4 kg) pork roast, boned and rolled
	salt and pepper
2 tbsp	(30 mL) peanut oil

■ Preheat oven to 400 °F (205 °C).

■ Spread open the pork roast and pound lightly to flatten. Season with salt and pepper and coat with stuffing of your choice then roll and tie, making sure to close off the ends.

■ In an oven-proof skillet, heat oil and sear stuffed pork roast on all sides over high heat. Season with salt and pepper and bake, approximately 20 minutes per pound (per 450 kg).

■ Remove from oven and let stand for 10 minutes, then slice.

Four Surprise Stuffings

Pine Nuts, Garlic, and Basil

- In a skillet, melt 1 tbsp (15 mL) butter, sauté 1 cup (250 mL) pine nuts, add 1 tbsp (15 mL) finely sliced garlic and 2 tbsp (30 mL) puréed basil or 1 tbsp (15 mL) fresh chopped basil, season with salt and pepper and refrigerate before stuffing.

Raspberry and Mint

- In a skillet, melt 1 tbsp (15 mL) butter, sauté but do not brown 1 tbsp (15 mL) chopped onion, 1 tsp (5 mL) finely sliced garlic and 2 tbsp (30 mL) finely sliced leeks or celery.

- Deglaze skillet with ¼ cup (60 mL) raspberry or wine vinegar, reduce liquid by half.

- Add 1 cup (250 mL) fresh or frozen unsweetened raspberries, stir well, season with salt and pepper.

- When raspberries begin to break apart, remove from heat, add 2 tsp (10 mL) chopped mint leaves and cool before stuffing.

Chick Peas, Wild Garlic, and Parsley

- Drain 14 oz (398 mL) can of chick peas. In a skillet, melt 1 tbsp (15 mL) butter, sauté chick peas, add 2 tsp (10 mL) finely sliced wild garlic and 2 tbsp (30 mL) chopped parsley, season with salt and pepper and cool before stuffing.

Artichoke Hearts and Pâté de Foie

- Drain 14 oz (398 mL) can of artichoke hearts, blanch for 3 minutes in boiling salted water, cool in cold water, drain and chop.

- In a bowl, using a fork, soften ¼ cup (125 mL) pâté de foie and spread it inside the roast and cover with artichoke hearts. Roll and tie the meat, and cook according to basic recipe.

HAM

In Roman times ham was considered a delicacy fit for emperors. In the days before refrigeration, it was an ideal meat for preserving by smoking and salting methods, and it is no surprise to find it a traditional favorite in many countries.

Strictly speaking, true ham comes from the shank half. However, a smoked shoulder can be made into similar smaller cuts and used in any ham recipe.

Different varieties of ham

Beer-flavored Ham

Using the tip of a knife, trace a diamond pattern on the ham and stud it with whole cloves to give it a festive look.

10 to 12 servings

5 lb	(2,3 kg) shoulder of ham
20	whole cloves
1 cup	(250 mL) molasses
2 tsp	(10 mL) dry mustard
1 tsp	(5 mL) pepper
1 cup	(250 mL) beer
1	large onion, cut into wedges

■ Preheat oven to 450 °F (230 °C).

■ Remove ham rind and stud ham surface with cloves. Line the bottom of a large roasting pan with aluminum foil and place ham in middle.

■ In a bowl, combine molasses, mustard, pepper and beer and pour over ham, then add onion pieces.

■ Wrap ham in aluminum foil, seal and bake in oven for 15 minutes per pound (450 g). Serve hot or cold.

Pressure-cooked Ham

This is the time to use up those celery leaves that have been sitting in the fridge. Put them in the pressure cooker with the other ingredients to add to the flavor of the meat.

4 to 6 servings

3 lb	(1,4 kg) boneless ham
2 cups	(500 mL) fresh milk
¼ cup	(60 mL) molasses or brown sugar
1 tsp	(5 mL) dry mustard
3	whole cloves
1	large onion, cut into wedges

■ Place all ingredients in pressure cooker, seal cover and cook for 30 minutes.

■ Remove ham when pressure cooker is cooled. Let ham cool completely before serving.

VARIATION

Braised Ham

• **Place all ingredients in a cast iron casserole, cover and let meat simmer slowly for 1 ½ hours. Let ham cool in its cooking juices.**

Ham Cubes in Sweet and Sour Sauce

A delicately sweetened sauce that allows the fragrant aromas of rosemary and coriander to mingle.

10 to 12 servings

3 tbsp	(45 mL) butter
3 cups	(750 mL) ham, diced
1	chopped onion
2	garlic cloves, chopped
10 oz	(284 mL) canned apricots
¼ cup	(60 mL) wine vinegar
¾ cup	(180 mL) beef stock
¾ cup	(180 mL) chicken stock
	salt and pepper
¼ tsp	(1 mL) rosemary
½ tsp	(2 mL) coriander
1 tsp	(5 mL) honey

■ In a skillet, melt butter and sauté ham, onion and garlic.

■ Add apricot syrup and wine vinegar and let liquid reduce by two-thirds.

■ Pour beef and chicken stocks into liquid, season with salt, pepper, rosemary and coriander, then add honey and halved apricots.

■ Let mixture simmer for 20 minutes and serve.

Oven-baked Ham Slices

For this recipe, use canned sliced pineapples in their juice. If you run out of pineapple juice, add some orange juice.

4 servings

4	large ham slices, 1 inch (2,5 cm) thick each
1 tbsp	(15 mL) prepared mustard
8	pineapple slices
1 cup	(250 mL) pineapple juice
	salt and pepper

■ Preheat oven to 400 °F (205 °C).

■ Baste ham slices with prepared mustard then place them in oven-proof dish. Arrange pineapple slices over ham, coat with juice, season with salt and pepper, cover, and bake in oven for 1 hour.

■ Remove cover 20 minutes before the meat is done.

Ham and Pork Meatballs

For that special occasion, replace the brown sugar and dry mustard with liquid honey and old-fashioned prepared mustard.

4 to 6 servings

Meatballs

³/₄ lb	(340 g) ground ham
³/₄ lb	(340 g) medium-lean ground pork
1 ¹/₂ cups	(375 mL) breadcrumbs
³/₄ cup	(180 mL) milk
2	eggs, beaten
	pinch of salt

Sauce

1 ¹/₂ cups	(375 mL) brown sugar
³/₄ cup	(180 mL) water
¹/₂ cup	(125 mL) vinegar
1 tbsp	(15 mL) dry mustard

■ Preheat oven to 325 °F (160 °C).

■ In a bowl, combine all meatball ingredients, shape into small meatballs, place in a shallow oven-proof dish and set aside.

■ In a bowl, combine all ingredients for sauce, pour over meatballs and bake for 40 minutes. Baste often during cooking process.

■ If you wish, garnish the meatballs with olives, secured with toothpicks.

Ham Turnover

For a lovely golden crust, baste the pastry top with a beaten egg.

4 servings

10 oz	(284 mL) canned cream of mushroom soup
¹/₂ cup	(125 mL) milk
1 tbsp	(15 mL) butter
1	chopped onion
¹/₄ cup	(60 mL) green bell pepper, slivered
3 cups	(750 mL) ground ham
	salt and pepper
	short pastry or puff pastry

■ Preheat oven to 400 °F (205 °C).

■ In a bowl, dilute cream of mushroom soup in milk and set aside.

■ In a skillet, melt butter, then sauté onion and green bell pepper slivers, add diluted cream of mushroom soup and ham, stir, season with salt and pepper, then set aside.

■ Roll out pastry dough into an 8 in x 12 in (20 cm x 32 cm) oval.

■ Spoon ham mixture onto pastry shell, fold into half-moon shape, pinch edges to seal and bake in oven 35 to 40 minutes.

191

Diet Pork Kebabs

Mushrooms won't split when you skewer them if you soak them in cold water for an hour.

4 servings

1 cup	(250 mL) white wine
½ cup	(125 mL) chicken stock
1 lb	(450 g) pork, cubed
16	mushrooms
16	green bell pepper wedges
1	pineapple, cut into chunks
16	onion wedges

■ Preheat oven to broil.

■ In a bowl, combine white wine and chicken stock, add pork cubes and marinate for 3 hours. Drain and pat the meat dry.

■ Prepare skewers, alternating pork with mushrooms, peppers, pineapple chunks and onion pieces.

■ Broil for 20 minutes. Baste with marinade sauce after 10 minutes of broiling.

Old-fashioned Stew

The perfect meal to serve on chilly days.

4 servings

4 cups	(1 L) chicken stock
2 cups	(500 mL) pork, cooked and cubed
1 cup	(250 mL) dark chicken meat
	pinch of mixed spices (rosemary, nutmeg, cinnamon, savory, thyme, parsley)
2 tbsp	(30 mL) grilled flour

■ In a stove-top casserole, pour chicken stock, add cubed pork and chicken pieces and simmer for 30 minutes, then flavor with spices.

■ Add a small amount of oven-browned (or commercial browned) flour to thicken sauce.

Cubed Pork in Cream Sauce

Serve this dish on a bed of egg noodles. By replacing ¹/₂ cup (125 mL) cream with an equal amount of plain yogurt, you'll be creating a whole new recipe.

4 to 6 servings

1 tbsp	(15 mL) oil
1 tbsp	(15 mL) butter
1 ¹/₂ lbs	(675 g) pork, cubed
¹/₂ cup	(125 mL) white wine
1 cup	(250 mL) 15% cream
¹/₂	red onion, cut into 3 pieces
	salt and pepper
¹/₄ tsp	(1 mL) nutmeg
2 tbsp	fine breadcrumbs
	chopped parsley

■ In a skillet, heat oil, melt butter and sauté pork. Remove meat from skillet and keep warm.

■ Deglaze skillet with white wine and reduce liquid by half. Add cream and red onion pieces, season with salt, pepper, and nutmeg and simmer over low heat, stirring constantly.

■ Place pork in a serving dish; pour the cream sauce over it and sprinkle with parsley.

* Illustrated recipe

VARIATION

• **Preheat oven to 350 °F (175 °C). Spread a layer of endive leaves in the bottom of an oven-proof dish. Place pork cubes on top, pour the cream sauce over meat and sprinkle with breadcrumbs. Cover with aluminum foil and bake in oven 20 to 25 minutes.**

Oven-baked Cubed Pork

If you'd like to teach your child the joy of cooking, why not start with this delicious and easy dish?

4 servings

Seasoned Flour

¹/₄ cup	(60 mL) flour
	pinch of thyme
	pinch of dry mustard
	pinch of onion salt
	pinch of garlic salt
	ground pepper
1 lb	(450 g) pork, cut into ¹/₂ inch (1,25 cm) cubes

Sauce

1 cup	(250 mL) ketchup
1 ¹/₂ cups	(375 mL) water
3 tbsp	(45 mL) brown sugar

■ In a bowl, combine all seasoned flour ingredients.

■ Preheat oven to 350 °F (175 °C).

■ Dredge pork cubes with seasoned flour, place in oven-proof dish and set aside.

■ In a bowl, combine the sauce ingredients. Pour the sauce over the meat and bake for 45 minutes.

193

PORK STRIPS

Pork Strips in Sweet and Sour Sauce

Spruce up this dish with a can of miniature corn cobs, stirred in with the meat 20 minutes before it's done.

8 servings

2 tbsp	(30 mL) oil
2 lbs	(900 g) pork, cut into strips
1	finely sliced garlic clove
1	chopped onion
1	zucchini, finely sliced
1	diced green bell pepper
1	diced sweet red pepper
12 oz	(341 mL) commercial sweet and sour sauce

■ Preheat oven to 350 °F (175 °C).

■ In a skillet, heat oil and sauté pork strips and garlic for 5 minutes.

■ Add onion, zucchini, green bell pepper, and sweet red pepper. Sauté mixture for 2 minutes, then pour mixture into an oven-proof dish and stir in the sweet and sour sauce.

■ Bake for 30 minutes or until meat is tender.

Serve this one-casserole meal with rice or pasta. If you have no sherry on hand, port is a good substitute.

6 servings

1 ½ lbs	(675 g) pork, cut into fine strips
1 tsp	(5 mL) sugar
1 tbsp	(15 mL) cornstarch
2 tbsp	(30 mL) sherry
3 tbsp	(45 mL) soy sauce
3 tbsp	(45 mL) oil
14 oz	(398 mL) canned green string beans
1	medium onion, finely sliced
14 oz	(398 mL) canned miniature corn cobs
½ tsp	(2 mL) salt

■ In a dish, spread pork strips, add sugar, cornstarch, sherry and soy sauce and stir.

■ In a cast iron skillet, heat oil and cook green string beans and onion for 1 minute. Add miniature corn cobs and half their juice, cover and cook for 1 minute. Drain vegetables and place in a serving dish.

■ Drain pork strips; reserve the marinade.

■ Reheat skillet, then add oil and brown half the pork strips. Take them out and add them to the vegetable mixture.

■ Brown the rest of the meat, combine it with all the cooked ingredients, add marinade, season with salt, heat and stir to mix well.

* Illustrated recipe

Pork Chop Suey

If possible, use fresh bean sprouts, rather than the canned variety.

4 servings

1 tsp	(5 mL) cornstarch
¼ cup	(60 mL) water
3 tbsp	(45 mL) vegetable oil
1 lb	(450 g) pork, cut into strips
½ cup	(125 mL) diced celery
2	medium onions, sliced
14 oz	(398 mL) canned or fresh bean sprouts, rinsed in cold water and drained
	salt and pepper
½ cup	(125 mL) water
3 tbsp	(45 mL) soy sauce

■ In a bowl, dissolve cornstarch in ¼ cup (60 mL) water and set aside.

■ In a skillet, heat oil and sauté pork strips, celery, and onions. Add bean sprouts and season with salt and pepper, then stir.

■ Add ½ cup (125 mL) water and soy sauce, cover and cook for 5 minutes.

■ Add dissolved cornstarch, cover and cook 1 minute longer.

Chinese Pork Strips

If you have to stretch the recipe to accommodate an unexpected guest, add a can of small shrimp.

4 servings

1 tbsp	(15 mL) butter
1	egg, beaten
1 tbsp	(15 mL) oil
1 lb	(450 g) pork, cut into strips
2 tbsp	(30 mL) green bell peppers, cut into strips
½	sweet red pepper, cut into strips
4	green onions, finely sliced
½ tsp	(2 mL) grated ginger
1	package Chinese fried rice
1 cup	(250 mL) bean sprouts, drained
1 tbsp	(15 mL) soy sauce
¼ cup	(60 mL) mushrooms, sliced
½ tsp	(2 mL) garlic powder

■ In a skillet, melt butter and cook beaten egg, then let stand to cool, crumble and set aside.

■ In a separate skillet, heat oil and sauté pork strips. Add green and red peppers, green onions and ginger, reduce heat and cook for 5 minutes.

■ Meanwhile, prepare Chinese fried rice according to package directions. Add bean sprouts, soy sauce, mushrooms and garlic powder, stir, then add crumbled egg.

■ Pour mixture into a serving dish and spoon pork and vegetables over it.

195

GROUND PORK

Ground Pork Parmentier

"Parmentier" means "with potatoes"—a reminder that Parmentier popularized the potato in France.

4 servings

2 tbsp	(30 mL) oil
1 lb	(450 g) ground pork
¾ cup	(180 mL) chopped onions
1 cup	(250 mL) carrots, diced
½ cup	(125 mL) celery, diced
½ tsp	(2 mL) thyme
3 cups	(750 mL) water
	salt and pepper
6	large potatoes, finely sliced
¼ cup	(60 mL) beef stock

■ In a skillet, heat oil and sauté pork and onions. Put them in a stove-top casserole, add carrots, celery, thyme, and water and let mixture simmer for 10 minutes over medium heat, then season with salt and pepper.

■ Add potatoes and beef stock, and cook for 15 minutes or until potatoes are done.

Bavarian Porkballs

Wash this hearty dish down with a foaming stein of Bavarian beer.

4 servings

1 lb	(450 g) ground pork
¼ cup	(60 mL) breadcrumbs
1	egg, lightly beaten
¼ cup	(60 mL) water
½ cup	(125 mL) chopped onion
2 tsp	(10 mL) horseradish
1 tsp	(5 mL) salt
1 tbsp	(15 mL) ketchup
¼ tsp	(1 mL) pepper
5	bacon slices

■ In a bowl, combine all the ingredients except the bacon, and shape into small meatballs measuring 1 ¼ inches (3 cm) in diameter.

■ In a skillet, cook bacon, crumble, and set aside.

■ Using the same skillet, cook pork meatballs in the bacon fat, drain, sprinkle with crumbled bacon and serve.

Porkballs in Tomato Sauce

If you're expecting guests, make tiny porkballs as appetizers.

4 servings		
1 lb	(450 g)	ground pork
½ lb	(225 g)	ground beef
½ cup	(125 mL)	chopped onion
½ tsp	(2 mL)	celery seeds
1 tsp	(5 mL)	flour
1		egg, beaten
1 tsp	(5 mL)	salt
2 tbsp	(30 mL)	oil

Sauce

28 oz	(796 mL)	canned ground tomatoes
5 oz	(142 mL)	tomato paste
½ cup	(125 mL)	chopped onion
½ tsp	(2 mL)	garlic salt or finely sliced garlic
1 tsp	(5 mL)	sugar
1 cup	(250 mL)	water
		salt and pepper

■ Preheat oven to 350 °F (175 °C).

■ Combine first 7 ingredients, shape into small meatballs 1 ½ inches (3,25 cm) in diameter.

■ In a skillet, heat oil and cook meatballs 8 to 10 minutes, then place in a baking dish and set aside.

■ In a bowl, combine all sauce ingredients, pour over meatballs, cover and bake for 1 hour.

Shepherd's Pork Pie

This is the traditional French-Canadian version of the familiar shepherd's pie, a nourishing one-dish meal.

4 servings		
4 cups	(1 L)	mashed potatoes
19 oz	(540 mL)	canned creamed corn
1 lb	(450 g)	leftover cooked ground pork
3 to 4		knobs of butter

■ Preheat oven to 350 °F (175 °C).

■ In a saucepan, cook potatoes and mash them.

■ In a small saucepan, heat creamed corn.

■ In an oven-proof dish, alternate layers of mashed potatoes, creamed corn, and ground pork, finishing with a layer of mashed potatoes.

■ Dot with knobs of butter and bake in oven for 15 minutes.

* Illustrated recipe

VARIATIONS

• **Replace creamed corn with 2 cups (500 mL) applesauce. Garnish with thin slices of apple sautéed in butter.**

• **Replace creamed corn with 19 oz (540 mL) canned asparagus coarsely chopped.**

Pork Rolls in Spinach Sauce

These pork rolls can also be served with a dash of ketchup or a tangy tomato sauce.

4 servings

2	bacon slices
1 ½ lbs	(675 g) lean ground pork
8	crumbled soda biscuits
	salt and pepper
1	beaten egg
½ cup	(125 mL) milk
	flour

Spinach Sauce

½ cup	(125 mL) cream
¼ cup	(60 mL) spinach, stemmed and blanched
½	chopped garlic clove
	salt and pepper

■ Preheat oven to 350 °F (175 °C).

■ Chop bacon in food processor, add ground pork and soda biscuits, and season with salt and pepper.

■ Stir in the egg and milk. Roll mixture in flour and shape into rolls.

■ Place rolls in a baking dish and bake for 15 minutes; cover with greased paper and cook 30 minutes longer.

■ Meanwhile, in a saucepan, mix together all sauce ingredients, bring to a boil and let mixture reduce one-third. Run sauce through a blender and serve with pork rolls.

Old-fashioned Pork and Cabbage Bake

Served with steamed potatoes, this traditional dish will bring back memories of "down home" cooking.

4 servings

2 tbsp	(30 mL) oil
1 ½ lbs	(675 g) ground pork
1	onion, finely chopped
10 oz	(284 mL) canned cream of tomato soup
1	cabbage cut into strips
10 oz	(284 mL) water
	salt and pepper

■ Preheat oven to 350 °F (175 °C).

■ In a skillet, heat oil and sauté ground pork and onions.

■ In a bowl, dilute cream of tomato soup in water.

■ In an oven-proof dish, place alternate layers of ground pork and cabbage strips, pour diluted cream of tomato soup over mixture and cook 45 to 60 minutes.

Pork Loaf with Pine Nuts

If you've run out of soda biscuits, use breadcrumbs instead.

8 servings

2 lbs	(900 g) ground pork
½ cup	(125 mL) chopped pine nuts
½ cup	(125 mL) finely sliced celery
½ cup	(125 mL) grated carrots
½ cup	(125 mL) sliced mushrooms
1 cup	(250 mL) tomato soup concentrate
1 ½ cups	(375 mL) soda biscuits, crumbled
2 tsp	(10 mL) parsley
½ cup	(125 mL) grated Parmesan cheese
¼ tsp	(1 mL) thyme
3 tbsp	(45 mL) tomato paste
	salt and pepper

■ Preheat oven to 350 °F (175 °C).

■ In a bowl, combine all ingredients and shape into loaf.

■ Place in a loaf pan and bake for 50 minutes.

Pork Liver

Make sure you pat liver slices dry before dredging them with flour.

4 servings

1 lb	(450 g) pork liver, cut into small strips
¼ cup	(60 mL) milk
5 tbsp	(75 mL) flour
8	bacon slices, cut into 1-inch (2,5-cm) pieces
1	large onion, coarsely chopped
5 ½ oz	(156 mL) tomato paste
¼ cup	(60 mL) cold water
½ tsp	(2 mL) barbecue steak spices
½ tsp	(2 mL) pepper

■ In a deep bowl, spread pork liver strips and coat with milk, refrigerate and let soak from 2 to 4 hours. Remove liver strips from milk, pat dry, then dredge with flour.

■ In a skillet, cook bacon, drain, and pat dry with paper towel and set aside.

■ Using the same skillet, sauté pork liver strips and onion over medium heat, stirring with a wooden spoon. Add tomato paste and water, stir, season with barbecue steak spices and pepper, then sprinkle with bacon and serve.

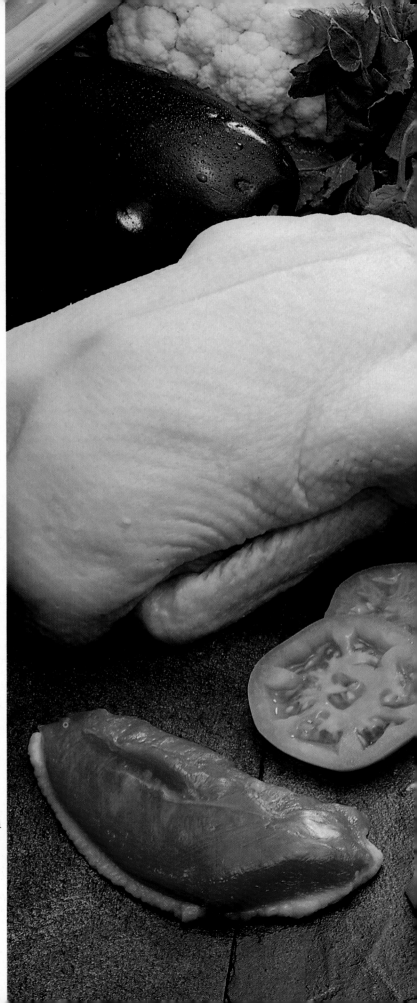

Game has traditionally been valued for its distinctive flavor. To palates conditioned to our modern, scientifically bred and raised meat, the taste of game is a discovery in itself.

Desirable game is available in many areas of North America, and antlered animals such as deer, elk and caribou are often important food sources for people living in wilderness areas. Small game offers a wide range of meats that include small animals and birds, many of which are considered delicacies.

Meat markets have a variety of small game and venison available in season or frozen. Some forms of game are now being raised commercially. Choose a reliable supplier, as the skinning, cleaning, hanging and general handling of game have a direct effect on the quality of the meat, from both the culinary and health point of view.

Try out the various recipes in this section as the occasion offers. They have been developed with game specially in mind, but many of them can be used with other, similar meat.

GAME

Duck Glazed with Apricots

Save the duck fat for future basting of drier meats.

4 servings

4 lb	(1,8 kg) duck
1 tbsp	(15 mL) butter
	salt and pepper
	pinch of chervil
10 oz	(280 mL) canned apricots
¼ cup	(60 mL) apricot jam
½ cup	(125 mL) orange juice
2	onions, halved and sliced

■ Preheat the oven to 350 °F (175 °C).

■ Truss the duck, smear it with butter, and season with salt, pepper and chervil.

■ Bake for about 90 minutes, basting with cooking juices every 20 minutes.

■ Drain the apricots and reserve the juice.

■ In a bowl, thoroughly blend the apricot juice, orange juice and apricot jam. After 20 minutes of cooking, baste the duck with 2 tbsp (30 mL) of this mixture.

■ After 60 minutes of cooking, take the duck out of the oven and pour off all the fat. Baste the duck with the remaining juice mixture and put it back in the oven.

■ Add onion and apricots after 15 minutes, and continue cooking for another 15 minutes. Take the roast out of the oven, sprinkle it with chervil and cover it with aluminum foil. Let it stand for 10 minutes before serving.

Stuffed Duck Breasts

This light rice and watercress stuffing absorbs the juices and helps keep the white meat moist.

4 servings

4	duck breasts
1 tbsp	(15 mL) oil
½ cup	(125 mL) rice, cooked
¼ cup	(60 mL) watercress, stemmed
1	egg
	salt and pepper

■ Preheat the oven to 400 °F (205 °C).

■ Nick the breast skin slightly to prevent it shrinking during cooking.

■ Blend the egg, rice and watercress in the food processor. Season with salt and pepper and set aside.

■ Slit the breasts in the tube-style method (p. 48), and stuff them.

■ In a skillet, heat the oil and brown the breasts on the skinless side. Season with salt and pepper and transfer directly to the oven. Cook for about 12 minutes.

■ Take them out of the oven and let them stand for 5 minutes. Slice them in thin strips and serve with a tomato coulis (p. 454).

QUAIL AND GUINEA FOWL

Quail and fowl have been considered delicacies throughout history. Our medieval ancestors ate them with their fingers, forks being a relatively recent addition to our domestic eating habits.

Quails are sometimes called partridge in the Deep South, although partridge is a name more commonly given, in the North, to ruffed grouse, another much valued small game bird. Remember that these birds tend to be dry. They are better cooked in a way that preserves moisture, and for this reason, stocks, wine, and liqueurs often figure in their recipes.

This recipe provides a Provençale touch.

4 servings

4 ½ lb	(2 kg) guinea fowl
1 tbsp	(15 mL) olive oil
1 tbsp	(15 mL) butter
3	onions, quartered
1 cup	(250 mL) mushrooms, finely sliced
¼ cup	(60 mL) black olives, pitted and quartered
2 tbsp	(30 mL) tomato paste
3 cups	(750 mL) chicken stock
1 tbsp	(15 mL) chopped parsley
	salt and pepper
2	tomatoes, seeded and julienned

■ Bone the guinea fowl, cutting each of the legs and breasts into two pieces.

■ In a stove-top casserole or heavy saucepan, heat the oil, melt the butter, and brown the pieces of guinea fowl on all sides.

■ Add onions, mushrooms, and olives. Sauté and stir well for about 4 minutes.

■ Add tomato paste and stir well. Add the chicken stock and parsley, and season with salt and pepper.

■ Bring to a boil, half cover, lower the heat, and simmer for about 1 hour.

■ When done, the flesh will come away easily from the bone. Correct the seasoning and serve, garnished with the julienned tomatoes.

Quail on a Rice Ring

A colorful, fragrant rice ring makes an attractive bed for the quails.

4 servings

Stuffing

2 cups	(500 mL) mushrooms, quartered
1 tbsp	(15 mL) melted butter
	a few pinches of thyme
8	quails
1 tbsp	(15 mL) oil
	salt and pepper

Rice

1 ½ cups	(375 mL) chicken stock
1 ½ cups	(375 mL) fast-cooking rice
¼ cup	(60 mL) red and green sweet peppers, finely diced
¼ cup	(60 mL) tomato juice
	salt and pepper

■ Preheat oven to 375 °F (190 °C)

■ Mix the stuffing ingredients. Divide it into eight, and stuff the quails.

■ In a skillet, heat the oil and sear the quails on all sides, season with salt and pepper, and put in the oven for about 15 minutes.

■ In the meantime, bring the chicken stock to a boil, add the rice, sweet peppers and tomato juice, and season with salt and pepper. Remove from heat, cover, and let stand for 10 minutes.

■ When the quails are done, serve them on a rice ring.

Quail Fricassee with Grapes and Almonds

The sweet tang of Amaretto, green grapes, almonds, and pink peppercorns makes this a festive dish.

4 servings

1 tbsp	(15 mL) oil
6	quails, boned
2 tbsp	(30 mL) almonds, slivered
¼ cup	(60 mL) green grapes
	salt and pepper
1 tsp	(5 mL) pink peppercorns
1 cup	(250 mL) chicken stock
2 tbsp	(30 mL) Amaretto (almond liqueur)

■ In a skillet, heat oil and sear the pieces of quail well on all sides. Add the almonds and grapes, and stir well. Add the Amaretto and stir well again.

■ Add salt and pepper, and the pink peppercorns, and pour in the chicken stock. Bring to a boil, then reduce heat and simmer, half-covered, for about 10 minutes.

■ When done, adjust the seasoning and serve with baby carrots.

DEER AND BUFFALO

Early settlers in North America from England and France must have been amazed at the abundance of venison. In their native lands, deer were the preserve of royalty and the aristocracy, and a man could be hanged for poaching.

The Virginia white-tailed deer is the species most commonly available in eastern North America, while the mule deer is widespread in the western half of the continent. Individual hunting quotas are severely restricted in most localities, although deer populations can become fairly high in favorable years.

Aspiring venison cooks needn't worry about endangering wild species. Deer and buffalo (as well as "beefalo") are now being raised commercially, and you should have no trouble finding a selection at a market in your area.

Witloof is the Flemish word for endive. The Belgians traditionally braise this vegetable.

4 servings		
3 tbsp	(45 mL)	peanut oil
2 tbsp	(30 mL)	butter
3 lb	(1,4 kg)	roast of deer
		salt and pepper
2 cups	(500 mL)	beef stock
½ tsp	(2 mL)	nutmeg
1		garlic clove, finely sliced
2 tsp	(10 mL)	chopped parsley
6		endives, halved

■ Preheat oven to 400 °F (205 °C).

■ In a stove-top casserole, heat oil and melt butter. Sear roast on all sides, season with salt and pepper, then cook in oven 15 minutes per pound (per 450 g) for rare meat.

■ Fifteen minutes into cooking process, add beef stock, nutmeg, garlic, and parsley and continue cooking.

■ Twenty-five minutes into cooking process, add endives to braise in the cooking juices.

■ When cooked, let roast stand for 10 minutes, then carve. Serve with braised endives, and baste with cooking juices before serving.

Buffalo Roast with Bourguignon or Madeira Sauce

Prepare the sauce using the cooking juices. For this recipe, you can also use beefalo meat, a cross between beef and buffalo.

8 servings

3 tbsp	(45 mL) black pepper, crushed
3 lb	(1,4 kg) buffalo roast
3 tbsp	(45 mL) peanut oil
1 cup	(250 mL) beef stock

Bourguignon Sauce

1 tbsp	(15 mL) butter
1	large red onion, finely sliced
1 cup	(250 mL) mushrooms, finely sliced
1 tbsp	(15 mL) flour
½ cup	(125 mL) meat juices
½ cup	(125 mL) red wine
	salt and pepper
	bouquet garni

■ Preheat oven to 400 °F (205 °C).

■ Sprinkle pepper over roast and baste with oil.

■ In a stove-top casserole, sear roast on all sides in hot oil, then bake 15 minutes per pound (per 450 g) for rare meat.

■ Fifteen minutes into cooking process, pour beef stock over meat and sprinkle with salt. Baste frequently.

Bourguignon Sauce

■ In a skillet, melt butter, add onion, mushrooms, and flour and stir. Pour meat juices and red wine over mixture, cook to desired thickness, and season with salt and pepper. Add bouquet garni and let mixture simmer for 10 minutes.

MADEIRA SAUCE

• In a skillet, melt 2 tbsp (30 mL) butter. Cook 1 large finely sliced onion (or several green onions) along with 3 oz (85 g) lardons, then add 4 tsp (20 mL) flour and stir.

• Pour ¾ cup (150 mL) meat juice or meat stock and ¾ cup (150 mL) dry white wine over mixture, and cook to desired thickness.

• Season with salt and pepper. Add bouquet garni and let mixture simmer over low heat for 10 minutes.

• Add ½ cup (125 mL) finely sliced mushrooms and cook for 5 minutes. Add ½ cup (125 mL) Madeira or port wine and stir well (see illustration on this page).

Venison and Rabbit

Cubed Venison in Beer Sauce

Try using a brown beer for this recipe.

4 servings

1 tbsp	(15 mL) oil
1 ½ lbs	(675 g) venison, cubed
2 tbsp	(30 mL) cornstarch
¼ cup	(60 mL) cold water
1	large carrot, grated
1	celery stalk, finely sliced
½ cup	(125 mL) fresh or canned mushrooms
1	medium-size onion, diced
1	large green onion, chopped
	salt and pepper
	pinch of paprika
	chopped parsley
1	bottle (340 mL) beer
	grilled croûtons

■ Preheat oven to 375 °F (190 °C).

■ In a skillet, heat oil and sear venison cubes over high heat, then set aside.

■ Dissolve cornstarch in cold water and set aside.

■ Place meat in a casserole dish, add all other ingredients, except croûtons, cover and cook in oven for 45 minutes.

■ About 4 to 5 minutes before the meat is done, pour dissolved cornstarch over the meat. Place on a serving dish, sprinkle with croûtons and serve.

Venison Kebabs with Vegetables

Any one of your favorite beef marinades will bring out the flavor of this dish.

4 servings

Marinade

¼ cup	(60 mL) red wine
¼ cup	(60 mL) oil
1 tsp	(5 mL) dry mustard
1 tbsp	(15 mL) soy sauce
1 lb	(450 g) venison meat, cubed
8	cherry tomatoes
1	onion, cut into 8 wedges
16	mushrooms
16	pieces of green bell pepper

■ Heat barbecue 20 minutes prior to cooking.

■ In a bowl, combine all marinade ingredients, add cubed venison and marinate for 6 hours.

■ Drain meat, then slip onto skewers, alternating with vegetables. Cook over barbecue, basting with marinade from time to time.

VARIATIONS

• Serve with spinach fettucine.

• Serve with a plum or cranberry sauce or with a cream of mushroom sauce.

Rabbit in Mustard Sauce

You might like to replace the brown sugar with honey.

4 servings

2 tbsp	(30 mL) oil
1 lb	(450 g) rabbit meat, cut into fine strips
2 tbsp	(30 mL) tomato sauce
⅓ cup	(80 mL) water
⅓ cup	(80 mL) chicken stock
1 tbsp	(15 mL) brown sugar
1 tbsp	(15 mL) Dijon mustard
1 tbsp	(15 mL) Worcestershire sauce
1	medium onion, thinly sliced
	old-fashioned mustard

■ In a skillet, heat oil and brown meat, then drain. Skim cooking fat from surface, then return meat to the skillet.

■ In a bowl, combine all other ingredients, pour over meat, cover and simmer for 30 minutes or until meat is tender.

■ Garnish each serving with 1 tsp (5 mL) old-fashioned mustard.

Game Meat Loaf

This is the ideal way to serve game to your family for the first time.

4 servings

1 lb	(450 g) ground rabbit meat
1 lb	(450 g) leftover ground game meat
4	slices bacon, cut into pieces
1	small package instant onion soup mix
1 ½ cups	(375 mL) breadcrumbs
2 tbsp	(30 mL) prepared mustard
¼ tsp	(1 mL) savory
2	eggs, lightly beaten
¾ cup	(180 mL) hot water
7 ½ oz	(220 mL) tomato sauce

■ Preheat oven to 400 °F (205 °C).

■ In a bowl, combine ground rabbit, leftover ground game meat, bacon, onion soup mix, breadcrumbs, mustard, and savory and stir well.

■ Add eggs, add water and stir.

■ Shape into a loaf and put in a loaf pan. Pour tomato sauce over meat, cover and cook in oven for 1 ½ hours.

■ Serve with mixed vegetables.

Fish, traditionally a Friday special, is a popular dinner party item for weight-conscious hosts and hostesses.

With fishmarkets offering an ever-increasing variety of fresh fish, there is a growing demand for recipes that make the most of this tender, delicate flesh.

Fresh fish offers all sorts of culinary possibilities that a frozen block does not. It can be served stuffed, cut into steaks, sautéed with the skin on, and in various ways that preserve the flavor and form, so pleasing to the palate and the eye.

Fish contains a complete range of proteins and a limited amount of fat. Even the eel—the fish with the highest fat content—has only 25%, the equivalent of pork or lamb.

FISH

FILLETING FISH—
FISH WITH TWO FILLETS

Salmon-like fish

- *Choose a nice, fresh fish, well scaled. Rinse it in very cold water and pat dry.*

- *To make your job easier, slice off the head, immediately behind the gills, as well as the dorsal and pectoral fins.*

- *You are now ready to remove the fillets from the bone.*

- *With the aid of a well-sharpened knife, slice along the back of the fish to locate the backbone.*

- *Rest the knife blade against the backbone. Continue to slice. Lift the fillet as it comes away from the bone.*

- *When the first fillet is removed, cut away the backbone to release the second fillet.*

- *Place the fillet flat (skin side down) and cut into it 1 inch (2,5 cm) from the tail. Rest the knife blade flat against the skin and, with a sawing motion, cut the fillet away, taking care not to tip the blade to avoid tearing the skin or damaging the fish meat.*

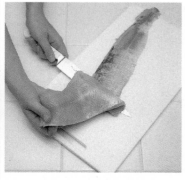

- *Clear the fish fillet from its skin.*

- *Lie the fillet flat, skin or outer side down, and remove the smaller bones with a tweezer.*

FILLETING FISH— FISH WITH FOUR FILLETS

Sole-like fish

- *Buy a nice, fresh fish. Rinse it in very cold water, pat it a little dry and lie it flat on a cutting board (white side down).*

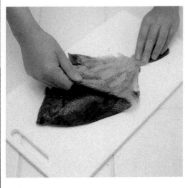

- *Make a small cut just above the tail. Turn up the skin. Hold the fish tail with one hand and pull the skin towards the head in one swift motion.*

- *Remove the skin from the fish.*

- *With a sharp-pointed knife, locate the central bone. Press the tip of the knife against the smaller bones. Lift off the first fillet.*

- *Repeat this procedure on the other side of the central bone to remove the second fillet.*

- *Turn the fish over. Remove the white skin. One by one, separate the third and fourth fillets from the central bone.*

- *You now have four fillets.*

Cutting up fish

These days, it's easy to buy fish whole (cleaned) or in pieces (sections, fillets or steaks). A visit to a modern-day fish market is an invitation to discovery: salmon, sardines, trout and sole lie next to Arctic char, mahi-mahi or even Boston bluefish.

Selecting fish

To make sure the fish you buy is fresh, watch for:

- *the smell: it mustn't be strong.*

- *the flesh: it must be firm and slightly elastic.*

- *the eye: it should be bright and not sunken into the eye socket.*

- *the gills: they should be bright red and damp.*

N.B.: Buy your fish from a fish market where fish is kept packed in ice and algae.

Sections

- *Lie the fish flat after having removed its fins and, if you wish, its skin.*

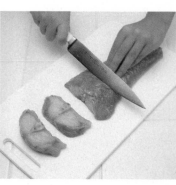

- *Slice the fish into equal pieces, about 2 to 5 inches (5 to 12,5 cm) thick.*

Steaks

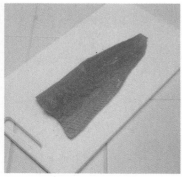

- *Remove the head and fins.*

- *Lie the fish flat on a cutting board.*

- *Cut into 1 to 2-inch (2,5 to 5 cm) thick steaks.*

Baby Fillets or Supremes

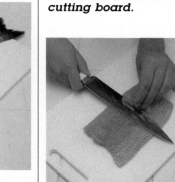

- *Use a fillet with no skin or bones left. Lie it flat on a cutting board.*

- *Slice lengthwise, keeping the knife at a 45° angle. Pieces should weigh 2 to 4 oz (60 to 120 g).*

214

Strips

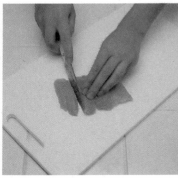

- Take a piece of fillet and cut it crosswise into equal widths.

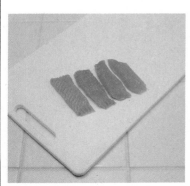

- Use the strips as they are, or cut them into finer slivers.

Checkerboard strips

- Slice 7 or 8 strips of equal length, half of one color, half another.

- Place 4 lengths of the same color side by side. One by one, weave in the strips of a different color, as shown.

- You get a checkerboard effect.

Sailor's knot

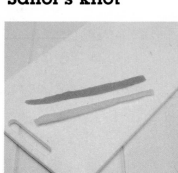

- Slice long thin strips of fillet.

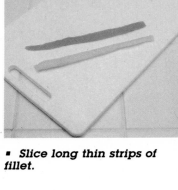

- Tie each one in a knot.

Braided strips

- Take two fish fillets of different colors.

- Slice them into long strips of equal width and line them up side by side, alternating colors.

- Braid the fish strips.

215

WHOLE FISH

Fried Smelts

Smelts are members of the salmon family. Their flesh is delicate and tasty. They are usually fried whole after being cleaned and washed. Smelts are generally sold frozen.

4 servings

	vegetable oil
1 lb	(450 g) smelts
1 cup	(250 mL) milk
	flour
	salt
	sprigs of parsley
2	lemons

■ In a deep fryer, heat oil to 375 °F (190 °C).

■ Pat smelts dry with paper towel. Dip smelts in milk, dredge with flour, then shake off excess flour.

■ Drop smelts into deep fryer and cook until golden. Let stand to drain on paper towel and season with salt.

■ Place smelts in a serving dish, garnish with parsley and lemon wedges.

Poached Trout

Simmer the trout in a poaching stock that is hot, but not boiling.

4 servings

2	carrots, sliced
2	celery stalks, chopped
1	onion, sliced into rings
1	leek
1 tbsp	(15 mL) lemon juice
1 tsp	(5 mL) black pepper, crushed
	pinch of thyme
1	bay leaf
1	bouquet of fresh parsley
3 cups	(750 mL) water
	salt
4	trout, ½ lb (225 g) each
1	lemon, sliced

■ In a saucepan, mix together all ingredients except trout and lemon slices. Bring to a boil and let mixture simmer lightly for 10 minutes.

■ Add trout, simmer for 5 minutes, then remove trout from stock and drain vegetables.

■ Place vegetables and trout in serving dish and garnish with lemon slices. Serve with hollandaise sauce.

Red Snapper with Corn Niblets

Red snapper will cook faster if you notch the flesh.

4 servings

4	corn husk leaves
2	red snappers, 1 lb (450 g) each
1 tbsp	(15 mL) corn oil
	salt and pepper
½ cup	(125 mL) tomato sauce
¼ cup	(60 mL) corn niblets

■ Preheat oven to broil 20 minutes before cooking time.

■ In a saucepan filled with salted boiling water, blanch corn husk leaves for 3 minutes.

■ Baste fish with oil and broil for 3 minutes on each side. Meanwhile, broil corn husk leaves for 1 minute and set aside.

■ In a saucepan, heat tomato sauce and mix in corn niblets.

■ Place fish on corn husk leaves and coat with sauce.

VARIATION

• **Remove fish fillets, lift skin from fish and wrap fillets in corn husk leaves. Broil (see illustrated recipe above).**

Samlets Amandine

Samlets are young salmon with a soft pink flesh. They make a very tempting dish.

4 servings

	salt and pepper
2	whole young salmon, 1 lb (450 g) each, cleaned
	flour
3 tbsp	(45 mL) butter
½ cup	(125 mL) slivered almonds
5 tsp	(25 mL) parsley
1 tbsp	(15 mL) lemon juice

■ Season inside and outside of samlets with salt and pepper and dredge in flour.

■ In a skillet, melt butter and cook fish over medium heat for 7 minutes each side.

■ Add the almonds, stir until golden. Add parsley and lemon juice, then remove from heat. Serve with a white butter sauce.

VARIATION

• **Preheat oven to 350 °F (175 °C). Coat the fish with crushed almonds. In a skillet, melt butter and sauté fish on both sides. Wrap fish in aluminum foil and finish cooking in oven.**

217

STUFFED WHOLE FISH

Stuffed Bass

Bass is considered a delicacy. Its firm, fine-grained flesh has very few bones.

4 servings

2 lb	(900 kg) bass
	salt and pepper
2 cups	(500 mL) breadcrumbs
2 tbsp	(30 mL) onions, finely sliced
1 tbsp	(15 mL) capers
1 tsp	(5 mL) chopped parsley
	pinch of paprika
¼ cup	(60 mL) hot water
2 tbsp	(30 mL) melted butter
¼ cup	(60 mL) 15% cream

■ Preheat oven to 400 °F (205 °C).

■ Season inside and outside of bass with salt and pepper and set aside.

■ Butter a baking dish.

■ In a bowl, combine breadcrumbs, onions, capers, parsley and paprika, then spoon stuffing into bass and close opening.

■ Place bass in baking dish and bake for 45 minutes, basting frequently with a mixture of hot water and melted butter.

■ Transfer stuffed bass to a serving dish. Arrange vegetables of your choice around it and keep warm.

■ Add cream to cooking juices, stir and cook over medium heat to desired thickness. Pour in a circle over vegetables to frame the fish.

Stuffed Trout

If you have some dry white wine left from a previous meal, use it instead of water in this recipe.

4 servings

1 tbsp	(15 mL) butter
¼ cup	(60 mL) onions, finely chopped
¼ cup	(60 mL) celery, finely chopped
1	garlic clove, finely sliced
	salt and pepper
	pinch of tarragon
½ cup	(125 mL) cooked rice
2 tbsp	(30 mL) water
4	trout, ½ lb (225 g) each
1 tbsp	(15 mL) chopped parsley

■ Preheat oven to 450 °F (230 °C).

■ In a skillet, melt butter and sauté onions, celery, and garlic; season with salt, pepper, and tarragon, then add rice and a small amount of water. Spoon stuffing loosely into trout, then close opening and set aside.

■ Butter a baking dish, put the stuffed trout in, cover loosely with aluminum foil and bake for 10 minutes.

■ Place stuffed trout in a serving dish, garnish with parsley and serve with shrimp sauce.

VARIATION

• **Replace rice with milk-soaked bread and add mushrooms to stuffing.**

218

Broiled Stuffed Sardines

Broil the sardines with their heads on. They are less likely to break when being turned.

4 servings

¼ cup	(60 mL) anchovies
2 tbsp	(30 mL) capers
¾ cup	(150 mL) breadcrumbs
½ cup	(125 mL) onions, chopped
2 tbsp	(30 mL) chopped parsley
2	garlic cloves, finely sliced
	pinch of thyme
¼ cup	(60 mL) milk
¼ cup	(60 mL) creamed butter
	salt and pepper
⅓ cup	(75 mL) stuffed olives
2 lbs	(900 g) sardines
2 tbsp	(30 mL) vegetable oil

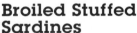

- Preheat oven to broil.

- In a bowl, combine all ingredients except sardines and oil.

- Spoon stuffing into sardines, then place them, well spaced, in a baking dish and season with salt and pepper.

- Baste with oil. Broil each side for 5 minutes, on the middle rack of the oven.

- Place in serving dish and serve.

Sole Stuffed with Mixed Vegetables

You don't need to peel the zucchini.

4 servings

1	small zucchini, diced
2	celery stalks, finely sliced
1	leek, finely sliced
2	small carrots, diced
4 tsp	(20 mL) butter
¼ cup	(60 mL) diced pork fat back (lardons)
	salt and pepper
10 oz	(284 mL) canned cream of celery soup
4	small sole, cleaned
¾ cup	(180 mL) fine breadcrumbs
4 tsp	(20 mL) chopped parsley

- Preheat oven to 375 °F (190 °C).

- In a saucepan, blanch vegetables for 3 minutes in boiling salted water, then drain.

- In a skillet, melt butter and sauté lardons and blanched vegetables, season with salt and pepper and cook over low heat for 3 minutes. Add cream of celery soup and cook 3 minutes longer.

- Stuff each sole with the vegetables and place in a baking dish. Pour a small amount of cream of celery soup over the fish, cover with aluminum foil and bake for 25 minutes.

- When cooked, sprinkle mixed breadcrumbs and parsley over the sole, broil for 1 minute or until golden. Spoon pan juices over the fish and serve.

219

FISH FILLETS

Doré Fillets with Tomatoes

The tender doré or yellow pike fillet is a delicacy that you can easily include in everyday meals.

4 servings

1 lb	(450 g) doré fillets, fresh or thawed
	salt and pepper
3 tbsp	(45 mL) green onions, chopped
2	tomatoes, cut into wedges
½ tsp	(2 mL) sugar
¼ cup	(60 mL) melted butter
1	lemon, sliced
¼ tsp	(1 mL) basil
2 tbsp	(30 mL) chopped parsley

■ Preheat oven to 450 °F (230 °C).

■ Remove skin from the fish. Butter a baking dish, arrange fillets over the chopped green onions in dish, season with salt and pepper and set aside.

■ In a bowl, gently mix tomatoes and sugar. Place them around the fish, baste with melted butter and bake for 10 minutes.

■ Place in a serving dish, garnish with lemon slices, sprinkle with parsley and basil and serve.

VARIATIONS

• When fish is cooked, run tomatoes and cooking juice through the blender, and pour this sauce over the fish.

• Prepare the recipe with green tomatoes and triple the amount of sugar. Slice the shallots in rings (see illustration).

• Dice the fish and tomatoes. Halve the zucchini lengthwise and blanch for 5 minutes in boiling salted water. Scoop pulp from zucchini halves, fill with fish and tomato mixture, sprinkle with ½ cup (125 mL) grated Cheddar cheese and brown lightly under the broiler (see illustration).

220

Halibut au Gratin

Halibut, fished from cold Atlantic waters, is very lean. This recipe is also good for turbot.

4 servings

2 lb	(900 g) halibut, cut into pieces
½ cup	(125 mL) chicken broth
2 tbsp	(30 mL) parsley
1 tsp	(5 mL) tarragon
½ cup	(125 mL) grated Cheddar cheese
1	egg white, beaten until stiff

■ Preheat oven to 400 °F (205 °C).

■ In a baking dish, place halibut pieces, add chicken stock, sprinkle with parsley and tarragon and bake for 10 minutes. Remove from oven, pour off excess liquid and set aside.

■ Heat the broiler.

■ In a bowl, add cheese to beaten egg white, spread over halibut pieces and broil au gratin.

VARIATIONS

• **Replace chicken stock with white wine.**

• **Wrap halibut pieces in blanched cabbage leaves.**

• **Top the halibut with anchovies.**

Haddock Fillets with Shrimp Sauce

Frozen haddock fillets are well suited to this recipe. For greater eye appeal, use fresh fillets or fillets frozen individually rather than in a block.

4 servings

2 tbsp	(30 mL) butter
2 tbsp	(30 mL) flour
1 cup	(250 mL) milk
½ tsp	(2 mL) salt
¼ tsp	(1 mL) pepper
1 tbsp	(15 mL) lemon juice
6 oz	(170 mL) canned shrimp, drained
1 lb	(450 g) halibut fillets
¾ cup	(150 mL) grated Mozzarella cheese
	paprika and parsley

■ In a measuring cup, combine butter, flour, milk, salt, and pepper.

■ Cook in microwave at HIGH, 3 to 4 minutes, stirring every minute. Add lemon juice and shrimp.

■ In a rectangular baking dish 6 x 8 inches (15 x 20 cm), place halibut fillets and cover with a paper towel. Cook at HIGH for 3 minutes.

■ Pour shrimp sauce over halibut fillets, sprinkle with cheese and paprika, garnish with parsley and cook 3 to 4 minutes longer.

Stuffed Fish Fillets

Stuffed Fillets of Sole

Vary the flavor of the tartare sauce with different sweet or sour pickles.

4 servings

1 lb	(450 g) fillet of sole

Stuffing

1	egg
1/2 cup	(125 mL) celery, diced
1/2 cup	(125 mL) soft part of bread toasted and crumbled
1/4 cup	(60 mL) milk
	salt and pepper

Tartare Sauce

2	French (dry) shallots, finely chopped
1 cup	(250 mL) béchamel sauce
1/2 cup	(125 mL) mayonnaise
1/4 cup	(60 mL) pickles, chopped
1/4 cup	(60 mL) olives, chopped
1/4 cup	(60 mL) parsley, chopped

■ Preheat oven to 375 °F (190 °C).

■ Pat sole fillets dry and set aside.

■ In a bowl, combine stuffing ingredients, spread between two fillets and set aside.

■ Butter a baking dish, add the stuffed fillets and bake for 15 to 20 minutes.

■ In a bowl, combine all tartare sauce ingredients and warm over low heat. Pour the sauce over the fish.

VARIATIONS

• Replace celery with mushroom pieces.

• Add grated cheese and finely sliced sweet red peppers to stuffing.

• Replace béchamel sauce with an equal amount of cream of celery soup.

• Roll sole fillets with the stuffing and secure with toothpick. Decorate dish with celery leaves as well as cucumber and tomato slices (see illustration).

Spinach-stuffed Angler

You won't need as many fillets if you use another type of fish.

4 servings

Stuffing

1/2 lb	(225 g) angler flesh
1/4 cup	(60 mL) spinach, cooked, drained
	salt and pepper
2	eggs
1/4 cup	(60 mL) 35% cream
12	small angler fillets
1/2 cup	(125 mL) clam and tomato juice

Au Gratin Mixture

1/4 cup	(60 mL) spinach, cooked, drained
2	egg yolks
1/3 cup	(80 mL) grated cheese
2 tbsp	(30 mL) butter

■ Preheat oven to 400 °F (205 °C).

■ In a food processor, chop angler flesh and spinach into fine pieces; season with salt and pepper. Add eggs, one by one and stir well after each addition. Dribble the cream over this, then spread mixture over angler fillets.

■ In a baking dish, place angler fillets one on top of the other, pour clam and tomato juice over the fish, cover and bake for 15 minutes.

■ Meanwhile, combine au gratin ingredients, spread over angler fillets and broil for 2 minutes. Transfer to a serving dish and keep warm.

■ Allow cooking juice to reduce, baste the fish lightly.

Salmon-stuffed Pike Fillets

Go easy on the curry!

4 servings

Stuffing

4	bread slices, buttered on both sides, cut in squares
1	egg
6	small pickles, chopped
1/2 tsp	(2 mL) paprika
	pinch of curry powder
	pinch of thyme
1/4 cup	(60 mL) milk
	salt and pepper
7 1/2 oz	(213 g) salmon, flaked
4	pike fillets, 1/4 lb (115 g) each
1/2 cup	(125 mL) water
2 tbsp	(30 mL) butter
2 tbsp	(30 mL) cheese spread
1	cucumber, sliced
1	tomato, diced

■ Preheat oven to 375 °F (190 °C).

■ In a bowl, combine all stuffing ingredients.

■ Butter a baking dish. Sandwich stuffing between fillets, place them in the dish and add water and butter. Bake for 30 minutes.

■ Pour cooking juices into a saucepan and reduce liquid by a quarter. Add cheese spread and pour this sauce over the fish. Garnish dish with cucumber slices and diced tomatoes, and serve.

FANCY FISH FILLETS

Angler and Salmon Checkerboard with Tomato Butter

The intriguing and appetizing appearance of woven or braided fish fillets, or the easy-to-serve sailor's knot, adds a certain panache to any meal. It's easier than you think, since the supple, boneless flesh of fillets can be manipulated without too much difficulty. Simply follow the instructions.

The rosy color of salmon is a nice contrast to the white flesh of the angler. You might like to try using plaice or turbot instead.

- Preheat oven to 400 °F (205 °C).

- Slice salmon and angler fillets into strips of even lengths.

- Place salmon fillet strips side by side. To obtain a checkerboard effect weave the pink and white fillets, as shown.

- Butter a baking dish. Add the fish, sprinkle with shallots, pour in wine, then cover with aluminum foil. Bake 12 to 15 minutes.

- Transfer to a serving dish and keep warm.

- Reduce cooking juices almost completely, add cream and simmer, stirring constantly, until cream thickens slightly. Remove from heat, still stirring, then add butter.

- Pour the sauce in a ring around the fish. Garnish with carrots and sprinkle with diced tomatoes and parsley.

4 servings		
1 lb	(450 g) salmon fillet, whole	
1 lb	(450 g) angler fillet, whole	
	salt and pepper	
2 tbsp	(30 mL) French (dry) shallots, finely sliced	
1/2 cup	(125 mL) white wine	
1/2 cup	(125 mL) 35% cream	
1/3 cup	(75 mL) butter	
	miniature carrots, halved, steamed	
1/4 cup	(60 mL) tomatoes, diced	
4 tsp	(20 mL) chopped parsley	

Braided Salmon and Sole Mimosa

Handle the braided fish carefully once it is cooked, as it falls apart easily. "Mimosa" refers to the attractive crumbled egg topping.

4 servings

8	long salmon fillets
8	long fillets of sole
½ cup	(125 mL) white wine
	salt and pepper
1 tsp	(5 mL) basil
¾ cup	(180 mL) 15% cream
2 tbsp	(30 mL) butter
4	hard-boiled egg yolks, pressed through sieve
	bouquet of chervil

■ Preheat oven to 425 °F (220 °C).

■ Braid 2 salmon fillets and 1 sole fillet for each serving.

■ Lightly butter a baking dish, place salmon and sole braids in it and baste with wine. Season with salt and pepper, cover and bake for 15 minutes.

■ Remove dish from oven and place braids on plates. Keep warm.

■ Pour cooking juice in a small saucepan, add basil, and reduce liquid by half, then add cream and cook until cream thickens slightly.

■ Remove from heat, add butter and beat with wire whisk.

■ Pour sauce over fish braids and sprinkle with egg yolk bits, then garnish with chervil sprigs.

VARIATION

• **Serve the fish braid as illustrated, on a bed of leeks that have been steamed for 5 minutes.**

Halibut Fillet in Puff Pastry Shell

Buy frozen puff pastry for these attractive little pies.

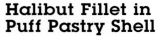

4 servings

Stuffing

¹⁄₃ cup	(80 mL)	mushrooms, finely sliced
8		shallots, chopped
4 tsp	(20 mL)	olive oil
2 tsp	(10 mL)	chives
2 tsp	(10 mL)	chervil
4 tsp	(20 mL)	tomatoes, diced
¹⁄₃ cup	(80 mL)	leek, julien-ned, blanched
		salt and pepper
2 tsp	(10 mL)	sherry
2 tsp	(10 mL)	lemon juice
4		halibut fillets, 7 oz (200 g) each
1 lb	(450 g)	puff pastry
2		egg yolks, beaten

■ Preheat oven to 375 °F (190 °C).

■ In a bowl, combine all stuffing ingredients and let stand for at least 1 hour.

■ Roll out puff pastry and cut into 8 identical fish shapes.

■ Place 1 halibut fillet in middle of pastry and spoon stuffing over it. Baste outer edge of pastry with water, then cover with a second crust and pinch edges to seal.

■ With a small knife, draw scales on pastry surface. Use a peppercorn for an eye and baste the pastry lightly with beaten egg yolks.

■ Repeat for the other halibut fillets, and bake for 30 minutes.

Sole Strips Verdurette

Use fresh herbs such as basil, thyme, chervil, and tarragon, as well as parsley.

4 servings

1 lb	(450 g)	fillet of sole
		salt and pepper
2 tbsp	(30 mL)	butter
2 tbsp	(30 mL)	French (dry) shallots, chopped
4 tsp	(20 mL)	chopped watercress
4 tsp	(20 mL)	chopped parsley
4 tsp	(20 mL)	chopped fines herbes
¹⁄₂ cup	(125 mL)	15% cream
		carrots, diced and steamed

■ Slice fillets of sole into very fine strips and season with salt and pepper.

■ In a skillet, melt butter and cook fish over medium heat for 6 minutes, then remove from skillet. Place in serving dish and keep warm.

■ Using the same skillet, combine all other ingredients except cream, reduce heat and cook for 2 minutes. Add cream, bring to a boil and let boil for 1 minute. Season with salt and pepper.

■ Put the fish in the sauce and reheat gently. Sprinkle with carrots and serve.

Sailor's Knots

Most fish sold today can readily be tied in these amusing and easy-to-serve sailor's knots. A few cooked, unpeeled shrimp or steamed mussels around the edge of the serving platter give added variety.

4 servings

1 lb	(450 g) fish fillets, cut into strips
4 tsp	(20 mL) butter
	salt and pepper
1	commercial seafood sauce mix

■ Preheat oven to 400 °F (205 °C).

■ Tie fish strips in loose knots.

■ Coat a baking pan lightly with butter. Place sailor's knots in baking pan and season with salt and pepper then bake for 12 minutes.

■ Meanwhile, prepare seafood sauce according to package directions and serve with fish.

VARIATION

• Place each fish knot on a blanched ½ inch (1,25 cm) thick cucumber slice (see illustration).

• Place one or two knots in a cooked pastry shell, coat with a little sauce and sprinkle with grated cheese, then brown under the broiler.

• Serve cold with a lime vinaigrette.

FISH STEAKS

Salmon Steaks Sautéed with Tomatoes

Steaks taken from the middle section of the salmon are considered to be the most delectable.

Sauté them in olive oil for a nicer flavor.

4 servings

2 tbsp	(30 mL) vegetable oil
4	salmon steaks, ³/₄ inch (2 cm) thick
2	garlic cloves, finely sliced
1	onion, chopped
4 tsp	(20 mL) chopped parsley
2 tsp	(10 mL) basil
1 tsp	(5 mL) fresh mint, trimmed
8	tomatoes, peeled, cut into wedges
	juice of 1 lemon
	salt and pepper

■ Preheat oven to 375 °F (190 °C).

■ In a skillet, heat oil and cook salmon steaks over medium heat for 2 minutes each side.

■ Bake in oven 8 to 10 minutes depending on thickness of steaks, then remove from oven, place in a serving dish and keep warm.

■ Using the same skillet, combine garlic, onion, and herbs and cook for 2 minutes over medium heat, stirring, then add tomatoes, lemon juice, salt, and pepper and cook for 4 minutes.

■ Place salmon steaks in a serving dish. Pour the sauce around the fish and serve.

VARIATION

• Replace lemon juice with juice of 2 oranges.

• Add 6 shelled, cooked mussels and their juice to sauce, as illustrated here.

• Let salmon steaks cool. Run sauce through blender and serve the fish with a tomato purée.

• Add 1 diced zucchini, 1 diced sweet red pepper, and ¹/₂ diced eggplant to sauce.

• Pour 8 oz (287 mL) cream of tomato soup into sauce for a more velvety texture.

• Add to sauce 2 chopped rhubarb stalks, cooked in water for 5 minutes.

Halibut Steaks with Crabmeat

Use canned or frozen crabmeat and make sure it is well drained.

For a health-conscious diet, cook steaks in equal parts of butter and oil.

4 servings

2 tbsp	(30 mL) butter
4	halibut steaks, 3/4 inch (2 cm) thick
	salt and pepper
6 oz	(170 mL) crabmeat
8 oz	(227 mL) cream of tomato soup
2 tbsp	(30 mL) chopped parsley or chervil

■ Preheat oven to 375 °F (190 °C).

■ In a skillet, heat butter and cook halibut steaks over medium heat for 3 minutes on each side, then season with salt and pepper.

■ Place halibut steaks in oven and bake for 8 minutes.

■ Remove from oven, place in serving dish and keep warm.

■ Using the same skillet, combine crabmeat and cream of tomato soup, cook a few minutes then pour sauce over halibut steaks. Garnish with chervil or parsley and serve.

Salmon Pepper Steaks

The succulent taste of thick salmon steaks is a treat fit for a gourmet. A dusting of flour and crushed peppers, plus a wine-flavored pan sauce, makes this cut especially tasty.

4 servings

1/4 cup	(60 mL) flour
4	1/2 inch (1,5 cm) thick salmon steaks
2 tsp	(10 mL) black pepper, ground
5 tsp	(25 mL) vegetable oil
1/4 cup	(60 mL) butter
1 tsp	(5 mL) salt
1/4 cup	(60 mL) dry white wine
1	lemon, sliced

■ Lightly dredge steaks with flour, press pepper firmly into salmon meat so it adheres well to flesh.

■ In a skillet, heat oil and melt 5 tsp (25 mL) butter. Cook steaks for 5 minutes or until flesh is opaque and falls apart easily. Half-way through cooking, turn steaks.

■ Remove from heat, place in a serving dish, season with salt and keep warm.

■ Using the same skillet, add rest of butter and wine and stir quickly. Pour the sauce mixture over the steaks, garnish with lemon slices and serve.

Fish stew

Angler Stew with Matelote Sauce

The term "matelote" refers to fish stewed in wine.

4 servings		
3 tbsp	(45 mL) butter	
1 lb	(450 g) angler, cut into pieces	
½ cup	(125 mL) pearl onions	
1 cup	(250 mL) mushrooms	
½ cup	(125 mL) leek, finely sliced	
¼ cup	(60 mL) carrots, diced	
3 tbsp	(45 mL) flour	
1 ½ cups	(375 mL) water	
1 cup	(250 mL) white wine	
	juice of ½ lemon	
	salt and pepper	
¾ cup	(180 mL) 35% cream	
3	egg yolks	
2 tbsp	(30 mL) fines herbes	

■ In a skillet, melt butter and sauté angler with pearl onions, mushrooms, leek, and carrots over medium heat for 3 minutes.

■ Add flour and cook for 3 minutes, stirring constantly.

■ Add water, wine and lemon juice and let mixture thicken, then season with salt and pepper. Blend in cream and cook for 10 minutes, then remove from heat.

■ Meanwhile, stir egg yolks into a small amount of sauce, add to first mixture, then add fines herbes and serve.

VARIATION

• **Replace cream and water with cream of mushroom soup.**

Halibut Stew with Cucumbers

Use long, slender "English" cucumbers, since they don't need to be seeded.

4 servings		
3 tbsp	(45 mL) butter	
1 lb	(450 g) halibut, cut in pieces	
2	cucumbers, peeled, seeded, finely sliced	
1	onion, chopped	
	salt and pepper	
2 cups	(500 mL) cream of celery soup	
4	vol-au-vent pastry shells	

■ In a skillet, melt butter, and sauté halibut with cucumbers and onion, season with salt and pepper. Add cream of celery soup and cook over medium heat until halibut is well done.

■ Heat vol-au-vent pastry shells in oven. Spoon halibut mixture into shells, garnish and serve.

Perch Fricassee

4 servings	
3 tbsp	(45 mL) butter
1 lb	(450 g) fillet of perch, skinned
	salt and pepper
6	slices bacon, finely chopped
½ cup	(125 mL) mushrooms, cut into pieces
¼ cup	(60 mL) apples, diced
¼ cup	(60 mL) pearl onions
3 tbsp	(45 mL) flour
2 cups	(500 mL) fish stock
¼ cup	(60 mL) lettuce, cut into strips
¾ tsp	(3 mL) fresh tarragon
	tomatoes, diced

■ In a skillet, melt butter and sauté perch fillets, season with salt and pepper, then remove from heat and keep warm. Pour off excess fat from skillet. Melt bacon, then sauté mushrooms, apples and pearl onions until liquid evaporates completely. Add flour, stir for 1 minute, then add fish stock and let it thicken for 7 to 8 minutes, stirring constantly.

■ Place warm fillets of perch in the sauce, cook 3 minutes, garnish with lettuce strips, fresh tarragon, and tomatoes.

Fish Pot-au-Feu, with Aurora Sauce

4 servings	
¼ lb	(115 g) sole
¼ lb	(115 g) angler
¼ lb	(115 g) haddock
¼ cup	(60 mL) turnip
¼ cup	(60 mL) celery
¼ cup	(60 mL) leeks
¼ cup	(60 mL) potatoes
¼ cup	(60 mL) carrots
¼ cup	(60 mL) butter
1	bay leaf
	pinch of thyme
	juice of ½ lemon
2 tbsp	(30 mL) flour
2 ½ cups	(625 mL) water
2 tbsp	(30 mL) tomato paste
	salt and pepper
4	cabbage leaves, blanched

■ Cut fish into strips and dice vegetables.

■ In a stove-top casserole, melt butter and sauté the vegetables over low heat. Cover and cook for 6 minutes more.

■ Add bay leaf, thyme, lemon juice, and flour and cook for 4 minutes, stirring constantly. Add water, tomato paste and the fish and let mixture thicken, then reduce heat to low and cook for 15 minutes. Season with salt and pepper.

■ Spread cabbage leaves in a serving dish and spoon fish in middle.

FISH STICKS

Fish Croquettes

Serve these delicious croquettes with a hot sauce or a cold tartare sauce.

4 servings

1 cup	(250 mL) milk
2	bay leaves
3 tbsp	(45 mL) butter
3 tbsp	(45 mL) flour
1	onion, finely sliced
1 tbsp	(15 mL) sweet red pepper
1 cup	(250 mL) cooked fish, crumbled
1	egg, beaten
2 tbsp	(30 mL) chopped parsley
2	eggs, beaten
	breadcrumbs
	oil

■ In a saucepan, heat milk and bay leaves. Remove from heat and let cool to lukewarm.

■ In a skillet, melt butter, add flour and cook a few minutes, stirring constantly, then remove from heat.

■ Add milk (without bay leaves) to flour mixture, then add onion and sweet red pepper, return to heat, and cook until sauce thickens.

■ Add crumbled fish, beaten egg and parsley, then pour into serving dish and let stand to cool for a few minutes. Refrigerate.

■ Dredge hands with flour and shape fish into sticks, dipping each fish stick into beaten eggs, then into breadcrumbs. Fry in hot oil until golden.

VARIATIONS

• Add ¼ cup (60 mL) grated Parmesan cheese for a Parmesan fish fondue.

• Add a small amount of tomato paste to color the croquette meat.

• Add ½ cup (125 mL) cooked, well-drained spinach to fish mixture for croquettes florentine (see illustration).

Jiffy Fish Sticks

This is an ingenious way of serving fish with cheese and vegetables. With a side dish of rice, these delicious fish sticks offer a healthy and complete meal in no time flat!

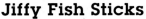

4 servings

2 cups	(500 mL) cooked vegetables, sliced
1 lb	(450 g) fish sticks
1	package cheese sauce

■ Preheat oven to 400 °F (205 °C).

■ Butter a baking dish, put in the vegetables, cover with fish sticks and set aside.

■ Prepare cheese sauce according to package directions, then pour over fish sticks, and bake 15 to 20 minutes.

VARIATION

• Combine fish sticks with frozen peas and cooked, curried rice. Cook in microwave at HIGH 4 to 6 minutes. Stir during cooking, and let stand for 5 minutes before serving.

Deep-fried Fish Sticks

You can partially prepare these fish sticks in advance by deep-frying them until half cooked, and then freezing them. To serve them, simply pop them in the oven while still frozen and finish cooking.

4 servings

1 tsp	(5 mL) oil
1/4 tsp	(1 mL) paprika
1/2 tsp	(2 mL) baking powder
1	egg
1/2 cup	(125 mL) milk
3/4 cup	(180 mL) flour
1/2 cup	(125 mL) soda biscuits, crumbled, or corn flakes
1 tsp	(5 mL) salt
1 lb	(450 g) frozen fish sticks

■ In a deep-fryer, heat oil to 400 °F (205 °C).

■ In a bowl, combine oil, paprika, baking powder, egg and milk. Add flour, soda biscuits or corn flakes, and salt. Stir.

■ Coat fish sticks with this mixture, then drop into deep-fryer and fry until golden. Drain well and serve with tartare sauce.

Portuguese Haddock Sticks

Portuguese cooking immediately conjures up the aroma of tomatoes and herbs.

4 servings

19 oz	(540 mL) canned tomatoes, drained
2	zucchini, diced
½ tsp	(2 mL) sugar
¼ tsp	(1 mL) basil
¼ tsp	(1 mL) pepper
¼ tsp	(1 mL) salt
1 lb	(450 g) haddock fillet, cut into sticks
4	shallots, finely sliced
¼ cup	(60 mL) chopped parsley
¼ cup	(60 mL) oil
2 tbsp	(30 mL) flour
1 tsp	(5 mL) paprika
4	hard-boiled eggs, pressed through sieve

■ In a rectangular microwave-safe dish, spread tomatoes and zucchini, sprinkle with sugar, basil, pepper, and salt, then place haddock sticks over mixture and set aside.

■ In a bowl, combine all other ingredients except hard-boiled eggs, pour mixture over fish sticks, and cover with a sheet of perforated plastic wrap.

■ Cook in microwave at HIGH 6 to 7 minutes, then let stand for 3 minutes and sprinkle with hard-boiled egg bits.

Low-cal Pike Fish Sticks

These fish sticks are low in calories, since the breading has been omitted. Cook them in a non-stick frying pan, and you won't need to add any butter either.

4 servings

1 tbsp	(15 mL) corn oil
4	pike fillets, cut into sticks
	salt and pepper
1 tbsp	(15 mL) butter
1 tbsp	(15 mL) chervil
1 tbsp	(15 mL) chives
1 tbsp	(15 mL) lemon juice

■ In a skillet, heat oil and sauté pike sticks for 3 minutes on each side, season with salt and pepper, then place in serving dish and set aside.

■ Using the same skillet, melt butter, then add herbs, cook for 1 minute, and sprinkle with lemon juice. Pour mixture over fish sticks and serve.

VARIATIONS

- Add 1 cup (250 mL) sliced mushrooms, and ⅓ cup (80 mL) finely chopped onions fried in butter.

- Before cooking, marinate pike sticks in a mixture of 1/4 cup (60 mL) vinegar, ½ cup (125 mL) oil, 2 tbsp (30 mL) fines herbes, 2 tsp (10 mL) paprika, and 1 tsp (5 mL) curry powder.

Fried Haddock Sticks

Haddock flesh contains only 1% fatty substances. It's the perfect choice for weight-conscious people.

4 servings

Batter

2		eggs, beaten
1 cup	(250 mL),	milk
1 tsp	(5 mL)	salt
1 cup	(250 mL)	flour
4		haddock fillets, cut into sticks

■ In a deep-fryer, heat oil to 400 °F (205 °C).

■ In a bowl, combine all batter ingredients and dip haddock sticks into it. Drop into deep-fryer, fry until golden, then remove, drain on paper towel, and serve.

VARIATIONS

- Marinate haddock sticks for 40 minutes in a mixture of ¼ cup (60 mL) vinegar, ¼ cup (60 mL) oil, 2 tsp (10 mL) finely sliced garlic, 2 tsp (10 mL) paprika, salt and pepper.

- Serve haddock sticks with a jiffy tartare sauce prepared as follows: Add 3 tbsp (45 mL) chopped pickles, 2 tbsp (30 mL) chopped onion, 5 tsp (25 mL) chopped parsley, 4 tsp (20 mL) capers, and 1 finely sliced garlic clove to 1 cup (250 mL) mayonnaise (see illustration).

- Replace capers with chopped pearl onions.

- Season cooked haddock sticks with a mixture of salt, pepper, and thyme.

FISH BROCHETTES

Trout Steak Shish Kebabs

Since this recipe calls for marinating the fish pieces once they're on the skewers, we recommend that you use wooden skewers.

4 servings	
4	small trout, 6 oz (175 g) each, cut into ½ inch (1 cm) steaks
8	small potatoes, sliced
1	onion, cubed
24	bacon pieces

Marinade

4	shallots, finely sliced
¼ cup	(60 mL) orange juice
¼ cup	(60 mL) white wine
½ cup	(125 mL) plain yogurt
2 tbsp	(30 mL) vegetable oil
2 tbsp	(30 mL) chopped parsley
½ tsp	(2 mL) thyme
	salt and pepper
2 tbsp	(30 mL) butter

■ Slide trout onto skewers, alternating with vegetables (place a piece of bacon on either side of the trout), then place skewered fish in a long, shallow dish.

■ In a bowl, combine marinade ingredients, pour over shish kebabs and marinate 24 hours, turning from time to time.

■ In a large skillet, melt butter and cook shish kebabs for 6 minutes on each side.

VARIATIONS

• Serve shish kebabs with avocado sauce prepared as follows: 1 ripe avocado, mashed, flavored with 2 tsp (10 mL) lemon juice, 1 finely sliced garlic clove, and 3 tbsp (45 mL) vegetable oil or mayonnaise (see illustration).

• Replace trout steaks with whole smelts or tom cod.

• Slice firm-fleshed fish into long thin fillets, tie into sailor's knots, slide onto skewer.

• Alternate trout steak pieces with cubed chicken and beef.

Salmon Shish Kebabs with Fruit

When in season, use fresh pineapple chunks.

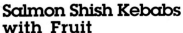

4 servings

1 ½ lb	(675 g) salmon cut into 1 inch (2,5 cm) thick cubes
2	peaches, in wedges
2	oranges, in wedges
1	zucchini, diced
1	sweet red pepper, diced

Marinade

½ cup	(125 mL) orange juice
2 tsp	(10 mL) coriander, crushed
	sesame seeds, to taste
1	small onion, chopped
2 tbsp	(30 mL) oil
2 tsp	(2 mL) curry
	salt and pepper

■ Slide salmon pieces onto skewers, alternating with fruit and vegetables.

■ In a bowl, combine all marinade ingredients.

■ Place shish kebabs in a dish, coat with marinade and marinate overnight.

■ Heat broiler and broil shish kebabs for 8 minutes. Baste often with marinade.

VARIATIONS

• Use any firm fruit of your choice (cantaloup, nectarine, grapes, etc.).

• Add 2 tbsp (30 mL) port, Madeira or sherry to marinade.

Tuna Shish Kebabs with Fennel

Keep the fennel bulb for another meal.

4 servings

1 ½ lbs	(675 g) tuna, cubed
2	tomatoes, in wedges
2	onions, in wedges
4	slices bacon
1	sweet red pepper, cubed

Marinade

¼ cup	(60 mL) lemon juice
¼ cup	(60 mL) tomato juice
½ tsp	(2 mL) tarragon
½ tsp	(2 mL) basil
3	garlic cloves, finely sliced
½ tsp	(2 mL) black pepper
2 tbsp	(30 mL) olive oil
2 tbsp	(30 mL) fresh fennel leaves, finely sliced
	salt and pepper

■ Slide tuna pieces onto skewers, alternating with vegetables, then place mixture in shallow dish.

■ In a bowl, combine marinade ingredients, then baste kebabs and marinate for 24 hours, turning from time to time.

■ Preheat the broiler. Broil shish kebabs for 8 minutes, basting frequently with marinade, and serve.

Seafood

Shrimp-stuffed Apples

Use an apple corer to remove the cores with a flick of the wrist.

6 servings	
6	apples
1 tbsp	(15 mL) lemon juice

Stuffing

3 tbsp	(45 mL) mayonnaise
1 tsp	(5 mL) tomato paste
	few drops of Tabasco sauce
2	dill pickles, finely sliced
4	stuffed olives, chopped
³/₄ cup	(180 mL) pink or grey shrimp, shelled, cooked
1 tbsp	(15 mL) chopped parsley

■ Slice top off apples and remove core, seeds and pulp, taking care not to pierce skin. Slice pulp into cubes and sprinkle with lemon juice.

■ In a bowl, combine apple cubes with stuffing ingredients.

■ Spoon stuffing into apples a few minutes before serving.

Frog's Legs Marinated in Garlic

Thaw the frozen frog's legs in the refrigerator before marinating them.

4 servings	

Marinade

1 cup	(250 mL) oil
	juice of 1 lemon
2 tbsp	(30 mL) fines herbes
	salt and pepper
2 lbs	(900 g) frog's legs
1	egg, beaten
¹/₂ cup	(125 mL) flour
1 cup	(250 mL) breadcrumbs
4 tsp	(20 mL) butter
3 or 4	garlic cloves, finely sliced
2 tbsp	(30 mL) chopped parsley

■ In a deep-fryer, heat oil to 375 °F (190 °C).

■ In a bowl, combine marinade ingredients and marinate frog's legs for 1 hour, turning from time to time. Drain and dredge with flour, then dip into egg, coat with breadcrumbs and fry in deep-fryer 4 to 5 minutes.

■ In a skillet, melt butter, and sauté garlic and parsley.

■ Place frog's legs in a serving dish, pour garlic butter over them and serve.

Seafood Pizza

If you don't have any fresh crabmeat, try using crab-flavored pollock strips instead.

4 servings

1 ½ cups	(375 mL) béchamel sauce
¾ cup	(180 mL) cooked shrimp
¾ cup	(180 mL) cooked scallops
1	pizza dough
¾ cup	(180 mL) crabmeat
1 cup	(250 mL) fresh mushrooms, finely sliced
2 cups	(500 mL) grated Mozzarella cheese

■ Preheat oven to 450 °F (230 °C).

■ In a bowl, combine béchamel sauce and seafood, then spread mixture over pizza dough, cover with finely sliced mushrooms and Mozzarella cheese. Bake in oven for 10 minutes.

Scallops Royale

If you use homemade breadcrumbs, make sure you grind them very finely so as not to lose the delicate texture of the scallops.

4 servings

1 lb	(450 g) scallops, fresh or frozen
1 cup	(250 mL) garlic vinaigrette
1 tbsp	(15 mL) milk
2	eggs, beaten
½ cup	(125 mL) cooked ham, chopped
½ cup	(125 mL) breadcrumbs
2 tbsp	(30 mL) grated Parmesan cheese
	salt
	oil
	commercial spicy sauce

■ In a deep-fryer, heat oil to 375 °F (190 °C).

■ Marinate scallops in the vinaigrette for 30 minutes.

■ Meanwhile combine milk and beaten eggs and set aside.

■ In a separate bowl, combine ham, breadcrumbs, and cheese, and season mixture with salt.

■ Drain scallops, dip into egg mixture, dredge with breadcrumb mixture, then cook in deep-fryer until slightly golden. Drain on paper towel and serve with spicy sauce.

239

MUSSELS

Mussels Provençale

Mussels need careful scrubbing and rinsing. Remove the byssus— the beard-like filaments at the hinges of the mussels shells.

4 servings

4 lbs	(2 kg) mussels
2 tbsp	(30 mL) butter
6	garlic cloves, finely sliced
2 tbsp	(30 mL) chopped parsley
2 tsp	(10 mL) lemon juice
1 ½ cups	(375 mL) tomato sauce
½ cup	(125 mL) bread-crumbs

■ Heat broiler.

■ Scrub and rinse mussels.

■ In a large saucepan, pour 1 inch (2,5 cm) water, add mussels, then cover, and boil over high heat until mussels open.

■ Drain and place in a dish to keep warm.

■ In a small saucepan, melt butter. Add garlic and parsley and cook over low heat for 1 minute, then add lemon juice and remove from heat.

■ Fill each mussel shell with a small amount of tomato sauce, coat with breadcrumbs and garlic butter and broil for 2 to 3 minutes.

VARIATIONS

- **Replace tomato juice with creamed spinach purée (see illustration).**

- **Remove mussels from their shells, place 10 or 12 mussels in small ramekins and follow recipe.**

- **Replace ramekins with puff pastry shells, and increase amount of tomato sauce.**

- **Before final broiling, add a small amount of Parmesan cheese and 6 bacon slices, cut into pieces (see illustration).**

- **Add ⅓ cup (80 mL) finely sliced stuffed olives and 2 tbsp (30 mL) anchovy fillets.**

- **Place shelled mussels on small skewers, and cook in skillet.**

Mussels Marinière

A fragrant herb sauce generously laced with white wine complements this distinctive French seafood dish.

4 servings

¼ cup	(60 mL) butter
⅓ cup	(80 mL) French (dry) shallots, finely sliced
4 tsp	(20 mL) parsley
2 tsp	(10 mL) chervil
½ tsp	(2 mL) tarragon
½ tsp	(2 mL) thyme
4 ½ lbs	(2 kg) mussels
¾ cup	(180 mL) white wine
	ground pepper
2 tbsp	(30 mL) kneaded butter (beurre manié)
	juice of ½ lemon

■ Clean and wash mussels.

■ In a large saucepan, melt butter and cook shallots and herbs over low heat. Add mussels, white wine and ground pepper, then cover and cook over high heat until mussels open.

■ With a skimmer, remove mussels and place in plates.

■ In a separate saucepan, bring cooking juice to a boil. With a wire whisk, stir in kneaded butter and keep stirring until sauce thickens. Pour sauce over mussels and serve.

Mussels Cremolata

Mussels must open during cooking, otherwise they aren't fit to eat. Throw away those that stay closed.

4 servings

4 ½ lbs	(2 kg) mussels
2 tbsp	(30 mL) butter
¼ cup	(60 mL) French (dry) shallots, finely sliced
½ cup	(125 mL) tomatoes, diced
2 tbsp	(30 mL) chopped parsley
½ tsp	(2 mL) thyme
1	garlic clove, finely sliced
¾ cup	(180 mL) white wine
⅓ cup	(80 mL) orange juice
1 cup	(250 mL) 35% cream
4 tsp	(20 mL) tomato paste
	salt and pepper

■ Scrub and rinse mussels well.

■ In a large saucepan, melt butter and cook shallots with tomatoes, parsley, thyme and garlic over low heat. Add white wine, orange juice and mussels. Cover and cook over high heat until mussels open.

■ With a skimmer, remove mussels and put them in individual bowls.

■ Reduce cooking liquid by ⅓, then add cream and cook until sauce is smooth. Add tomato paste, season with salt and pepper and pour over mussels.

FISH MOUSSES AND LOAVES

Fish mousses and loaves may be served as a first or main course. They are easy to shape because of their consistency, and can be very decorative. However, as they tend to be somewhat on the dry side, we recommend serving them with a sauce.

Fish Log

Use a piece of frozen rather than fresh fish for this recipe. The loaf will be just as tasty but far more economical.

4 servings

10	cooked potatoes
	salt and pepper
2 tbsp	(30 mL) butter
1	onion, finely chopped
2 tbsp	(30 mL) chopped parsley
1 lb	(450 g) cooked fish
	water
1	egg white, beaten

Spicy Sauce

3 tbsp	(45 mL) butter
1	onion, finely chopped
1	garlic clove, finely sliced
½ cup	(125 mL) ketchup
½ cup	(125 mL) water
1 tsp	(5 mL) Worcestershire sauce
1 tbsp	(15 mL) vinegar
¾ tsp	(3 mL) sugar

■ Preheat oven to 375 °F (190 °C).

■ Make a thick potato purée and season with salt and pepper.

■ In a skillet, melt butter, then sauté and stir together onions, parsley, and fish. Stir mixture into potato purée.

■ Spread mixture on a sheet of waxed paper and roll to shape, then remove waxed paper.

■ In a bowl, add a small amount of water to beaten egg and coat log with this mixture, then bake for 20 minutes or until log becomes golden.

■ Serve with spicy sauce.

Spicy Sauce
■ In a saucepan, melt butter, then sauté onion, add other ingredients and let mixture simmer for approximately 30 minutes.

Salmon Mousseline with Mushrooms in Sauce

You can bake the mousseline in individual ramekins or in a small decorative mold to be turned out onto a serving dish.

4 servings	
4 tsp	(20 mL) butter
1 cup	(250 mL) mushrooms, cut into wedges
1 tbsp	(15 mL) flour
⅓ cup	(80 mL) white wine
	salt and pepper

Mousse

½ lb	(225 g) fresh salmon, finely chopped
	salt and pepper
4	eggs
1 ¼ cups	(310 mL) 35% cream
4 tsp	(20 mL) tomato paste

■ Preheat oven to 350 °F (175 °C).

■ In a skillet, melt butter and cook, but do not brown, mushrooms until liquid has completely evaporated.

■ Add flour and stir, then pour wine over mixture. Season with salt and pepper and cook until mixture thickens. Remove from heat, then let stand to cool and refrigerate.

■ Put chopped salmon into mixer and season with salt and pepper. Add eggs, one at a time then pour cream in a thin trickle, add tomato paste and mix until slightly thick. Set mousseline aside.

■ Coat bottom and sides of 4 ramekins with butter, fill to half with mousseline, then add a little of the mushrooms and sauce, and cover with rest of mousseline.

■ Place ramekins in a baking dish containing 1 inch (2,5 cm) water. Cover ramekins with aluminum foil and bake 35 to 40 minutes. Serve with White Butter Sauce (p. 457).

243

FISH AND SHELLFISH MARINATED AND SMOKED

Dill-marinated Baby Salmon

Why not try marinating fish yourself? It's so easy, you'll be pleasantly surprised!

4 servings

Marinade

1 tsp	(5 mL) salt
1 tbsp	(15 mL) sugar
2 tsp	(10 mL) black pepper, crushed
5 tsp	(25 mL) fresh dill, chopped
¼ cup	(60 mL) lemon juice
¼ cup	(60 mL) olive oil
1	baby salmon, 1 lb (450 g), skinned and cut into fillets
1	onion, sliced
1	lemon, sliced
	sour cream
	chives

■ In a small bowl, combine all marinade ingredients.

■ Place fillets side by side in a dish, outer side up, and baste with marinade. Refrigerate 4 to 6 hours, turning every hour.

■ Cut fillets into long, thin slices, garnish with onion rings, lemon slices, capers, sour cream and chives.

Marinated Scallop Flower

The marinade "cooks" the scallops in just a few hours. Take them out of the refrigerator 30 minutes before serving.

4 servings

1 lb	(450 g) fresh scallops
⅓ cup	(80 mL) lime juice
1	garlic clove, finely sliced
¼ cup	(60 mL) olive oil
3 tbsp	(45 mL) tomato, diced
5 tsp	(25 mL) chopped parsley
2 tbsp	(30 mL) French (dry) shallots, chopped
	salt and pepper
	salmon caviar

■ Cut scallops into thin slices.

■ In a bowl, combine other ingredients except for salmon caviar, then add scallops to mixture, cover with plastic wrap, and marinate for 4 hours in refrigerator.

■ Arrange in the shape of a flower in a serving dish and garnish with salmon caviar.

Classic Smoked Salmon

Put a pepper mill and a jug of pure olive oil on the table, and let your family or guests help themselves.

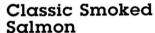

4 servings	
24	slices smoked salmon
1	onion, sliced
8	small pickles, finely sliced
2 tbsp	(30 mL) capers
12	pearl onions
	parsley bouquet

■ Place salmon slices in a serving dish and garnish with other ingredients, then serve.

Smoked Trout in Avocados

You'll find smoked trout (as well as smoked mackerel) in any gourmet shop.

4 servings	
2	avocados, halved
2	fillets of trout, cut into bite-size pieces
2 tbsp	(30 mL) mayonnaise
¼ cup	(60 mL) sweet red pepper, diced
2 tsp	(10 mL) lime juice
	salt and pepper
2	endives, finely sliced
1	lime, sliced

■ Remove half the pulp from avocado halves and dice.

■ Mix together all other ingredients except for endives and lime slices, then stuff avocado halves with this mixture.

■ Serve on a bed of finely sliced endive leaves and garnish with lime slices.

245

VEGETABLES

Folk wisdom has always attributed healing properties to vegetables. A potato in the pocket is said to ward off rheumatism, for instance, and a mushroom tonic will guarantee long life.

Modern research indicates that the healing or preventive properties of certain vegetables are real. Many studies point out, for example, that eating vegetables from the cabbage family can help prevent cancer. However true this may or may not be, there is no doubt that vegetables should figure high on the list in any well-balanced meal.

ARTICHOKES

From top to bottom:
Artichoke Lily • Cheese-stuffed
Artichoke Bottoms • Paté-stuffed
Artichoke Bottoms

Artichoke Lily

4 servings

4 tsp	(20 mL)	salt
2 tbsp	(30 mL)	flour
2 tbsp	(30 mL)	lemon juice
5 tbsp	(75 mL)	milk
4		artichokes
⅓ cup	(80 mL)	vinaigrette or mayonnaise
1		tomato, diced

■ In a saucepan filled with water, combine salt, flour, lemon juice, and milk. Beat ingredients with a wire whisk and bring to a boil. Add artichokes and cook until artichoke stems are tender or until tip of knife glides easily through artichoke bottom. Let stand to cool.

■ Arrange outer leaves in a circle on a large dish. Remove the hairy part of the heart, then peel slightly. Dice the heart and the bottom and toss the pieces in vinaigrette or mayonnaise. Put the diced artichoke in the center of the dish, and spoon vinaigrette or mayonnaise over the outer leaves.

■ Top the "lily" with diced tomatoes.

Cheese-stuffed Artichoke Bottoms

4 servings

12	canned artichoke bottoms
1 cup	(250 mL) cheese spread
2	round slices tomatoes, cut into 6 wedges each
3	black olives, cut into wedges
12	small celery leaves

■ Fill artichoke bottoms with cheese spread, then garnish each with 1 tomato wedge, 1 olive wedge and 1 celery leaf.

Paté-stuffed Artichoke Bottoms

4 servings

12	canned artichoke bottoms
1 cup	(250 mL) pâté or mousse de foie gras
6	small pickles, sliced in fans

■ Fill artichoke bottoms with pâté or mousse. Garnish with fan-shaped pickles and serve.

Fresh artichokes, steamed and coated with melted butter or a salad dressing, are quite delicious. When not in season, you can buy canned artichoke hearts or bottoms.

Artichoke Hearts Marinated with Olives

2 ½ cups (625 mL)

12	canned artichoke hearts
12	black olives
12	green olives
½ cup	(125 mL) olive oil
1 tsp	(5 mL) ground coriander
1 tsp	(5 mL) garlic, finely sliced
4 tsp	(20 mL) chopped parsley
½ tsp	(2 mL) thyme
1 tsp	(5 mL) oregano
1	bay leaf
2 tbsp	(30 mL) vinegar
1	sweet red pepper, diced
	lettuce leaves
	garlic croûtons

■ In a large bowl, combine all ingredients except lettuce leaves and garlic croûtons and cover with plastic wrap. Refrigerate and marinate for 24 hours.

■ Arrange on a bed of lettuce leaves and garnish with garlic croûtons.

Egg-stuffed Artichoke Bottoms

4 servings

4	hard-boiled eggs, chopped
2 tbsp	(30 mL) mayonnaise
12	canned artichoke bottoms
36	capers
36	pink peppercorns

■ In a bowl, mix together hard-boiled eggs and mayonnaise, then spoon mixture into artichoke bottoms. Garnish with capers and pink peppercorns.

Tuna-stuffed Artichoke Bottoms

4 servings

6 ½ oz	(184 g) canned, flaked tuna
1 tbsp	(15 mL) mayonnaise
1 tsp	(5 mL) chili sauce
12	canned artichoke bottoms
2	round lemon slices, cut into 6 wedges each
12	small parsley sprigs
12	baby shrimp

■ In a bowl, combine tuna, mayonnaise, and chili sauce. Spoon mixture into artichoke bottoms. Garnish each with lemon wedges and parsley. Place 1 baby shrimp on each artichoke.

From top to bottom:
Artichoke Hearts Marinated with Olives ▪ Egg-stuffed Artichoke Bottoms ▪ Tuna-stuffed Artichoke Bottoms

249

ASPARAGUS

Asparagus Glazed with Sorrel

4 servings	
24	asparagus spears, cooked
1 tbsp	(15 mL) commercial sorrel purée
⅓ cup	(80 mL) hollandaise sauce

■ Place asparagus spears on 4 plates.

■ Mix together sorrel purée and hollandaise sauce in a small bowl. Pour sauce over bottom ends of the asparagus, leaving top visible.

VARIATION

• **Replace sorrel with a purée of basil or tomato paste.**

Danish Asparagus Tips

4 servings	
36	asparagus tips
2 tbsp	(30 mL) orange juice
½ cup	(125 mL) plain yogurt
4 tsp	(20 mL) chives
8	slices of smoked salmon
	salt and pepper
4	lettuce leaves
1	hard-boiled egg, sliced
	orange wedges

■ In a saucepan filled with lightly salted boiling water, cook asparagus tips for 5 minutes, then rinse under cold water. Drain and set aside.

■ In a bowl, combine orange juice, yogurt, chives, and 4 chopped smoked salmon slices. Season lightly with salt and pepper.

■ Garnish each of 4 plates with a lettuce leaf. Place asparagus tips on top. Coat with sauce and set aside.

■ Julienne 4 smoked salmon slices and spread over asparagus tips. Garnish with hard-boiled egg and orange wedges.

VARIATION

• **Replace smoked salmon with smoked trout or smoked sturgeon.**

Asparagus Glazed with Sorrel
Danish Asparagus Tips

However it is finally served, asparagus must first be steamed or boiled. Green asparagus breaks easily and has the most flavor. White and purple asparagus can also be found in vegetable markets.

Asparagus Tips Mousseline
Asparagus with Citrus Fruit

Asparagus Tips Mousseline

4 servings		
2 tbsp	(30 mL)	whipped cream
1 tsp	(5 mL)	chopped parsley
24		cooked asparagus tips
1/3 cup	(80 mL)	hollandaise sauce

■ Preheat broiler.

■ In a bowl, mix hollandaise sauce, whipped cream, and chopped parsley.

■ Place asparagus tips in a baking dish and coat with sauce mixture.

■ Broil until golden.

Asparagus with Citrus Fruit

4 servings		
2		oranges
1		white grapefruit
1		pink grapefruit
1/4 cup	(60 mL)	mayonnaise
1 cup	(250 mL)	lettuce, finely shredded
24		asparagus spears, cooked

■ Peel fruit, including white underskin. Separate into small segments. Keep juice.

■ In a bowl, mix together mayonnaise and fruit juice and set aside.

■ Spread shredded lettuce on 4 salad plates and top with 6 asparagus on each.

■ With a pastry bag and fine nozzle attachment, pipe a ribbon of mayonnaise diagonally across asparagus spears. Garnish with citrus fruit segments.

EGGPLANT

Eggplant and Tomato Torte

about 2 cups (500 mL)

¼ cup	(60 mL) salted boiling water
1	large eggplant, peeled, sliced
3 tbsp	(45 mL) onion, chopped
2	eggs, beaten
1 cup	(250 mL) breadcrumbs
2 tbsp	(30 mL) butter, melted
½ tsp	(2 mL) oregano
4	large tomatoes, sliced
¼ cup	(60 mL) grated Cheddar cheese
¼ cup	(60 mL) grated Parmesan cheese
1 tsp	(5 mL) paprika

■Preheat oven to 375 °F (190 °C).

■ Place eggplant slices in a skillet, filled with lightly salted boiling water, then cover, cook for 10 minutes and drain.

■ In a bowl, purée eggplant, onion, eggs, breadcrumbs, butter, and oregano.

■ In a buttered baking dish, spread a layer of tomatoes. Cover with a thick layer of eggplant purée, then spread a second layer of tomatoes. Top with grated cheeses and sprinkle with paprika. Bake for 45 minutes.

Eggplant Sautéed with Onions

about 2 cups (500 mL)

2 tbsp	(30 mL) oil
1	medium-size eggplant, unpeeled, diced
½ cup	(125 mL white onion, sliced
½ cup	(125 mL) red onion, sliced
¼ cup	(60 mL) pearl onions, halved
1	garlic clove, finely sliced
	salt and pepper
2 tsp	(10 mL) chopped parsley
½ tsp	(2 mL) chopped basil
½ cup	(125 mL) tomato juice

■ In a skillet, heat oil and sauté eggplant with white and red onion for approximately 5 minutes, stirring constantly.

■ Add pearl onions and garlic, season with salt and pepper, sprinkle with basil and parsley and stir. Coat mixture with tomato juice and cook over low heat for 3 minutes.

Eggplant and Tomato Torte
Eggplant Sautéed with Onions

The eggplant or aubergine has a shiny purple skin and a cream-colored flesh with a distinctive flavor that blends well with tomato and zucchini. It absorbs all fatty elements, so make sure your skillet is only lightly coated with butter or oil.

Eggplant and Tomatoes with Tarragon

about 3 cups (750 mL)		
1		medium-size eggplant, peeled, cubed
5 tbsp	(75 mL)	oil
1		garlic clove, finely sliced
1/2 tsp	(2 mL)	salt
1		very small hot red pepper
3		medium-size onions, sliced
3		large canned tomatoes
1 tsp	(5 mL)	sugar
1 tbsp	(15 mL)	vinegar
2 tsp	(10 mL)	fresh tarragon, chopped

■ In a saucepan filled with lightly salted boiling water, cook eggplant for 5 minutes, then drain.

■ In a skillet, heat oil. Add garlic, salt and hot red pepper, then stir in the onion and cook until slightly golden. Add eggplant, tomatoes, and sugar and bring to a boil.

■ Pour vinegar over mixture. Cover and cook over very low heat for 1 hour, stirring every 10 minutes. Adjust seasoning. Let stand to cool, then refrigerate.

■ Sprinkle with tarragon, and serve.

Eggplant and Tomatoes with Tarragon
Baked Eggplant

Baked Eggplant

4 servings		
1		large eggplant, cut into 12 slices
2 tbsp	(30 mL)	olive oil
		salt and pepper
1 cup	(250 mL)	zucchini, sliced
		sliced tomatoes
3		slices Mozzarella cheese, each cut into 4 slices

■ Preheat oven to 350 °F (175 °C).

■ Baste eggplant slices with oil and place in a baking dish. Season with salt and pepper. Garnish each slice with 3 zucchini slices. Season with salt and pepper. Top with sliced tomatoes and baste with oil. Season with salt and pepper.

■ Bake in oven for 12 minutes. Spread Mozzarella cheese slices over vegetables and bake 3 minutes longer or until cheese begins to melt.

AVOCADO

California Avocado

4 servings

2	avocados
1	cucumber, peeled and sliced
2	pink grapefruit, cut into segments
1	orange, cut into segments
1/3 lb	(150 g) cooked shrimp
1/2 cup	(125 mL) mayonnaise
2 tbsp	(30 mL) chives
1 tbsp	(15 mL) ketchup
	Tabasco sauce, to taste
	salt and pepper
	chives (optional)
	celery seeds (optional)
	lemon slices

■ Slice avocados in half and scoop out pulp without damaging shell, then cut pulp into pieces and set aside.

■ In a bowl, combine all other ingredients except for the chives, celery seeds and lemon. Add avocado pulp, fill shells with mixture and garnish with chives, celery seeds or lemon slices.

Marinated Avocado

about 1 cup (250 mL)

2	avocados, fairly firm
1/4 cup	(60 mL) olive oil
2 tbsp	(30 mL) wine vinegar
1 tsp	(5 mL) sugar
1/2	garlic clove, finely sliced
1/2 tsp	(2 mL) shallot, finely sliced
2 tsp	(10 mL) chopped parsley
	juice of 1 lemon
2	endives, separated into leaves

■ Peel and slice avocados and place in a bowl.

■ In a separate bowl, combine all other ingredients, except endive leaves. Pour mixture over avocado slices, refrigerate to marinate for 2 hours.

■ Serve on a bed of endive leaves.

California Avocado
Marinated Avocado

The avocado is, in fact, a fruit, although we use it as a vegetable. There are several varieties, including those with smooth and shiny green skins, and the rougher brownish-black type. All ripe avocados have a beautiful pale green pulp that is easily removed from the skin and stone. A warning to the diet-conscious: avocados have a high fat content.

Avocado with Mixed Vegetables

6 servings		
¼ cup	(60 mL) cauliflower, in small flowerets	
¼ cup	(60 mL) broccoli, in small flowerets	
¼ cup	(60 mL) sweet red peppers, finely diced	
¼ cup	(60 mL) sweet yellow peppers, finely diced	
¼ cup	(60 mL) peas	
¼ cup	(60 mL) carrots, diced	
¼ cup	(60 mL) celery, finely sliced	
¼ cup	(60 mL) red onion, finely sliced	
3	avocados	
¾ cup	180 mL) sour cream	
12	dill leaves	

■ In a saucepan filled with lightly salted boiling water, blanch vegetables for 4 minutes, drain and refrigerate.

■ Slice avocados in half, remove the stone. Cut fine grooves in pulp, without separating the flesh from the skin.

■ In a bowl, combine sour cream and blanched vegetables and spoon mixture into avocado halves. Garnish with dill leaves.

"Guacamole" (Avocado Purée)

about 2 cups (500 mL)		
4	ripe avocados, peeled	
¼ tsp	(1 mL) Tabasco sauce	
4 tsp	(20 mL) lemon juice	
4 tsp	(20 mL) parsley	
	salt and pepper	
1	tomato, diced	
1	cucumber, sliced	
8	tortillas (or chips, or raw vegetables)	

■ In a bowl, purée avocados, then add Tabasco sauce, lemon juice, parsley, salt and pepper. Garnish with tomatoes and cucumbers.

■ Stuff tortillas with mixture or serve as dip with chips or raw vegetables.

Avocado with Mixed Vegetables
"Guacamole" (Avocado Purée)

BEETS

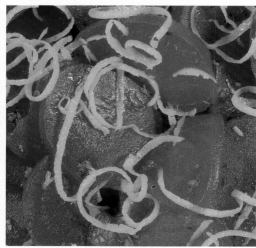

From Top to Bottom:
Buttered Beet Valentines ▪
Beets with Tarragon and
Lemon ▪ *Beets in Spinach*

Buttered Beet Valentines

about 1 ½ cups (375 mL)

4	large beets
3 tbsp	(45 mL) butter
	salt and pepper
2 tbsp	(30 mL) parsley

▪ In a saucepan filled with lightly salted boiling water, cook beets for 1 hour, then drain.

▪ Slice beets and carve each slice into a heart shape.

▪ In a skillet, melt butter and gently sauté beet hearts. Season with salt and pepper. Garnish with parsley and serve.

Beets with Tarragon and Lemon

about 3 cups (875 mL)

24	small new beets, with 2 inch (5 cm) stems, washed
⅓ cup	(80 mL) butter
1 tsp	(5 mL) tarragon, chopped
½ tsp	(2 mL) finely grated lemon peel
2 tsp	(10 mL) lemon juice
	salt and pepper
1 tbsp	(15 mL) chopped parsley

▪ Place beets in a saucepan filled with lightly salted boiling water, cover and cook for 30 minutes or until tender. Drain, rinse under cold water, then gently remove skin and cut stems and roots.

▪ In a heavy skillet, heat butter over medium heat until foamy, then add beets, tarragon, lemon peel and juice. Season with salt and pepper. Place in a warm serving dish. Garnish with parsley and serve.

Beets in Spinach

about 2 cups (500 mL)

16	small beets
16	large spinach leaves
	salt and pepper
2 tbsp	(30 mL) melted butter

▪ In a saucepan filled with lightly salted boiling water, cook beets for approximately 30 minutes.

▪ Remove stems from spinach leaves and blanch leaves for 30 seconds.

▪ Spread spinach leaves flat on a cutting board. Place 1 beet on each spinach leaf, season with salt and pepper. Wrap each beet in its spinach leaf, baste leaves with melted butter and serve.

The ruby-colored beet brightens any table. It has the advantage of keeping well in cool, dry conditions, retaining its color and food value right through the winter. Beet greens can be prepared like spinach. Cook beets in their skins to preserve their distinctive color and flavor.

Marinated Beets

---
about 1 cup (250 mL)

4	beets, cooked
½ cup	(125 mL) water
1 cup	(250 mL) wine vinegar
2 tsp	(10 mL) sugar
½ tsp	(2 mL) salt
	pinch of chopped chives
	pinch of chopped tarragon
	pinch of chopped fennel
	mayonnaise, to taste

■ In a saucepan filled with lightly salted boiling water, cook beets, then drain and cut into sticks. Place in a bowl and set aside.

■ In a separate saucepan, combine water, wine vinegar, sugar, salt, and herbs and bring to a boil. Let mixture boil for 1 minute.

■ Pour mixture over beets. Let mixture marinate at least 2 hours. Serve with mayonnaise.

Beets and Red Cabbage

---
about 1 cup (250 mL)

2	beets, cooked "al dente"
½ cup	(125 mL) red cabbage, grated
2 tbsp	(30 mL) red wine
	salt and pepper
2 tbsp	(30 mL) butter
½	garlic clove, finely sliced

■ Cut beets into small sticks.

■ In a bowl, combine red cabbage and wine. Season with salt and pepper.

■ In a skillet, melt butter and sauté garlic, then add beets and cabbage.

■ Stir mixture. Cook over low heat for 5 minutes.

Beets with Garlic and Sesame Seeds

---
about 1 cup (250 mL)

4	large beets, cooked
2 tbsp	(30 mL) butter
1	garlic clove, chopped
2 tbsp	(30 mL) sesame seeds
1 tbsp	(15 mL) chopped parsley
	salt and pepper

■ Slice beets into sticks.

■ In a skillet, melt butter and sauté beet sticks with garlic for 2 minutes.

■ Add sesame seeds, parsley, salt and pepper and stir gently.

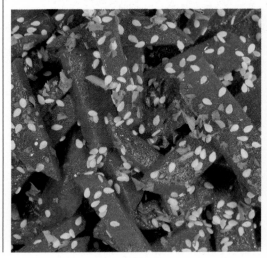

From Top to Bottom: Marinated Beets ▪ Beets and Red Cabbage ▪ Beets with Garlic and Sesame Seeds

Broccoli

Breaded Broccoli Fritters with Tartare Sauce

about 3 cups (750 mL)	
1	broccoli, cut into flowerets, 1 inch (2,5 cm) in diameter

Batter

½ cup	(125 mL) flour
1 cup	(250 mL) beer or water
2 tbsp	(30 mL) melted butter
	pinch of salt
1	egg yolk
1	egg white, salted and beaten into stiff peaks

■ Preheat deep-fryer to 400 °F (205 °C).

■ In a saucepan filled with lightly salted boiling water, cook broccoli for 4 minutes. Rinse under cold water, drain and set aside.

■ In a bowl, mix batter ingredients together (except egg white) with a wooden spoon, and stir until smooth. Gently fold in egg white, beaten into stiff peaks.

■ Dip 6 or 7 broccoli flowerets into batter and cook in deep-fryer. Remove and drain on paper towel. Serve with tartare sauce.

Broccoli with Almonds

about 2 cups (500 mL)	
2 tbsp	(30 mL) butter
3 tbsp	(45 mL) slivered almonds
3 tbsp	(45 mL) 35% cream
	salt and pepper
1 ½ cups	(375 mL) cooked broccoli, cut into flowerets

■ In a skillet, melt butter and lightly cook almonds until golden. Pour cream into mixture, season with salt and pepper and let liquid reduce to half.

■ Meanwhile, heat broccoli flowerets in boiling water, then drain.

■ Arrange broccoli flowerets in a crown, then pour cream and almond mixture over the crown.

Broccoli is a close cousin of cauliflower. The most obvious difference is the green or purplish flowerets. Choose broccoli with straight stalks and compact heads. Before cooking, peel the stalks so that they will cook in the same time as the more tender flowerets. If you cut the stalks off, chop them into chunks and freeze them for later use in a delicious cream of vegetable soup.

Broccoli with Cheddar and Mustard

about 2 ½ cups (625 mL)	
1 ½ cups	(375 mL) broccoli, cut into flowerets, cooked
1 cup	(250 mL) béchamel sauce
¼ cup	(60 mL) grated Cheddar cheese
4 tsp	(20 mL) Dijon mustard
	breadcrumbs
2 tbsp	(30 mL) melted butter

■ Preheat oven to 425 °F (220 °C).

■ In an au gratin dish, arrange broccoli flowerets and set aside.

■ Prepare béchamel sauce. Add mustard and half the cheese and pour mixture over broccoli. Sprinkle with other half of cheese and breadcrumbs, then coat with melted butter.

■ Bake in oven for 10 minutes or until top becomes slightly golden.

Broccoli with Sesame Seeds

about 1 ½ cups (375 mL)	
1 ½ cups	(375 mL) broccoli, cut into flowerets
1 tsp	(5 mL) butter
2 tbsp	(30 mL) sesame seeds
	salt and pepper
	knobs of butter
1	lemon slices, cut into wedges

■ In a saucepan filled with lightly salted boiling water, blanch broccoli for 4 minutes then let stand to cool, drain and set aside.

■ In a skillet, melt butter and cook sesame seeds until golden.

■ Place broccoli flowerets in microwave-safe dish. Sprinkle with sesame seeds, season with salt and pepper. Place a knob of butter on each floweret, then cook in microwave at HIGH for 1 minute. Garnish with lemon wedges.

CARROTS

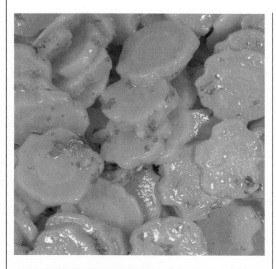

Vichy Carrots

about 2 cups (500 mL)

2 cups	(500 mL) carrots, sliced
2 tsp	(10 mL) granulated sugar
2 tbsp	(30 mL) butter
2 tsp	(10 mL) chopped parsley
¼ tsp	(1 mL) ground black pepper

■ Place sliced carrots in a saucepan, cover with lightly salted water, add sugar, butter, parsley and pepper and bring to a boil. Cook "al dente," then drain, adjust seasoning and serve.

VARIATION
• **Boil carrots in mineral water of your choice.**

Carrots with Chives

about 2 cups (500 mL)

2 tbsp	(30 mL) butter
2 tsp	(10 mL) honey
2 cups	(500 mL) carrots, cut into sticks, blanched for 3 minutes
2 tsp	(10 mL) finely sliced chives
	salt and pepper

■ In a skillet, melt butter and add honey.

■ Sauté carrots in this mixture for 3 minutes.

■ Sprinkle with chives, season with salt and pepper, and serve.

Carrot Sticks with Tarragon

about 2 cups (500 mL)

2 cups	(500 mL) carrots, cut into thin sticks
2 tsp	(10 mL) granulated sugar
2 tbsp	(30 mL) butter
2 tsp	(10 mL) tarragon, chopped
	salt and pepper

■ Follow same recipe as Vichy Carrots and replace parsley with tarragon.

From top to bottom:
Vichy Carrots ▪ Carrots with
Chives ▪ Carrot Sticks with
Tarragon

Carrots are an excellent source of vitamin A. These succulent and colorful root vegetables go well with numerous dishes. Young carrots don't even need peeling: a good scraping and rinsing is enough. Prepare carrots just before cooking, if you want to retain all the vitamins.

Carrots and Onions au Gratin

about 6 cups (1,5 L)

| 1 cup | (250 mL) onions, finely sliced |
| 2 cups | (500 mL) carrots, diagonally sliced |

Seasoned Flour

3 tbsp	(45 mL) flour
1 tsp	(5 mL) salt
1/2 tsp	(2 mL) pepper
1 tsp	(5 mL) savory

1 cup	(250 mL) broccoli, cut into flowerets
1 cup	(250 mL) grated Cheddar cheese or Emmenthal cheese
2	potatoes, sliced
1 cup	(250 mL) milk

■ Preheat oven to 375 °F (190 °C).

■ Lightly butter a baking dish. Spread half the onions and half the carrots in the bottom of the baking dish and set aside.

■ In a bowl, mix together seasoned flour ingredients, then sprinkle 1/3 this mixture over carrots and onions. Cover this mixture with rest of carrots and onions, and sprinkle with another 1/3 of seasoned flour.

■ Place broccoli flowerets over mixture and sprinkle with 1/3 cheese, then with rest of seasoned flour and again with 1/3 cheese. Add sliced potatoes and coat with milk. Cover and bake for 45 minutes.

■ Sprinkle baked mixture with rest of cheese and bake, uncovered, for another 15 minutes.

Carrot Salad

about 4 cups (1 L)

2 lbs	(900 g) carrots, thinly sliced in rounds
1	green bell pepper, finely sliced
8 oz	(237 mL) canned cream of tomato soup
3/4 cup	(180 mL) white vinegar
1 cup	(250 mL) sugar
1/2 cup	(125 mL) vegetable oil
1 tsp	(5 mL) Worcestershire sauce
1 tsp	(5 mL) dry mustard
	salt and pepper

■ Cook carrots "al dente" in a saucepan filled with lightly salted boiling water. Drain.

■ In a salad bowl, mix together all other ingredients. Add carrots, then place in a serving dish.

Dijon Carrots

about 2 cups (500 mL)

1 1/2 cups	(375 mL) carrots, sliced in rounds
2 tbsp	(30 mL) butter
5 tbsp	(75 mL) onions, finely sliced
4 tsp	(20 mL) flour
1/2 cup	(125 mL) milk
1 tbsp	(15 mL) strong mustard
	salt and pepper
2 tbsp	(30 mL) chopped parsley

■ Cook carrots in a saucepan filled with lightly salted boiling water. Drain.

■ In a skillet, over low heat, melt butter and sauté onions for 2 minutes. Add carrots and flour and stir.

■ Pour milk slowly into mixture and stir until thickened. Add mustard, salt and pepper and stir.

■ Heat for a few minutes, sprinkle with parsley and serve.

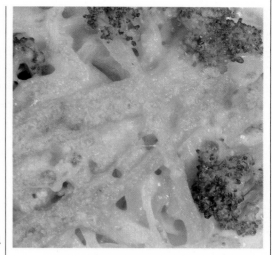

From Top to Bottom:
Carrots and Onions au Gratin ▪
Carrot Salad ▪ Dijon Carrots

CELERY

Braised Celery

4 servings

2	celery hearts, cut in half
2 tsp	(10 mL) butter
2 cups	(500 mL) chicken stock
	salt and pepper
	pinch of nutmeg

■ In a saucepan filled with lightly salted boiling water, blanch celery for 5 minutes, then drain and set aside.

■ In a skillet, melt butter and cook celery gently for 2 minutes. Fill half the skillet with chicken stock, season with salt, pepper, and nutmeg, then cover partially and braise for 15 minutes.

Celery with Fennel Seeds

about 1 ½ cups (375 mL)

1 ½ cups	(375 mL) celery, finely sliced
1 tbsp	(15 mL) butter
1 tsp	(5 mL) fennel seeds
	salt and pepper

■ In a saucepan filled with lightly salted boiling water, blanch celery for 3 minutes, then drain and set aside.

■ In a skillet, melt butter and sauté fennel seeds until golden. Add celery and sauté for 2 minutes. Season with salt and pepper.

Braised Celery
Celery with Fennel Seeds

Celery is available all year round, but you'll find the quality better during winter months. Choose bunches with green leaves and tightly-packed, pale green or white stalks. The darker the stalks, the stringier the celery. Don't throw away any part of this useful vegetable. The stronger-tasting leaves and outer stalks are good for adding a pleasant tang to salads, thick soups, and stocks.

Celery Fricassée with Mornay Sauce

about 1 cup (250 mL)

1 ¼ cups	(300 mL) celery, finely sliced
2 tbsp	(30 mL) butter
4 tsp	(20 mL) flour
½ cup	(125 mL) milk
	salt and pepper
	pinch of nutmeg
	cayenne pepper, to taste
2	egg yolks
5 tbsp	(75 mL) grated cheese
1 tsp	(5 mL) parsley

■ Preheat broiler.

■ In a saucepan filled with lightly salted boiling water, cook celery for 7 minutes, drain and set aside.

■ In a cast-iron saucepan, melt butter and lightly sauté celery. Add flour and stir for 1 minute.

■ Add milk, season with salt, pepper, nutmeg, and cayenne pepper and cook until mixture thickens. Add egg yolks and cheese and stir.

■ Place mixture in an oven-proof serving dish, sprinkle with parsley, broil for a few minutes until golden.

Home-style Celery

about 2 cups (500 mL)

	celery sticks, cut into 3-inch (7,5-cm) pieces

Sauce

8 oz	(237 mL) canned beef consommé
¼ cup	(60 mL) ketchup
1 tbsp	(15 mL) Worcestershire sauce
3 tbsp	(45 mL) cornstarch
3 tbsp	(45 mL) cold water
	parsley or tarragon, to taste

■ In a saucepan filled with lightly salted boiling water, cook celery "al dente" then drain, place in a serving dish and keep warm.

■ In a separate saucepan, combine beef consommé, ketchup and Worcestershire sauce and bring to a boil.

■ Meanwhile, in a bowl, dissolve cornstarch in water.

■ Add dissolved cornstarch to sauce and bring to a boil, stirring constantly. Let mixture boil for 2 minutes. Pour over celery, then garnish with parsley or tarragon and serve.

Celery Fricassée with Mornay Sauce
Home-style Celery

MUSHROOMS

Oyster Mushrooms Sautéed in Garlic

about 1 cup (250 mL)	
2 cups	(500 mL) oyster mushrooms
3 tbsp	(45 mL) butter
4 tsp	(20 mL) French (dry) shallots, chopped
1 tsp	(5 mL) garlic, finely sliced
4 tsp	(20 mL) chopped parsley
	salt and pepper
2 tbsp	(30 mL) white wine

■ Remove mushroom stems and slice the caps coarsely.

■ In a skillet, melt butter. Sauté oyster mushrooms for 2 minutes. Add shallots, garlic, and parsley, then season with salt and pepper. Cook 1 minute longer and stir. Add white wine, heat for 30 seconds and serve.

Creamed Mushrooms

about 2 cups (500 mL)	
3 tbsp	(45 mL) butter
1 ½ lbs	(675 g) mushrooms, cleaned, cut into segments
3	egg yolks
⅓ cup	(80 mL) 35% cream
	salt and pepper
¼ cup	(60 mL) grated Gruyère cheese

■ Preheat oven to 400 °F (205 °C).

■ In a skillet, melt butter and sauté mushrooms, stirring with a wooden spoon until liquid evaporates completely. Place mushrooms in a baking dish and set aside.

■ In a bowl, combine egg yolks, cream, salt, and pepper. Pour mixture over mushrooms. Sprinkle with Gruyère and bake for 10 to 15 minutes.

Remember that mushrooms don't like water. Wipe the caps with a damp cloth, and if they are really dirty, rinse them quickly in cold water and pat them completely dry. On the other hand, if you buy dried wild mushrooms, soak them in water before cooking, and they will regain their original shape and tenderness.

Stuffed Mushroom Caps

4 servings

24	large mushrooms
3 tbsp	(45 mL) butter
3 tbsp	(45 mL) carrots, diced
3 tbsp	(45 mL) zucchini, diced
1 tsp	(5 mL) garlic, finely sliced
1 tbsp	(15 mL) chopped parsley
4 tsp	(20 mL) breadcrumbs
	salt and pepper
6 oz	(170 mL) canned cream of mushroom soup
1 tsp	(5 mL) paprika

■ Preheat oven to 350 °F (175 °C).

■ Remove mushroom stems, finely chop and set aside.

■ In a skillet, melt butter and sauté mushroom stems with diced carrots and zucchini. Add garlic, parsley and breadcrumbs, season with salt and pepper and cook for 3 minutes. Add cream of mushroom soup and cook a few minutes over medium heat.

■ Spoon mixture into mushroom caps. Sprinkle with paprika. Place stuffed mushroom caps on a lightly oiled baking sheet and bake for 12 minutes.

Tiny Mushroom Cake

4 servings

3 tbsp	(45 mL) butter
3 cups	(750 mL) mushrooms, cleaned, finely sliced
1 tbsp	(15 mL) white wine
4	eggs
¼ cup	(60 mL) grated cheese
¼ cup	(60 mL) 35% cream
	salt and pepper
2 tbsp	(30 mL) butter
8 oz	(237 mL) canned cream of mushroom soup

■ Preheat oven to 375 °F (190 °C).

■ In a skillet, melt butter and sauté mushrooms for 4 minutes. Pour wine over mushrooms and cook until liquid has completely evaporated.

■ Meanwhile, in a bowl, combine eggs, cheese, and cream. Season with salt and pepper.

■ Generously butter an oven-proof mold, then pour mushroom mixture into mold and bake, standing in a pan of water, for 35 minutes.

■ Remove from oven and let stand for 5 minutes. Flip over and unmold. Serve with heated cream of mushroom soup.

CABBAGE

Braised Cabbage with Sesame Seeds

about 2 cups (500 mL)

3 tbsp	(45 mL) butter
4	drops sesame oil
1	red onion
2 cups	(500 mL) green cabbage, cut into thin strips
¼ cup	(60 mL) white wine
¼ cup	(60 mL) water
	juice of 1 lemon
1 tbsp	(15 mL) honey
2 tbsp	(30 mL) chopped parsley
2 tbsp	(30 mL) sesame seeds
	salt and pepper

■ In a skillet, melt butter and add the drops of sesame oil then sauté onion and cabbage. Stir, then reduce heat to low, cover and cook for 3 minutes.

■ Increase heat. Add wine, water, lemon juice, honey, parsley and sesame seeds. Season with salt and pepper and bring to a boil. Reduce heat to low, cover and simmer for 30 minutes, stirring from time to time.

Chinese Cabbage with Garlic

about 1 cup (250 mL)

3 tbsp	(45 mL) butter
2	garlic cloves, chopped
2 cups	(500 mL) Chinese cabbage, cut into fine strips
	salt and pepper
	chives, chopped

■ In a skillet, melt butter, and sauté garlic. Add cabbage and season. Continue cooking for 3 minutes. Garnish with chives and serve.

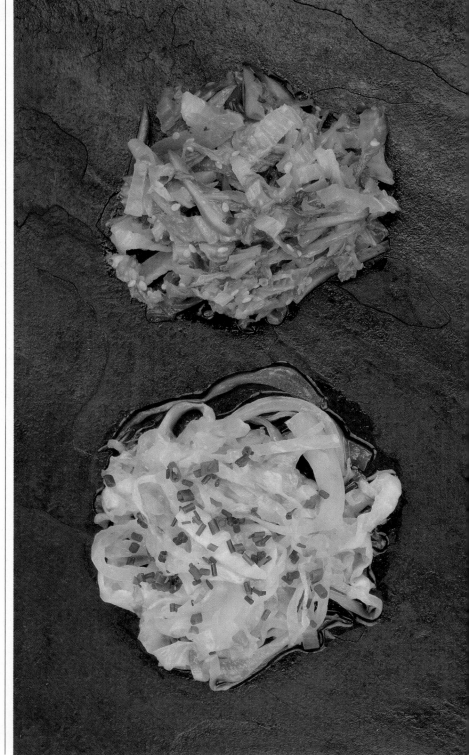

Braised Cabbage with Sesame Seeds
Chinese Cabbage with Garlic

Members of the large cabbage family differ as much in size as in color. Be sure you know whether the cooking time should be short or long, and avoid filling the house with the characteristically unpleasant sulphur odor of overcooked cabbage.

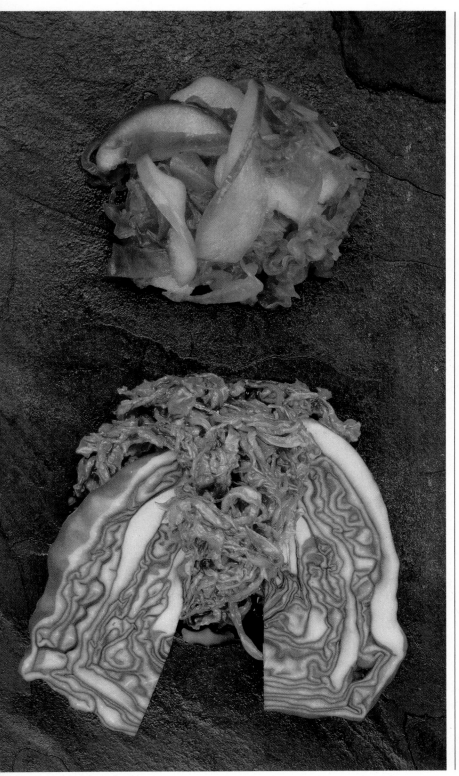

Red Cabbage and Apples

about 1 cup (250 mL)

1 cup	(250 mL) red cabbage, finely sliced
2 tbsp	(30 mL) butter
2	apples, finely sliced
1 tbsp	(15 mL) brown sugar
1 tbsp	(15 mL) vinegar

■ In a saucepan filled with lightly salted boiling water, cook red cabbage for 5 minutes, then drain.

■ In a skillet, melt butter and sauté red cabbage and apples. Add brown sugar and cook until mixture begins to caramelize, then add vinegar and serve.

Red Cabbage Marmalade

about 1 ½ cups (375 mL)

1 ½ cups	(375 mL) red cabbage, chopped
5 tbsp	(75 mL) sugar
2 tbsp	(30 mL) vinegar
¼ cup	(60 mL) red wine

■ In a stove-top casserole or heavy iron saucepan, combine all ingredients and bring to a boil, then reduce heat and simmer for about 30 minutes. Let stand to cool, then refrigerate.

■ Serve on canapés or with cold cuts.

Red Cabbage and Apples
Red Cabbage Marmalade

BRUSSELS SPROUTS

From Top to Bottom:
Sautéed Brussels Sprouts ▪
Brussels Sprouts with Tomatoes ▪
Brussels Sprouts with Leeks in
Butter

Sautéed Brussels Sprouts

about 2 cups (500 mL)

1 ½ cups	(375 mL) Brussels sprouts
2 tbsp	(30 mL) butter
	salt and pepper
	pinch of nutmeg
2 tsp	(10 mL) lemon juice
2 tbsp	(30 mL) chopped parsley

▪ Cut a cross on the base of each Brussels sprout and place in a saucepan filled with lightly salted boiling water. Cook for 20 minutes. Drain and set aside.

▪ In a skillet, melt butter and brown Brussels sprouts. Season with salt, pepper, and nutmeg. When butter turns slightly brown, add lemon juice and parsley.

Brussels Sprouts with Tomatoes

about 4 cups (1 L)

3 tbsp	(45 mL) butter
1	onion, chopped
1	garlic clove, finely sliced
½	green bell pepper, diced
14 oz	(398 mL) canned tomatoes
1 ½ cups	(375 mL) Brussels sprouts, halved
½ tsp	(2 mL) chopped basil
	salt and pepper

▪ In a skillet, melt butter over medium heat and sauté onion, garlic, and pepper for 4 minutes. Add tomatoes and Brussels sprouts.

▪ Season mixture with basil, salt, and pepper and bring to a boil. Cover and cook over low heat for 20 minutes.

Brussels Sprouts with Leeks in Butter

about 3 cups (750 mL)

3 cups	(375 mL) Brussels sprouts
1 cup	(250 mL) leeks, sliced
3 tbsp	(45 mL) butter
½ cup	(125 mL) onion, finely sliced
¼ cup	(60 mL) 15% cream

▪ In a saucepan filled with lightly salted boiling water, blanch Brussels sprouts and leeks for 4 minutes, then drain.

▪ In a skillet, melt butter and sauté Brussels sprouts with leeks over low heat for about 10 minutes.

▪ Add onions. Season with salt and pepper, then pour cream into mixture.

▪ Stir until mixture is smooth and creamy and cook for another 5 minutes.

Brussels sprouts must always be cooked. Cut the stems off, remove a few outer leaves, and soak them for a few minutes in water with a little vinegar.

Brussels Sprouts Flavored with Hazelnuts

about 2 cups (500 mL)

1 tbsp	(15 mL) butter
¼ cup	(60 mL) lardons or chopped bacon
1½ cups	(375 mL) Brussels sprouts
3 tbsp	(45 mL) ground hazelnuts
4 tsp	(20 mL) chopped parsley
	salt and pepper

■ In a skillet, melt butter and sauté lardons or bacon over medium heat for 3 minutes. Add Brussels sprouts, cover and cook for 7 minutes, stirring from time to time.

■ Add hazelnuts and parsley. Season with salt and pepper.

Green on Green

about 2 cups (500 mL)

8	Brussels sprouts, halved
½ cup	(125 mL) broccoli, cut into flowerets
½ cup	(60 mL) snow peas, finely sliced
4 tsp	(20 mL) butter
12 oz	(341 mL) canned green peas
	salt and pepper
	nutmeg
¼ cup	(60 mL) raw spinach, finely shredded

■ In a saucepan filled with lightly salted boiling water, blanch Brussels sprouts for 4 minutes. Add broccoli and snow peas and boil for 2 minutes. Drain under cold running water and set aside.

■ In a skillet, melt butter and sauté Brussels sprouts, snow peas and broccoli for 2 minutes, then add green peas, and season with salt, pepper, and nutmeg.

■ Add spinach just before serving.

Brussels Sprouts with Miniature Corn

about 3 cups (750 mL)

1 tbsp	(15 mL) butter
¼ cup	(60 mL) lardons or chopped bacon
1½ cups	(375 mL) Brussels sprouts
1 cup	(250 mL) miniature corn
3 tbsp	(45 mL) chopped hazelnuts
4 tsp	(20 mL) chopped parsley
	salt and pepper

■ Follow same method as recipe for Brussels Sprouts Flavored with Hazelnuts.

■ Add miniature corn to Brussels sprouts 2 minutes before end of cooking process.

From Top to Bottom:
Brussels Sprouts Flavored with Hazelnuts ▪ Green on Green
▪ Brussels Sprouts with Miniature Corn

CAULIFLOWER

Cauliflower au Gratin

about 3 cups (750 mL)

1	cauliflower, cut into flowerets, cooked
1 cup	(250 mL) béchamel sauce
¼ cup	(60 mL) grated Parmesan cheese

■ Preheat oven to broil.

■ Place cauliflower in a small au gratin dish, coat with béchamel sauce, sprinkle with Parmesan and cook au gratin for approximately 5 minutes.

Cauliflower with Saffron and Chives

about 1 cup (250 mL)

1 cup	(250 mL) cauliflower, cut into flowerets
	salt and pepper
	pinch of saffron
	or
1 tsp	(5 mL) curry powder
4 tsp	(20 mL) butter
4 tsp	(20 mL) chives

■ In a saucepan filled with lightly salted boiling water, cook cauliflower for 4 minutes with salt, pepper, saffron or curry powder. Remove from heat, and let mixture steep for 15 minutes, then drain.

■ In a skillet, melt butter and lightly sauté cauliflower. Add chives, stir and serve.

Cauliflower is the most easily digestible of all the members of the cabbage family. Choose a head that is very white, with tight, unspotted flowerets. Stalks that snap crisply are a sure sign of freshness.

Polish Cauliflower

about 2 cups (500 mL)

4 tsp	(20 mL) butter
1 ½ cups	(375 mL) cauliflower, cut into flowerets, cooked
	salt and pepper
3	hard-boiled eggs, chopped
4 tsp	(20 mL) fines herbes, chopped
4 tsp	(20 mL) breadcrumbs, lightly browned in butter

■ In a saucepan, melt butter and sauté cauliflower. Season with salt and pepper, then place in a serving dish. Sprinkle with chopped eggs, fines herbes and breadcrumbs.

Greek Cauliflower

about 4 cups (1 L)

2 tbsp	(30 mL) oil
¼ cup	(60 mL) carrots, diced
¼ cup	(60 mL) onions, finely sliced
¼ cup	(60 mL) celery, sliced diagonally
2 cups	(500 mL) cauliflower, cut into flowerets
½ cup	(125 mL) white wine
½ cup	(125 mL) water
1 cup	(250 mL) tomato juice
	salt and pepper
	pinch of thyme
1	bay leaf
	pinch of coriander
	juice of 1 lemon

■ In a skillet, heat oil and sauté but do not brown carrots, onions, and celery. Add cauliflower and sauté for 1 minute.

■ Pour white wine, water, and tomato juice into mixture. Add spices and lemon juice and bring to a boil. Remove from heat and let mixture stand in cooking juice.

CUCUMBERS

Marinated Cucumbers

3 to 4 servings

1	large cucumber, thinly sliced
1	tomato, diced
¼ cup	(60 mL) oil
2 tbsp	(30 mL) cider vinegar
	juice of ½ lemon
	salt and pepper
½ tsp	(2 mL) sugar
4	mint leaves, chopped

■ In a bowl, combine all ingredients and marinate for 2 hours. Arrange mixture on lettuce leaves and serve.

Sliced Cucumbers with Chives

4 servings

3 tbsp	(45 mL) butter
2	cucumbers, peeled, seeded, finely sliced
2 tbsp	(30 mL) chives
¼ cup	(60 mL) 35% cream
	salt and pepper
	pinch of nutmeg

■ In a skillet, melt butter and sauté cucumbers until they begin to shine.

■ Add other ingredients and heat over low heat, stirring constantly. Place in serving dish.

Marinated Cucumbers
Sliced Cucumbers with Chives

Cucumbers, often eaten raw, have a mild, refreshing taste. They contain lots of water and very few calories. Although they make an ideal salad food, they can be cooked in much the same way as squash or zucchini, in water, sautéed, baked or braised. They should be peeled and seeded before cooking.

Stuffed Cucumbers Bayaldi

4 servings

2	English cucumbers, peeled, cut into 1 ½ inch (3,75 cm) segments
4 tsp	(20 mL) olive oil
3	tomatoes, diced
2 tbsp	(30 mL) fresh mint
	salt and pepper

■ Blanch cucumbers for 2 minutes in salted boiling water. Rinse under cold water and drain.

■ Scoop out pulp of cucumbers and set aside.

■ In a skillet, heat oil and sauté tomatoes, then add mint and season with salt and pepper.

■ Spoon stuffing into cucumbers and place in a daisy steamer for 5 minutes.

Braised Cucumbers

2 servings

3 tbsp	(45 mL) butter
1	large cucumber, peeled, diced
	juice of 1 lemon
1 tsp	(5 mL) honey
½ tsp	(2 mL) paprika
	salt and pepper

■ In a skillet, melt butter and sauté cucumber for 2 minutes. Add other ingredients and stir.

■ Reduce heat to low, cover and braise slowly for another 5 minutes.

Stuffed Cucumbers Bayaldi
Braised Cucumbers

ZUCCHINI

Zucchini Sticks

about 1 cup (250 mL)

2	zucchini, cut into thin sticks
2 tbsp	(30 mL) butter
	salt and pepper

- In a saucepan filled with lightly salted boiling water, blanch zucchini for 30 seconds.

- In a skillet, melt butter and sauté zucchini, season with salt and pepper and serve.

Breaded Zucchini

about 1 cup (250 mL)

2	small zucchini
	seasoned flour
2	eggs, beaten
½ cup	(125 mL) breadcrumbs

- Heat deep-fryer to 425 °F (220 °C).

- Cut zucchini lengthwise into thin slices.

- In a saucepan filled with lightly salted boiling water, cook zucchini slices. Rinse under cold water, drain and pat dry.

- Dredge zucchini slices with seasoned flour, dip into beaten eggs, coat with breadcrumbs, then drop into hot oil and fry. Drain on paper towel.

Zucchini with Mustard Cream

about 1 cup (250 mL)

1 tbsp	(15 mL) butter
1 cup	(250 mL) zucchini, cut into thin sticks
2 tsp	(10 mL) old-fashioned mustard
¼ cup	(60 mL) 35% cream
	salt and pepper

- In a small skillet, heat butter and sauté zucchini sticks for 2 minutes.

- Add mustard seeds and cream, season with salt and pepper and simmer over low heat for 5 minutes.

From Top to Bottom: Zucchini Sticks ▪ Breaded Zucchini ▪ Zucchini with Mustard Cream

Zucchini is a form of squash much favored in Mediterranean cuisine. Tender zucchini doesn't need to be peeled before cooking.

Zucchini Pastilles

about 1 cup (250 mL)

2	zucchini, thinly sliced in rounds
2 tbsp	(30 mL) butter
	salt and pepper
¼ tsp	(1 mL) fennel seeds
½ tsp	(2 mL) chopped parsley

■ In a saucepan filled with lightly salted boiling water, blanch zucchini slices for 30 seconds, then drain and set aside.

■ In a skillet, melt butter and sauté zucchini slices. Season with salt and pepper. Add fennel seeds, sprinkle with parsley and serve.

Parmesan-flavored Zucchini

about 1 cup (250 mL)

2	zucchini, thinly sliced
½	sweet red pepper, cut into strips
2 tbsp	(30 mL) butter
2 tbsp	(30 mL) grated Parmesan cheese
	salt and pepper

■ In a saucepan filled with lightly salted boiling water, blanch zucchini and sweet red peppers for 30 seconds. Drain.

■ In a skillet, melt butter and sauté zucchini and peppers for about 4 minutes.

■ Sprinkle with Parmesan, season with salt and pepper, and serve.

Tomato-flavored Zucchini Tambourines

about 6 tambourines

2	zucchini
2 tbsp	(30 mL) butter
1	garlic clove, finely sliced
4 tsp	(20 mL) shallots, finely sliced
1	tomato, diced
	salt and pepper
2 tbsp	(30 mL) Parmesan cheese

■ Preheat oven to 400 °F (205 °C).

■ Slice zucchini into 1 ½ inch (3,75 cm) chunks.

■ In a saucepan filled with lightly salted boiling water, cook zucchini pieces for 5 minutes. Rinse under cold water and drain.

■ Scoop out pulp, but not too deeply.

■ Chop pulp and set aside.

■ In a skillet, melt butter and cook zucchini pulp along with garlic, shallots and diced tomatoes until liquid has completely evaporated. Season with salt and pepper and sprinkle with Parmesan.

■ Garnish each zucchini tambourine with stuffing. Heat in oven for 5 minutes and serve.

From Top to Bottom: Zucchini Pastilles • Parmesan-flavored Zucchini • Tomato-flavored Zucchini Tambourines

ENDIVES

Endives and Spinach

about 1 cup (250 mL)	
3 tbsp	(45 mL) butter
1	garlic clove, finely sliced
2 tsp	(10 mL) shallots, chopped
1 cup	(250 mL) endives, sliced
¼ cup	(60 mL) leeks, thinly sliced
¼ tsp	(1 mL) nutmeg
	salt and pepper
	juice of 1 lemon
1 cup	(250 mL) spinach, finely shredded

■ In a skillet, melt butter and sauté but do not brown garlic and shallots. Add endives and leeks, season with nutmeg, salt, and pepper and sauté for 4 minutes.

■ Add lemon juice and spinach. Cook until spinach wilts, then remove from heat.

VARIATION

• Replace spinach with beet leaves, shredded Chinese cabbage or red cabbage, lightly blanched for 5 minutes.

Endives with Tomatoes

about 1 ½ cups (375 mL)	
3 tbsp	(45 mL) butter
1 tbsp	(15 mL) onion, chopped
1	garlic clove, chopped
1 tbsp	(15 mL) pine nuts
1 cup	(250 mL) endives, finely sliced
½ cup	(125 mL) tomatoes, diced
2 tbsp	(30 mL) chopped parsley
	salt and pepper

■ In a skillet, melt butter and sauté but do not brown onion and garlic.

■ Add pine nuts, endives and tomatoes and sauté mixture for 3 minutes.

■ Add chopped parsley, season with salt and pepper, and serve.

Endives (sometimes called Belgian or French endives) have been part of the culinary scene for little more than a century. This unusual, compact vegetable is grown in the dark from a chicory root. Since the heart is more bitter than the rest of the plant, remove it by inserting the point of a small knife in the base and scooping out the central cone of leaves.

Ham-rolled Endives

4 servings	
3 tbsp	(45 mL) butter
8	endives
8	slices ham, cooked
3 cups	(750 mL) hot béchamel sauce
¼ tsp	(1 mL) nutmeg
1 tbsp	(15 mL) grated Parmesan cheese
	salt and pepper
¼ cup	(60 mL) grated cheese

■ Preheat oven to 350 °F (175 °C). Butter a baking dish.

■ In a skillet, melt butter and cook endives.

■ Place 1 endive on each ham slice, roll, secure with a toothpick and place in baking dish.

■ In a saucepan containing béchamel sauce, add nutmeg and Parmesan cheese. Season with salt and pepper then pour mixture over endive-ham rolls, cover and bake for 30 minutes. Remove from oven. Heat broiler.

■ Sprinkle endive-ham rolls with grated cheese broil to brown.

Friday's Endives

4 servings	
3 tbsp	(45 mL) butter
8	endives
8	slices of smoked salmon
3 cups	(750 mL) hot béchamel sauce
¼ tsp	(1 mL) nutmeg
1 tbsp	(15 mL) grated Parmesan cheese
	salt and pepper
¼ cup	(60 mL) grated cheese
16	baby shrimp

■ Follow same recipe as Ham-rolled Endives; simply replace ham with smoked salmon.

■ Just before baking au gratin, place 2 baby shrimp on each roll.

FENNEL

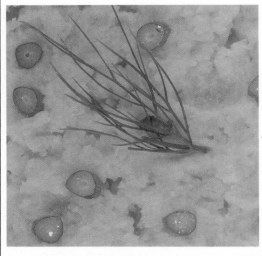

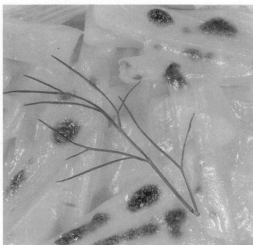

Fennel Purée

about 1 cup (250 mL)	
⅓ cup	(80 mL) potatoes, diced
1 cup	(250 mL) fennel, cut into pieces
3 tbsp	(45 mL) butter
	salt and pepper

■ In a saucepan filled with lightly salted boiling water, cook potatoes. Drain, place in a bowl, then mash to purée and set aside.

■ In a separate saucepan filled with lightly salted boiling water, cook fennel for about 20 minutes. Drain, place in a separate bowl, then mash to purée and combine with potato purée.

■ With a wire whisk, add other ingredients to potatoes and fennel. Place in a serving dish. Garnish and serve.

Fennel au Gratin

about 1 cup (250 mL)	
1 ½ cups	(375 mL) fennel, finely sliced
	salt and pepper
	pinch of nutmeg
¼ cup	(60 mL) hollandaise sauce
1 tbsp	(15 mL) Parmesan cheese

■ Preheat oven to broil.

■ In a saucepan filled with lightly salted boiling water, blanch fennel for 5 minutes. Drain.

■ Place in a baking dish, season with salt, pepper and nutmeg, coat with hollandaise sauce, sprinkle with Parmesan cheese and broil to brown.

Fennel Boulangère

about 2 cups (500 mL)	
1 ½ cups	(375 mL) fennel, finely sliced
½ cup	(125 mL) onion, finely sliced
	salt and pepper
½ tsp	(2 mL) thyme
1 cup	(250 mL) chicken stock
4 tsp	(20 mL) lemon juice

■ Preheat oven to 375 °F (190 °C).

■ In a bowl, combine fennel, onion, salt, pepper, and thyme and pour mixture into a baking dish. Pour chicken stock over mixture along with lemon juice and bake until liquid has completely evaporated.

From Top to Bottom:
Fennel Purée ■ Fennel au Gratin
■ Fennel Boulangère

Fennel comes to us from Italy, and is cooked in the same way as celery heart. Its light aniseed taste goes very well with fish.

Spinach and Fennel with Tomatoes

about 3 cups (750 mL)	
1 ½ cups	(375 mL) fennel, cut into sticks
½ cup	(125 mL) tomatoes, diced
2 cups	(500 mL) spinach, stems removed
2 tbsp	(30 mL) butter
¼ cup	(60 mL) tomato juice
	salt and pepper

■ In a saucepan filled with lightly salted boiling water, blanch fennel for 8 minutes, and drain.

■ In a skillet, melt butter and sauté fennel with tomatoes for 2 minutes.

■ Add spinach and tomato juice to mixture and season with salt and pepper.

■ Cook until spinach leaves have completely wilted.

Mustard-flavored Fennel

about 2 cups (500 mL)	
2 cups	(500 mL) fennel, finely sliced
2 tbsp	(30 mL) butter
¼ cup	(60 mL) 35% cream
2 tbsp	(30 mL) old-fashioned mustard
	salt and pepper

■ In a saucepan filled with lightly salted boiling water, blanch fennel for 10 minutes and drain.

■ In a skillet, melt butter and sauté fennel for 5 minutes.

■ Add cream and mustard and season with salt and pepper. Cook until sauce begins to thicken.

Fennel Vinaigrette

about 3 cups (750 mL)	
2 cups	(500 mL) fennel, cut into sticks
1 ½ cups	(375 mL) plain yogurt
1	garlic clove, finely sliced
¼ cup	(60 mL) cucumber, finely diced
½ tsp	(2 mL) chopped dill
½ tsp	(2 mL) Worcestershire sauce
	salt and pepper

■ In a saucepan filled with lightly salted boiling water, blanch fennel for 8 minutes. Rinse under cold water, drain and set aside.

■ In a bowl, combine yogurt and all other ingredients. Add fennel, cover, then refrigerate for 1 hour.

From Top to Bottom: Spinach and Fennel with Tomatoes ▪ Mustard-flavored Fennel ▪ Fennel Vinaigrette

BEAN SPROUTS

Bean Sprouts with Mayonnaise

about 3 cups (750 mL)	
2 cups	(500 mL) bean sprouts
2 tbsp	(30 mL) soy sauce
½ cup	(125 mL) celery, diced
⅓ cup	(80 mL) onions or shallots, finely chopped
¼ cup	(60 mL) green bell pepper or sweet red pepper, finely chopped
3 tbsp	(45 mL) mayonnaise
	juice of 1 lemon
	salt and pepper

■ Place bean sprouts in colander, scald in boiling water and drain.

■ In a bowl, place bean sprouts and add soy sauce. Let stand a few minutes, stirring often. Drain.

■ In a salad bowl, combine other ingredients. Add bean sprout mixture and stir.

Bean Sprouts au Gratin

about 4 cups (1 L)	
2	large potatoes, cooked, sliced
2 cups	(500 mL) bean sprouts, scalded
1 ½ cups	(375 mL) hot béchamel sauce
¼ cup	(60 mL) grated Parmesan cheese
	salt and pepper
½ tsp	(2 mL) nutmeg

■ Preheat oven to 375 °F (190 °C).

■ In a buttered, ovenproof baking dish, place overlapping layers of potatoes and bean sprouts. Complete process with layer of bean sprouts. Coat with béchamel sauce, sprinkle with Parmesan cheese and season with salt, pepper, and nutmeg.

■ Bake until golden, then turn off oven, cover baking dish with sheet of aluminum foil and let stand for 10 minutes.

Bean Sprouts with Mayonnaise
Bean Sprouts au Gratin

Keep the children amused by growing your own sprouts on the kitchen windowsill from a handful of Mung beans. Fresh bean sprouts can be bought in bulk or bagged if you prefer, and taste infinitely better than the canned variety.

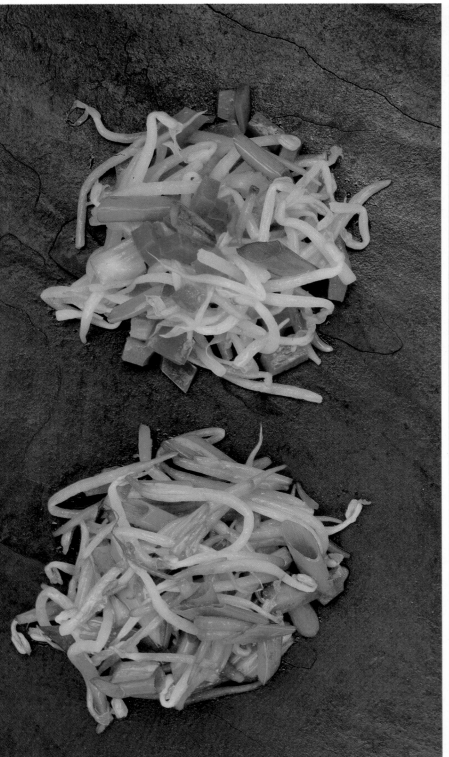

Multi-colored Bean Sprouts

about 3 cups (750 mL)

3 tbsp	(45 mL) butter
1 tbsp	(15 mL) onion, chopped
1	garlic clove, finely sliced
¼ cup	(60 mL) shallots, finely sliced
½ cup	(125 mL) sweet red pepper, diced
2 cups	(500 mL) bean sprouts
3 tbsp	(45 mL) soy sauce
	salt and pepper

■ Follow same recipe as Sautéed Bean Sprouts.

■ Add sweet red peppers along with the shallots.

Sautéed Bean Sprouts

about 2 cups (500 mL)

3 tbsp	(45 mL) butter
1 tbsp	(15 mL) onion, chopped
1	garlic clove, finely sliced
¼ cup	(60 mL) green onions, finely sliced
2	cups (500 mL) bean sprouts
3 tbsp	(45 mL) soy sauce
	salt and pepper

■ In a skillet, melt butter and sauté onion, garlic, and green onions without browning for 3 minutes, stirring constantly. Add bean sprouts and soy sauce, season with salt and pepper, stir and cook over low heat 5 minutes longer.

Multi-Colored Bean Sprouts
Sautéed Bean Sprouts

281

Green and Wax Beans

From Top to Bottom:
Green Beans Amandine ▪ Wax Beans Provençale ▪ Green Beans with Sesame Seeds

Green Beans Amandine

about 2 cups (500 mL

1 ½ cups	(375 mL) green beans, tips removed
	salt and pepper
3 tbsp	(45 mL) butter
¼ cup	(60 mL) almond slivers
2 tbsp	(30 mL) chopped parsley

▪ In a saucepan filled with lightly salted boiling water, cook green beans for 5 minutes, drain, season with salt and pepper, then set aside.

▪ In a skillet, melt butter and sauté almonds. Add green beans and parsley, stir and serve.

Wax Beans Provençale

about 3 cups (750 mL)

3 tbsp	(45 mL) butter
5 tbsp	(75 mL) onion, finely sliced
1 tbsp	(15 mL) garlic, finely sliced
2 tbsp	(30 mL) chopped parsley
2	tomatoes, diced
1 ½ cups	(375 mL) wax beans, cooked, sliced in half
8 oz	(237 mL) canned cream of tomato soup
	salt and pepper
4	hard-boiled eggs, chopped

▪ In a skillet, melt butter and sauté onion and garlic.

▪ Add parsley, tomatoes, and wax beans; stir, then add cream of tomato soup, season with salt and pepper, cover and cook over medium heat for 10 minutes.

▪ Place in serving dish, sprinkle with chopped eggs and serve.

Green Beans with Sesame Seeds

about 2 cups (500 mL)

2 cups	(500 mL) green beans, tips removed
	salt and pepper
2 tbsp	(30 mL) butter
¼ tsp	(1 mL) sesame oil
2 tbsp	(30 mL) sesame seeds
2 tbsp	(30 mL) chopped parsley
2 tsp	(10 mL) lemon juice

▪ In a saucepan filled with lightly salted boiling water, cook beans for 5 minutes. Drain, season with salt and pepper, and let stand.

▪ In a skillet, melt butter, add sesame oil, and sauté sesame seeds.

▪ Add cooked beans and parsley, sprinkle with lemon juice and toss lightly.

Wax or yellow pod beans and green beans are often served with meat or as a decoration, but these vitamin-and mineral-rich vegetables make a nourishing dish on their own.

Mixed Bundles

4 servings	
20	wax beans, tips removed
20	green beans, tips removed
2	slices bacon, sliced in half
	salt and pepper

■ Slice beans into 3-inch (7,5-cm) lengths.

■ In a saucepan filled with lightly salted boiling water, blanch beans for 2 minutes and drain. Separate beans into 4 bundles.

■ Place each bean bundle over a bacon slice, wrap bacon around bundles, then season with salt and pepper.

■ Place bundles in a microwave-safe dish and cook in microwave at MEDIUM for 4 minutes.

Bean Bouquet

about 3 cups (750 mL)		
1 cup	(250 mL) green beans, sliced in half	
1 cup	(250 mL) wax beans, sliced in half	
½ cup	(125 mL) egg-plant, unpeeled, diced	
¼ cup	(60 mL) carrots, diced	
¼ cup	(60 mL) sweet red pepper, diced	
2 tbsp	(30 mL) butter	
¼ cup	(60 mL) tomato juice	
1 tbsp	(15 mL) chopped parsley	
	salt and pepper	

■ In a saucepan filled with lightly salted boiling water, blanch all vegetables together. Drain.

■ In a skillet, melt butter and sauté all vegetables for 3 minutes.

■ Pour tomato juice over vegetables and sprinkle with parsley. Season with salt and pepper and cook 3 minutes more.

Green Beans with Fennel

about 2 cups (500 mL)	
1 ½ cups	(375 mL) green beans, sliced in half
¼ cup	(60 mL) fennel bulb, diced
2 tbsp	(30 mL) fennel leaves
	juice of ½ lemon
	salt and pepper
	water
	slivers of lemon peel (optional)

■ In a bowl, combine all ingredients except for lemon peel, place in daisy steamer and cook for 6 minutes. Garnish with slivers of lemon peel.

VARIATION

• Replace fennel bulb with equal amount of diced celery, and replace fennel leaves with equal number of celery leaves.

*From Top to Bottom:
Mixed Bundles ▪ Bean Bouquet
▪ Green Beans with Fennel*

LEGUMES

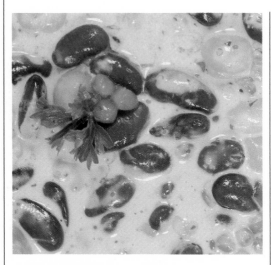

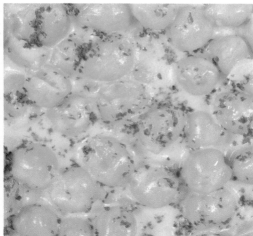

Broad Bean Medley with Mustard Sauce

about 3 cups (750 mL)	
2 tbsp	(30 mL) butter
1 cup	(250 mL) lentils
1 cup	(250 mL) chick peas
1 cup	(250 mL) red kidney beans
2 tbsp	(30 mL) old-fashioned mustard
¼ cup	(60 mL) 35% cream
	chopped parsley
	salt and pepper

■ In a skillet, melt butter and sauté lentils, chick peas and kidney beans for 3 minutes.

■ Add mustard and cream. Stir, then add parsley, and season with salt and pepper. Cook until cream begins to thicken.

Chick Peas with Garlic Cream

about 2 cups (500 mL)	
1 tbsp	(15 mL) butter
2	garlic cloves, finely sliced
14 oz	(398 mL) canned chick peas, drained and rinsed
¼ cup	(60 mL) 35% cream
2 tsp	(10 mL) parsley
	salt and pepper

■ In a skillet, melt butter and sauté garlic.

■ Add chick peas and sauté another 4 minutes.

■ Add cream and remove from heat when cream begins to boil, then add parsley and season with salt and pepper.

Chick Pea Croquettes

about 4 cups (1 L)	
1 cup	(250 mL) cooked rice
½ cup	(125 mL) ground sunflower seeds
1 cup	(250 mL) chick peas
8 oz	(237 mL) tofu, crumbled
½ cup	(125 mL) grated cheese
1 tbsp	(15 mL) onion powder
	pinch of basil
	pinch of sage
2 tbsp	(30 mL) fines herbes

■ Heat deep fryer to 425 °F (220 °C).

■ In a bowl, combine all ingredients and shape into croquettes.

■ Drop into deep-fryer and fry. Drain. Serve with sauce of your choice, in hamburger buns or on a bed of spinach leaves, accompanied with sliced tomatoes.

From Top to Bottom:
Broad Bean Medley with Mustard Sauce ▪ Chick Peas with Garlic Cream ▪ Chick Pea Croquettes

Protein-rich dried legumes are an important food staple for many people in the world. Chick peas from North Africa, red kidney beans from Latin America, and many other legumes have found their way into our cooking. They are an excellent meat substitute when eaten with a cereal, giving a full range of proteins. Try serving legumes with such cereal foods as whole-wheat bread, semolina pasta, or corn tortillas.

White Kidney Beans with Fines Herbes au Gratin

about 2 cups (500 mL)

14 oz	(348 mL) canned white kidney beans, drained and rinsed
2 tsp	(10 mL) chopped parsley
1/2 tsp	(2 mL) chopped chives
1/2 tsp	(2 mL) chopped chervil
1/4 tsp	(1 mL) chopped tarragon
1 cup	(250 mL) 35% cream
1/4 tsp	(60 mL) grated cheese

■ Preheat oven to broil.

■ In an ovenproof dish, place white kidney beans and sprinkle with herbs, then season with salt and pepper. Pour 35% cream over mixture and sprinkle with grated cheese. Broil and serve.

Spicy Red Kidney Beans

about 2 cups (500 mL)

1 tbsp	(15 mL) butter
14 oz	(398 mL) canned red kidney beans, rinsed and drained
1/4 tsp	(1 mL) pimento, crushed
	pinch of chili powder
	salt
1/4 cup	(60 mL) tomato juice
1/2 tsp	(2 mL) Worcestershire sauce

■ In a skillet, melt butter and sauté kidney beans, then add pimento, chili powder, and salt, and stir. Add tomato juice and Worcestershire sauce and stir.

Lentils with Spinach

about 3 cups (750 mL)

2 tbsp	(30 mL) butter
1	garlic clove, finely sliced
1	French (dry) shallot, chopped
4 cups	(1 L) spinach, washed and drained
14 oz	(398 mL) canned lentils, rinsed and drained
	salt and pepper

■ In a skillet, melt butter and sauté garlic with shallot, then add spinach and lentils. Season with salt and pepper, stir and cook until spinach wilts.

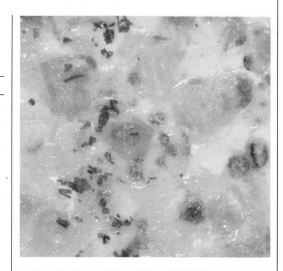

From Top to Bottom: White Kidney Beans with Fines Herbes au Gratin • Spicy Red Kidney Beans • Lentils with Spinach

CORN

Corn Chunks with Parsley

4 servings	
4 cups	(1 L) chicken stock
2 tbsp	(30 mL) chopped parsley
1	garlic clove
4	ears of corn, cut into 8 pieces
	salt and pepper
12	pats of butter

▪ In a large saucepan bring chicken stock and parsley to a boil. Add garlic clove to season stock.

▪ Cook corn chunks in stock for 10 minutes, then drain, and season with salt and pepper. Serve with butter.

Corn Mousse au Gratin

6 to 8 servings	
1 cup	(250 mL) canned corn niblets
½ cup	(125 mL) puréed potatoes
2	eggs
2 tbsp	(30 mL) 35% cream
2 tbsp	(30 mL) Cheddar cheese
	salt and pepper
8 oz	(237 mL) canned cream of tomato soup

▪ Preheat oven to 350 °F (175 °C).

▪ Drain corn.

▪ In a bowl, mix together corn niblets, puréed potatoes, eggs, cream and cheese. Season with salt and pepper and stir.

▪ Butter small ramekins and fill with corn mixture. Bake in large pan partially filled with water for 35 minutes.

▪ Remove from oven, unmold, then serve with a tomato sauce.

Garlic Creamed Corn

about 3 cups (750 mL)	
1 tbsp	(15 mL) butter
2	garlic cloves, chopped
12 oz	(341 mL) canned creamed corn
12 oz	(341 mL) canned corn niblets
2 tbsp	(30 mL) chopped parsley
	salt and pepper

▪ In a skillet, melt butter and sauté garlic without browning.

▪ Add creamed corn, corn niblets and season with salt and pepper.

▪ Add parsley and cook for 4 minutes.

Fresh corn is delicious, but frozen corn kernels are just as good in these recipes. Thaw them in the refrigerator first.

Corn Fritters

about 1 cup (250 mL)

³/₄ cup	(180 mL) canned corn niblets
³/₄ cup	(180 mL) sifted flour
	pinch of salt
³/₄ tsp	(3 mL) baking powder
1	egg yolk
1	egg white, beaten into stiff peaks

■ Preheat deep-fryer to 375 °F (190 °C).

■ Drain corn niblets. In a bowl, combine all ingredients except egg white, then gently fold in egg white.

■ Drop spoonfuls of mixture into deep-fryer and fry until golden. Drain on paper towel.

Miniature Corn and Vegetable Mix

about 2 cups (500 mL)

1 ¹/₂ cups	(375 mL) miniature corn on the cob
¹/₂ cup	(125 mL) green peas
¹/₄ cup	(60 mL) carrots, diced
	salt and pepper
3 tbsp	(45 mL) butter

■ In a daisy steamer, cook all vegetables for 5 minutes, then place in a serving dish and dot with knobs of butter.

Miniature Corn on a Bed of Tomatoes

about 3 cups (750 mL)

2 tbsp	(30 mL) butter
2	red onions, finely sliced
1 cup	(250 mL) tomatoes, diced
12 oz	(341 mL) canned miniature corn on the cob
1 cup	(250 mL) chicken stock
	salt and pepper

■ In a skillet, melt butter and sauté onions and tomatoes for 5 minutes. Season with salt and pepper.

■ Meanwhile, heat miniature corn on the cob in chicken stock.

■ Shape a bed of onions and tomatoes, then place miniature corn in the middle.

From Top to Bottom: Corn Fritters ▪ Miniature Corn and Vegetable Mix ▪ Miniature Corn on a Bed of Tomatoes

TURNIP AND PARSNIP

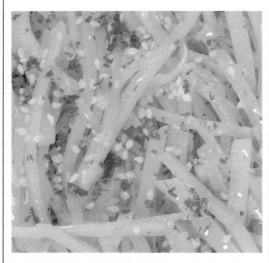

Julienned Turnips with Sesame Seeds

about 2 cups (500 mL)		
2 cups	(500 mL) julienned turnips	
1 tbsp	(15 mL) butter	
1 tbsp	(15 mL) sesame seeds	
1 tbsp	(15 mL) chopped parsley	
	salt and pepper	

■ In a saucepan filled with lightly salted boiling water, blanch turnips for 2 minutes, then drain.

■ In a skillet, melt butter and sauté sesame seeds until golden.

■ Add turnips, season with salt and pepper, sprinkle with parsley, stir and serve.

Roquefort-stuffed White Turnips

4 servings		
4	equal-sized white turnips, peeled	
2 tbsp	(30 mL) Roquefort cheese	
	pinch of nutmeg	
1 tbsp	(15 mL) chives	
	salt and pepper	

■ In a saucepan filled with lightly salted boiling water, cook turnips.

■ Cut a slice off top of each turnip and set aside.

■ Scoop out pulp.

■ In a bowl, combine turnip pulp and Roquefort cheese and run through blender.

■ Add nutmeg and chives. Season with salt and pepper.

■ Garnish turnips with stuffing and serve.

Garlic-seasoned Turnips

about 2 cups (500 mL)		
2 cups	(500 mL) turnips, diced	
1 tbsp	(15 mL) butter	
1	garlic clove, finely sliced	
1/4 cup	(60 mL) 35% cream	
1 tsp	(5 mL) parsley, chopped	
	salt and pepper	

■ In a saucepan filled with lightly salted boiling water, blanch turnips for 5 minutes, then drain.

■ In a skillet, melt butter and sauté garlic. Add turnips, cream and parsley. Season with salt and pepper, stir, cook 4 minutes and serve.

From Top to Bottom:
Julienned Turnips with Sesame Seeds ▪ Roquefort-stuffed White Turnips ▪ Garlic-seasoned Turnips

Turnips, rutabagas (Swedes), and parsnips are root vegetables. The outer skin of the turnip is purplish at the base, and its flesh is white and crunchy. Stronger-tasting rutabagas, on the other hand, have a firm, yellow flesh. Parsnips are sweet, almost fruity in taste and have an attractive ivory flesh that has a rather floury consistency when cooked.

Roasted White Turnips

about 3 cups (750 mL)		
3	large white turnips	
½ cup	(125 mL) breadcrumbs	
	salt and pepper	
1	egg, beaten	
¼ cup	(60 mL) butter	
	parsley	

■ In a saucepan filled with lightly salted boiling water, cook turnips until tender, then drain, slice and set aside.

■ In a bowl combine breadcrumbs, salt and pepper. Dip each turnip slice into beaten egg, then into seasoned breadcrumbs and set aside.

■ In a skillet, melt butter and cook turnips until golden. Place in a serving dish, decorate with parsley sprigs and serve.

Parsnip Soufflé

about 2 cups (500 mL)		
2	parsnips, diced	
2 tbsp	(30 mL) melted butter	
1 cup	(250 mL) thick béchamel sauce	
½ cup	(125 mL) grated cheese	
4	egg yolks, beaten	
	salt and pepper	
4	egg whites, beaten into stiff peaks	

■ Preheat oven to 350 °F (175 °C).

■ In a saucepan filled with lightly salted boiling water, cook parsnips, then drain, press through sieve into a bowl. Add butter, béchamel sauce, half the cheese, and the egg yolks. Season with salt and pepper.

■ Gently fold in egg whites.

■ Coat small ramekins with butter and half fill with mixture. Sprinkle with cheese and bake for 15 to 20 minutes.

Parsnips with Curry and Basil

about 2 cups (500 mL)		
1 ½ cups	(375 mL) chicken stock	
½ tsp	(2 mL) curry powder	
3	parsnips, diced	
	salt and pepper	
2 tsp	(10 mL) chopped basil	

■ In a saucepan, pour chicken stock and curry powder and bring to a boil. Cook parsnips in stock for 6 minutes, then drain.

■ Pour mixture into a large bowl, season with salt and pepper and sprinkle with basil.

From Top to Bottom: Roasted White Turnips ■ Parsnip Soufflé ■ Parsnips with Curry and Basil

289

ONIONS

From Top to Bottom:
Fried Onions ▪ Onion Shells
Jardinière ▪ Fried Onions with
Mixed Vegetables

Fried Onions

about 2 cups (500 mL)

4	medium-size onions
2 tsp	(10 mL) peanut oil
2 tsp	(10 mL) butter
	pinch of onion salt
	pinch of garlic salt
¼ tsp	(1 mL) pepper
1 tsp	(5 mL) Worcestershire sauce

■ Slice each onion into 8 wedges and set aside.

■ In a skillet, heat oil, melt butter and fry onions until golden. Season with onion salt, garlic salt, and pepper and cook for 2 minutes. Add Worcestershire sauce.

Onion Shells Jardinière

4 servings

2	large onions, peeled
2 tbsp	(30 mL) sugar
1 cup	(250 mL) water
¼ cup	(60 mL) spinach, chopped, cooked
½ cup	(125 mL) mixed vegetables (corn kernels, diced carrots and peas), cooked
2 tbsp	(30 mL) butter

■ Preheat oven to 400 °F (205 °C).

■ Slice onions in 2 along the width and set aside.

■ In a saucepan, place onion halves, then add sugar and pour water over onions. Cover and cook over low heat for 10 minutes, then drain.

■ Scoop inner layers out of onions and stuff each half with layer of spinach, then mixed vegetables. Place a pat of butter over each stuffed onion half and bake for 10 minutes.

Fried Onions with Mixed Vegetables

about 3 cups (750 mL)

4	medium-size onions
1 tbsp	(15 mL) peanut oil
2 tsp	(10 mL) butter
⅓ cup	(80 mL) corn kernels
⅓ cup	(80 mL) green peas
½ cup	(80 mL) carrots, blanched, diced
	salt and pepper
1 tsp	(5 mL) Worcestershire sauce

■ Slice each onion into 8 wedges and set aside.

■ In a skillet, heat oil, melt butter and fry onions until golden. Season with salt and pepper. Add corn kernels, green peas and carrots and cook for 2 minutes. Add Worcestershire sauce and serve.

White, yellow, or red, the onion is an indispensable culinary ingredient, whether as a food in itself or a flavoring. One way of preventing tears when peeling onions is to put them in the refrigerator for an hour before cutting.

Veal-stuffed Onions

4 servings		
4		onions
2 tbsp	(30 mL)	butter
1/4 lb	(115 g)	mushrooms, sliced
1/3 lb	(150 g)	ground veal
1		garlic clove, finely sliced
2 tbsp	(30 mL)	breadcrumbs
2 tbsp	(30 mL)	parsley, chopped
		salt and pepper
2 tbsp	(30 mL)	oil
1 cup	(250 mL)	cream of tomato soup

■ Preheat oven to 350 °F (175 °F).

■ In a saucepan filled with lightly salted boiling water, cook onions for 10 minutes, then drain.

■ Slice top off each onion and set aside. Scoop out pulp of onion.

■ In a skillet, melt butter and sauté onion pulp with mushrooms.

■ Pour mixture into a bowl and add ground veal, garlic, breadcrumbs, and parsley. Season with salt and pepper, stir, then stuff onion shells with mixture. Place top over each onion.

■ In a baking dish, pour oil, add onions over oil and bake for 20 minutes. Pour off fat. Add cream of tomato soup, cover and bake for 30 minutes.

Boiled Onions

4 servings		
8		medium onions
1/2 tsp	(2 mL)	salt
		pepper
2 tsp	(10 mL)	chopped parsley
8		knobs butter

■ In a saucepan filled with lightly salted boiling water, cook onions, then drain. Place in a serving dish, season with pepper to taste and sprinkle with parsley. Decorate each onion with a pat of butter and let butter melt.

Onions Provençale

about 2 cups (500 mL)		
2 tbsp	(30 mL)	butter
1 1/2 cups	(375 mL)	onions
2 tbsp	(30 mL)	green bell pepper, diced
1		garlic clove, finely sliced
1/4 cup	(60 mL)	canned tomatoes, diced
1/4 cup	(60 mL)	tomato juice
		salt and pepper

■ In a skillet, melt butter and sauté onions for 4 minutes. Add green pepper and garlic and cook 2 minutes longer.

■ Add tomatoes and tomato juice, season with salt and pepper and simmer for 3 minutes.

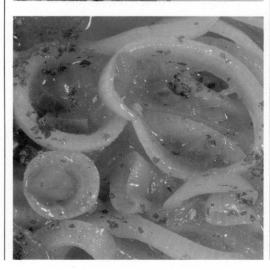

From Top to Bottom:
Veal-stuffed Onions ▪ Boiled Onions ▪ Onions Provençale

Leeks

Leeks Marinated in Yogurt

4 servings

4	leeks
	salt and pepper
½ cup	(125 mL) plain yogurt
½ cup	(125 mL) vinaigrette
4	hard-boiled eggs, chopped
	assorted julienned vegetables, cooked
2 tbsp	(30 mL) chopped parsley

■ Slice leeks through middle almost to the bottom and wash.

■ In a saucepan filled with lightly salted boiling water, cook leeks for 10 minutes. Drain, cut into pieces 4 to 6 in (10 to 15 cm) long, and set aside.

■ In a bowl, combine yogurt and vinaigrette, then add leek pieces and marinate overnight.

■ Place leeks in a serving dish, sprinkle with chopped eggs, julienned vegetables, and parsley.

Leeks and Eggplant on a Spinach Bed

3 cups (750 mL)

	butter
2	leek stalks, sliced into ½ inch (1 cm) thick rounds
¼ cup	(60 mL) eggplant, un-peeled, diced
	juice of ½ lemon
¼ cup	(60 mL) tomato juice
	salt and pepper
1 tsp	(5 mL) chopped chives
4	large spinach leaves, blanched

■ In a skillet, melt butter and sauté leek pieces with-out browning for 5 minutes, then add eggplant and lemon juice.

■ Cook over low heat for 5 minutes. Add tomato juice, season with salt and pepper and sprinkle with chives.

■ Arrange on a bed of blanched spinach leaves.

292

Leeks, the national vegetable of Wales, are the keynote ingredients of vichyssoise, the cold potato-leek-and-cream soup that is a summer favorite. Look for leeks that are smooth at the base, with the green upper half firm and straight, not broken or floppy. To get "leek whites," cut off the roots and base, and chop off the green upper half as well. Keep the latter for soups, using it as you would an onion. Be sure to wash the sand out of the upper outer layers as you peel them off.

Leek Fondue

about 1 cup (250 mL)	
2 tbsp	(30 mL) butter
2	leek stalks (mostly the white part), sliced
	salt and pepper
2 tsp	(10 mL) ground pink peppercorns

■ In a skillet, melt butter and sauté leeks without browning for 10 minutes over low heat until they begin to separate. Season with salt, pepper and pink peppercorns, stir and serve.

VARIATIONS

• Add sliced, stuffed olives to mixture, 1 minute before end of cooking. In this case, do not add pink peppercorns.

• Add thinly sliced black olives to mixture, 1 minute before end of cooking.

Ham-rolled Leeks with Mozzarella Topping

4 servings	
2	leek stalks
2 tbsp	(30 mL) butter
4	slices ham
8 oz	(237 mL) canned cream of tomato soup
2 tbsp	(30 mL) parsley
2 tbsp	(30 mL) breadcrumbs
1/3 cup	(80 mL) Mozzarella cheese

■ Preheat oven to 350 °F (175 °C).

■ Slice leek stalks in half lengthwise and wash.

■ In a saucepan filled with lightly salted boiling water, cook leeks, then drain, slice in half and set aside.

■ In a skillet, melt butter and cook leek halves until golden. Remove from skillet and roll ham slices around leek halves.

■ In an oven-proof dish, place ham-rolled leeks and coat with cream of tomato soup. Sprinkle with parsley, breadcrumbs, and Mozzarella cheese and bake for 10 minutes.

GREEN PEAS

Green Peas Bonne Femme

about 3 cups (750 mL)	
2 tbsp	(30 mL) butter
½ lb	(225 g) lardons
⅓ cup	(80 mL) pearl onions
½	onion, finely sliced
1½ cups	(375 mL) frozen green peas
4 tsp	(20 mL) sugar
	salt and pepper
	mint leaves

■ In a stove-top casserole, melt butter and sauté onions and lardons without browning. Add green peas, and sugar. Stir; cover and cook over low heat for 10 minutes. Season with salt and pepper.

■ Place in a serving dish, garnish with mint leaves, and serve.

Green Peas with Tomatoes

about 2 cups (500 mL)	
2 tbsp	(30 mL) butter
¼ cup	(60 mL) onion, finely sliced
1	garlic clove, finely sliced
2 tbsp	(30 mL) tomato paste
1	tomato, diced
1⅓ cups	(330 mL) green peas
	salt and pepper
1 tbsp	(15 mL) fresh basil, chopped

■ In a skillet, melt butter and sauté onion and garlic over low heat.

■ Add tomato paste and tomatoes, stir, then add green peas. Cook for 10 minutes over medium heat. Season with salt and pepper, add basil and serve.

Old-fashioned Mixed Vegetables

about 3 cups (750 mL)	
½ cup	(125 mL) carrots, diced
½ cup	(125 mL) turnip, diced
1 tbsp	(15 mL) butter
¼ cup	(60 mL) onion, finely sliced
12 oz	(341 mL) canned green peas
	salt and pepper
2 tsp	(10 mL) honey

■ In a saucepan filled with lightly salted boiling water, blanch carrots and turnip for 5 minutes, then drain and set aside.

■ In a skillet, melt butter and sauté onion, then add carrots and turnip. Add green peas, season with salt and pepper and pour honey over mixture.

From Top to Bottom:
Green Peas Bonne Femme ■
Green Peas with Tomatoes ■
Old-fashioned Mixed Vegetables

Green peas are probably our most popular vegetable. The delicate snow pea is a great favorite, as it can be eaten whole and only needs to have the ends snipped off before being cooked. Its subtle flavor makes it a pleasant accompaniment for numerous dishes.

Snow Pea Succotash

about 2 cups (500 mL)	
2 tbsp	(30 mL) butter
1 ½ cups	(375 mL) snow peas, diagonally cut
¼ cup	(60 mL) corn kernels
¼ cup	(60 mL) sweet red pepper, julienned
1 tbsp	(15 mL) chopped parsley
	salt and pepper

■ In a skillet, melt butter and sauté snow peas for 3 minutes.

■ Add corn kernels and peppers, season with salt and pepper and cook for 5 minutes, stirring constantly.

■ Sprinkle with parsley and serve.

Julienned Snow Peas with Wild Garlic

about 2 cups (500 mL)	
2 tbsp	(30 mL) butter
1	wild garlic clove, chopped
2 cups	(500 mL) snow peas, julienned
¼ cup	(60 mL) 35% cream
	salt and pepper

■ In a skillet, melt butter and sauté snow peas and wild garlic for 3 minutes.

■ Add cream and season with salt and pepper.

■ Cook until mixture begins to thicken, then serve.

Gourmet Snow Pea Fan

4 servings	
20	snow peas
4	cloves
2 tbsp	(30 mL) hollandaise sauce
¼ tsp	(1 mL) paprika
½ tsp	(2 mL) chopped parsley

■ In a saucepan filled with lightly salted boiling water, blanch snow peas for 4 minutes and drain.

■ Slice snow pea tips diagonally. Group in 5 bundles of 5 snow peas each and join together with a clove. Open fan-like.

■ Coat each fan lightly with a ribbon of hollandaise sauce. Garnish with paprika and parsley.

From Top to Bottom:
Snow Pea Succotash ▪ Julienned
Snow Peas with Wild Garlic ▪
Gourmet Snow Pea Fan

Sweet peppers

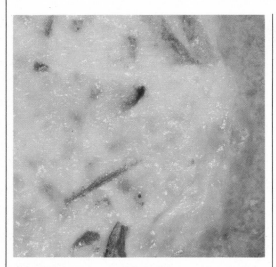

Sweet Pepper Quiche

6 to 8 servings

1	pie crust, uncooked
4	green bell peppers and sweet red peppers, diced
2 tbsp	(30 mL) oil
1 tsp	(5 mL) garlic, finely sliced
	salt and pepper
2	eggs
1 cup	(250 mL) 15% cream
1/4 cup	(60 mL) grated cheese
4 tsp	(20 mL) chopped parsley

■ Preheat oven to 375 °F (190 °C).

■ Line a pie plate with crust and set aside.

■ In a saucepan filled with lightly salted boiling water, blanch peppers. Drain.

■ In a skillet, heat oil and sauté peppers in oil until liquid evaporates completely. Add garlic, season with salt and pepper and stir. Remove from heat and set aside.

■ In a bowl, combine other ingredients, then add peppers. Pour into pie crust and bake for 35 minutes.

Sautéed Sweet Peppers

about 3 cups (750 mL)

2 tbsp	(30 mL) butter
4	different colored peppers, cut into chunks
1/2	white onion, finely sliced
1/2	red onion, finely sliced
	salt and pepper

■ In a skillet, melt butter and sauté peppers with onions for 6 minutes. Season with salt and pepper and serve.

Sweet Red Pepper Jam

about 4 cups (1 L)

12	large sweet red peppers, chopped
1 1/2 cups	(375 mL) cider vinegar
1 tbsp	(15 mL) coarse salt
1/2 cup	(125 mL) water
1	lemon, un-peeled, cut into wedges
3 cups	(750 mL) sugar

■ Sprinkle sweet red peppers with coarse salt and let stand for 3 hours, then drain.

■ In a large saucepan, combine all ingredients except sugar, cover and cook over low heat for 30 minutes.

■ Remove lemon wedges. Add sugar and continue cooking process for 1 hour or until mixture has the consistency of jam. Stir from time to time.

■ Pour mixture into hot sterilized jars. Coat with paraffin wax. Serve with meat dishes or on toast.

From Top to Bottom:
Sweet Pepper Quiche ■ *Sautéed*
Sweet Peppers ■ *Sweet Red*
Pepper Jam

Colorful sweet peppers, as delicious raw as they are cooked, are an excellent source of vitamin C. Surprisingly light for a vegetable of their size, they can be used in a variety of ways. If you want to peel sweet peppers to make them more digestible, first put them in the oven at 350 °F (175 °C) for 10 or 12 minutes, then put them in a tightly closed plastic bag for a further ten minutes before peeling.

Sweet Pepper Fritters

4 servings

4	sweet peppers
	salt and pepper
½ cup	(125 mL) flour
2	eggs, beaten
½ cup	(125 mL) breadcrumbs
3 tbsp	(45 mL) butter

■ Preheat broiler.

■ Slice peppers in half lengthwise and place on a cookie sheet, then broil until peel begins to brown. Remove from heat, place in a plastic bag and close tightly.

■ After 10 minutes, peel pepper halves with small paring knife and remove seeds. Slice halves in half and season with salt and pepper.

■ Dredge pepper strips with flour, dip into beaten egg, coat with breadcrumbs and set aside.

■ In a skillet, melt butter and cook pepper slices on all sides until golden. Drain on paper towel and serve.

Sweet Pepper Rainbow

4 to 6 servings

4	peppers of different colors
2	medium-size tomatoes, peeled and diced
1	cucumber, peeled, seeded, diced

Sauce

3 tbsp	(45 mL) lemon juice
¼ cup	(60 mL) plain yogurt
1 tbsp	(15 mL) chopped parsley
¼ tsp	(1 mL) garlic, finely sliced

■ Clean out peppers and place in a saucepan filled with lightly salted boiling water. Blanch for 5 minutes, then drain. Cut into ¼ inch (0,5 cm) strips and place in a salad bowl.

■ Add tomatoes and cucumbers, and toss lightly.

■ In a bowl, mix sauce ingredients and pour over vegetables. Cover and refrigerate for 30 minutes. Arrange on a bed of lettuce and serve as an appetizer.

Marinated Sweet Pepper Strips

about 2 cups (500 mL)

⅓ cup	(80 mL) olive oil
5	sweet red and green peppers, seeded and cut in strips
1	large onion, finely sliced
2 tbsp	(30 mL) vinegar
2 tbsp	(30 mL) chopped parsley
1 tsp	(5 mL) garlic, chopped
1 tsp	(5 mL) chopped tarragon
	salt and pepper

■ In a skillet, heat oil and sauté peppers, then drain and set aside.

■ In a bowl, combine other ingredients. Add peppers and soak for a few hours.

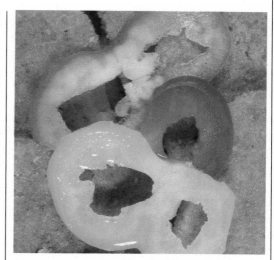

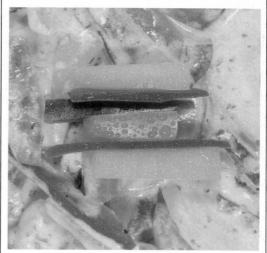

From Top to Bottom: Sweet Pepper Fritters ▪ Sweet Pepper Rainbow ▪ Marinated Sweet Pepper Strips

POTATOES

Potatoes Bolognese

about 3 cups (750 mL)	
½ lb	(225 g) potatoes, unpeeled
⅓ cup	(80 mL) skim milk
	salt
1 tbsp	(15 mL) oil
1	onion, chopped
¼ cup	(60 mL) mushrooms
¼ lb	(115 g) lean ground beef
¼ cup	(60 mL) tomatoes, ground

■ Preheat oven to 250 °F (120 °C).

■ In a saucepan filled with lightly salted boiling water, cook potatoes. Mash. Add milk and salt. Spread mixture evenly in a ring mold and keep warm.

■ In a skillet, heat oil and sauté onion, mushrooms, and ground beef. Add tomatoes and simmer for 20 minutes.

■ Unmold potato crown onto a warm serving dish, and put the meat and vegetable mixture in the center.

VARIATION

• Spread meat mixture between two layers of puréed potatoes, then unmold and garnish middle with vegetables and meat, as shown.

Potatoes with Onions au Gratin

about 4 cups (1L)	
1 lb	(450 g) potatoes, peeled, cut into chunks
⅓ cup	(80 mL) butter
½ lb	(225 g) onions, finely sliced
1	egg, beaten
	salt and pepper
	pinch of nutmeg
3 tbsp	(45 mL) grated Gruyère or Parmesan cheese

■ Preheat oven to 400 °F (205 °C).

■ In a saucepan filled with lightly salted boiling water, cook potatoes, then drain, purée in the food processor and set aside.

■ In a skillet, melt 4 tbsp (60 mL) butter and sauté onions and add onion mixture to purée. Add egg, season with salt, pepper, and nutmeg and stir mixture.

■ Butter a baking dish, then spread purée evenly. Sprinkle with cheese and dot with butter. Bake for 20 minutes or until golden crust forms.

Potatoes Bolognese (variation)
Potatoes with Onions au Gratin

Sir Walter Raleigh revolutionized the eating habits of Europe when he brought the potato back to England from Virginia. Nutritious and durable, the potato became a staple food. In eighteenth-century France it was popularized as a table vegetable by the scientist Antoine Augustin Parmentier— hence "potage parmentier."

Puréed Potatoes:
Bacon and Onions ▪ Fines
Herbes ▪ Carrots and Turnips ▪
Broccoli

Puréed Potatoes

about 4 cups (1 L)	
1 lb	(450 g) potatoes, peeled
½ tsp	(2 mL) salt
1	egg, beaten
2 tbsp	(30 mL) butter
2 tbsp	(30 mL) milk
¼ tsp	(1 mL) nutmeg
	salt and pepper

▪ Preheat oven to 300 °F (150 °C).

▪ In a saucepan filled with lightly salted boiling water, cook potatoes, then drain, place in an oven-proof dish and dry in oven for 15 minutes.

▪ In a bowl, mash potatoes. Add other ingredients and mix until smooth and creamy.

VARIATIONS

Bacon and Onions

- Add 1 finely sliced onion sautéed in 2 tbsp (30 mL) butter and 2 tbsp (30 mL) cooked, crumbled bacon to the puréed potatoes.

Fines Herbes

- Sprinkle the puréed potatoes with small amount of chives, tarragon, chervil, and chopped parsley.

Carrots and Turnips

- Cook potatoes with ¼ cup (60 mL) carrots and ¼ cup (60 mL) turnips.

Broccoli

- Fold ½ cup (125 mL) cooked, puréed broccoli into puréed potatoes.

From Top to Bottom:
Cheddar-flavored Potato
Croquettes • Sautéed Potatoes
and Sweet Peppers • Sautéed
Potatoes with Carrots and
Zucchini

Cheddar-flavored Potato Croquettes

about 24 croquettes

2 lbs	(900 g) potatoes, peeled, cut into chunks
1 cup	(250 mL) flour
½ cup	butter, softened
1	egg
1 cup	(250 mL) grated Cheddar cheese
	salt and pepper
	pinch of nutmeg
	pinch of cayenne pepper
⅓ cup	(80 mL) butter

■ In a saucepan filled with lightly salted boiling water, cook potatoes, then drain.

■ In a bowl, purée potatoes. Add flour, softened butter, egg, and cheese. Season with salt, pepper, nutmeg, and cayenne pepper.

■ Shape into a roll measuring 2 inches (5 cm) in diameter. With a sharp knife, slice 1 ¼ inch (3 cm) thick slices.

■ In a skillet, melt butter and sauté potato slices. Turn when golden.

Sautéed Potatoes and Peppers

about 4 cups (1 L)

1 lb	(450 g) potatotes, diced
¼ cup	(60 mL) oil
¼ cup	(60 mL) red and green sweet peppers, finely chopped
	salt and pepper

■ In a saucepan filled with lightly salted boiling water, blanch potatoes for 4 minutes, then drain.

■ In a large skillet, heat oil and sauté potatoes on all sides. Add peppers and cook for 1 minute. Season with salt and pepper.

Sautéed Potatoes with Carrots and Zucchini

about 4 cups (1 L)

1 lb	(450 g) potatoes, diced
¼ cup	(60 mL) oil
¼ cup	(60 mL) grated carrot
¼ cup	(60 mL) zucchini, cut into thin sticks
	salt and pepper

■ In a saucepan filled with lightly salted boiling water, blanch potatoes for 4 minutes, then drain.

■ In a large skillet, heat oil and sauté potatoes on all sides.

■ Add carrots and zucchini, season with salt and pepper and cook for 3 minutes longer.

Potatoes Dauphinoise

about 2 cups (500 mL)

1 ½ cups	(375 mL) pota-toes, sliced in rounds
	salt and pepper
2 tsp	(10 mL) garlic, finely sliced
4 tsp	(20 mL) thyme
½ cup	(125 mL) 35% cream
	milk

■ Preheat oven to 375 °F (190 °C).

■ In a large bowl, combine potatoes seasoned with salt, pepper, garlic, and thyme and stir.

■ Spread mixture in an oven-proof dish, pour cream over potatoes, then add milk up to halfway level and bake for 40 minutes or until liquid has reduced and top is golden.

VARIATION

• Before pouring cream over potatoes, add ¼ tsp (1 mL) of each of the following chopped fines herbes: chives, basil, tarragon, and parsley, as shown.

Tomato-flavored Potatoes

about 2 cups (500 mL)

1 ½ cups	(375 mL) pota-toes, sliced into rounds
	salt and pepper
2 tsp	(10 mL) thyme
½ cup	(125 mL) 35% cream
	milk
¼ cup	(60 mL) toma-toes, diced

■ Follow same recipe as for Potatoes Dauphinoise, then add diced tomatoes 10 minutes before end of cooking time.

Sautéed Potatoes Lyonnaise

about 2 cups (500 mL)

1 tbsp	(15 mL) vegetable oil
1 tbsp	(15 mL) butter
4	potatoes, cooked "al dente," sliced
¼ cup	(60 mL) onion, finely sliced
	salt and pepper
1 tbsp	(15 mL) parsley
1 tsp	(5 mL) garlic, finely sliced

■ In a skillet, over high heat, heat oil and melt butter.

■ Add potatoes and onions and cook until slightly browned. Stir gently, season with salt and pepper and sprinkle with chopped parsley. Add garlic, then remove from heat.

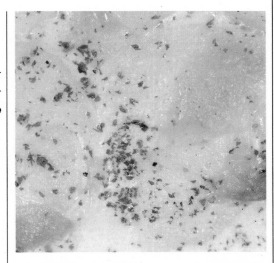

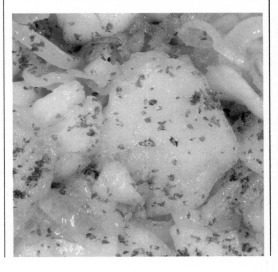

From Top to Bottom:
Potatoes Dauphinoise (variation)
■ Tomato-flavored Potatoes ■
Sautéed Potatoes Lyonnaise

301

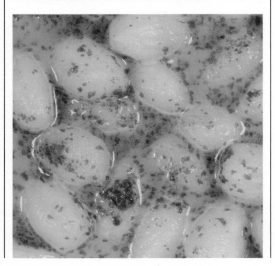

From Top to Bottom:
Steamed Potatoes with Fines
Herbes Butter ▪ Potato Balls with
Tomatoes ▪ Potato Balls with
Spinach

Steamed Potatoes with Fines Herbes Butter

about 2 cups (500 mL)

2 cups	(500 mL) potatoes, diced

Seasoned Butter

3 tbsp	(45 mL) butter, softened
2 tsp	(10 mL) parsley
2 tsp	(10 mL) tarragon
1 tsp	(5 mL) thyme
2 tsp	(10 mL) basil
1 tsp	(5 mL) garlic, finely sliced
1 tbsp	(15 mL) green onions, chopped
1 tbsp	(15 mL) lemon juice
½ tsp	(2 mL) ground pepper
	salt, to taste

▪ In a daisy steamer, cook potatoes.

▪ Meanwhile, in a large bowl, combine all other ingredients, then add potatoes and stir gently to allow potatoes to absorb herb butter. Place in a serving dish.

Potato Balls with Tomatoes

about 2 cups (500 mL)

8	large potatoes
4 cups	(1 L) water or chicken stock
1 cup	(250 mL) tomato juice
	salt and pepper

▪ With the aid of a melon-ball spoon, shape potatoes into balls.

▪ In a saucepan, pour water or chicken stock and cook potato balls for 6 minutes, then drain.

▪ In a separate saucepan, heat tomato juice, then add potato balls and let them absorb juice. Season with salt and pepper.

Potato Balls with Spinach

about 2 cups (500 mL)

8	large potatoes
4 cups	(1 L) chicken stock
½ cup	(125 mL) spinach, stems removed
	salt and pepper

▪ With the aid of a melon ball spoon, shape potatoes into balls.

▪ In a saucepan, heat chicken stock and poach spinach leaves for 4 minutes, then purée in a food processor.

▪ Bring chicken stock to a boil and cook potato balls for 6 minutes. Serve with spinach juice.

Curried Potatoes

about 2 cups (500 mL)	
2 cups	(500 mL) potatoes, diced
1 cup	(250 mL) chicken stock
1 tsp	(5 mL) curry powder
	pinch of saffron
	salt and pepper
1 tbsp	(15 mL) chopped parsley

■ In a saucepan, mix together all ingredients except parsley, and bring to a boil. Cover and simmer for 15 minutes. Sprinkle with parsley and serve.

Buttered Potatoes

about 2 cups (500 mL)	
½ lb	(225 g) bacon, cut into pieces
¼ cup	(60 mL) pearl onions
1 cup	(250 mL) chicken stock
1 ½ cups	(375 mL) potatoes, cut into large cubes
1 tbsp	(15 mL) parsley
1	bay leaf
	pinch of thyme
1 tsp	(5 mL) garlic, finely sliced
	salt and pepper
¼ cup	(60 mL) butter

■ In a stove-top casserole, melt the bacon and cook onions until transparent.

■ Pour chicken stock over mixture. Add all other ingredients except butter, cover and cook 25 to 30 minutes.

■ Remove from heat, add butter, cover and let stand for 10 minutes before serving.

Glazed Potato Sticks

about 2 cups (500 mL)	
2 cups	(500 mL) potatoes, cut into sticks
	salt and pepper
½ oz	(18 g) package of commercial hollandaise sauce
1 tbsp	(15 mL) grated Parmesan cheese

■ Heat broiler.

■ In a daisy steamer, cook potato sticks "al dente," then season with salt and pepper.

■ Meanwhile, prepare hollandaise sauce according to package directions.

■ Arrange potato sticks in an oven-proof serving dish, coat with sauce and sprinkle with grated Parmesan. Broil until golden.

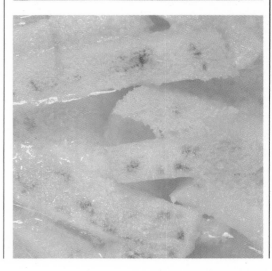

From Top to Bottom:
Curried Potatoes ▪ Buttered
Potatoes ▪ Glazed Potato Sticks

Cheese-stuffed Potatoes

4 servings

4	large potatoes
3 tbsp	(45 mL) butter
1	egg
½ cup	(125 mL) grated cheese
3 tbsp	(45 mL) milk
	salt and pepper
	breadcrumbs

- Preheat oven to 400 °F (205 °C).

- Wrap each potato in a sheet of aluminum foil, then pierce aluminum with fork and bake for 90 minutes.

- Cut a ¼ inch (0,5 cm) cap off top of each potato, scoop out pulp without damaging skin.

- Purée pulp in a food processor. Add all other ingredients except breadcrumbs.

- Garnish potatoes with mixture and sprinkle with breadcrumbs. Broil until golden.

Ham-stuffed Potatoes

4 servings

4	large potatoes
3 tbsp	(45 mL) butter
1	egg
½ cup	(125 mL) grated cheese
3 tbsp	(45 mL) milk
	salt and pepper
1 tsp	(5 mL) bread-crumbs
¼ cup	(60 mL) cooked ham, cut into strips

- Follow same recipe as Cheese-stuffed Potatoes. Simply add ham to puréed potatoes before stuffing.

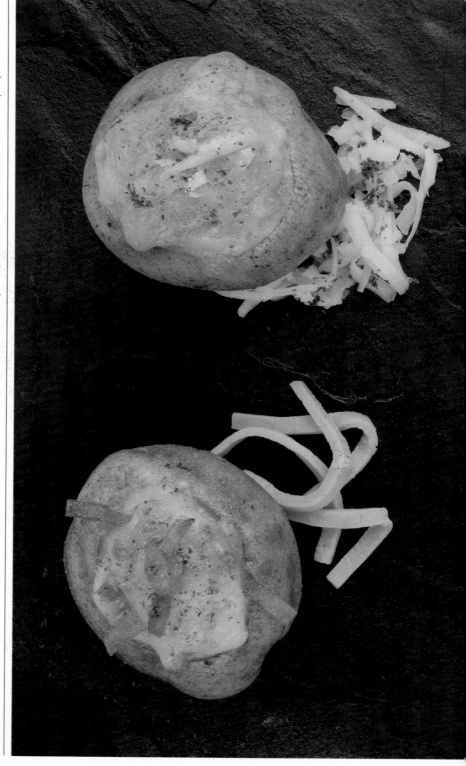

Cheese-stuffed Potatotes
Ham-stuffed Potatoes

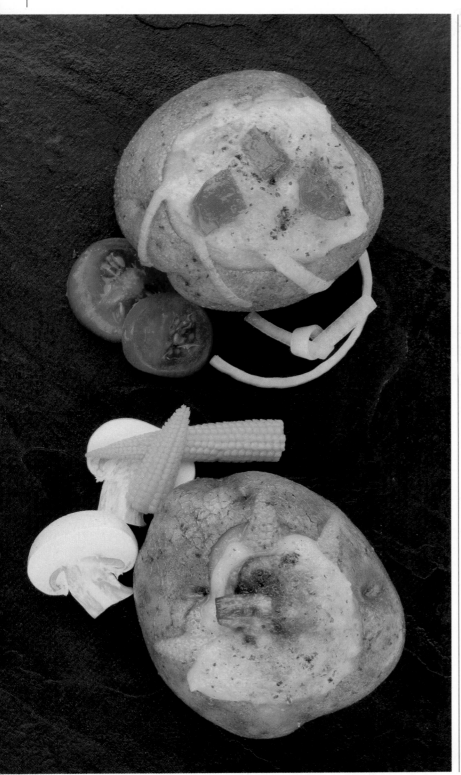

Tomato-stuffed Potatoes

	4 servings
4	large potatoes
3 tbsp	(45 mL) butter
1	egg
½ cup	(125 mL) grated cheese
3 tbsp	(45 mL) milk
	salt and pepper
1 tsp	(5 mL) bread-crumbs
½ cup	(125 mL) tomatoes, diced

■ Follow same recipe as for Cheese-stuffed Potatoes. Simply add diced tomatoes to puréed potatoes before stuffing.

Potatoes Stuffed with Mushrooms and Miniature Corn

	4 servings
4	large potatoes
3 tbsp	(45 mL) butter
1	egg
½ cup	(125 mL) grated cheese
3 tbsp	(45 mL) milk
	salt and pepper
1 tsp	(5 mL) bread-crumbs
¼ cup	(60 mL) mushrooms, sliced, sautéed in butter
12	miniature ears of corn, sliced in half

■ Follow same recipe as for Cheese-stuffed Potatoes. Simply add mushrooms and miniature ears of corn to puréed potatoes before stuffing.

Tomato-stuffed Potatoes
Potatoes Stuffed with Mushrooms and Miniature Corn

FIDDLEHEAD GREENS

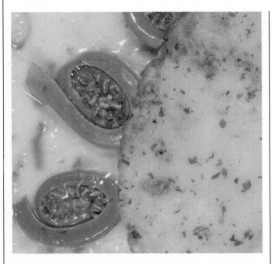

Fiddlehead Crêpes

6 servings

5 tbsp	(75 mL) butter
¼ cup	(60 mL) flour
1	leek white, chopped
2	French (dry) shallots, finely sliced
1 lb	(450 g) fiddlehead greens
3 cups	(750 mL) chicken stock
¼ cup	(60 mL) water-cress
2 tbsp	(30 mL) parsley
¼ cup	(60 mL) 15% cream
6	small crêpes, 6 inches (15 cm) in diameter

■ In a skillet, melt ¼ cup (60 mL) butter, then add flour, stir and set aside.

■ In a saucepan, melt 1 tbsp (15 mL) butter and sauté leek whites and shallots until transparent.

■ Meanwhile, set aside 18 fiddlehead greens for garnish. Dice remaining fiddlehead greens, add to leek-shallot mixture.

■ Pour chicken stock over vegetables and simmer until vegetables are tender to taste. Remove from heat and pass vegetables through sieve. Set cooking juice aside.

■ In a separate sauce-pan, pour cooking juice and add butter-flour roux to liquid and cook over medium heat.

■ Add vegetables, wa-tercress, parsley and cream and adjust sea-soning, then set aside.

■ Arrange crêpes in serving dishes. Garnish each crêpe with ½ cup (125 mL) fiddlehead velouté and fold crêpe. Garnish each crêpe with 3 whole fiddlehead greens.

VARIATION

• **Add to chicken stock 3 tbsp (45 mL) diced carrots and 6 mini-ature ears of corn, sliced into 4 pieces. Serve this mixture on crêpes, without folding, as shown.**

Fiddlehead Greens and Pearl Onion Croustade

4 servings

2 tbsp	(30 mL) butter
⅔ cup	(160 mL) fiddle-head greens
24	pearl onions
	salt and pepper
1	French (dry) shallot, finely sliced
¼ cup	(60 mL) brown gravy
2 tbsp	(30 mL) chopped parsley
4	vol-au-vent pastry shells

■ In a skillet, melt butter and sauté fiddlehead greens with pearl onions. Season with salt and pepper, add shallots and stir.

■ Pour brown gravy over vegetables and bring to a boil. Remove from heat and sprinkle with parsley. Fill vol-au-vent pastry shells with mixture and serve.

From Top to Bottom:
Fiddlehead Crêpes ■ (Variation)
■ Fiddlehead Greens and Pearl Onion Croustade

Fiddleheads, the curly new leaves of woodland ferns, were welcome greens for early settlers after the hard North American winter. Today we eat this spring delicacy sautéed in butter or steamed and sprinkled with lemon juice. Their pretty shape and color, as well as their subtle taste, make them a worthwhile addition to many dishes.

Marinated Fiddlehead Greens

4 to 6 servings

2 cups	(500 mL) fiddlehead greens
½ cup	(125 mL) olive oil
¼ cup	(60 mL) white wine vinegar
	salt and pepper
½ tsp	(2 mL) chopped tarragon
	juice of ½ lemon
1 tsp	(5 mL) sugar
2	tomatoes, thinly sliced
8	black olives

■ In a bowl, combine all ingredients except tomatoes and olives and marinate for 2 hours.

■ Spread mixture over thinly sliced tomatoes. Garnish with black olives and serve.

Fiddlehead Greens Sautéed in Butter

4 servings

2 cups	(500 mL) fiddlehead greens
2 tbsp	(30 mL) butter
	salt and pepper

■ In a saucepan filled with lightly salted boiling water, blanch fiddlehead greens for 4 minutes, then drain.

■ In a skillet, melt butter and sauté fiddlehead greens for 3 minutes. Season with salt and pepper.

Fiddlehead Greens with Garlic and Chives

4 servings

2 cups	(500 mL) fiddlehead greens
1 cup	(250 mL) sour cream or plain yogurt
2	garlic cloves, finely sliced
¼ tsp	(1 mL) Worcestershire sauce
	juice of ½ lemon
	salt and pepper
1 tsp	(5 mL) chives, chopped

Garnish

4	spinach leaves
¼ cup	(60 mL) grated carrots

■ In a bowl, combine all ingredients except for garnish ingredients and marinate for 1 hour.

■ Pour mixture over spinach leaves. Garnish with grated carrots.

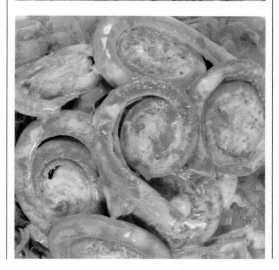

From Top to Bottom: Marinated Fiddlehead Greens ▪ Fiddlehead Greens Sautéed in Butter ▪ Fiddlehead Greens with Garlic and Chives

TOMATOES

Tomato Pizza

6 to 8 wedges

5	large tomatoes, cored, sliced
1	uncooked pizza crust
3 tbsp	(45 mL) Dijon mustard
1	knob of butter or small amount of oil
3	medium-size onions, peeled, sliced
	basil (optional)
1/2 lb	(225 g) Emmenthal cheese, cut into thin strips
8	mushrooms, sliced
	salt and pepper
1 tbsp	(15 mL) olive oil
1	garlic clove, finely sliced

■ Preheat oven to 350 °F (175 °C).

■ Spread pizza dough with mustard and set aside.

■ In a skillet, heat butter or oil, and lightly sauté onions, then spread over top of crust and sprinkle with basil.

■ Cover mixture with cheese strips. Arrange tomato slices and mushrooms so as to overlap, and season with salt and pepper.

■ In a bowl, combine olive oil and garlic and pour mixture over tomatoes.

■ Bake for 30 minutes. Garnish with black olives and basil leaves. Serve hot or warm.

Cheese-stuffed Tomatoes

4 servings

8	slices bacon
1 tbsp	(15 mL) bacon grease
2 tbsp	(30 mL) mayonnaise or vinaigrette
2 tsp	(10 mL) vinegar
1/4 tsp	(1 mL) basil
1/2 cup	(125 mL) celery, diced
1 1/2 cups	(375 mL) cottage cheese
4	tomatoes, hollowed out
	chives

■ In a skillet, cook bacon until crunchy, then crumble and set aside.

■ In a bowl, combine bacon grease, mayonnaise or vinaigrette, vinegar, basil, and bacon. Add celery and cottage cheese and stir gently. Cover and refrigerate for 1 hour. Stuff mixture into tomatoes and garnish with chives. Serve cold.

Tomato Pizza
Cheese-stuffed Tomatoes

The tomato, an excellent source of vitamins, A, B, and C, is actually a fruit. Its development as a table food has changed cooking the world over, and it is one of the few fruits that adapt, raw or cooked, to such a wide variety of dishes. To ripen tomatoes that are still firm, put them in a tightly closed paper bag for a few days.

Cherry Tomatoes Provençale

8 tomatoes

3 tbsp	(45 mL) breadcrumbs
2 tsp	(10 mL) chopped parsley
1	garlic clove, finely sliced
	salt and pepper
2 tsp	(10 mL) vegetable oil
8	cherry tomatoes, halved
2 tsp	(10 mL) Parmesan cheese, grated

■ Preheat oven to 400 °F (205 °C).

■ In a bowl, combine breadcrumbs, parsley, garlic, salt, and pepper.

■ Lightly coat each tomato half with oil, then cover with breadcrumb mixture, sprinkle with Parmesan and bake for 5 minutes.

Tomatoes au Gratin

4 to 6 servings

3 tbsp	(45 mL) olive oil
6	large tomatoes, cut into ½ inch (2 cm) thick slices
1 tbsp	(15 mL) oregano or marjoram
2 tbsp	(30 mL) capers
¼ tsp	(1 mL) salt
	pepper
¼ cup	(60 mL) breadcrumbs
¼ cup	(60 mL) grated Parmesan cheese

■ Preheat oven to 450 °F (220 °C).

■ Coat a baking dish with 1 tbsp (15 mL) olive oil and spread half the tomato slices in bottom, then sprinkle with oregano and add half the capers. Season with salt and pepper.

■ Arrange rest of tomatoes and capers over mixture. Sprinkle with breadcrumbs and cheese, and coat with rest of olive oil. Bake for 20 minutes. Serve hot or cold.

*Cherry Tomatoes Provençale
Tomatoes au Gratin*

VEGETABLE JUICES

Tomato Juice Cocktail

about 4 cups (1 L)

2 tbsp	(30 mL) chopped parsley
2 tbsp	(30 mL) chopped chives
1 tbsp	(15 mL) sweet pepper, grated
½	stalk celery, grated
¼ cup	(60 mL) cucumber, grated
4 cups	(1 L) tomato juice
1 tsp	(5 mL) salt
1 tsp	(5 mL) sugar
1 tbsp	(15 mL) Worcestershire sauce
	Tabasco sauce (optional)
1 tbsp	(15 mL) lemon juice
	lemon, cut into thin slices and lemon peel
	fennel sprigs

■ In a bowl, combine parsley, chives, pepper, celery, cucumber, and tomato juice and steep for 2 hours, then pass mixture through sieve.

■ Add other ingredients, stir and refrigerate until thoroughly chilled.

■ Drop 1 or 2 ice cubes into each glass and pour tomato juice cocktail over ice cubes. Garnish with lemon slices and fennel sprigs.

Carrot and Apple Juice

about 2 cups (500 mL)

4	medium carrots
2	celery stalks
1	red apple

■ Put all vegetables through juice extractor and pour into tall glasses. Garnish with celery leaves and a slice of apple.

Tomato Juice Cocktail
Carrot and Apple Juice

It's always a good idea to relax for a few minutes before a meal. Instead of opening a beer or pouring the usual apéritif, why not replenish your system with a tall glass of liquid vitamins?

Velvety Cucumber Juice

about 2 cups (500 mL)

2	cucumbers, peeled, seeded
¼ cup	(60 mL) 35% cream
¼ cup	(60 mL) milk
	pinch of salt
	pinch of pepper
4	fennel leaves
	crushed ice

■ Put all ingredients except ice through blender, pour into glasses ¼ full of crushed ice. Garnish with skewered vegetables (1 cherry tomato, 1 cucumber slice, 1 red onion wedge, 1 sweet pepper wedge).

Tomato and Melon Beverage

about 4 cups (1 L)

8	tomatoes, peeled, seeded
1	melon, peeled, seeded
2 tbsp	(30 mL) lemon juice
	pinch of cayenne pepper
½ tsp	(2 mL) Worcestershire sauce
	pinch of salt
	crushed ice
1 tsp	(5 mL) paprika

■ In a blender, combine all ingredients except paprika and ice, stir and pour into glasses ¼ full of crushed ice. Sprinkle with paprika.

■ Serve with skewered cherry tomatoes and melon balls.

Velvety Cucumber Juice
Tomato and Melon Beverage

You can let your culinary imagination run free when it comes to salads. Green salads, for example, can feature all sorts of leaf vegetables: the traditional iceberg, Boston, and romaine lettuces, plus chicory, lamb's lettuce (corn salad), endive, watercress, spinach, and even dandelion leaves! Then there are one-of-a-kind salads such as coleslaw, potato, rice or macaroni salad, bound with a mayonnaise, vinaigrette, or mustard dressing. Mixed salads are the most colorful, with combinations of bright and dark reds, yellows and oranges, and a whole range of greens. Most useful of all are salads that offer a one-plate meal, such as the Mediterranean standby, salade niçoise, which combines tuna, green beans, and eggs, to name just a few of its many ingredients.

SALADS

Green salads

Monday Salad

4 servings

1	iceberg lettuce, torn into large shreds
10	radishes, sliced
8	chive sprigs, finely sliced
4	celery stalks, finely sliced
3 tbsp	(45 mL) mayonnaise

■ In a salad bowl, combine all ingredients. Fold in mayonnaise. Toss.

VARIATION
• **Add diced apples and julienned carrots to salad. Garnish with parsley.**

Simple Salad

4 servings

¼ cup	(60 mL) peanut oil
2 tbsp	(30 mL) lemon juice
½ tsp	(2 mL) dry mustard
½ tsp	(2 mL) paprika
½ tsp	(2 mL) salt
¼ tsp	(1 mL) pepper
1	curly lettuce, washed, dried, hand-torn
	tomato slices
	hard-boiled egg slices
	pickles
	radishes, thinly sliced

■ In a small bowl, combine oil, lemon juice, and dry mustard. Season with paprika, salt, and pepper. Stir.

■ Spread shredded leaf lettuce in large salad bowl. Coat with dressing. Toss.

■ Garnish with sliced tomatoes, hard-boiled egg slices, pickles and radishes.

Green Salad Italiana

	8 servings
2	Boston lettuces, washed, drained, hand-torn
1/4 cup	(60 mL) celery leaves, washed, dried
1/4 cup	(60 mL) spinach, washed, dried
1	onion, chopped
2	small garlic cloves, finely sliced
2 tbsp	(30 mL) lemon
1 tbsp	(15 mL) corn oil
1 tbsp	(15 mL) mayonnaise
3/4 tsp	(3 mL) Dijon mustard
1 tsp	(5 mL) oregano
	salt and pepper
1/3 cup	(80 mL) grated Parmesan cheese

■ In a large salad bowl, combine lettuce, spinach, and celery leaves and set aside.

■ In a small bowl, combine other ingredients (except cheese). Pour mixture over salad. Sprinkle with grated Parmesan and serve.

Romaine and Cucumber Salad

	4 servings
1	cucumber, peeled
1	romaine lettuce, washed, dried, hand-torn
3 tbsp	(45 mL) sour cream
1	garlic clove, finely sliced
1 tsp	(5 mL) chopped chives
	salt and pepper

■ Slice cucumber in half lengthwise. Scoop out seeds and pulp. Cut into thin slices.

■ In a salad bowl, combine lettuce and cucumber and set aside.

■ In a small bowl, mix other ingredients. Pour over vegetables. Toss lightly.

* Illustrated recipe

Salad Duet

6 servings	
1	small Boston lettuce, washed, dried, hand-torn
1	small red lettuce, washed, dried, hand-torn
3 tbsp	(45 mL) mayonnaise
1 tsp	(5 mL) honey
1 tsp	(5 mL) sesame seeds
	salt and pepper

■ In a large salad bowl, toss together both lettuces and set aside.

■ In a small bowl, combine other ingredients. Pour dressing over lettuce. Toss.

Festive Salad

4 servings	
1	Boston lettuce, washed, dried, hand-torn
1	avocado, thinly sliced
1/2	sweet red pepper, diced
2	shallots, chopped
1/2 cup	(125 mL) tofu, diced
2 tbsp	(30 mL) sesame seeds, roasted

Garlic Dressing

3	garlic cloves, finely sliced
2 tbsp	(30 mL) lemon juice
3/4 cup	(180 mL) sunflower oil
1/4 tsp	(1 mL) dry mustard
1/2 tsp	(2 mL) dill
1 tsp	(5 mL) dried parsley

■ In a serving dish, place each ingredient in order listed, and set aside.

■ In a small bowl, combine all garlic dressing ingredients and pour over salad.

VARIATIONS

• Replace avocado with fiddlehead greens, blanched for 5 minutes and cooled.

• Replace tofu with cubed cheese.

• Replace sesame seeds with sunflower seeds.

316

Mixed Salad

Winter Salad

Mixed Salad

4 servings

Dressing

	juice of 1 lemon
3 tbsp	(45 mL) soya oil or sunflower oil with 2 drops soy sauce
½	iceberg lettuce
½	romaine lettuce
½ cup	(125 mL) broccoli, broken into flowerets
½ cup	(125 mL) cauliflower, broken into flowerets
¼ cup	(60 mL) radishes, sliced
¼ cup	(60 mL) cucumber, sliced
1 or 2	green onions, chopped
1	celery stalk, diced
3 to 5	fresh mushrooms, sliced
	chopped parsley
½ cup	(125 mL) Cheddar cheese, diced
	salt and pepper

■ In a small bowl, combine all dressing ingredients and set aside.

■ In a salad bowl, combine all other ingredients. Coat with dressing. Toss gently.

Winter Salad

4 servings

1	escarole lettuce, washed, dried, hand-torn
1	Boston lettuce, washed, dried, hand-torn
1	package of water-cress, washed, dried
1 cup	(250 mL) radishes, sliced
1	leek white, julienned

Vinaigrette

3 tbsp	(45 mL) wine or sherry vinegar
½ tsp	(2 mL) Dijon mustard
½ tsp	(2 mL) fresh parsley
½ cup	(125 mL) oil

■ Arrange shredded lettuce leaves in individual serving bowls or in large salad bowl. Garnish middle with radishes and leek whites. Coat with vinaigrette.

317

Crunchy Salad

4 servings	
1 tbsp	(15 mL) butter
¾ cup	(180 mL) mush-rooms, chopped
¾ cup	(180 mL) celery, diced
1 ½ cups	(375 mL) pork meat, cooked, diced
2 tbsp	(30 mL) green bell pepper, diced
2 tbsp	(30 mL) slivered almonds
1	medium red apple, unpeeled, diced
¼ tsp	(1 mL) salt
	pepper
¼ cup	(60 mL) vinaigrette or mayonnaise
4	leaves Boston lettuce, washed, dried
1	tomato, sliced
½	cucumber, sliced

■ In a skillet, melt butter; cook mushrooms and celery until slightly golden. Let stand to cool.

■ Add pork meat, pepper, and almonds, stir lightly and set aside.

■ When ready to serve, add diced apple. Season with salt and pepper. Coat with dressing. Toss gently.

■ Arrange mixture on a bed of lettuce leaves. Garnish with tomatoes and cucumbers.

Fresh and Easy Salad

4 servings	
1	curly lettuce, washed, dried, hand-torn
8 oz	(225 g) spinach, washed, hand-torn
8 oz	(225 g) frozen green peas
2 cups	(500 mL) grated Canadian Cheddar cheese
½ cup	(125 mL) green onions
1 tbsp	(15 mL) chives
½ cup	(125 mL) bacon, cut into pieces (optional)
6	hard-boiled eggs, sliced

Vinaigrette

1 cup	(250 mL) mayonnaise
1 cup	(250 mL) sour cream or natural yogurt
2 tsp	(10 mL) green onions, chopped

■ In a salad bowl, mix all ingredients and set aside.

■ In a small bowl, combine all vinaigrette ingredients. Pour over salad and serve.

Egg Salad

4 servings

8	hard-boiled eggs
1 cup	(250 mL) mayonnaise
1 tbsp	(15 mL) prepared mustard
½ cup	(125 mL) chicken or ham, cooked, diced
½ cup	(125 mL) celery, finely sliced
	salt and pepper
8	olives, halved
4	leaves Boston lettuce
1	tomato, sliced
	chopped parsley

■ Cut eggs in half, lengthwise. Gently remove egg yolks. Place in salad bowl. Set egg whites aside.

■ In a bowl, mash egg yolks with a fork. Add mayonnaise, mustard, chicken or ham, and celery. Season with salt and pepper and toss.

■ Fill each egg white shell with mixture.

■ In a serving dish, spread lettuce leaves and arrange stuffed egg whites in middle. Decorate with sliced tomatoes and olive halves. Sprinkle with parsley and serve.

Bean Ceasar Salad

8 servings

1	romaine lettuce, washed, dried, hand-torn
¾ cup	(180 mL) Italian vinaigrette
1	egg
1 ½ cups	(375 mL) green beans, cooked, sliced
⅓ cup	(80 mL) grated Parmesan cheese
1 cup	(250 mL) croûtons
8	anchovy filets, rolled

■ In a salad bowl, arrange lettuce leaves and set aside.

■ In a small bowl, combine vinaigrette and egg, and coat lettuce leaves with mixture. Add green beans. Sprinkle with grated Parmesan, toss and add croûtons. Garnish with anchovy filets.

Boston Salad with Fruit and Shrimp

4 servings

1	medium grapefruit
2	oranges
1	Boston lettuce, washed, dried, hand-torn
1	small green bell pepper, seeded, finely sliced
1	small sweet red pepper, seeded, finely sliced
	salt and pepper
1 cup	(250 mL) baby shrimp

■ Peel grapefruit and oranges. Divide into wedges.

■ In a salad bowl, combine all ingredients. Coat with a light dressing.

Chicken Salad Supreme

6 servings

2 cups	(500 mL) chicken, cooked, diced
1 cup	(250 mL) pineapple, diced
½ cup	(125 mL) celery, diced
1 cup	(250 mL) green peas
2 tbsp	(30 mL) radishes, sliced
¾ cup	(180 mL) mayonnaise
	Boston lettuce leaves

■ In a salad bowl, gently toss all ingredients except Boston lettuce leaves and refrigerate for 30 minutes.

■ In a serving dish, spread Boston lettuce leaves and spoon salad on top.

VARIATION

• Add seedless green grapes to salad.

Grape Salad

4 servings

4	Boston lettuce leaves
4	romaine lettuce leaves
8	chicory or curly endive lettuce leaves
5	beet leaves
2	green onions, finely sliced
1	celery stalk, diced
2	carrots, shredded
8	red grapes, seeded, halved
8	seedless green grapes, halved
	nuts and/or almonds, finely chopped

Dressing

2 tbsp	(30 mL) mayonnaise
2 tbsp	(30 mL) plain yogurt
1 tbsp	(15 mL) lemon juice
	salt and pepper

■ Wash, dry, and tear up lettuce leaves and beet leaves.

■ In a salad bowl, combine salad ingredients and set aside.

■ Combine all dressing ingredients. Pour over salad and toss.

"Moon in June" Salad

4 servings

1 cup	(250 mL) Boston lettuce, cut into strips
1	bouquet of watercress
2 cups	(500 mL) spinach leaves
1 tsp	(5 mL) chives
2 tbsp	(30 mL) cold-pressed olive oil
	juice of 1/2 lemon
	salt and pepper
4	cabbage leaves, shell-shaped
4	artichoke bottoms
1	white onion, finely sliced
1	garlic clove, finely sliced
2	medium-size carrots, grated

■ In a large salad bowl, combine lettuce, watercress, spinach leaves, chives, oil, and lemon juice. Season with salt and pepper.

■ Put mixture on shell-shaped cabbage leaves. Garnish with artichoke bottoms, onion, and garlic. Arrange grated carrots in a circle around the cabbage leaves.

Warm salads

Creole-style Brussels Sprouts

4 servings

3 tbsp	(45 mL) butter
1	large onion, chopped
1	green bell pepper, chopped
1	garlic clove, finely sliced
14 oz	(398 mL) canned tomatoes
2 cups	(500 mL) Brussels sprouts
	salt and pepper
½ tsp	(2 mL) basil
4	Chinese lettuce leaves

■ In a skillet, melt butter and sauté onion, pepper, and garlic for 4 minutes. Add tomatoes and Brussels sprouts. Season with salt, pepper, and basil. Reduce heat. Cover and cook 15 to 20 minutes. Arrange on Chinese lettuce leaves and serve.

4 to 6 servings

4 cups	(1 L) cooked rice
2 cups	(500 mL) romaine lettuce, hand-torn
1	cucumber, peeled, seeded, finely sliced
3 tbsp	(45 mL) white vinegar
3 tbsp	(45 mL) soy sauce
2 tsp	(10 mL) sesame oil
1 tsp	(5 mL) sugar
2 tbsp	(30 mL) vegetable oil
3	eggs, beaten, slightly seasoned with salt and pepper
1 tbsp	(15 mL) grated ginger, (optional)
2	carrots, sliced very thinly on the diagonal
¼ lb	(115 g) snow peas, diagonally sliced
¼ lb	(115 g) mushrooms, sliced
½ cup	(125 mL) currants
½	sweet red pepper, sliced into strips
½ cup	(125 mL) chicken stock
2	green onions, chopped

■ In a large salad bowl, combine rice, lettuce and cucumber and set aside.

■ In a small bowl, mix vinegar, soy sauce, sesame oil, and sugar and set aside.

■ In a wok or a skillet, heat 1 tbsp (15 mL) oil. Pour eggs into wok. Cook over medium heat. Remove from wok or skillet. Cut into 1 x ½ inch (2 x 1 cm) strips and set aside.

■ Heat rest of oil. Sauté ginger and carrots for 2 minutes. Add snow peas, mushrooms, currants, and sweet red pepper. Sauté for 1 minute.

■ Pour chicken stock over mixture and bring to a boil. Cover and simmer for 30 seconds. Remove cover for 30 seconds.

■ Pour mixture over rice. Stir. Add egg strips and soy sauce mixture. Sprinkle with green onions.

* Illustrated recipe

Warm Chicken Liver Salad

4 servings	
4 cups	(1 L) spinach, stalks removed
2 tsp	(10 mL) olive oil
	salt and pepper
1 tsp	(5 mL) peanut oil
½ cup	(125 mL) bacon, cut into pieces
1 cup	(250 mL) chicken livers, cut into pieces
1	garlic clove, finely sliced
2	French (dry) shallots, chopped
1 tbsp	(15 mL) port
¼ cup	(60 mL) wine vinegar

■ In a bowl, mix together spinach leaves and olive oil. Season with salt and pepper and set aside.

■ In a skillet, heat oil. Sauté bacon for 2 minutes. Sear chicken livers over high heat. Remove from skillet and set aside.

■ Using same skillet, sauté garlic and shallots. Stir. Deglaze skillet with port and wine vinegar. Let liquid reduce to half, then remove from heat.

■ Pour mixture over spinach. Toss lightly. Put chicken livers and bacon pieces on top of mixture.

Illustrated recipe

Leaf Lettuce with Chicken

4 servings	
4 cups	(1 L) curly lettuce, washed, dried, hand-torn
2 tsp	(10 mL) olive oil
	salt and pepper
1 tsp	(5 mL) peanut oil
½ cup	(125 mL) bacon, cut into pieces
1 cup	(250 mL) cooked chicken, cut into strips
1	garlic clove, finely sliced
2	green onions, chopped
2 tbsp	(30 mL) sesame seeds
1 tbsp	(15 mL) white vermouth
¼ cup	(60 mL) champagne vinegar

■ Place lettuce leaves in a salad bowl. Coat with olive oil. Season with salt and pepper. Toss lightly and set aside.

■ In a skillet, heat peanut oil. Sauté bacon for 2 minutes. Add chicken strips and sear.

■ Add garlic, green onions, and sesame seeds. Stir. Deglaze skillet with white vermouth and champagne vinegar. Reduce liquid by half, then remove from heat.

■ Pour mixture over lettuce. Toss lightly.

■ Sprinkle with chicken strips and bacon pieces.

Cabbage salads

Cabbage and Carrot Salad

6 to 8 servings

1	medium-size green cabbage, finely chopped
1	medium-size onion, finely chopped
1	carrot, finely chopped
¼ cup	(60 mL) sugar

Dressing

½ cup	(125 mL) vinegar
1 tbsp	(15 mL) prepared mustard
1 tsp	(5 mL) celery seeds
½ cup	(125 mL) vegetable oil

■ In a large salad bowl, toss all vegetables. Add sugar, then toss and set aside.

■ In a small saucepan, combine dressing ingredients. Bring to a boil. Remove from heat. Pour over salad and toss lightly.

Red Cabbage Salad

4 to 6 servings

½	small red cabbage, finely chopped
1	small cucumber, diced
½ cup	(125 mL) onion, sliced
½ cup	(125 mL) celery leaves, finely cut

Dressing

¼ cup	(60 mL) plain yogurt
	parsley
1 tsp	(5 mL) lemon juice

■ In a salad bowl, combine red cabbage, cucumber, onion, and celery leaves and set aside.

■ In a small bowl, combine all dressing ingredients. Fold into red cabbage salad.

324

Fancy Coleslaw

4 to 6 servings

½	green cabbage, grated
1	white onion, chopped
2	celery stalks, diced
2	carrots, grated
2	apples, unpeeled, diced
½	cucumber, sliced
4 to 5	radishes, sliced
½	package of alfalfa sprouts
1 tbsp	(15 mL) parsley
	pinch of thyme
	salt and pepper
¼ cup	(60 mL) walnuts, chopped
¼ cup	(60 mL) raisins
1	tomato, diced
¼ cup	(60 mL) 35% cream
¼ cup	(60 mL) sour cream
½ cup	(125 mL) grated cheese

■ In a large salad bowl, combine cabbage, onion, celery, carrots, apples, cucumber, and radishes.

■ Add alfalfa sprouts, parsley, and thyme. Season with salt and pepper. Toss. Add nuts, cheese, raisins, and diced tomato.

■ Just before serving, fold in 35% cream and sour cream.

* Illustrated recipe

VARIATION

• Add fiddlehead greens or any other seasonal vegetable to mixture. Serve with a vinaigrette of your choice.

Multi-colored Salad

6 servings

1 ½ cups	(375 mL) cabbage, chopped
1 cup	(250 mL) lettuce, chopped
1 cup	(250 mL) beets, cooked, diced
½ cup	(125 mL) spinach leaves, diagonally sliced
1 cup	(250 mL) plain yogurt
2 tsp	(10 mL) prepared mustard
1	onion, finely chopped
	salt and pepper
	chopped parsley

■ In a salad bowl, combine first 4 ingredients and set aside.

■ In a small bowl, mix together yogurt, mustard, and onion and pour over vegetables.

■ Season with salt and pepper. Toss gently. Sprinkle with parsley.

VEGETABLE SALADS

Potato Salad

4 servings

4	large potatoes, cooked, diced
1	small onion, finely chopped
½	green bell pepper, diced
½	sweet red pepper, diced
1	celery stalk, finely chopped
2	green onions, finely chopped
2 tbsp	(30 mL) parsley
	salt and pepper

Dressing

2 tbsp	(30 mL) mayonnaise
3 tbsp	(45 mL) oil
1 tbsp	(15 mL) vinegar

■ In a salad bowl, combine all vegetables and seasonings and set aside.

■ In a small bowl, mix together dressing ingredients. Pour over salad and toss gently. Refrigerate for a few hours before serving.

Carrot Salad

4 servings

3 cups	(750 mL) carrots, thinly sliced
1	medium-size onion, finely chopped
1	green bell pepper, julienned

Dressing

5 oz	(142 mL) canned tomato soup
¼ cup	(60 mL) sugar
¼ cup	(60 mL) vegetable oil
⅓ cup	(80 mL) vinegar
¼ tsp	(1 mL) pepper
½ tsp	(2 mL) salt
2 tsp	(10 mL) prepared mustard
½ tsp	(2 mL) Worcestershire sauce

■ In a saucepan filled with lightly salted boiling water, cook carrots "al dente." Drain, place in a salad bowl and cool.

■ Add onion and green pepper. Toss lightly and set aside.

■ In a mixer, beat dressing ingredients. Pour over carrots. Refrigerate mixture for a few hours before serving.

Cucumber Salad

	4 servings
1	cucumber, peeled, finely sliced
1	celery stalk, diced
1	carrot, peeled, grated
¼ cup	(60 mL) plain yogurt
1 tsp	(5 mL) lemon juice
1 tbsp	(15 mL) chopped parsley
	pepper
	celery seeds
4	lettuce leaves
2	tomatoes, cut into wedges

■ In a large salad bowl, combine cucumber, celery and carrot and set aside.

■ In a small bowl, combine yogurt, lemon juice, parsley, pepper, and celery seeds.

■ Spread lettuce leaves on a serving dish with vegetables in the middle. Coat with yogurt dressing. Decorate with tomato wedges.

Beet Salad

	4 servings
2 tbsp	(30 mL) green onions, finely sliced
2 tbsp	(30 mL) onions, chopped
1 tbsp	(15 mL) parsley
1 tbsp	(15 mL) chives
19 oz	(540 mL) canned diced beets, drained

Dressing

1 tbsp	(15 mL) dry mustard
2 tbsp	(30 mL) red wine vinegar
¾ cup	(180 mL) vegetable oil
	salt and pepper

■ In a salad bowl, combine all vegetables and herbs and set aside.

■ In a small bowl, mix together dressing ingredients. Pour over salad.

■ Refrigerate for a few hours to marinate.

* *Illustrated recipe*

Bean Sprout Salad

4 servings

8 oz	(225 g) canned bean sprouts, washed, drained
2	celery stalks, finely sliced
1	carrot, diced
1/4	green bell pepper, diced
1/4	sweet red pepper, diced
1	tomato, diced
4	green beans, cut into pieces

Dressing

1/2 cup	(125 mL) soy sauce
2 tbsp	(30 mL) vegetable oil
	juice of 1/2 lemon
1/4 cup	(60 mL) honey
1	garlic clove, finely sliced

■ In a salad bowl, combine all vegetables, then set aside.

■ In a small bowl, mix together dressing ingredients and pour over salad. Refrigerate for at least 3 hours to marinate before serving.

Beet, Endive and Watercress Salad

4 servings

2	medium beets
1/4 cup	(60 mL) water
3	endives
2 cups	(500 mL) watercress leaves, loosely packed

Green Onion Dressing

1 tbsp	(15 mL) white wine vinegar
1 tbsp	(15 mL) green onions, chopped
1 tsp	(5 mL) Dijon mustard
1/4 tsp	(1 mL) salt
	pinch of sugar
	pinch of pepper
1/4 cup	(60 mL) vegetable oil

■ Pour water into a 6-cup (1,5 L) microwave-safe dish and add beets. Cover and cook at HIGH from 10 to 12 minutes or until beets are tender to taste. Drain, then refrigerate. Peel and slice.

■ Spread out endive leaves on one side of a dish or salad bowl, and put the watercress on the other, with the beets in the center.

■ In a small bowl, whisk vinegar, green onions, mustard, salt, sugar, and pepper. Add oil in thin stream while beating constantly. Pour dressing over salad and serve.

Endives and Tomatoes with Artichokes

4 servings

4	endives
2	tomatoes, sliced
8	artichoke hearts, halved
2 tbsp	(30 mL) olive oil
1 tbsp	(15 mL) wine vinegar
	salt and pepper
1 tbsp	(15 mL) chopped parsley

■ In a serving dish, arrange endive leaves, sliced tomatoes and artichoke halves and set aside.

■ In a small bowl, blend oil, vinegar, salt, and pepper. Pour mixture over salad. Sprinkle with parsley.

Cooked Vegetable Salad

4 servings

2	sweet peppers, sliced in half lengthwise, and seeded
1 cup	(250 mL) carrots, cooked, sliced in rounds
1/2 cup	(125 mL) turnip, cooked, diced
1/2 cup	(125 mL) potato, cooked, diced
1/2 cup	(125 mL) celery, diced
1/2 cup	(125 mL) green peas, cooked
1/2 cup	(125 mL) unpeeled apple, diced
2	small green onions, finely chopped
1 cup	(250 mL) chicken (veal or ham), cooked, diced
	salt and pepper
1/4 cup	(60 mL) mayonnaise

■ In a saucepan filled with lightly salted boiling water, blanch pepper halves for 5 minutes, then drain and refrigerate.

■ Meanwhile, in a salad bowl, mix together all other ingredients.

■ Spoon mixture into pepper halves.

LEGUME SALADS

Friday's Baked Beans with a Sunday Flair

4 servings	
2 cups	(500 mL) traditional baked beans with pork, (canned or cooked)
1	green onion, finely chopped
½ cup	(125 mL) celery, finely sliced
½ cup	(125 mL) green bell pepper, finely chopped

Dressing

3 tbsp	(45 mL) oil
1 tsp	(5 mL) dry mustard
	salt and pepper
1 tbsp	(15 mL) vinegar
1 tsp	(5 mL) sugar

■ In a salad bowl, combine vegetables and set aside.

■ In a small bowl, combine dressing ingredients. Pour over vegetables. Marinate for a few hours and serve.

Lentil and Rice Salad

4 servings	
1 ½ cups	(375 mL) lentils, cooked
1 ½ cups	(375 mL) cooked rice
¼ cup	(60 mL) chopped parsley
1	onion, finely chopped
2	garlic cloves, finely sliced

Dressing

¼ cup	(60 mL) olive oil or corn oil
	juice of 1 lemon
	pinch of basil
	pinch of savory
2 tbsp	(30 mL) soy sauce
	salt and pepper

■ In a salad bowl, combine all ingredients. Let stand for 15 minutes.

VARIATION

• Serve this salad warm.

Mexican Salad

4 to 6 servings	
19 oz	(540 mL) canned red kidney beans, drained
19 oz	(540 mL) canned corn niblets, drained
1	sweet red pepper, cut into strips

Spicy Dressing

1/4 cup	(60 mL) light oil
2 tbsp	(30 mL) soy sauce
1 tbsp	(15 mL) lemon juice
1	garlic clove, finely sliced
1/2	green bell pepper, seeded, finely chopped
	salt and pepper
	pinch of chili powder

■ In a salad bowl, combine kidney beans, corn niblets and pepper and set aside.

■ In a small bowl, mix together all dressing ingredients. Pour over vegetables.

* Illustrated recipe

Two-Bean Salad

4 servings	
10 oz	(284 mL) canned lima beans
10 oz	(284 mL) canned green beans
10 oz	(284 mL) canned green beans, seasoned
1/2	green bell pepper, finely sliced
6	mushrooms, finely sliced
3	green onions, chopped
	chopped parsley
	dried mint

Dressing

1/4 cup	(60 mL) lemon juice
1/4 cup	(60 mL) oil
	salt and pepper
	garlic, finely sliced

■ In a salad bowl, combine vegetables and herbs, and set aside.

■ In a bowl, mix together all dressing ingredients. Pour over vegetables and serve.

PASTA SALADS

Yuppie Salad

4 servings	
2	tomatoes, diced
½ cup	(125 mL) canned red pimento
2 cups	(500 mL) Italian salami, diced
¼ cup	(60 mL) cashews
¾ cup	(180 mL) grated cheese
½ tsp	(2 mL) pepper
¾ tsp	(3 mL) salt
2 cups	(500 mL) cooked tortellini, drained
¼ cup	(60 mL) vegetable oil

■ In a large salad bowl, combine first 7 ingredients.

■ Add cooked tortellini. Coat with oil and toss gently.

Tuna and Pasta Salad

4 servings	
3 cups	(750 mL) pasta shells, cooked
7 oz	(198 g) canned tuna, drained
1 cup	(250 mL) celery, finely sliced
¼ cup	(60 mL) onion, chopped
½ cup	(125 mL) Italian dressing
2 cups	(500 mL) broccoli, broken into flowerets
1 cup	(250 mL) cherry tomatoes, halved
½ cup	(125 mL) grated Parmesan cheese
1 tsp	(5 mL) basil
2 cups	(500 mL) Boston lettuce
2 cups	(500 mL) romaine (or other) lettuce

■ In a large salad bowl, combine shells, tuna, celery, and onion. Pour dressing over mixture, and set aside. Marinate for a few hours.

■ Add broccoli flowerets and tomatoes. Sprinkle with Parmesan and basil.

■ In a large salad bowl, combine all ingredients and serve.

VARIATIONS

• Replace tuna with salmon, shrimp or lobster. Replace pasta shells with rotini, elbow macaroni or small bows. Replace Italian dressing with creamy dressing.

Macaroni Salad

4 servings	
2 cups	(500 mL) macaroni
¹/₂ cup	(125 mL) celery, diced
¹/₂ cup	(125 mL) carrots, grated
1	green or red sweet pepper, diced
3	green onions, chopped
¹/₂ cup	(125 mL) sweet gherkins, diced
¹/₂ cup	(125 mL) green peas, drained
	salt and pepper

Dressing

¹/₂ cup	(125 mL) mayonnaise
2 tbsp	(30 mL) prepared mustard
	juice of ¹/₂ lemon
	salt and pepper
1	hard-boiled egg, sliced

■ In a large saucepan filled with lightly salted boiling water, cook macaroni for 10 minutes. Rinse under cold running water and drain. Pour macaroni into a large salad bowl. Add other salad ingredients except for hard-boiled egg, and set aside.

■ In a small bowl, combine all dressing ingredients. Coat macaroni mixture with dressing. Garnish with hard-boiled egg slices.

* Illustrated recipe

Penne Salad

6 servings	
2 cups	(500 mL) cooked penne pasta, drained
1	chicken leg, cooked, diced
1	slice ham, cooked, chopped
2	green onions, chopped
¹/₄ cup	(60 mL) celery, diced
¹/₄ cup	(60 mL) green bell pepper, cut into strips
4	radishes, sliced
¹/₂	cucumber, diced
1	carrot, grated
2	hard-boiled eggs, chopped
1	tomato, diced
	salt and pepper
	pinch of sugar
¹/₂ cup	(125 mL) mayonnaise
	parsley

■ In a large salad bowl, combine all ingredients. Refrigerate for a few hours before serving.

Rice salads

Rice Salad

4 servings	
¹/₂	cucumber, sliced
2 tbsp	(30 mL) oil
1 tbsp	(15 mL) wine vinegar
2 cups	(500 mL) water, lightly salted
1 cup	(250 mL) rice
4 oz	(125 g) cream cheese
2 tbsp	(30 mL) mayonnaise
¹/₄	onion, finely chopped
8	stuffed olives, finely sliced
¹/₂ cup	(125 mL) green bell pepper or sweet red pepper, diced
	parsley
1	celery stalk, diced
	salt and pepper

■ In a bowl, combine cucumber, oil, and vinegar. Marinate.

■ Meanwhile, pour lightly salted water in a saucepan, bring to a boil, and add rice. Put the cooked rice in a salad bowl, and let stand to cool.

■ In a separate bowl, combine mayonnaise and cream cheese. Fold into cooled rice. Add other ingredients. Toss.

Ham and Rice Salad

4 servings	
¹/₂ cup	(125 mL) bacon, cut into pieces
1	small onion, chopped
2	green bell peppers, cut into strips
1	garlic clove, finely sliced
19 oz	(540 mL) canned tomatoes, diced
2 cups	(500 mL) cooked rice
¹/₂ tsp	(2 mL) thyme
	salt and pepper
1 cup	(250 mL) cooked ham, diced

■ Preheat oven to 350 °F (175 °C).

■ In an ovenproof skillet, melt bacon and sauté onion, green peppers, and garlic.

■ Add other ingredients. Cover and cook in oven for 10 minutes. Remove from oven and let stand to cool. Serve warm or cold.

Chinese Salad

4 servings

1 cup	(250 mL) mushrooms, finely sliced
	juice of ½ lemon
2 cups	(500 mL) cooked rice, cooled
2 cups	(500 mL) spinach, washed, dried
⅓ cup	(80 mL) raisins
1 cup	(250 mL) bean sprouts
3	celery stalks, diced
1	green bell pepper, diced
2 tbsp	(30 mL) chopped parsley
¼ cup	(60 mL) green onions, chopped
1 cup	(250 mL) cashews

Dressing

¼ cup	(60 mL) soy sauce
½ cup	(125 mL) oil
1	garlic clove, finely sliced

■ Sprinkle mushrooms with lemon juice and place in large salad bowl. Add other ingredients and set aside.

■ In a bowl, combine all dressing ingredients. Pour over vegetable salad. Toss. Marinate for 1 hour before serving.

* Illustrated recipe

Rice and Chicken Salad

4 servings

1 cup	(250 mL) cooked chicken, diced
2 cups	(500 mL) cooked rice
¼ cup	(60 mL) green bell pepper, diced
1 cup	(250 mL) celery, diced
¼ tsp	(1 mL) thyme
	salt and pepper
¼ cup	(60 mL) mayonnaise
4	lettuce leaves
	chopped parsley

■ In a salad bowl, combine all salad ingredients except lettuce leaves and toss.

■ In a serving dish, spread lettuce leaves and spoon salad mixture in the middle. Garnish with parsley.

OIL AND VINEGAR DRESSINGS

Garlic Dressing

about 1 cup (250 mL)

³/₄ cup	(180 mL) olive oil
¹/₂ cup	(125 mL) white wine vinegar or champagne vinegar
3	garlic cloves, finely sliced
1	wild garlic clove, finely sliced
¹/₄ tsp	(1 mL) Worcestershire sauce
	salt and pepper

■ In a small bowl, combine all ingredients, and adjust seasoning to taste.

Tarragon Dressing

about 1 cup (250 mL)

³/₄ cup	(180 mL) olive oil
¹/₂ cup	(125 mL) tarragon vinegar
1 tbsp	(15 mL) dried tarragon
	salt and pepper

■ In a small bowl, combine all ingredients, and adjust seasoning to taste.

N.B.: You can replace the tarragon vinegar with wine vinegar. Simply double the amount of dried tarragon in the dressing.

Chili Dressing

about 1 ¹/₄ cups (300 mL)

³/₄ cup	(180 mL) sunflower oil
1 tbsp	(15 mL) dried chili pepper, crushed
1 tbsp	(15 mL) sweet red pepper, finely chopped
1 tsp	(5 mL) paprika
4	drops Tabasco sauce
	salt and pepper
¹/₂ cup	(125 mL) wine vinegar

■ In a small saucepan, heat all ingredients except vinegar, but do not boil. Let stand to cool, pour vinegar into mixture, and adjust seasoning.

Chives, Dill and Fennel Dressing

about 1 ¹/₄ cups (300 mL)

³/₄ cup	(180 mL) olive oil
¹/₂ cup	(125 mL) champagne vinegar
2 tsp	(10 mL) dried chives
2 tsp	(10 mL) dried dill leaves
2 tsp	(10 mL) dried fennel
	salt and pepper

■ In a small bowl, mix together all ingredients, and adjust seasoning to taste.

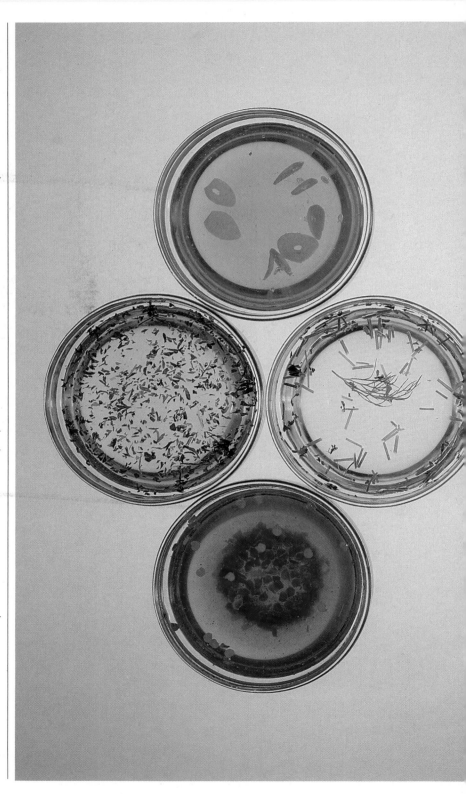

Clockwise from the top:
Garlic ▪ Chives, Dill and Fennel ▪ Chili ▪ Tarragon

Oil, vinegar, salt and pepper—these are the basic ingredients of the versatile vinaigrette. Buy top quality oil (olive, sunflower seed, or a nut oil) and if possible a wine or cider vinegar flavored with tarragon, green onions, basil, raspberry or other aromatic agents.

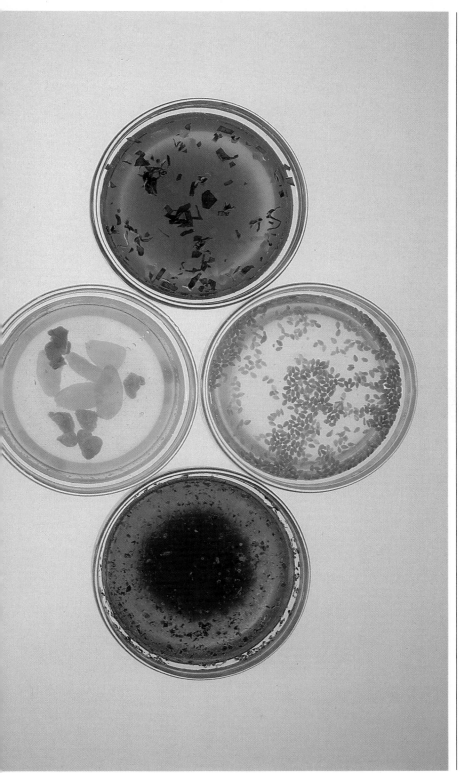

Tomato Dressing

about 1 ½ cups (375 mL)

¾ cup	(180 mL) vegetable oil
½ cup	(125 mL) wine vinegar
2 tbsp	(30 mL) ketchup
1 tsp	(5 mL) sugar
1 tbsp	(15 mL) tomatoes, chopped
2 tsp	(10 mL) basil
	salt and pepper

■ In a small bowl, mix together all ingredients. Adjust seasoning to taste.

Mustard Dressing

about 1 ¼ cups (300 mL)

¾ cup	(180 mL) vegetable oil
¼ cup	(60 mL) wine vinegar
1 tbsp	(15 mL) Dijon mustard
1 tbsp	(15 mL) old-fashioned mustard
2 tsp	(10 mL) chopped parsley
	salt and pepper

■ In a small bowl, mix all ingredients, and adjust seasoning to taste.

Sesame Seed Dressing

about 1 ¼ cups (300 mL)

1 tbsp	(15 mL) butter
3 tbsp	(45 mL) sesame seeds
¼ cup	(180 mL) sunflower oil
⅓ cup	(80 mL) white wine vinegar
1 tsp	(5 mL) sugar
	salt and pepper

■ In a skillet, melt butter and sauté sesame seeds until golden. Let stand to cool. Add other ingredients, and mix well.

Nut Dressing

about 1 ¼ cups (300 mL)

1 tbsp	(15 mL) butter
2 tbsp	(30 mL) slivered almonds
1 tbsp	(15 mL) crushed hazelnuts
¾ cup	(180 mL) peanut oil
1 tsp	(5 mL) walnut oil
⅓ cup	(80 mL) champagne vinegar
1 tsp	(5 mL) sugar

■ In a skillet, melt butter and sauté almonds and hazelnuts until golden. Let stand to cool. Add other ingredients, and mix well.

Clockwise from the top:
Tomato ▪ Sesame Seed ▪
Mustard ▪ Nut

MAYONNAISE DRESSINGS

French Dressing

about 1 ½ cups (375 mL)

1 cup	(250 mL) mayonnaise
¼ cup	(60 mL) wine vinegar
1 tbsp	(15 mL) Dijon mustard
2	French (dry) shallots, chopped
1 tsp	(5 mL) chopped tarragon
½ tsp	(2 mL) chopped chervil
¼ tsp	(1 mL) chopped thyme
1 tsp	(5 mL) chopped parsley
	salt and pepper

■ In a bowl, mix together all ingredients, and adjust seasoning to taste.

Citrus Dressing

about 1 ½ cups (375 mL)

¼ cup	(60 mL) orange wedges
¼ cup	(60 mL) grapefruit wedges
	juice of ½ lemon
¾ cup	(180 mL) mayonnaise
½ tsp	(2 mL) pink peppercorns
1 tsp	(5 mL) honey
2 tbsp	(30 mL) grapefruit juice
¼ cup	(60 mL) sour cream

■ Chop orange and grapefruit wedges into chunks and place in a bowl. Add other ingredients and stir well. Adjust seasoning to taste.

Caesar Dressing

about 1 cup (250 mL)

1 cup	(250 mL) mayonnaise
1	anchovy fillet, chopped
2	garlic cloves, finely sliced
1 tsp	(5 mL) capers, chopped
½ tsp	(2 mL) Worcestershire sauce
2	drops Tabasco sauce
1 tbsp	(15 mL) Parmesan cheese, grated
	salt and pepper

■ In a bowl, mix together all ingredients, and adjust seasoning to taste.

Catalina Dressing

about 1 ½ cups (375 mL)

1 cup	(250 mL) mayonnaise
¼ cup	(60 mL) ketchup
2 tbsp	(30 mL) wine vinegar
2 tsp	(10 mL) sugar
2 tsp	(10 mL) paprika
2	drops Tabasco sauce
	salt and pepper

■ In a bowl, mix together all ingredients, and adjust seasoning to taste.

Clockwise from the top:
French ▪ Citrus ▪
Caesar ▪ Catalina

All sorts of ingredients can be added to mayonnaise. Judicious blends of fines herbes, spices, garlic and capers, to name a few, can transform a salad.

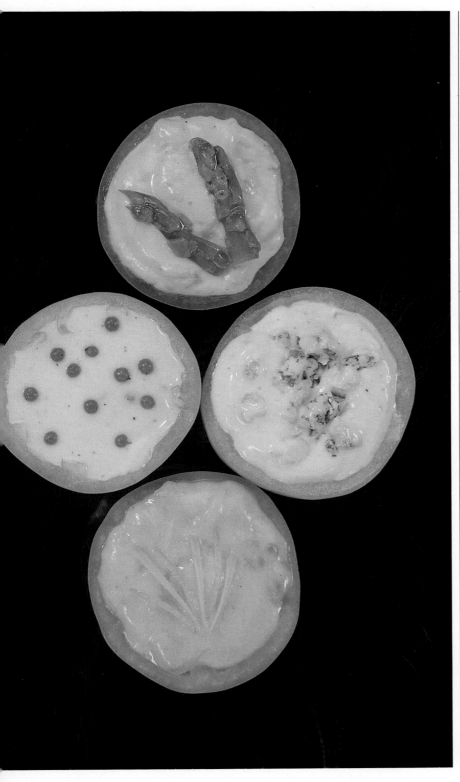

Avocado Dressing

about 1 cup (250 mL)

¼ cup	(60 mL) avocado, very ripe
	juice of 1 lemon
¾ cup	(180 mL) mayonnaise
½ tsp	(2 mL) Worcestershire sauce
2	drops Tabasco sauce
½ tsp	(2 mL) julienned lemon peel
2 tsp	(10 mL) chili sauce
	salt and pepper

■ In a food processor or blender, purée avocado and lemon juice. Add other ingredients and mix well. Adjust seasoning to taste.

Roquefort Dressing

about 1 cup (250 mL)

¾ cup	(180 mL) mayonnaise
¼ cup	(60 mL) yogurt
2 tbsp	(30 mL) white wine vinegar
1	green onion, chopped
1	garlic clove, finely sliced
¼ tsp	(1 mL) Worcestershire sauce
3	drops Tabasco sauce
1 tbsp	(15 mL) Roquefort or blue cheese, crumbled
	salt and pepper

■ In a bowl, mix together all ingredients, and adjust seasoning to taste.

Creamy Dressing

about 1 ½ cups (375 mL)

¾ cup	(180 mL) mayonnaise
3 tbsp	(45 mL) white wine vinegar
2 tbsp	(30 mL) honey
1 tsp	(5 mL) pink peppercorns
⅓ cup	(80 mL) milk
	salt and pepper

■ In a bowl, whisk together all ingredients, except for milk, until smooth and creamy. Add milk, stir, and adjust seasoning to taste.

Clockwise from the top:
Asparagus ▪ Roquefort ▪
Avocado ▪ Creamy

Asparagus Dressing

about 1 cup (250 mL)

¼ cup	(60 mL) canned asparagus
1 tbsp	(15 mL) wine vinegar
¾ cup	(180 mL) mayonnaise
1 tsp	(5 mL) Dijon mustard
½ tsp	(2 mL) Worcestershire sauce
	salt and pepper

■ In a food processor or blender, purée asparagus and vinegar. Add other ingredients and mix well. Adjust seasoning to taste.

PASTA

Contrary to popular belief, pasta was invented by the Chinese, not the Italians. The great explorer, Marco Polo, brought the recipe back to Italy. It made its way to France with Catherine de Medici, who married the French king. French, Italian and Chinese cooking have contributed much to North American cuisine, and it's therefore not surprising to find pasta in various forms on tables from coast to coast.

Pasta comes in literally hundreds of shapes. There are slender soup pastas (pennini, vermicelli, etc.), more substantial main course pastas (noodles, spaghetti, macaroni, rigatoni), and pastas especially designed for layering (lasagna), or stuffing (cannelloni, ravioli, or tortellini), to name just a few.

In recent years fresh pasta has gained in popularity over the traditional dry variety. But whether fresh or dry, there is only one basic cooking rule: pasta must be cooked "al dente," that is, tender but firm, and still a little chewy in the center. The cooking time depends on the thickness of the pasta and the ingredients used in making it.

Spaghetti, Basic Recipe

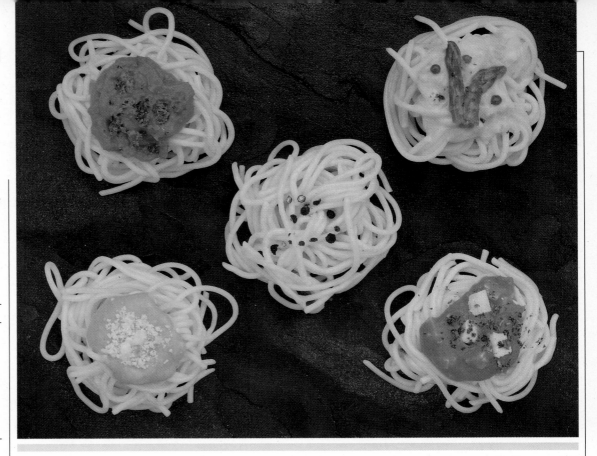

Give spaghetti an individual touch by serving different-colored pasta on the same plate, blending such subtle flavors as spinach, tomato, saffron, and so on.

4 servings		
16 cups	(4 L) water	
1 tbsp	(15 mL) oil	
2 tsp	(10 mL) salt	
1 lb	(450 g) spaghetti	
3 tbsp	(45 mL) butter	
	salt and pepper	

■ Pour water into a saucepan. Add oil and salt and bring to a boil. Add spaghetti and cook according to package directions. Rinse under cold running water, then in hot water. Drain and set aside.

■ In a skillet, melt butter and sauté cooked spaghetti. Season with salt and pepper.

■ Pour spaghetti into heated plates. Coat with a sauce or garnish of your choice.

Center: Spaghetti with Butter Clockwise from the top left: Quick and Easy Meat Sauce ▪ Asparagus Spear Sauce ▪ Chicken Sauce ▪ Salsa Rosa

Quick and Easy Meat Sauce

4 servings		
1 tbsp	(15 mL) oil	
8 oz	(225 g) ground meat	
1	onion, finely sliced	
1	garlic clove, finely sliced	
1 tsp	(5 mL) chopped parsley	
	pinch of each of fines herbes: basil, oregano, thyme, and rosemary	
14 oz	(398 mL) canned tomato sauce	

■ In a skillet, heat oil and sear ground meat. Add onion, garlic, parsley and fines herbes and cook for 4 minutes, stirring from time to time. Pour tomato sauce into mixture and bring to a boil. Simmer for 5 minutes, then pour over pasta.

Chicken Sauce

■ Follow same procedure as recipe for Quick And Easy Meat Sauce. Replace ground meat with 1/2 cup (125 mL) diced chicken.

Salsa Rosa

4 servings		
2 tsp	(10 mL) butter	
1	garlic clove, finely sliced	
2	French (dry) shallots, chopped	
14 oz	(398 mL) canned tomato sauce	
3 tbsp	(45 mL) grated Parmesan cheese	
1/4 cup	(60 mL) 35% cream	

■ In a skillet, melt butter and cook garlic and shallots until soft but not browned. Add tomato sauce and cook over medium heat for 5 minutes. Add grated Parmesan and cream and simmer for 5 minutes. Pour sauce over pasta.

Asparagus Spear Sauce

4 servings		
2 tsp	(10 mL) butter	
1	garlic clove, finely sliced	
1 tbsp	(15 mL) onion, chopped	
10 oz	(284 mL) canned asparagus spears, drained, sliced into bite-size pieces	
10 oz	(284 mL) canned cream of asparagus soup	
1/2 tsp	(2 mL) dried coriander salt and pepper	
1/2 tsp	(2 mL) pink peppercorns	

■ Set some asparagus tips aside for garnish.

■ In a skillet, melt butter and cook garlic and onion until soft but not browned. Add other ingredients, except reserved asparagus tips and pink peppercorns, and simmer for 10 minutes. Adjust seasoning. Pour mixture over cooked pasta. Garnish dish with asparagus spears and pink peppercorns.

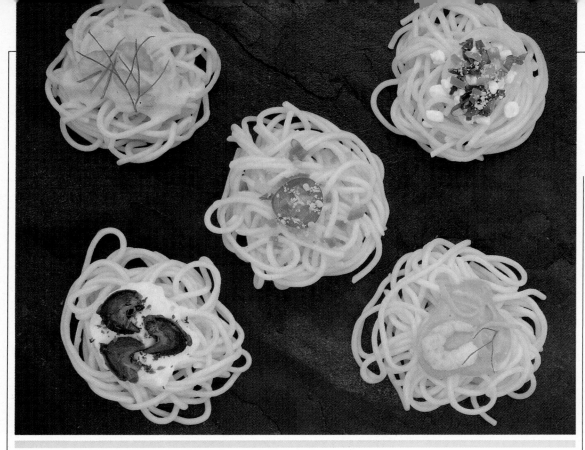

Sweet Pepper and Chili Sauce

	4 servings
1 tbsp	(15 mL) butter
¼ cup	(60 mL) sweet red and yellow peppers, finely chopped
1	small chili cut into thin rounds
1	garlic clove, finely sliced
2 tbsp	(30 mL) grated Parmesan cheese
1 tsp	(5 mL) chopped chili

■ In a skillet, melt butter and cook sweet peppers, chili rounds and garlic until soft but not browned. Add cooked pasta and heat for a few minutes. Sprinkle with grated Parmesan and chopped chili.

Shrimp Sauce

	4 servings
	Salsa Rosa
½ cup	(125 mL) baby shrimp
1 tbsp	(15 mL) julienned lemon peel
4	small fennel sprigs

■ Follow same procedure as in Salsa Rosa recipe. Add shrimp along with cream and pour mixture over pasta. Garnish with lemon peel and fennel.

Center: Sweet Pepper and Chili
Clockwise from top left:
Celery ▪ Tomato, Ricotta and Spinach
▪ Shrimp ▪ Escargot

Celery Sauce

	4 servings
2 tsp	(10 mL) butter
1	garlic clove, finely sliced
1 tbsp	(15 mL) onion, chopped
¼ cup	(60 mL) celery, diced
½ tsp	(2 mL) dried fennel
¾ tsp	(3 mL) chopped chives
	salt and pepper
10 oz	(284 mL) canned cream of celery soup

■ In a skillet, melt butter and cook garlic, onion, and celery until soft but not browned. Add other ingredients and simmer for 10 minutes. Pour over cooked pasta.

Escargot Sauce

	4 servings
1 tbsp	(15 mL) butter
2	garlic cloves, finely sliced
1	French (dry) shallot, finely sliced
24	escargots, halved
½ tsp	(2 mL) fennel seeds
2 tbsp	(30 mL) white wine
1 cup	(250 mL) 35% cream
	salt and pepper
1 tbsp	(15 mL) chopped parsley

■ In a skillet, melt butter and cook garlic, shallot, escargots and fennel seeds until soft. Add white wine and cream. Season with salt and pepper and simmer for 4 minutes, stirring constantly. Add cooked pasta to mixture and stir to warm. Arrange in a serving dish and sprinkle with parsley.

Tomato, Ricotta and Spinach Sauce

	4 servings
2 tsp	(10 mL) butter
1	garlic clove, finely sliced
1	French (dry) shallot, chopped
½ cup	(125 mL) tomatoes, diced
½ cup	(125 mL) spinach, cut into strips
½ cup	(125 mL) ricotta cheese
	salt and pepper
2 tbsp	(30 mL) grated Parmesan cheese

■ In a skillet, melt butter and cook garlic, shallot and tomatoes until soft but not browned. Add shredded spinach and ricotta. Season with salt and pepper. Heat for a few minutes. Pour mixture over pasta. Sprinkle with Parmesan and serve.

343

Tomato and Cheese Macaroni

Always cook pasta in plenty of boiling water with a spoonful of oil to prevent sticking.

6 servings

4 cups	(1 L) macaroni, cooked
14 oz	(398 mL) canned tomatoes
½ cup	(125 mL) grated cheese
3 tbsp	(45 mL) breadcrumbs
¼ cup	(60 mL) butter
	salt and pepper

■ Preheat oven to 350 °F (175 °C).

■ Spread cooked macaroni in a baking dish.

■ Pour tomatoes and grated cheese over macaroni, sprinkle with breadcrumbs and dot with butter. Bake in oven 25 to 30 minutes.

Sausage Macaroni

For an appetizer, you should calculate 1 to 2 oz (25 to 50 g) of un-cooked pasta per person, and for a main dish, 3 to 4 oz (75 to 100 g) per person.

6 servings

3 tbsp	(45 mL) butter
12	smoked sausages, cut into bite-size pieces
¼ cup	(60 mL) green bell pepper, diced
2	celery stalks, diced
10 oz	(284 ml) canned mushrooms, drained
	salt and pepper
4 cups	(1 L) macaroni, cooked
1 tbsp	(15 mL) soy sauce
½ cup	(125 mL) 15% cream
3 tbsp	(45 mL) green onions, finely sliced

■ In a skillet, melt butter and sauté sausages, green pepper, celery, and mushrooms and season with salt and pepper. Add cooked macaroni, soy sauce and cream, and stir. Spoon mixture onto warmed plates and decorate with finely sliced green onions.

* Illustrated recipe

Penne with Corn Niblets

Penne is a short section of macaroni with the ends cut on a slant.

6 servings	
4 cups	(1 L) cooked penne
10 oz	(284 mL) canned corn niblets, drained
¼ cup	(60 mL) butter
	salt and pepper
1 ½ cups	(375 mL) lightly-textured béchamel sauce
	parsley

■ Preheat oven to 350 °F (175 °C).

■ In a buttered baking dish, spread alternate layers of penne and corn niblets. Dot each layer with tiny knobs of butter and season with salt and pepper Coat with light béchamel sauce and bake for 30 minutes. Garnish with parsley and serve.

Salmon and Egg Pennine

The Italian name recalls the goose quill our ancestors used for writing.

6 servings	
4 cups	(1 L) cooked pennine
¼ cup	(60 mL) butter
2 tbsp	(30 mL) flour
	salt and pepper
2 ½ cups	(625 ml) milk
1 cup	(250 mL) canned green peas
3	hard-boiled eggs, sliced
7 ¾ oz	(220 mL) canned salmon, drained
2 tbsp	(30 mL) onion, finely sliced
1 tsp	(5 mL) paprika
2 tsp	(10 mL) chopped parsley

■ Spread cooked pennine in large serving dish. Keep warm in oven.

■ In a skillet, melt butter, add flour, and season with salt and pepper. Cook for a few minutes.

■ Pour milk into mixture in thin stream, stirring until sauce is smooth and creamy. Gently fold in green peas, hard-boiled egg slices, salmon and onion. Adjust seasoning to taste.

■ Stir sauce into pennine and sprinkle with paprika and parsley.

* Illustrated recipe

Fettucine Alfredo with Chicken

Alfredo sauce is a classic for creamed noodles. We offer you this slight variation.

4 servings

¼ cup	(60 mL) butter
1 tsp	(5 mL) flour
12 oz	(385 mL) evaporated milk
¾ cup	(150 mL) grated Parmesan cheese
1 tsp	(5 mL) chopped parsley
1 ½ cups	(375 mL) cooked chicken, julienned
	½ cup (125 mL) bacon, cooked, crumbled
	freshly ground pepper
4 cups	(1 L) cooked fettucine

■ In a skillet, melt butter, add flour and cook for a few minutes. Pour milk into mixture in thin stream and stir with wire whisk. Add cheese and parsley, and fold in cooked chicken and crumbled bacon. Season with ground pepper. Cook for a few minutes to desired thickness. Add fettucine and serve.

Spinach and Ricotta Fettucine

The green of the spinach noodles forms a pleasing background for the darker chopped spinach.

4 servings

1 lb	spinach fettucine
	salted water
2 tsp	butter
1	clove garlic, chopped
1	French (dry) shallot, chopped
2 cups	(500 mL) spinach, cut in strips
1 cup	(250 mL) ricotta cheese
½ cup	(125 mL) 15% cream
1 tsp	(5 mL) chives, chopped
2 tsp	(10 mL) parsley
	salt and pepper

■ Cook the noodles in boiling water according to package directions, rinse them under cold water and drain.

■ In a skillet, melt the butter and sauté the garlic and shallot but do not brown. Stir in the spinach, ricotta cheese, cream and herbs. Season with salt and pepper. Cook over low heat for about 5 minutes, stirring continually.

■ Plunge the cooked noodles in boiling water to heat them up, then drain them, put them on a serving dish, and pour the spinach and ricotta sauce on top.

* Illustrated recipe

346

Vegetable Lasagna

The wavy lasagna helps to hold the sauce in each layer.

6 to 8 servings

¹/₂ cup	(125 mL) carrots, diced
¹/₂ cup	(125 mL) celery, diagonally sliced
¹/₂ cup	(125 mL) broccoli, broken into flowerets
¹/₂ cup	(125 mL) cauliflower, broken into flowerets
15	cooked lasagna, drained
28 oz	(796 mL) canned tomato sauce
20 oz	(568 mL) canned cream of mushroom soup, undiluted
	salt and pepper
2 cups	(500 mL) grated cheese
¹/₂ cup	(125 mL) grated Parmesan cheese
3 tbsp	(45 mL) chopped parsley
2 tbsp	(30 mL) butter

■ Preheat oven to 350 °F (175 °C).

■ Blanch vegetables in lightly salted boiling water for 4 minutes. Drain and set aside.

■ Cook lasagna according to package directions. Drain and set aside.

■ Lightly butter a baking dish and spread a thin layer of tomato sauce and a layer of lasagna on the bottom. Follow with a layer of cream of mushroom soup and blanched vegetables and season with salt and pepper. Add a layer of tomato sauce and sprinkle with grated cheese.

■ Repeat operation twice. Sprinkle top with grated Parmesan and dot with knobs of butter. Bake for 25 minutes. Garnish with parsley and serve.

Ham and Chicken Lasagna

Since the canned chicken and ham are already salty, only use a little salt in the béchamel sauce.

6 to 8 servings

8 oz	(225 g) canned, flaked ham
28 oz	(796 mL) canned tomato sauce
1 tsp	(5 mL) paprika
8 oz	(225 g) canned, flaked chicken
2 cups	(500 mL) béchamel sauce
¹/₂ tsp	(2 mL) curry powder
2 cups	(500 mL) spinach, stemmed
15	cooked lasagna, drained
¹/₂ cup	(125 mL) grated cheese
	salt and pepper

■ Preheat oven to 350 °F (175 °C).

■ Cook lasagna according to package directions, drain and set aside.

■ In a bowl, mix together ham and tomato sauce. Season with paprika and set aside.

■ In a separate bowl, fold chicken into béchamel sauce. Season with curry powder and set aside.

■ Butter a baking dish and spread successive layers of tomato sauce, spinach, lasagna, béchamel sauce, then another layer of spinach and a layer of lasagna. Repeat operation twice, and finish with a layer of tomato sauce. Sprinkle grated cheese over tomato sauce and bake for about 25 minutes. Let stand to cool for 10 minutes before serving.

* Illustrated recipe

347

Mushroom Linguini

Flat, thin linguini are cooked in the same way as spaghetti.

6 to 8 servings

1 lb	(450 g) linguini
3 tbsp	(45 mL) butter
1	garlic clove, finely sliced
1 cup	(250 mL) mushrooms, quartered
½ cup	(125 mL) asparagus, cut into rounds
½ cup	(125 mL) artichoke bottoms, quartered
10 oz	(284 mL) undiluted canned cream of mushroom soup

■ Cook linguini in boiling salted water according to package directions. Rinse under cold running water. Drain and set aside.

■ In a skillet, melt butter and sauté garlic, mushrooms, asparagus and artichoke bottoms for 3 minutes.

■ Add cream of mushroom soup and heat over moderate heat for 10 minutes, stirring constantly. Fold in cooked linguini and stir.

Linguini with Mixed Vegetables

Save time by cooking the vegetables in the microwave.

6 to 8 servings

½ cup	(125 mL) carrots, julienned
½ cup	(125 mL) zucchini, julienned
1 lb	(450 g) linguini
3 tbsp	(45 mL) butter
1	garlic clove, finely sliced
1	green onion, chopped
¾ tsp	(3 mL) chopped basil
2 tsp	(10 mL) chopped parsley
1 cup	(250 mL) spinach
	salt and pepper
2 cups	(500 mL) vegetable juice
¼ cup	(60 mL) canned tomatoes, ground

■ Blanch carrots for 3 minutes in boiling salted water. Blanch zucchini for 1 minute. Drain and set aside.

■ In a separate saucepan cook linguini in boiling water according to package directions. Rinse under cold running water, then drain and set aside.

■ In a skillet, melt butter and cook garlic and green onion until soft. Add blanched carrots and zucchini and sauté for 3 minutes. Add basil, parsley and spinach. Season with salt and pepper. Pour vegetable juice and ground tomatoes into mixture and heat. Fold in linguini. Stir and serve.

Illustrated recipe

348

Ham and Pineapple Tagliatelli

Tagliatelli are often arranged in an attractive nest.

6 to 8 servings

1 lb	(450 g)	tagliatelli
¼ cup	(60 mL)	butter
1 cup	(250 mL)	cooked ham, cubed
½		onion, chopped
1		garlic clove, finely sliced
1 cup	(250 mL)	pineapple, drained, cubed
		salt and pepper
1 tbsp	(15 mL)	cornstarch
2 tbsp	(30 mL)	cold water
2 cups	(500 mL)	unsweetened pineapple juice
		pinch of clove
1 tbsp	(15 mL)	chopped parsley
¼ tsp	(1 mL)	paprika

■ Cook tagliatelli in boiling salted water according to package directions. Rinse under cold running water, then drain and set aside.

■ In a skillet, melt 2 tbsp (30 mL) butter and sauté ham, onion, garlic and pineapple. Season with salt and pepper, then set aside.

■ In a small bowl, dissolve cornstarch in cold water and set aside.

■ Heat pineapple juice in a small saucepan. Add dissolved cornstarch and clove, stir and simmer until mixture thickens. Remove from heat.

■ In a large skillet, melt rest of butter and heat tagliatelli. Add ham and pineapple mixture and sauce. Stir gently. Garnish with parsley and paprika.

* Illustrated recipe

Russian Tagliatelli

Be sure to get the sauce good and hot before pouring it over the pasta.

6 to 8 servings

1 lb	(450 g)	tagliatelli
1 tbsp	(15 mL)	peanut oil
2 tsp	(10 mL)	butter
½ tsp	(2 mL)	freshly ground black pepper
½ tsp	(2 mL)	chopped basil
¼ cup	(60 mL)	vodka
1 cup	(250 mL)	tomato juice
		salt

■ Cook tagliatelli in boiling salted water according to package directions. Rinse under cold running water and drain.

■ In a skillet, heat oil, melt butter and sauté cooked tagliatelli. Add ground pepper and basil. Deglaze skillet with vodka. Pour tomato juice over mixture and season with salt. Heat for a few minutes. Stir and serve.

Garnished Tortellini, Basic Recipe

Doughnut-shaped tortellini are stuffed with meat, fish or cheese.

6 to 8 servings

1 lb	(450 g) tortellini

- Cook tortellini in boiling salted water according to package directions. Rinse under cold running water and drain.

- Place tortellini in serving dish, coat with sauce or garnish of your choice and serve.

Roquefort Cream

6 to 8 servings

2 tsp	(10 mL) butter
1/2	onion, chopped
1	garlic clove, finely sliced
1 1/2 cups	(375 mL) 15% cream
1/4 cup	(60 mL) grated Parmesan cheese
2 tsp	(10 mL) Roquefort cheese, crumbled
	salt and pepper
	meat-stuffed tortellini, cooked

- In a skillet, melt butter and cook onion and garlic until soft. Pour cream over mixture. Add grated Parmesan and Roquefort. Season with salt and pepper and reduce until smooth.

- Add tortellini and heat to warm. Sprinkle with Roquefort and serve.

Chicken Sauce

6 to 8 servings

10 oz	(284 mL) canned cream of chicken soup
5 oz	(140 mL) milk
6 oz	(180 g) canned flaked chicken
	cheese-stuffed tortellini, cooked
	salt and pepper

- In a saucepan, heat cream of chicken soup and milk.

- Add flaked chicken and tortellini season with salt and pepper and heat for 3 minutes.

Spinach and Goat's Cheese Sauce

- Follow same procedure as in Roquefort Cream Sauce recipe. Use chicken-stuffed tortellini. Replace Roquefort with goat's cheese. When adding tortellini to mixture include 1/2 cup (125 mL) spinach, stemmed and cut into strips. Stir to mix well and serve.

Seafood Sauce

6 to 8 servings

1 tbsp	(15 mL) cornstarch
2 tbsp	(30 mL) tomato juice
1 1/2 cups	(375 mL) canned lobster bisque
1/2 cup	(125 mL) baby shrimp
	fish-stuffed tortellini, cooked
1 tbsp	(15 mL) chopped parsley

- Dissolve cornstarch in tomato juice and set aside.

- In a saucepan, stir and heat lobster bisque with dissolved cornstarch. Add shrimp, then add tortellini. Simmer for 2 minutes. Sprinkle with parsley.

Gruyère and Onion Sauce

6 to 8 servings

2 tsp	(10 mL) butter
2 tbsp	(30 mL) onion, chopped
	meat-stuffed tortellini, cooked
1 1/2 cups	(375 mL) canned tomato sauce
	salt and pepper
1/2 cup	(125 mL) grated Gruyère cheese

- In a skillet, melt butter and cook onion until soft. Add tortellini, coat with tomato sauce, season with salt and pepper. Stir and simmer to warm. Sprinkle with Gruyère and serve.

Center: Seafood Sauce
Clockwise from top left: Gruyère and Onions ▪ Chicken ▪ Spinach and Goat's Cheese ▪ Roquefort Cream

Cappelletti, Basic Recipe

6 to 8 servings
1 lb   (450 g) cappelletti

■ Cook cappelletti in boiling salted water according to package directions.

Cappelletti in Pure Olive Oil

6 to 8 servings	
2 tbsp	(30 mL) olive oil
	cooked cappelletti
3 tbsp	(45 mL) black olives, julienned
½ cup	(125 mL) tomatoes, diced
½ tsp	(2 mL) dried crushed pimento
	salt and pepper
2 tbsp	(30 mL) chopped parsley

■ In a skillet, heat oil and sauté cappelletti, olives, tomatoes, and pimento. Stir, season with salt and pepper, and sprinkle with parsley.

Fennel Sauce

6 to 8 servings	
10 oz	(284 mL) canned cream of celery soup
5 oz	(140 mL) milk
¼ cup	(60 mL) fennel bulb, blanched and diced
	cooked cappelletti
1 tsp	(5 mL) fennel leaves

■ In a saucepan, heat cream of celery and milk, add the diced fennel, and cook for 5 minutes. Stir in the cappelletti and heat it in the sauce for a few minutes. Garnish with fennel leaves and serve.

Mushroom Cream Sauce

6 to 8 servings	
10 oz	(284 mL) canned cream of mushroom soup
5 oz	(140 mL) milk
½ cup	(125 mL) mushrooms, cut into pieces
	salt and pepper
¼ tsp	(1 mL) nutmeg
	chopped parsley
	cappelletti, cooked

■ In a saucepan, heat cream of mushroom soup and milk.

Add mushrooms, and season with salt, pepper, and nutmeg. Add cappelletti and heat for a few minutes. Sprinkle with parsley.

Center: Cappelletti in Olive Oil
Clockwise from top left: Tomato,
Chive and Basil ▪ Mushroom Cream ▪
Curry and Saffron ▪ Fennel

Tomato, Chive and Basil Sauce

6 to 8 servings	
2 tsp	(10 mL) butter
1	French (dry) shallot, finely sliced
1	garlic clove, finely sliced
½ cup	(125 mL) tomatoes, diced
½ tsp	(2 mL) chopped chives
½ tsp	(2 mL) chopped basil
1 ½ cups	(375 mL) vegetable juice
	salt and pepper
	cappelletti, cooked

■ In a skillet, melt butter and cook shallot and garlic until soft but not browned. Add tomatoes, chives and basil. Pour vegetable juice over mixture. Season with salt and pepper. Add cappelletti, stir, and heat.

Curry and Saffron Sauce

6 to 8 servings	
2 tsp	(10 mL) butter
½	garlic clove, finely sliced
1	French (dry) shallot, finely sliced
1 ½ cups	(375 mL) 15% cream
¼ tsp	(1 mL) saffron
¼ tsp	(1 mL) curry
	cappelletti, cooked

■ In a skillet, melt butter and cook garlic and shallot until soft. Pour cream into mixture. Add saffron and curry and cook until sauce is smooth. Add cappelletti and heat for a few minutes.

Rosy Creamed Cannelloni

Ricotta is a mild curd cheese made with whey.

6 to 8 servings

12	ricotta-stuffed cannelloni
2 tbsp	(30 mL) water
2 tsp	(10 mL) butter
1/2	garlic clove, finely sliced
1	French (dry) shallot, chopped
1/4 cup	(60 mL) tomatoes, diced
1 tbsp	(15 mL) tomato paste
1 1/2 cups	(375 mL) 35% cream
	salt and pepper
1/4 tsp	(1 mL) rosemary

■ Preheat oven to 350 °F (175 °C).

■ Spread cannelloni in a buttered baking dish. Sprinkle lightly with water. Place the butter-coated side of a sheet of aluminum foil over cannelloni and bake for 10 minutes.

■ In a skillet, melt butter and cook garlic, shallot and tomatoes until soft but not browned. Add tomato paste and cream to mixture and stir. Season with salt, pepper, and rosemary. Simmer for 5 minutes.

■ Place cannelloni in the sauce and turn once.

* Illustrated recipe

Cannelloni au Gratin

Cannelloni are usually stuffed with meat or a spinach mixture. We've chosen a stuffing for seafood lovers.

6 to 8 servings

12	shrimp-stuffed cannelloni, cooked
2 tbsp	(30 mL) water
1 1/2 cups	(375 mL) commercial seafood sauce
2 tbsp	(30 mL) grated Parmesan cheese
	salt and pepper
1/2 cup	(125 mL) grated cheese

■ Preheat oven to 350 °F (175 °C).

■ Spread cannelloni in a buttered baking dish. Lightly sprinkle with water. Place the butter-coated side of a sheet of aluminum foil over cannelloni and bake for 10 minutes.

■ Heat sauce in a saucepan and add grated Parmesan. Season with salt and pepper. Pour sauce over cannelloni and sprinkle with grated cheese. Broil for 4 minutes until topping is golden brown.

Classic Ravioli

You can change this recipe slightly by replacing meat- and cheese-stuffed ravioli with the zucchini-stuffed variety.

6 to 8 servings

1 lb	(450 g) veal-stuffed ravioli
2 tbsp	(30 mL) butter
1	French (dry) shallot, chopped
1	garlic clove, finely sliced
1 ½ cups	(375 mL) tomato sauce
	salt and pepper
½ tsp	(2 mL) chopped basil
¼ tsp	(1 mL) chopped chives
	pinch of dried thyme
3 tbsp	(45 mL) grated Parmesan cheese

■ Cook ravioli in boiling salted water. Rinse under cold running water, then drain and set aside.

■ In a skillet, melt butter and cook shallot and garlic. Add tomato sauce. Season with salt, pepper, basil, chives and thyme, and simmer for 5 minutes.

■ Add ravioli and stir. Sprinkle with Parmesan and serve.

Pesto Ravioli

Traditional pesto is made with herbs, nuts and cheese. You can use walnuts instead of pine nuts. Don't serve more cheese with the sauce.

6 to 8 servings

1 lb	(450 g) meat and cheese-stuffed ravioli
2 tbsp	(30 mL) butter
2	garlic cloves, finely sliced
2 tsp	(10 mL) chopped basil
1 tbsp	(15 mL) pine nuts
	salt and pepper
1 tbsp	(15 mL) chopped parsley

■ Cook ravioli in boiling salted water. Rinse under cold running water. Drain and set aside.

■ In a skillet, melt butter and cook garlic until soft but not browned. Add basil, pine nuts and season with salt and pepper. Add ravioli. Sprinkle with parsley, and heat for a few minutes.

* Illustrated recipe

A good many of us think that cereals are confined to breakfast foods. But the nutritious cereal family is a large one and constitutes the staple diet of many peoples. Think of rice, oats, barley, corn, millet, and sorghum (Indian millet), all of them belonging to the *Gramineae* family of edible grasses.

Rice, for example, is the main ingredient in Italian risoto, Spanish paella, and Indian curry. Throughout Asia and parts of Africa, it is consumed daily.

North Americans frequently serve converted or pretreated rice that has been steamed before "polishing," in order to preserve some of the nutrients. The highly popular precooked or "minute" rice is partially cooked before packaging.

Health experts have been stressing the benefits of a high-fiber diet for some time now. More and more people are serving wild rice (not really a rice, but a marsh plant), whole or brown rice, or even basmati, a long-grained Indian rice.

CEREALS

RICE

Spanish Rice

4 servings

1 ¼ cups	(310 mL) rice, uncooked
1 ½ cups	(375 mL) chicken stock
14 oz	(398 mL) canned spiced tomatoes
1 tbsp	(15 mL) butter
2 tsp	(10 mL) chili powder
¾ tsp	(3 mL) oregano
½ tsp	(2 mL) garlic salt
1 tbsp	(15 mL) green onion, chopped

■ Combine all ingredients, except the green onion, in a saucepan, and bring to a boil. Reduce heat and simmer for 25 minutes.

■ Spoon mixture into a serving dish, garnish with chopped green onion and serve.

VARIATION

• **Add cooked chicken pieces.**

Shrimp Fried Rice

4 servings

2 tbsp	(30 mL) oil
2	green onions, finely sliced
1 cup	(250 mL) baby shrimp
10 oz	(284 mL) canned mushrooms, drained
3 tbsp	(45 mL) soy sauce
2 cups	(500 mL) rice, cooked
	salt and pepper
1	egg, beaten

■ In a skillet, heat oil and sauté onions and shrimp for 3 minutes. Add mushrooms, soy sauce and rice. Season with salt and pepper, and fry for 5 minutes. Pour in beaten egg and cook 3 to 4 minutes, stirring constantly.

Vegetable Rice

4 servings

2 cups	(500 mL) fast-cooking rice
1 ¾ cups	(430 mL) water
1 tsp	(5 mL) butter
	pinch of salt
2 tbsp	(30 mL) oil
½ cup	(125 mL) mushrooms, sliced
½ cup	(125 mL) celery, chopped
½ cup	(125 mL) green bell pepper, chopped
¼ cup	(60 mL) sweet red pepper, chopped
	salt and pepper
	parsley
	thyme
	onion salt
¼ cup	(60 mL) garlic butter

■ Place first 4 ingredients in microwave-safe dish and cover. Cook in microwave for 2 minutes at HIGH. Stir, cover and cook 3 minutes longer. Let stand for a few minutes.

■ In a skillet, heat oil and sauté vegetables over medium heat until tender.

■ Put rice in the center of plates and spoon vegetables around it. Pour garlic butter over each and serve.

Oven-cooked Rice

4 servings

4 cups	(1 L) hot water
10 oz	(284 mL) canned mushroom pieces, in their juice
¼ cup	(60 mL) oil
¼ cup	(60 mL) beef stock
3 tbsp	(45 mL) soy sauce
2 cups	(500 mL) long-grained rice

■ Preheat oven to 375 °F (190 °C).

■ Combine all ingredients in a baking dish, cover and bake for 1 hour.

357

Ham and Rice

4 servings

1 tbsp	(15 mL) oil
2 cups	(500 mL) cooked ham, cubed
½	green bell pepper, chopped
2 tbsp	(30 mL) cornstarch
1 cup	(250 mL) water
½ cup	(125 mL) pineapple juice
1 tbsp	(15 mL) brown sugar
1 ½ tsp	(7 mL) dry mustard
½ tsp	(2 mL) ginger (optional)
1 cup	(250 mL) pineapple chunks
2 cups	(500 mL) cooked rice, hot

■ In a skillet, heat oil and sauté ham and green pepper and set aside.

■ In a small bowl, mix together cornstarch, water, pineapple juice, brown sugar, mustard and ginger, and pour over ham mixture. Cook over medium heat, stirring constantly until sauce is smooth and transparent. Add pineapple chunks and heat for 3 minutes. Serve over rice.

* Illustrated recipe

Flavored Rice

4 servings

1	small package instant onion soup mix
2 cups	(500 mL) water
2 cups	(500 mL) fast-cooking rice

■ Pour onion soup mix in water and bring to a boil. Add rice, cover and remove from heat. Let stand for 6 minutes, adjust seasoning and serve.

VARIATIONS

- **When serving meat dishes, replace onion soup mix with chicken noodle soup mix.**

- **When serving fish or seafood, replace onion soup mix with shrimp soup mix.**

Rice Patties

4 servings

1 ¼ cups	(310 mL) all-purpose flour
½ tsp	(2 mL) salt
1 ½ tsp	(7 mL) baking powder
1 ¼ cups	(310 mL) milk
1 ¼ cups	(310 mL) rice, cooked
1	egg, beaten
5 tsp	(25 mL) butter, melted

■ Sift together flour, salt and baking powder. Pour milk over dry ingredients and stir to moisten flour. Add other ingredients and stir gently.

■ In a skillet, melt butter and spoon batter in small patties. Fry on both sides until golden and serve.

Creamy Rice Pudding

4 to 6 servings

2	eggs
1 cup	(250 mL) milk
1 tsp	(5 mL) vanilla extract
⅓ cup	(80 mL) honey
2 cups	(500 mL) long-grained, fast-cooking rice
⅓ cup	(80 mL) raisins
½ tsp	(2 mL) cinnamon
	pinch of nutmeg
1 cup	(250 mL) plain yogurt

■ Preheat oven to 350 °F (175 °C).

■ Mix together eggs, milk, vanilla, and honey; stir in all other ingredients, except yogurt.

■ Spread mixture in a square 8 inch (20 cm) pan and bake for 25 minutes, stirring from time to time. Remove from oven and let stand for 10 minutes. Ladle yogurt over pudding.

Rice au Gratin

4 to 6 servings

2 cups	(500 mL) brown rice
1 tsp	(10 mL) oil
1 tsp	(10 mL) butter
1	onion, finely chopped
½ cup	(125 mL) celery, chopped
⅔ cup	(160 mL) green bell pepper, chopped
¼ cup	(60 mL) sweet red pepper, chopped
1 lb	(450 g) crabmeat
2	hard-boiled eggs, sliced
2 cups	(500 mL) béchamel sauce
	salt and pepper
	pinch of thyme
½ tsp	(2 mL) chopped parsley
¼ lb	(115 g) grated Cheddar or Mozzarella cheese
	breadcrumbs

■ Preheat oven to 350 °F (170 °C).

■ In a saucepan filled with 4 cups (1 L) boiling water, cook brown rice for about 20 minutes and drain.

■ In a skillet, heat oil, melt butter and sauté vegetables for a few minutes. Add rice and remove from heat. Butter a baking dish and spoon in alternate layers of rice, crabmeat and egg slices. Set aside.

■ In a bowl, pour béchamel sauce and season with salt, pepper, and thyme. Add ⅓ the amount of cheese and pour over the rice mixture. Sprinkle rest of cheese and breadcrumbs over mixture and bake for 30 minutes. Broil until cheese and breadcrumb layer is golden.

Cold Rice

4 to 6 servings

1	avocado, diced
	juice of 1 lemon
1 ½ cups	(375 mL) white rice, cooked
½ cup	(125 mL) brown rice, cooked
1	onion, chopped
2	tomatoes, diced
1	celery stalk, chopped
2 tbsp	(30 mL) chopped parsley
4 oz	(113 g) canned tuna, drained
2 tbsp	(30 mL) oil
1 tbsp	(15 mL) vinegar
1 tbsp	(15 mL) chili sauce
	salt and pepper

■ Sprinkle avocado with lemon juice.

■ Combine avocado and other ingredients in a large salad bowl, toss and serve.

Scrambled Rice

4 to 6 servings

1 tbsp	(15 mL) oil
1 tsp	(5 mL) butter
1	onion, chopped
1	garlic clove, finely sliced
½ cup	(125 mL) celery, diagonally sliced
½ cup	(125 mL) green peas
2	eggs
	salt and pepper
2 cups	(500 mL) brown rice, cooked

■ In a skillet, heat oil, melt butter and sauté onion, garlic, celery and green peas for about 4 minutes. Add eggs. When eggs begin to cook, stir mixture. Season with salt and pepper. Add rice, stir and serve.

Tri-color Rice

4 to 6 servings

½ cup	(125 mL) white rice
	pinch of saffron
½ cup	(125 mL) brown rice
½ cup	(125 mL) wild rice
3 tbsp	(45 mL) oil
	salt and pepper
1 tsp	(5 mL) curry
	pinch of chili powder
½ tsp	(2 mL) Worcestershire sauce
1 tbsp	(15 mL) chopped parsley

■ In 2 separate saucepans, pour 1 ½ cups (310 mL) water and cook white rice and brown rice separately for about 20 minutes. (Add a pinch of saffron to white rice.)

■ In a third saucepan filled with 2 cups (500 mL) water, cook wild rice for 20 to 30 minutes until rice begins to split open.

■ In a skillet, heat oil and sauté cooked rice. Season with salt, pepper, curry powder, chili powder and Worcestershire sauce, stirring constantly. Sprinkle with parsley and serve.

Illustrated recipe

Rice with Citrus Fruit

4 to 6 servings

1 ½ cups	**(375 mL) water**
¼ cup	**(60 mL) orange juice**
½ cup	**(125 mL) white rice**
1 ½ cups	**(375 mL) water**
¼ cup	**(60 mL) grapefruit juice**
½ cup	**(125 mL) brown rice**
3	**oranges, peeled, separated into segments**
2	**grapefruit, peeled, separated into segments**
	juice of 2 lemons
	peel of ½ lemon, coarsely grated
1 tsp	**(5 mL) fresh mint, chopped**
	salt and pepper

■ In a saucepan filled with 1 ½ cups (375 mL) water, pour orange juice and cook white rice for about 20 minutes.

■ In a separate saucepan filled with 1 ½ cups (375 mL) water, pour grapefruit juice and cook brown rice for about 20 minutes.

■ In a bowl, mix cooked white and brown rice with oranges, grapefruit, lemon juice, lemon peel and chopped mint. Season with salt and pepper and toss. Serve this dish hot, warm or cold.

Rice with Raisins

4 to 6 servings

1 cup	**(250 mL) instant brown rice**
1 cup	**(250 mL) water**
¼ cup	**(60 mL) raisins**
1 tsp	**(5 mL) honey**
	salt and pepper

■ In a saucepan, mix all ingredients and bring to a boil. Remove from heat, cover and let stand for 6 minutes. Adjust seasoning to taste and serve.

Rice with Almonds

4 to 6 servings	
2 ½ cups	(625 mL) water
½ tsp	(2 mL) sesame oil
1 cup	(250 mL) rice
2 tbsp	(30 mL) butter, melted
¼ cup	(60 mL) almonds, toasted
1 tbsp	(15 mL) sesame seeds
	salt and pepper
2 tsp	(10 mL) Amaretto (almond liqueur)

■ In a saucepan, pour water and add sesame oil. Cook rice according to package directions.

■ Add other ingredients, toss and serve.

Rice with Fruit

4 to 6 servings	
½ cup	(125 mL) milk
2 cups	(500 mL) brown rice, cooked
1	apple, diced
2 tbsp	(30 mL) brown sugar
	pinch of cinnamon
1 tsp	(5 mL) honey
	fresh fruit (optional)

■ In a saucepan, heat milk without letting it come to a boil. Add other ingredients and stir. Garnish with fresh fruit and serve.

OTHER CEREALS

Human beings depend largely on cultivated cereals for food. In Europe and North America this means wheat and oats for the most part. Latin American countries, on the other hand, favor corn or maize as a staple, while millet and sorghum are major cereal crops in many African and Asian countries. Grains are usually toasted after being harvested, and must absorb water in order to swell and soften for eating.

Cereals are rich in protein and go well with vegetables, meat, and fish. When served with nuts or legumes, they can actually replace meat in our diet.

Beef Polenta

Polenta, made with cornmeal, is a staple dish in northern Italy. Cook it in a ring mold and put meat or fish in the center.

4 to 6 servings

1 ¾ cups	(430 mL) water
½ cup	(125 mL) cornmeal
2 tbsp	(30 mL) vegetable oil
1 cup	(250 mL) strong Cheddar cheese, grated
1	garlic clove, finely sliced
⅓ cup	(80 mL) onions, finely sliced
⅓ cup	(80 mL) carrots, sliced
⅓ cup	(80 mL) celery, chopped
1 lb	(450 g) ground beef
19 oz	(540 mL) canned tomatoes, drained and chopped
2 tbsp	(30 mL) tomato paste
2 tsp	(10 mL) basil
	salt and pepper
1 tbsp	(15 mL) chopped parsley
	grated cheese

■ In a 12-cup (3 L) microwave-safe dish, mix together water, cornmeal and oil; cover and cook in microwave at HIGH for 5 minutes. Stir and cook 3 minutes longer or until liquid is completely absorbed. Spread cheese evenly over cornmeal.

■ In an 8-cup (2 L) microwave-safe, combine garlic, onions, carrots and celery. Cover and cook in microwave at HIGH 3 to 5 minutes.

■ Add ground beef and cook 5 minutes longer or until meat is done.

■ Break ground beef apart with a fork. Add tomatoes, tomato paste and basil, cover and cook in microwave at HIGH for 10 minutes or until mixture has thickened. Stir once or twice during cooking process. Season with salt and pepper.

■ Pour mixture over polenta, sprinkle with parsley and grated cheese.

Healthy Casserole

Millet cooks in 20 minutes in double the amount of milk, water or stock. Serve it plain as you would rice.

4 to 6 servings

³/₄ cup	(180 mL) millet
3	cheese slices
	pinch of sage
6	tomato slices
	pinch of sugar
	salt and pepper
1	small leek, finely sliced
¹/₂	green bell pepper, sliced
	knobs of butter

■ Preheat oven to 350 °F (175 °C).

■ In a saucepan containing 2 cups (500 mL) boiling water, cook millet for about 20 minutes.

■ Butter a baking dish and spread a layer of cooked millet in dish, then spread a layer of cheese slices on top. Sprinkle with sage.

■ Place sliced tomatoes over mixture, sprinkle with sugar and season with salt and pepper. Garnish with finely sliced leek and sliced green bell pepper. Dot with knobs of butter and bake for 25 minutes.

Friday's Delight

This is a good recipe for canned salmon. If you want to increase the calcium content of your recipe, crush the soft salmon cartilege into the flesh.

4 to 6 servings

1 cup	(250 mL) cornmeal, cooked
³/₄ cup	(180 mL) salmon, cooked
1	small onion, finely chopped
	pinch of thyme
	salt and pepper
1	egg
3 tbsp	(45 mL) milk
2 tbsp	(30 mL) cornmeal, uncooked
2 tsp	(10 mL) oil

■ In a saucepan containing 2 cups (500 mL) boiling water, cook 1 cup cornmeal for about 10 minutes.

■ In a bowl, combine cooked cornmeal, salmon and onion. Season with salt, pepper, and thyme. Refrigerate for 3 hours.

■ Meanwhile, beat egg, add milk and set aside.

■ Shape cold cornmeal mixture into croquettes. Dip into beaten egg and dredge in uncooked cornmeal.

■ In a skillet, heat oil and fry croquettes on both sides until golden.

* Illustrated recipe

365

Bread—the staff of life. Each nation has its own special bread. Whether leavened or unleavened, made of rice, maize, or rye, our daily bread has been with us since the time of the ancient Egyptians and earlier. Bread comes in all shapes and sizes: cottage loaves, baguettes, pitas, brioches, croissants, cornmeal muffins, scones and rolls, all reflecting the influence of geography and cultural traditions. There is something fundamentally hospitable about a loaf on the table and the smell of fresh bread baking.

BREADS

FLAVORED BREADS

French Toast

Who invented French toast? Perhaps it really was the thrifty French, who never like to waste food. It's a handy substitute for pancakes and makes a nourishing breakfast.

4 servings

2	eggs, beaten
1 cup	(250 mL) milk
½ tsp	(2 mL) vanilla
	pinch of cinnamon
½ tsp	(2 mL) cocoa
8	slices of bread
3 tbsp	(45 mL) butter
	chocolate chips

■ In a bowl, combine eggs, milk, vanilla, cinnamon, and cocoa.

■ Soak bread slices in mixture. Drain. Melt butter in a skillet and toast each slice of bread on both sides until golden. Sprinkle with chocolate chips.

■ Serve with maple syrup, honey, or stewed fruit sauce (p. 498).

VARIATION

• **Replace chocolate chips with pieces of fresh fruit.**

Cheese and Herb Bread

This crisp and tasty bread is a perfect accompaniment for soups and salads. Use Cheddar, Brie or even a Saint-Paulin cheese.

4 servings

1	baguette
½ cup	(125 mL) butter
2	garlic cloves, finely sliced
½ tsp	(2 mL) chopped tarragon
½ tsp	(2 mL) chopped oregano
½ tsp	(2 mL) chopped chervil
½ tsp	(2 mL) chopped basil
1 tsp	(5 mL) chopped parsley
4 oz	(115 g) cheese

■ Preheat oven to 350 °F (175 °C).

■ Slice baguette every ¾ inch (2 cm) without cutting completely.

■ In a skillet, melt butter and sauté garlic and herbs. Set aside.

■ Cut cheese into about 20 slices.

■ Coat one slice of baguette with herb butter. Put cheese in next slice, and repeat operation until baguette is completely garnished.

■ Wrap baguette in sheet of aluminum foil and bake for about 15 minutes.

Apricot Bread

Serve this bread at a special breakfast or brunch.

10 to 12 servings

1 1/2 cups	(375 mL) all-purpose flour
2/3 cup	(160 mL) sugar
1/2 cup	(125 mL) wheat germ
1 tsp	(5 mL) baking soda
1/4 tsp	(1 mL) salt
1/4 tsp	(1 mL) cinnamon
1/4 tsp	(1 mL) nutmeg
1/2 cup	(125 mL) softened butter, cut into pieces
2	eggs
1/2 cup	(125 mL) sour cream
1 cup	(250 mL) dried apricots, quartered

■ Preheat oven to 350 °F (175 °C).

■ In a bowl, combine flour, sugar, wheat germ, baking soda, salt, cinnamon, and nutmeg. Blend in butter with a fork.

■ In a small bowl, mix eggs and sour cream and add to first mixture. Stir well. Add apricots and stir gently.

■ Lightly grease a loaf pan with butter and sprinkle with flour. Pour batter into pan and bake for 1 hour. Remove from oven and let stand to cool for 10 to 15 minutes before unmolding.

Banana Bread

Make good use of those over ripe bananas sitting on your counter!

10 to 12 servings

3	very ripe bananas
2	eggs
3/4 cup	(180 mL) sugar
2 cups	(500 mL) flour
1/2 tsp	(2 mL) salt
1 tsp	(5 mL) baking soda
1/2 cup	(125 mL) chopped nuts

■ Preheat oven to 350 °F (175 °C).

■ In a large bowl, mash bananas. Add eggs and beat until foamy.

■ In a separate bowl, sift dry ingredients. Fold into foamy mixture and add nuts.

■ Lightly grease a 4 x 8 1/2 in (10 x 21 cm) loaf pan. Pour in batter and bake for 1 hour.

* Illustrated recipe

369

Baguettes

Stuffed Baguette

4 servings

1	baguette, cut into 4 lengths
	or
4	ficelles (small, slender French bread)

■ Scoop out the soft part of the bread and stuff the crust with mousse of your choice. Wrap tightly in plastic wrap and chill for at least 2 hours before serving.

Shrimp Mousse

4 servings

1 1/2 cups	(375 mL)	baby shrimp, cooked
1/3 cup	(80 mL)	mayonnaise
1 tbsp	(15 mL)	chili sauce
1 tsp	(5 mL)	horseradish in vinegar
1/2 cup	(125 mL)	cream cheese
2 tbsp	(30 mL)	butter
1		garlic clove, finely sliced
		salt and pepper
1/4 tsp	(1 mL)	Worcestershire sauce

■ Mix 1/2 cup (125 mL) baby shrimp and all other ingredients in a food processor. Gently fold in 1 cup (250 mL) baby shrimp with a fork.

Vegetable Mousse

4 servings

1/4 cup	(60 mL)	broccoli, cut into tiny flowerets
1/4 cup	(60 mL)	cauliflower, cut into tiny flowerets
1/4 cup	(60 mL)	yellow or orange pepper, diced
1/4 cup	(60 mL)	snow peas, diagonally sliced
1/4 cup	(60 mL)	carrots, julienned
1/4 cup	(60 mL)	tomatoes, diced
2		garlic cloves, finely sliced
2		green onions
3/4 cup	(180 mL)	cream cheese
1/4 cup	(60 mL)	mayonnaise
1/4 tsp	(1 mL)	Worcestershire sauce
		salt and pepper

■ In a saucepan filled with lightly salted boiling water, blanch all vegetables except tomatoes for 2 minutes. Rinse under cold running water and drain.

■ Combine other ingredients in a food processor and mix until smooth and creamy. Gently fold in vegetables.

Shrimp Mouse
Vegetable Mouse

If you're having people in, prepare a variety of stuffed baguettes and use the different-colored slices to make up attractive trays to pass round.

Ham Mousse

4 servings

½ cup	(125 mL) mayonnaise
½ cup	(125 mL) cream cheese
2 tbsp	(30 mL) butter
1	green onion, finely sliced
1	garlic clove, finely sliced
	salt and pepper
¼ tsp	(1 mL) Worcestershire sauce
1 ½ cups	(375 mL) cooked ham, chopped

■ Mix all ingredients in a food processor except ham. Gently fold in chopped ham with a fork.

Liver Mousse

4 servings

½ cup	(125 mL) chicken livers, trimmed
½	garlic clove, finely sliced
1	French (dry) shallot, chopped
1 tsp	(5 mL) brandy
2	eggs
	salt and pepper
1 cup	(250 mL) 35% cream
1 cup	(250 mL) cream cheese, softened
1 tbsp	(15 mL) chopped parsley

■ Preheat oven to 300 °F (150 °C).

■ In blender, mix all ingredients except cream, cream cheese and parsley. Press mixture through sieve. Add cream and stir.

■ Pour mixture into a lightly greased mold. Cover and cook in oven, in a pan of water, for about 15 minutes. Let stand to cool completely. Add cream cheese topping, and sprinkle with parsley.

Ham Mousse
Liver Mousse

ENGLISH MUFFINS

If a light lunch is in order or you want a television snack, garnish handy English muffins with a variety of appetizing foods.

English Muffins, Basic Recipe

4 servings

2	English muffins
1 to 2 tsp	(5 to 10 mL) butter
	a few drops of olive oil

■ Preheat oven to 400 °F (205 °C).

■ Slice muffins in half. Let dry in oven for 4 minutes.

■ Remove from oven. Baste with butter. Garnish with any one of the following preparations. Pour a few drops of olive oil over mixture. Bake for 10 to 12 minutes.

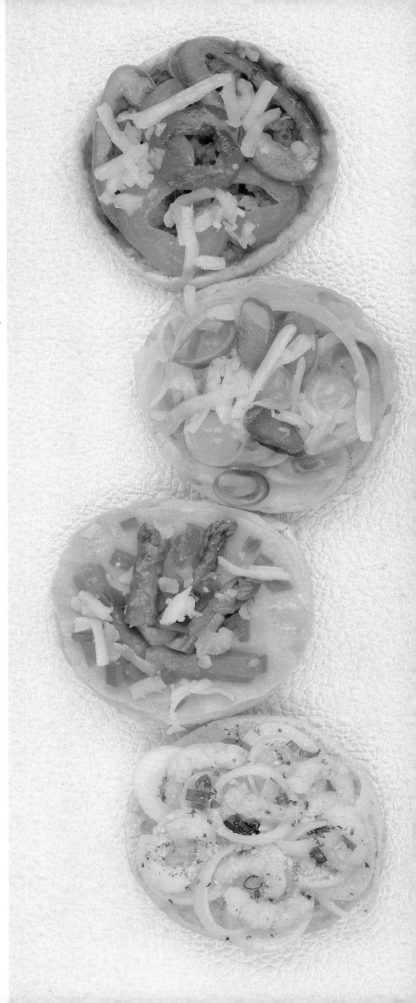

Eight Garnishes

First column

Sweet Peppers

- Spread ¹/₂ tsp (2 mL) chili sauce on each muffin. Garnish with blanched green pepper slices and a few drops of Worcestershire sauce. Sprinkle with grated cheese.

Onions

- Cover each muffin with a slice of cheese (same size as muffin). Add sliced red and yellow onion rings, lightly sautéed in butter. Garnish with small pickles and pearl onions. Season with salt and pepper. Sprinkle with grated cheese.

Ham

- Cover each muffin with a slice of cheese (same size as muffin) and a slice of cooked ham (same size as muffin). Place canned asparagus tips over cheese and ham. Decorate with diced tomatoes. Season with salt and pepper. Sprinkle with grated cheese.

Shrimp

- Cover each muffin with thinly sliced, blanched leek whites. Add cooked baby shrimp. Sprinkle with a pinch of chopped fines herbes (chives, tarragon, oregano and parsley). Season with salt and pepper. Sprinkle with grated Parmesan cheese.

Second Column

Italian

- Cover each muffin with a ¹/₂ tsp (2 mL) chili sauce. Top with 2 tomato slices. Place 3 anchovy fillets on top and garnish with 3 sliced black olives. Season with salt and pepper and sprinkle with 1 tbsp (15 mL) grated cheese.

Mushrooms

- Cover each muffin with a layer of canned, sliced mushrooms and a layer of grated Gruyère cheese. Repeat operation. Season with salt and pepper. Sprinkle with 2 tsp (10 mL) chopped parsley.

Spinach and Cheese

- Cover each muffin with ¹/₂ tsp (2 mL) chili sauce. Top each muffin with a slice of cheese (same size as muffin) and cover with 2 tbsp (30 mL) blanched spinach leaves. Add 2 tomato slices. Season with salt and pepper. Sprinkle with 2 tsp (10 mL) grated Cheddar cheese.

Eggplant

- Cover each muffin with 1 thin slice of eggplant (same size as muffin). Sprinkle ¹/₄ finely sliced garlic clove over eggplant. Top with 3 thin onion slices. Season with salt and pepper. Sprinkle garnished muffin with 1 tbsp (15 mL) grated Cheddar cheese.

CROISSANTS

Deli Croissants

If you're lucky enough to live near a croissant bakery, get fresh plain or butter croissants. If not, try frozen croissants. They're a better bet than croissants packed in plastic.

4 servings

4	croissants
4	smoked sausages
1 cup	(250 mL) sauerkraut in vinegar, drained
1 tbsp	(15 mL) Dijon mustard

■ Preheat oven to 400 °F (205 °C).

■ Slice croissants in half.

■ Slice sausages in half, lengthwise.

■ Baste inside of each croissant half with Dijon mustard. Place halved sausage and small amount of sauerkraut into each croissant. Close croissant and bake for 12 minutes.

* Illustrated recipe

Vegetable Croissants

Perfect for a special dinner on short notice.

4 servings

4	croissants
¼ cup	(60 mL) broccoli, cut into tiny flowerets
¼ cup	(60 mL) cauliflower, cut into tiny flowerets
¼ cup	(60 mL) carrots, julienned
¼ cup	(60 mL) celery, diced
¼ cup	(60 mL) leek, finely sliced
¼ cup	(60 mL) sweet red pepper, diced
¼ cup	(60 mL) grated Cheddar cheese
¼ cup	(60 mL) béchamel sauce
	salt and pepper

■ Preheat oven to 400 °F (205 °C).

■ Slice croissants in half and set aside.

■ In a saucepan filled with lightly salted boiling water, blanch vegetables for 2 minutes. Rinse under cold running water. Drain.

■ In a bowl, mix blanched vegetables, cheese and béchamel sauce. Season with salt and pepper.

■ Spoon mixture into croissants. Bake for 12 minutes.

Chocolate Croissants

Use semi-sweet, good quality baker's chocolate, grated, or cut small bits of dark Swiss chocolate from a bar.

4 servings	
4	croissants
¼ cup	(60 mL) chocolate, slivered
½ cup	(125 mL) canned pears, sliced
2 tbsp	(30 mL) liquid honey
½ cup	(125 mL) 35% cream
1 tsp	(5 mL) icing sugar
2	drops rum extract
1 tsp	(5 mL) fresh mint leaf, chopped

■ Preheat oven to 400 °F (205 °C).

■ Slice croissants in half. Place chocolate slivers and sliced pears on one half, and spread layer of liquid honey on other half. Close croissant. Bake for 8 minutes. Let stand for 5 minutes to cool.

■ Meanwhile, in a bowl, whip cream, icing sugar and rum extract.

■ Garnish each croissant with mixture. Decorate with chopped mint leaves.

Almond Croissants

Use smooth peanut butter so as not to mask the subtle flavor of the almonds.

4 servings	
4	croissants
½ cup	(125 mL) peanut butter
¼ cup	(60 mL) slivered almonds
2 tbsp	(30 mL) butter
12	dates
1 tbsp	(15 mL) liquid honey
1 tbsp	(15 mL) roasted almonds

■ Preheat oven to 400 °F (205 °C).

■ Slice croissants in half.

■ Mix peanut butter, almonds and butter in a food processor. Spoon mixture evenly over croissant halves. Place 3 halved dates on each croissant. Close and baste lightly with honey. Heat in oven for 8 minutes. Remove and sprinkle with roasted almonds.

* Illustrated recipe

375

PITA BREAD

Stuffed Pitas

Pitas are a sort of edible wallet, ideal for carrying on picnics or for take-out meals. You can put an amazing variety of food in them, and they won't leak.

4 servings	
4	pitas
	finely shredded lettuce
2 cups	(500 mL) stuffing

■ Slice pitas in half. Spoon stuffing into middle of each half. Garnish with shredded lettuce and close.

Turkey Stuffing

4 servings	
6 ½ oz	(184 g) canned turkey, flaked
¼ cup	(60 mL) green bell pepper, diced
2 tbsp	(30 mL) sour cream
¼ cup	(60 mL) canned cranberries, drained
	salt and pepper

■ Drain flaked turkey. In a saucepan filled with lightly salted boiling water, blanch green bell pepper for 2 minutes.

■ Mix all ingredients in a bowl.

Tuna Stuffing

4 servings	
6 ½ oz	(184 g) canned tuna, flaked
2 tbsp	(30 mL) mayonnaise
1 tsp	(5 mL) wine vinegar
1	tomato, diced
1	celery stalk, diced
1 tsp	(5 mL) chopped chives
	salt and pepper

■ Drain tuna.

■ Mix all ingredients in a bowl.

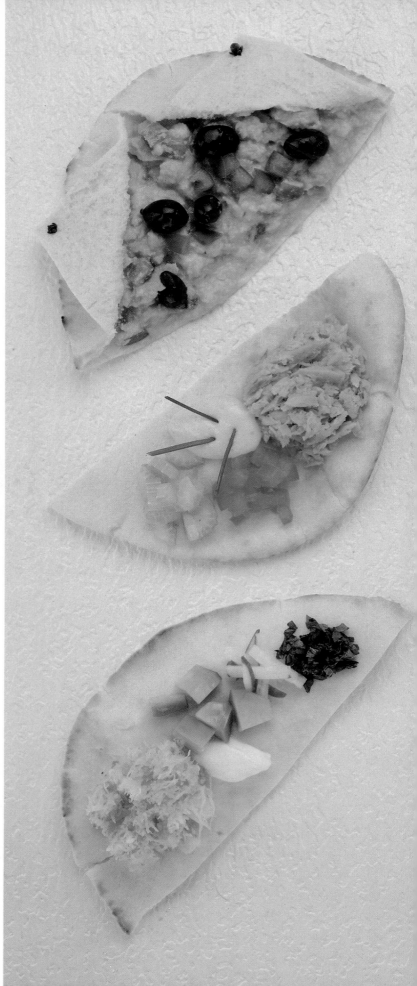

Top to bottom:
Turkey ▪ Tuna ▪ Crabmeat

Crabmeat Stuffing

4 servings

6 ½ oz	(184 g) canned crabmeat
	juice of ½ lemon
1	avocado, peeled, diced
2 tbsp	(30 mL) sour cream
4	radishes, cut into thin sticks
	salt and pepper
1 tsp	(5 mL) chopped mint

■ Drain crabmeat.

■ In a bowl, pour lemon juice, then add avocado. Stir. Add other ingredients.

Ham Stuffing

4 servings

6 ½ oz	(184 g) canned ham, flaked
¼ cup	(60 mL) alfalfa sprouts
¼ cup	(60 mL) cucumber, peeled, seeded, diced
1	tomato, diced
	salt and pepper
¼ cup	(60 mL) mayonnaise
1 tsp	(5 mL) wine vinegar

■ Drain flaked ham.

■ Mix all ingredients in a bowl.

Chicken Stuffing

4 servings

6 ½ oz	(184 g) canned chicken, flaked
¼ cup	(60 mL) carrots, diced
2 tbsp	(30 mL) mayonnaise
1 tsp	(5 mL) wine vinegar
¼ cup	(60 mL) canned asparagus, sliced into 3 pieces
	salt and pepper
1 tsp	(5 mL) chopped tarragon

■ Drain chicken. Meanwhile, in a saucepan filled with lightly salted boiling water, blanch carrots. Rinse under cold running water and drain.

■ Mix all ingredients in a bowl.

Salmon Stuffing

4 servings

6 ½ oz	(184 g) canned salmon, flaked
1 tbsp	(15 mL) mayonnaise
1 tbsp	(15 mL) plain yogurt
2 tbsp	(30 mL) onion, chopped
1	garlic clove, finely sliced
2 tsp	(10 mL) capers
2	anchovy filets, chopped
	salt and pepper

■ Drain salmon.

■ Mix all ingredients in a bowl.

Top to bottom:
Chicken ▪ Ham ▪ Salmon

377

DAIRY PRODUCTS

Cows have been a symbol of fertility and wealth since ancient times, and the milking of cows was often part of rituals or religious festivals.

Even today, milk is considered a veritable elixir of health. Although we think of milk as being vital for very young children, adults need their share as well. Milk is considered particularly important for women; it helps prevent osteoporosis.

Partially skimmed milk contains only 2% fat, with few calories and a high calcium content. But milk isn't the only dairy product. There are dozens of derivatives and numerous varieties of creams, butters, cheeses and yogurts, to name a few, that make it easy and pleasant to eat some form of dairy product with every meal.

YOGURT AND SOUR CREAM

Tsatziki

This Greek specialty makes a delightful party dip.

about 1 cup (250 mL)

½	cucumber, peeled, seeded
1 to 2	cloves garlic, finely sliced
1	French (dry) shallot, chopped
¾ cup	(180 mL) plain yogurt
1 tsp	(5 mL) chopped dill
½ tsp	(2 mL) chopped fennel
½ tsp	(2 mL) chopped chives
	juice of ½ lemon
	salt and pepper

■ Mix all ingredients in a food processor. Chill at least one hour before serving.

Mexican Dressing

Sour cream gives a smooth richness to this dressing.

about 1 ½ cups (375 mL)

½ cup	(125 mL) plain yogurt
½ cup	(125 mL) sour cream
1	garlic clove, finely sliced
¼ cup	(60 mL) chili sauce
2 tbsp	(30 mL) green bell pepper, finely diced
	juice of ½ lemon
	pinch of chili powder
	salt and pepper

■ Combine all dressing ingredients in a bowl. Chill at least one hour before serving.

Asparagus Dressing

Canned cream of asparagus soup is sometimes highly salted. It's good idea not to add any salt to this recipe until you've tasted it.

about 1 cup (250 mL)

½ cup	(125 mL) canned cream of asparagus soup, undiluted
¼ cup	(60 mL) plain yogurt
¼ cup	(60 mL) sour cream
6 to 8	canned asparagus, drained, diced
	juice of ½ lemon
	salt and pepper

■ Combine all dressing ingredients in a bowl. Chill for at least ½ hour before serving.

Grapefruit Dressing

Citrus fruit segments should have all the white membrane removed before being used in a recipe.

about 1 cup (250 mL)

1	white grapefruit
1	pink grapefruit
½ cup	(125 mL) sour cream
1 tsp	(5 mL) liquid honey
	salt and pepper
1 tsp	(5 mL) chopped fresh mint (optional)

■ Peel grapefruit, including white membrane. Separate into segments and coarsely chop each piece.

■ Mix all dressing ingredients in a bowl. Chill for at least 2 hours before serving.

■ Garnish with fresh mint.

Strawberry Yogurt Popsicles

Young and old will enjoy this healthy frozen treat.

about 4 cups (1 L)	
2 cups	(500 mL) strawberries
2 cups	(500 mL) strawberry yogurt
2 tbsp	(30 mL) strawberry jam

■ Mix all ingredients in a food processor. Pour into individual popsicle molds. Freeze. After ¹/₂ hour, place a popsicle stick in the middle of each mold. Freeze until popsicles harden.

VARIATION

• **Replace strawberries with your choice of fruit, such as apricots, blueberries or raspberries, and do the same for the yogurt and the jam.**

Frozen Yogurt with Pears

With a slimming dessert like this one, avoid smothering it in a chocolate sauce, which adds needless calories. Sprinkle some chopped almonds over it instead.

about 2 ¹/₂ cups (625 mL)	
1 ¹/₂ cups	(375 mL) canned pears, drained
1 cup	(250 mL) plain yogurt
2 tbsp	(30 mL) sugar
1 tbsp	(15 mL) icing sugar
1 tsp	(5 mL) lemon juice

■ Mix all ingredients in a food processor.

■ Pour into narrow container. Freeze.

■ When mixture is partially frozen, return to food processor for 20 seconds. Remove frozen particles that stick to sides of bowl.

■ Chill in freezer until mixture is frozen solid. Remove from freezer 10 minutes before serving.

* Illustrated recipe

VARIATION

• **Replace pears with canned peaches.**

381

MILK SHAKES

Vanilla Milk Shake

1 serving

³/₄ cup	(180 mL) or 2 scoops of vanilla ice cream
¹/₂ cup	(125 mL) milk
¹/₄ tsp	(1 mL) vanilla extract

■ Mix all ingredients in blender until smooth. Pour into glasses and serve chilled, with a vanilla stick.

Chocolate Milk Shake

1 serving

³/₄ cup	(180 mL) or 2 scoops of chocolate ice cream
¹/₂ cup	(125 mL) milk
1 tbsp	(15 mL) chocolate syrup

■ Mix all ingredients in blender until smooth. Pour into glasses and garnish each milk shake with chocolate shavings.

Foreground: Vanilla Milk Shake
Background: Chocolate Milk Shake

Wondering what to do with that leftover fruit? If it's over ripe or too bruised to be eaten raw, purée it. In a minute or so you'll have an excellent base for milk shakes.

Strawberry Milk Shake

1 serving

¾ cup	(180 mL) or 2 scoops of strawberry ice cream
½ cup	(125 mL) milk
2	strawberries

■ Mix all ingredients in blender until smooth. Pour into glasses and serve chilled.

Egg Nog

1 serving

1	egg
1 cup	(250 mL) milk
2 tsp	(10 mL) chocolate syrup
½ tsp	(2 mL) liquid honey

■ Mix all ingredients in blender until smooth and foamy. Serve with a cinnamon stick.

*Foreground: Egg Nog
Background: Strawberry Milk Shake*

BUTTER

Preparing butter medallions

- *Fold a sheet of aluminum foil in half down the middle and spread butter mixture into fold.*

- *Fold aluminum foil over butter and hold in place with one hand.*

- *Push the butter toward the center to form a roll with the other hand.*

- *Roll the butter-filled foil into a cylinder and twist one end to close.*

- *Squeeze butter to eliminate air bubbles and twist the other end.*

A little butter goes a long way toward making a variety of foods taste better. Spread on a sandwich, melting atop a succulent steak, or dripping over a steaming corn cob, butter adds a special touch. The trick is to use it to the best advantage, and not abuse it, since butter is about 82% animal fat.

Butter can be bought unsalted ("sweet"), half-salted, and salted. The seasoned butter recipes we give here use salted butter. If you use the unsalted variety as a rule, remember to add a little salt.

Seasoned butter or "beurre composé" as the French call it, comes in dozens of flavors and colors, and can combine fresh or cooked ingredients. These should be finely chopped or puréed before being added.

Keep the seasoned butter wrapped until the very last moment. If you want to keep the butter pats cold, put them in a dish with a little water and some ice cubes on the bottom.

- Allow butter to reach room temperature. Mix all ingredients in a food processor.
- Prepare a butter roll as shown here.
- Refrigerate it for at least 1 hour, and cut into rounds before serving.

Garlic Butter

about 1 cup (250 mL)	
8 oz	(225 g) butter
4	cloves garlic
½ tsp	(2 mL) Worcestershire sauce
	pepper

Tomato Butter

about 1 cup (250 mL)	
8 oz	(225 g) butter
2 tbsp	(30 mL) tomato paste
2 tbsp	(30 mL) tomatoes, diced
½	garlic clove
	pepper

Watercress Butter

about 1 cup (250 mL)

8 oz	(225 g) butter
2 tbsp	(30 mL) watercress, blanched, cooled
1 tbsp	(15 mL) parsley
½ tsp	(2 mL) Worcestershire sauce
	pepper

Citrus Butter

about 1 cup (250 mL)

8 oz	(225 g) butter
1 tbsp	(15 mL) orange pulp, thoroughly peeled
1 tbsp	(15 mL) pink grapefruit pulp, thoroughly peeled
2 tsp	(10 mL) lime pulp, thoroughly peeled
1 tbsp	(15 mL) orange, grapefruit, and lime peel, grated
½ tsp	(2 mL) Worcestershire sauce
	pepper

Blue Cheese Butter

about 1 cup (250 mL)

8 oz	(225 g) butter
2 tbsp	(30 mL) blue cheese
1	garlic clove
½ tsp	(2 mL) Worcestershire sauce
	pepper

Herb Butter

about 1 cup (250 mL)

8 oz	(225 g) butter
1 tsp	(5 mL) chopped tarragon
1 tsp	(5 mL) chopped oregano
1 tsp	(5 mL) chopped basil
1 tbsp	(15 mL) chopped parsley
½	garlic clove
½ tsp	(2 mL) Worcestershire sauce
	pepper

Left to Right:
Watercress ▪ Citrus ▪ Herb ▪ Tomato ▪
Garlic and Blue Cheese Butters

CHEESE

Pepper Dip

What better temptation to eat raw vegetables than a tasty dip? Instead of chips, arrange a large tray of carrot sticks, cauliflower flowerets, sliced mushrooms, and strips of green and red sweet peppers. You'll find it a refreshing change!

about 2 cups (500 mL)

8 oz	(225 g) cream cheese
1/2 cup	(125 mL) plain yogurt
1/4 cup	(60 mL) sour cream
2 tsp	(10 mL) hot pepper, finely chopped
2 tbsp	(30 mL) green bell pepper, chopped
1/2 tsp	(2 mL) Worcestershire sauce
4	drops of Tabasco sauce
	salt and pepper

■ Combine all ingredients in a bowl. Chill for at least 30 minutes before serving.

Lefthand platter:
Pepper Dip • Avocado Dip
Righthand platter:
Chive Dip • Indian Dip

Avocado Dip

about 2 cups (500 mL)

4 oz	(115 g) cream cheese
2	very ripe avocados, peeled
	juice of 1/2 lemon
1/2 cup	(125 mL) plain yogurt
1	garlic clove
1/2 tsp	(2 mL) Worcestershire sauce
2	drops of Tabasco sauce
	salt and pepper

■ Mix all ingredients in a food processor. Chill for at least 1 hour before serving.

Chive Dip

about 2 cups (500 mL)

8 oz	(225 g) cream cheese
1 cup	(250 mL) plain yogurt
1/4 cup	(60 mL) sour cream
2 tbsp	(30 mL) chopped chives
2 tsp	(10 mL) chopped dill
1 tbsp	(15 mL) chopped parsley
1/2 tsp	(2 mL) strong mustard
3	drops of Tabasco sauce
	salt and pepper

■ Blend cream cheese, yogurt and sour cream in a bowl. Fold in other ingredients. Chill at least 30 minutes before serving.

Indian Dip

about 2 cups (500 mL)

8 oz	(225 g) cream cheese
1/2 cup	(125 mL) mayonnaise
1/4 cup	(60 mL) sour cream
1 tsp	(5 mL) curry powder
1	garlic clove
	salt and pepper
1/2 tsp	(2 mL) celery seeds
1/2 tsp	(2 mL) poppy seeds

■ Combine first 7 ingredients in a bowl.

■ Add celery seeds and poppy seeds. Chill for at least 30 minutes before serving.

Olive Mousseline

The color and texture of mousselines make them a feast for the eye as well as the palate.

Put the mousseline mixture in a pastry bag with a fluted nozzle and pipe it into the scooped-out half of a tomato, cucumber, sweet pepper, or avocado.

Once you've tried our suggested recipes, you'll find it easy to invent your own.

about 1 cup (250 mL)

8 oz	(225 g) cream cheese
¼ cup	(60 mL) sour cream
¼ cup	(60 mL) green and black olives, pitted, drained
1 tsp	(5 mL) olive oil
2 tsp	(10 mL) lemon juice
	salt and pepper

■ Mix all ingredients in a food processor. Chill at least 30 minutes before serving.

Beet Mousseline

about 1 cup (250 mL)

8 oz	(225 g) cream cheese
¼ cup	(60 mL) sour cream
¼ cup	(60 mL) cooked beets, drained, diced
1 tbsp	(15 mL) lemon juice
2 tsp	(10 mL) chopped parsley
2 tsp	(10 mL) Worcestershire sauce
	salt and pepper

■ Mix all ingredients in a food processor. Chill at least 30 minutes before serving.

Roquefort Mousseline

about 1 cup (250 mL)

8 oz	(225 g) cream cheese
¼ cup	(60 mL) sour cream
1 tbsp	(15 mL) lemon juice
2 tbsp	(30 mL) Roquefort cheese, crumbled
¾ tsp	(3 mL) Worcestershire sauce
2 tsp	(10 mL) chopped parsley
	salt and pepper

■ Mix all ingredients in a food processor. Chill at least 30 minutes before serving.

Spinach Mousseline

about 1 cup (250 mL)

8 oz	(225 g) cream cheese
2 tbsp	(30 mL sour cream
¼ cup	(60 mL) spinach, blanched, drained
1	garlic clove, finely sliced
1 tbsp	(15 mL) chopped parsley
¾ tsp	(3 mL) Worcestershire sauce
	salt and pepper

■ Mix all ingredients in a food processor. Chill at least 30 minutes before serving.

In the Sweet Pepper: Olive Mousseline
In the Avocado: Roquefort Mousseline
In the Tomato: Spinach Mousseline
In the Cucumber: Beet Mousselline

Healthy Platter

A healthy one-plate meal par excellence! Serve it with a vegetable juice, and a light dessert such as a flan.

1 serving

1	hard-boiled egg
1	Italian tomato
¼ cup	(60 mL) tofu, diced
2 tbsp	(30 mL) tomato juice
2 tsp	(10 mL) chopped parsley
4	lettuce leaves
½ cup	(125 mL) cottage cheese
½ cup	(125 mL) ricotta cheese
2	slices of cantaloup
1	slice of watermelon
1	small cluster of green grapes
1	small cluster of purple grapes

■ Slice hard-boiled egg.

■ Slice tomato without cutting completely to the bottom.

■ Place 1 egg slice between each tomato wedge and set aside.

■ Meanwhile, mix tofu, tomato juice, and parsley in a bowl.

■ Arrange lettuce leaves in a serving dish and place cheese over lettuce. Spread other ingredients over lettuce and cheese in a colorful arrangement.

Cheese Chutney

Homemade chutney? Nothing could be simpler. Use this cheese chutney on hamburgers or add a few spoonfuls to a green salad.

4 servings

1 cup	(250 mL) cottage cheese
1 cup	(250 mL) ricotta cheese
¼ cup	(60 mL) pearl onions, marinated, quartered
¼ cup	(60 mL) sour pickles, chopped
¼ cup	(60 mL) tomato, diced
2 tbsp	(30 mL) spinach, finely shredded
¾ tsp	(3 mL) Worcestershire sauce
	salt and pepper
1 tsp	(5 mL) sugar (optional)

■ Combine all ingredients in a bowl. Chill.

Illustrated recipe

388

Cottage Cheese Pie

To make this pie more colorful, add a few canned peach slices with the cheese, or replace part of the sugar with strawberry or raspberry jam.

4 servings

2 tbsp	(30 mL) lemon juice
2	egg yolks
1	packet unflavored gelatin
¼ cup	(60 mL) hot milk
¼ cup	(60 mL) sugar
2 cups	(500 mL) cottage cheese
	graham cracker pie crust

■ In a blender, mix lemon juice, egg yolks and gelatin at high speed for a few seconds. Gradually pour in hot milk and sugar and blend for about 1 minute or until gelatin is dissolved. Reduce speed. Add cottage cheese gradually until mixture is smooth and creamy. Pour mixture into pie crust. Chill at least 2 hours before serving.

■ Garnish with fruit, nuts, or bits of chocolate.

VARIATION

• Reduce the amount of sugar to 1 tbsp (15 mL). Garnish pie with tiny pieces of blanched vegetables (shown opposite) or sprinkle with fresh, chopped fines herbes.

389

Cheese Balls

Serve these cheese appetizers with drinks or at a buffet. Be careful to use garlic powder, not garlic salt, otherwise the cheese balls will be too salty.

4 servings	
4 oz	(115 g) cream cheese
3 cups	(750 mL) strong Cheddar cheese, grated
4 tsp	(20 mL) prepared mustard
1 tsp	(5 mL) Worcestershire sauce
1/2 tsp	(2 mL) garlic powder
4 tsp	(20 mL) chili powder

■ Soften cream cheese in a bowl. Add other ingredients except 2 tsp (10 mL) chili powder. Stir well.

■ Shape into tiny balls, about 1/2 inch (1,25 cm) wide. Sprinkle cheese balls with 2 tsp (10 mL) chili powder. Chill before serving.

Cheese Kebabs

Get your family or friends to help you. Even novice cooks can succeed with this recipe.

You can use a variety of cheeses, replacing the brick cheese with Emmenthal, for example.

16 skewers	
1/4 cup	(60 mL) yellow Cheddar cheese, cubed
1/4 cup	(60 mL) cubed brick cheese
16	green grapes
16	red grapes
16	stuffed olives

■ Freeze grapes for 2 hours.

■ Meanwhile, break small wooden skewers in half.

■ Prepare kebabs, alternating 1 green grape, 1 cube of brick cheese, 1 olive, 1 cube of Cheddar, and 1 red grape. Arrange kebabs on a bed of lettuce leaves.

Cheddar Marinated in Port Wine

Served at the end of the evening with a glass of fine red wine ... mmmm! Any firm cheese could be used instead of the Cheddar suggested here.

---

about 3 cups (750 mL)

---

2 cups   (500 mL) extra strong Cheddar cheese, cubed

Marinade

½ cup   (125 mL) red wine

½ cup   (125 mL) port

2 tsp   (10 mL) sesame seeds

1   French (dry) shallot, chopped

■ Place cheese cubes in a bowl and set aside.

■ In a separate bowl, combine marinade ingredients. Pour over cheese cubes and marinate for 12 hours to 4 days. Drain and pat dry before serving.

Stuffed Cheese

This colorful appetizer is always a great success. Be sure to use high quality ham sliced fairly fine.

The Mozzarella could be replaced with a Swiss cheese.

---

4 servings

---

8   Mozzarella slices

8   ham slices

½ cup   (125 mL) cream cheese, softened

16   small sweet pickles

■ Coat each Mozzarella slice with cream cheese and place ham slice over cheese. Spread another layer of cream cheese over ham.

■ Place 2 pickles end to end on top of each slice. Roll tightly. Wrap each roll in plastic wrap. Chill at least 3 hours before serving.

■ Serve in a roll, or cut it into wheels before serving, as shown.

Center: Cheddar Marinated in Port Wine
Outside: Stuffed Cheese

391

Fried Camembert

Warm Goat's Cheese

For deep frying, it's best to use an oil from a single vegetable source (peanut, sunflower seed, corn) rather than a blend.

4 servings

1	Camembert cheese
2	beaten eggs
2 cups	(500 mL) breadcrumbs
	oil
1 tsp	(5 mL) paprika
2 tsp	(10 mL) chopped parsley
2	oranges, peeled, in segments
1 tbsp	(15 mL) mayonnaise
	orange peel, julienned

■ Slice cheese into 8 wedges.

■ Dip each wedge into beaten eggs and coat with breadcrumbs. Repeat operation.

■ Fry in hot oil for 2 minutes. Drain on paper towel. Sprinkle fried Camembert with paprika and parsley. Arrange on a platter and set aside.

■ Toss the oranges in the mayonnaise and put them in the center of the platter. Garnish with julienned orange peel.

It's very simple to prepare, but worthy of the finest restaurants. The key to success is to choose only the freshest ingredients.

4 servings

16	spinach leaves
	butter
4	goat cheese rounds
1 tbsp	(15 mL) olive oil
	pinch of oregano
	pinch of basil
	pinch of chervil

■ In a saucepan filled with lightly salted boiling water, blanch spinach leaves for 15 seconds.

■ Divide blanched spinach into 4 servings on a greased cookie sheet and garnish each serving with a round of goat's cheese.

■ Lightly baste cheese rounds with oil and sprinkle with fines herbes. Heat in microwave at MEDIUM for 20 seconds.

Cheese Fondue

Cheese fondue is traditionally served with chunks of bread and long forks. And don't forget another tradition: those who drop their bread into the fondue dish must kiss their lefthand neighbor ... or pay a forfeit of a bottle of wine!

4 servings

2 tsp	(10 mL) cornstarch
1 tbsp	(15 mL) cold water
1	garlic clove
1 ³/₄ cups	(430 mL) dry white wine
1 lb	(450 g) grated Emmenthal cheese
¹/₄ tsp	(1 mL) nutmeg
	salt and pepper
3 tbsp	(45 mL) kirsch

■ Stir cornstarch until smooth in cold water and set aside.

■ Rub inside of fondue pot with garlic clove.

■ Add wine and bring to a boil. Reduce heat, add Emmenthal cheese, and stir constantly until cheese has completely melted.

■ Add cornstarch. Season with nutmeg, salt, and pepper. Pour kirsch into mixture and stir.

Raclette

For raclette lovers who don't own a special raclette-maker, we offer this variation.

4 servings

4	small baked potatoes
20	marinated pearl onions
20	small marinated sour pickles
20	stuffed olives
	salt and pepper
	pinch of nutmeg
	butter
4	slices of Raclette or Emmenthal cheese

■ Preheat oven to 400 °F (205 °C).

■ Lightly butter 4 individual baking dishes.

■ Divide potatoes, onions, pickles, and olives equally into each serving dish. Season with salt, pepper, and nutmeg. Top each portion with a slice of cheese. Heat in oven for about 8 minutes or until cheese has melted.

* Illustrated recipe

Are you looking for the perfect food? One that, for example, contains only 80 calories, is 12% protein, rich in vitamins and minerals, and inexpensive? The egg is the perfect answer.

Eggs have figured in the culinary scene since the earliest times. We have learned not only how to cook them in the shell, but how to incorporate them in dishes and use them to make sauces thicken, custards firm, and soufflés rise. It's worth noting that even fledgling cooks can do wonders with eggs.

If you want to be sure that you're eating good quality, fresh eggs, only buy what you need for two weeks. Put them in the refrigerator as soon as you get home. An egg loses as much freshness in one hour sitting on the counter as it would in a day if kept cool.

A hint from the experts: buy medium-sized eggs as much as possible. They are less expensive and don't make a bit of difference to the recipe.

EGGS

BOILED EGGS

Jellied Eggs in Red Wine

Don't overcook boiled eggs. The white will become rubbery and an unattractive green circle will surround the yolk.

4 servings

4	eggs
1	packet unflavored gelatin
3 tbsp	(45 mL) cold water
	juice of ¹/₂ lemon
¹/₂ cup	(125 mL) red wine or port
¹/₃ cup	(80 mL) mushrooms, finely sliced (optional)
¹/₄ cup	(60 mL) sweet almond oil
¹/₄ cup	(60 mL) mayonnaise
	lettuce leaves

■ Boil eggs. Peel and set aside in cold water.

■ Pour 3 tbsp (45 mL) cold water into a bowl. Add gelatin and let stand 5 minutes. Add lemon juice and wine. Heat in top of double-boiler until gelatin has dissolved. Add mushrooms, (optional).

■ Lightly grease 4 small oval-shaped molds or 4 medium-size custard cups with sweet almond oil. Pour a thick layer of gelatin mix into each mold and chill until firm.

■ Spoon a layer of mayonnaise over firm gelatin. Place hard-boiled egg in middle of each mold and pour the rest of the gelatin over egg. Chill until firm. Unmold jellied eggs and place on a bed of lettuce leaves.

Garnished Soft-Boiled Eggs

A soft-boiled egg has a yolk that is thickened but still runny.

4 servings

4	eggs
	salt and pepper

Garnishes

2 tbsp	(30 mL) melted cheese
	or
2 tbsp	(30 mL) crabmeat, mixed with
2 tsp	(10 mL) mayonnaise
	or
2 tbsp	(30 mL) blanched spinach, finely chopped
	or
2 tbsp	(30 mL) diced tomatoes, mixed with
2 tsp	(10 mL) chili sauce

■ Place eggs in a small saucepan filled with cold water. After water begins to boil, cook over high heat for 6 minutes. Remove saucepan from heat and cool eggs in cold running water. Let stand 1 minute.

■ Cut off narrow tip of boiled egg and season with salt and pepper. Garnish with the mixture of your choice.

* Illustrated recipe:
Left: Crabmeat and Mayonnaise
Right: Melted Cheese

Devilled Eggs

Use week-old eggs for hard boiling. When eggs are too fresh, the shell is difficult to remove.

4 servings

4	eggs
	stuffing

■ Place eggs in a small saucepan filled with cold water. After water begins to boil, cook eggs over high heat for 10 minutes.

■ Slice eggs in half, or in 4, or cut into thick slices and gently scoop out yolks. Mix yolk with stuffing of your choice. Using a pastry bag or a spoon, stuff the egg whites.

STUFFINGS

Tarragon Stuffing

- Mix together 2 tbsp (30 mL) mayonnaise, ½ tsp (2 mL) finely sliced garlic and ½ tsp (2 mL) chopped tarragon.

- Decorate with tarragon leaves.

Cocktail Stuffing

- Mix together 4 tsp (20 mL) mayonnaise, 2 tsp (10 mL) chili sauce and ½ tsp (2 mL) vinegar-flavored horseradish.

- Decorate with julienned tomatoes.

Mustard Stuffing

- Mix together 4 tsp (20 mL) mayonnaise, 2 tsp (10 mL) prepared mustard and 1 tsp (5 mL) chopped red onion.

- Decorate with chopped parsley.

Carrot Stuffing

- Mix together 5 tsp (25 mL) mayonnaise, 2 tsp (10 mL) grated carrot and ¼ tsp (1 mL) Worcestershire sauce.

- Decorate with yellow onion, julienned.

Watercress Stuffing

- Mix together 4 tsp (20 mL) mayonnaise, 2 tsp (10 mL) chopped watercress and 1 tsp (5 mL) relish.

- Decorate with finely sliced radishes.

Shrimp Stuffing

- Mix together 5 tsp (25 mL) mayonnaise, 2 tsp (10 mL) chopped shrimp, and ½ tsp (2 mL) lemon juice.

- Decorate with small shrimp and fennel leaves.

Clockwise, from top left, stuffings: Cocktail ▪ Mustard ▪ Carrot ▪ Watercress

SCRAMBLED EGGS

Scrambled Eggs On Waffles

To get scrambled eggs that are an even, golden color, stir them constantly during cooking and don't let them stick to the pan. If possible, use a non-stick skillet.

4 servings	
4	waffles
4	eggs
1/4 cup	(60 mL) grated Cheddar cheese
2 tbsp	(30 mL) sweet red pepper, finely chopped
2 tbsp	(30 mL) green onion, finely sliced
	salt and pepper
1 tbsp	(15 mL) butter

■ Toast waffles and set aside.

Beat eggs in a bowl. Add cheese, sweet red pepper, and onion. Season with salt and pepper and stir.

In a skillet, melt butter and cook eggs, stirring constantly. Spoon scrambled eggs onto waffles.

* Illustrated recipe

Scrambled Eggs with Sausage

Last-minute guests? Cook a few crêpes and fill them with this satisfying sausage-and-egg mixture.

4 servings	
2 tsp	(10 mL) oil
1 tsp	(5 mL) butter
6	sausages, cut into bite-size pieces
1	French (dry) shallot, chopped
1	large garlic clove, finely sliced
6	eggs
	salt and pepper
1/2 tsp	(2 mL) chervil

■ In a skillet, heat oil and melt butter. Sauté sausages until lightly browned. Add shallot and garlic and cook for 30 seconds.

■ Lightly beat eggs in a bowl. Pour over sausage mixture. Season with salt and pepper. Cook over medium heat, stirring from time to time. Sprinkle with chervil and serve.

Scrambled Eggs with Tomatoes

Keep stirring the eggs as they cook, to remove all trace of the white and to keep the mixture from browning.

4 servings

6	eggs
2 tsp	(10 mL) chili sauce
1 tsp	(5 mL) tomato paste
1 tbsp	(15 mL) butter
1/4 cup	(60 mL) red tomato, diced
1/4 cup	(60 mL) green tomato, diced
	salt and pepper
1/4 tsp	(1 mL) chopped basil

■ In a bowl, beat eggs with chili sauce and tomato paste.

■ In a skillet, melt butter and cook eggs over medium heat. Stir from time to time. Halfway through cooking process, add tomatoes. Season with salt, pepper and basil.

* Illustrated recipe on the left

Scrambled Eggs with Spinach

To get a creamy consistency, beat the eggs until yolks and whites are fully blended.

4 servings

1 tsp	(5 mL) oil
8	bacon slices, cut into bite-size pieces
6	eggs
1 tsp	(5 mL) butter
1 cup	(250 mL) spinach, stemmed, finely shredded
1 tsp	(5 mL) chopped chives
	salt and pepper
1 tsp	(5 mL) pink peppercorns

■ In a skillet, heat oil and fry bacon.

■ Meanwhile, beat eggs in a bowl.

■ When bacon is almost crisp, remove excess fat from skillet. Melt butter and pour eggs into skillet. Cook over medium heat, stirring from time to time.

■ Halfway through cooking process, drop shredded spinach and chives into egg mixture and season with salt and pepper. Decorate with pink peppercorns.

* Illustrated recipe on the right

OMELETS

Apple Omelet

Coat the bottom of the skillet generously with butter to prevent sticking, then cook omelet over medium heat, stirring constantly to spread the eggs until the bottom of the omelet turns golden-brown.

4 servings

4	**eggs**
1 tbsp	**(15 mL) flour**
1 tbsp	**(15 mL) sugar**
3 tbsp	**(45 mL) milk**
2 tbsp	**(30 mL) butter**

Garnish

2	**apples, sliced**
2 tbsp	**(30 mL) Calvados (or Cognac)**
2 tsp	**(10 mL) icing sugar**

■ Beat eggs in a bowl. Add flour, sugar, and milk and mix well.

■ In a skillet, melt 1 tbsp (15 mL) butter. Cook sliced apples until golden. Add 1 tbsp (15 mL) Calvados or Cognac and set aside.

■ In a separate skillet, melt rest of butter and cook eggs over medium heat.

■ Spread cooked apple slices over omelet. Place garnished omelet on a warm serving dish and fold in half. Sprinkle with icing sugar. Pour rest of Calvados or Cognac over apple-stuffed omelet and flambé. Serve hot.

VARIATION

Strawberry Omelet

• **Replace apples with strawberries. Roll omelet just before serving. Slice into individual portions and garnish with fresh strawberries and whipped cream.**

Top: Apple Omelet
Bottom: Strawberry Omelet

Stuffed Omelet

To transfer the omelet smoothly from the pan to the hot serving dish, tip the skillet and let the omelet slide out.

4 servings

6	eggs
¹/₄ cup	(60 mL) milk
¹/₂	garlic clove, finely sliced
1	French (dry) shallot, finely sliced
	salt and pepper
2 tbsp	(30 mL) butter
	choice of garnish
	grated Parmesan cheese
	fines herbes

■ In a bowl, beat eggs with milk, garlic, and shallot. Season with salt and pepper.

■ In a skillet, melt 1 tbsp (15 mL) butter and sauté your choice of garnish. Sprinkle with Parmesan and fines herbes and set aside.

■ In a separate skillet, melt rest of butter and cook egg mixture over medium heat. When cooking is three-quarters done, spread garnish on one side of omelet. Continue cooking until omelet is done, then fold the other side over. Slide omelet onto a serving dish. Divide into individual servings.

* Illustrated recipe: Omelet, with leek stuffing

STUFFINGS

Eggplant

• Mix together 1 cup (250 mL) diced eggplant, 1 tbsp (15 mL) vegetable oil and ¹/₂ tsp (2 mL) chopped chervil. Season with salt and pepper.

White Poultry Meat

• Mix together 1 cup (250 mL) white poultry meat, cut into strips with 1 tbsp (15 mL) vegetable oil and ¹/₂ tsp (2 mL) curry powder. Season with salt and pepper.

Fiddlehead Greens

• Mix together 1 cup (250 mL) fiddlehead greens, 1 tbsp (15 mL) butter and ¹/₂ tsp (2 mL) chopped dill. Season with salt and pepper.

Leek

• Mix together ³/₄ cup (180 mL) finely sliced leek whites, ¹/₄ cup (60 mL) finely sliced leek greens, 1 tbsp (15 mL) butter and ¹/₂ tsp (2 mL) chopped basil. Season with salt and pepper.

Smoked Salmon and Shrimp

• Mix together ¹/₂ cup (125 mL) smoked salmon, cut into thin strips, ¹/₂ cup (125 mL) baby shrimp, 1 tbsp (15 mL) butter and ¹/₂ tsp (2 mL) chopped chives. Season with salt and pepper.

401

POACHED EGGS

Egg Surprise

You can make this a dish for special occasions by cutting the bread in appropriate shapes: hearts for St. Valentine's, fir trees for Christmas, and so on.

4 servings

2 tbsp	(30 mL) butter
4	slices of bread
4	eggs
	salt and pepper
4	lettuce leaves
8	cherry tomatoes, cut into 6 wedges each
12	chive stalks
	sprig of parsley

■ Coat both sides of bread slices with 2 tsp (10 mL) butter. With a round cookie cutter, cut a 2-inch (5 cm) circle in the middle of each bread slice. Keep both parts.

■ In a skillet, melt rest of butter and cook bread slices and bread circles over low heat. Take out the circles and set aside. Break an egg in the center of each slice. Season with salt and pepper. Gently turn slices and cook other side.

■ Garnish individual serving dishes with lettuce leaves. Place egg/bread slices on lettuce leaves and top with browned bread circles. Decorate with cherry tomato wedges. Garnish with chives and parsley.

Egg-stuffed Tomatoes

These handy eggs-in-tomatoes make a one-plate lunch when served with rice or a few slices of whole-wheat bread.

4 servings

4	firm tomatoes
4	eggs
	salt and pepper
4 tsp	(20 mL) grated Parmesan cheese
1 tbsp	(15 mL) olive oil
1/2 tsp	(2 mL) chopped basil
1/2	large garlic clove, finely sliced

■ Slice top off tomato and scoop out pulp without damaging the outer skin.

■ Break 1 egg into each tomato and season with salt and pepper. Sprinkle with Parmesan.

■ In a small bowl, mix together olive oil, basil, and garlic. Brush tomato skin with oil mixture.

■ Cook in microwave at HIGH for 1 1/2 minutes. Check the eggs for doneness. If necessary, cook for another 30 seconds.

* Illustrated recipe

Classic Poached Eggs

Two spoonfuls of vinegar in the poaching water helps the whites coagulate. The surface of the water should be quivering when you put the eggs in.

4 servings

4 cups	(1 L) water
2 tbsp	(30 mL) white vinegar
4	eggs
16	spinach leaves, blanched
2	English muffins, halved, toasted
¼ cup	(60 mL) hollandaise sauce

■ Heat the broiler.

■ In a saucepan, heat water and vinegar almost to boiling. Poach eggs for 1 minute.

■ Gently remove eggs and wrap them in blanched spinach leaves. Put them on toasted English muffins and coat with hollandaise sauce. Broil for 1 minute.

* *Illustrated recipe*

VARIATION

• **Instead of spinach, use finely sliced leek sautéed in butter.**

Poached Eggs Orly

The egg will keep its oval shape if you push the egg white toward the yolk during poaching.

4 servings

4 cups	(1 L) water
1 tbsp	(15 mL) white vinegar
1 cup	(250 mL) tomato juice
4	eggs
¼ cup	(60 mL) carrots, julienned, blanched
¼ cup	(60 mL) leek whites, julienned, blanched
¼ cup	(60 mL) tomato, julienned, blanched
¼ cup	(60 mL) turnip, julienned, blanched
	salt and pepper
¼ cup	(60 mL) cream of tomato soup

■ In a saucepan, heat water, vinegar and tomato juice almost to boiling. Poach eggs for 1 minute.

■ Gently remove eggs and place them on a bed of blanched vegetables. Season with salt and pepper and coat with cream of tomato soup.

QUICHES

Goat's Cheese Quiche

If you're counting calories, make a crustless quiche. Oil the pie plate to keep the quiche filling from sticking.

4 servings

4	eggs
1 cup	(250 mL) milk
1 cup	(250 mL) 35% cream
	salt and pepper
¼ tsp	(1 mL) nutmeg
2 tbsp	(30 mL) butter
1	large garlic clove, finely sliced
1	green onion, finely sliced
2 cups	(500 mL) spinach, stemmed
½ cup	(125 mL) goat's cheese, crumbled
1	9-inch (22-cm) pie crust, uncooked

■ Preheat oven to 400 °F (205 °C).

■ In a bowl, beat eggs with milk and cream. Season with salt, pepper, and nutmeg, and set aside.

■ In a skillet, melt butter and sauté garlic, green onion, and spinach.

■ When spinach becomes limp, remove from skillet and spoon mixture into pie crust. Sprinkle with cheese. Cover with egg mixture and bake for 20 minutes.

■ Reduce oven temperature to 325 °F (160 °C) and bake for 15 minutes.

VARIATION

• Replace spinach with 1 large finely sliced onion. Replace goat's cheese with ¾ cup (180 mL) grated Gruyère cheese.

404

Assorted Miniature Quiches

An ideal meal for people who can't make up their minds. Put these miniature quiches on a tray in the center of the table, and let everyone help themselves.

4 servings	
5	eggs
2 cups	(500 mL) milk
	salt and pepper
	nutmeg
	grated Parmesan cheese
12	small tart shells
¹/₂ cup	(125 mL) grated Cheddar cheese

■ Preheat oven to 400 °F (205 °C).

■ In a bowl, beat eggs. Add milk, salt, pepper, nutmeg and Parmesan and set aside.

■ Spoon garnish of your choice into tart shells and pour egg mixture over garnish. Sprinkle with grated Cheddar. Bake for 10 minutes. Reduce heat to 325 °F (160 °C) and bake for 15 minutes longer.

GARNISHES

Zucchini and Crabmeat

• Mix together 1 cup (250 mL) zucchini, julienned, and ¹/₂ cup (125 mL) canned crabmeat.

Ham and Mushroom

• Mix together ³/₄ cup (180 mL) canned mushrooms, finely sliced and ³/₄ cup (180 mL) cooked ham, chopped or flaked.

Chicken and Olive

• Mix together 1 cup (250 mL) cooked chicken, diced (or flaked) and ¹/₂ cup (125 mL) stuffed olives, thinly sliced.

Watercress and Apple

• Mix together 1 cup (250 mL) diced apples and ¹/₂ cup (125 mL) watercress.

Left to Right, Garnished Quiches :
Top: Zucchini and Crabmeat ▪ Ham and Mushroom
Bottom: Watercress and Apple ▪ Chicken and Olive

CRÊPES

Crêpes, Basic Recipe

Crêpes are always better if you let the batter stand for a while before cooking.

Once the crêpes are in the skillet, wait until bubbles burst on the surface before turning them.

4 servings	
1 cup	(250 mL) flour
1 ½ cups	(375 mL) milk
2	eggs
1 tbsp	(15 mL) melted butter
¼ tsp	(1 mL) salt

■ In a bowl, mix all ingredients and refrigerate for 2 hours.

■ In a lightly buttered skillet, pour ¼ cup (60 mL) crêpe mixture, spread evenly on skillet surface. Cook for 1 minute over medium heat. Turn crêpe and cook on other side for 30 seconds.

■ Garnish crêpes with your choice of stuffing. Roll crêpe or fold in half before serving.

N.B.: For sweet crêpes, add 1 tbsp (15 mL) of honey to the batter.

Stuffings for Sweet Crêpes

Cherry

• Spoon 3 tbsp (45 mL) whipped cream and 8 canned cherries on each crêpe. Sprinkle with brown sugar and fold crêpe.

Apricot

• Spoon 3 tbsp (45 mL) whipped cream and 6 canned apricot halves on each crêpe. Sprinkle with icing sugar and fold crêpe.

Pear

• Spoon 3 tbsp (45 mL) cottage cheese and 1 canned pear half on each crêpe. Sprinkle with chocolate chips and fold crêpe.

Strawberry

• Spoon 3 tbsp (45 mL) cream cheese on each crêpe and place 6 finely sliced strawberries over cheese. Coat with liquid honey and fold crêpe.

* Illustrated recipe: Apricot-stuffed Crêpe

Stuffings for Savory Crêpes

Mushroom

- Sauté 2 cups (500 mL) quartered mushrooms in butter, and coat with 1 ½ cups (375 mL) béchamel sauce. Add ½ cup (125 mL) grated Gruyère cheese to mixture and stir until cheese has melted. Garnish crêpes with mixture and roll.

Brussels Sprouts

- Cook 1 cup (250 mL) bacon, cut into bite-size pieces. Halfway through cooking process, add 1 cup (250 mL) Brussels sprouts, blanched and sliced in half. Cook over medium heat for 1 minute and season with salt and pepper. Degrease skillet. Add ¾ cup (180 mL) béchamel sauce. Heat, stirring occasionally, and garnish crêpes with mixture. Fold in half.

Sweet Pepper

- Sauté 1 ½ cups (375 mL) sweet peppers, julienned, in butter. Pour 1 cup (250 mL) canned, undiluted cream of tomato soup over sautéed peppers and garnish crêpes with mixture. Fold in half.

Asparagus

- Heat 1 cup (250 mL) canned, undiluted cream of asparagus soup. Add 1 cup (250 mL) canned asparagus and ½ cup (125 mL) blanched cauliflower flowerets. Season with salt and pepper and garnish crêpes with mixture. Fold in half.

Top: Asparagus-stuffed Crêpe
Bottom: Brussels Sprout-stuffed Crêpe

TOFU, NUTS AND SEEDS

North American families devote most of their grocery budget to protein foods. But it's worth noting that proteins are present in a good many foods other than the eternal beef steak. Fish, cheese and eggs are common substitutes, but soya, nuts and seeds are gaining in popularity. These foods contain incomplete proteins, and that means we have to eat complementary foods at the same time to make up the full range of proteins required for health. For example, you can serve tofu with rice or whole-wheat macaroni, both vegetarian dishes that are on a par with meat and poultry dishes.

Nuts are another excellent source of protein. Youngsters who love peanut butter have the right idea, especially if they spread it on whole-wheat bread!

Tofu is an ideal food for people who are concerned about excess fats or calories in their food. Nuts and seeds, although an equally good source of protein, contain a fair amount of oil and calories.

TOFU

Chinese Tofu

Tofu is made from ex-tracted soya-bean milk, and looks very much like cream cheese.

4 servings	
1 lb	(450 g) tofu
1 tbsp	(15 mL) oil
1/2 cup	(125 mL) soy sauce
2	celery stalks, diago-nally sliced
1	green bell pepper, diced
2 to 3	onions, finely sliced
	boiling water
	ground ginger
2 tbsp	(30 mL) cornstarch
	salt and pepper

■ Cut tofu into cubes or tri-angles and pat dry. In a skillet, heat oil and fry tofu cubes until golden. Deglaze skillet with 1/4 cup (60 mL) soy sauce, remove tofu from skillet and set aside.

■ Using the same skillet, sauté all vegetables until cooked but still crunchy. Cover with boiling water, add rest of soy sauce and ginger, stir well and set aside.

■ Dilute cornstarch in cold water and add to vegetable mixture. Season with salt and pepper, add tofu and stir gently. Heat and serve.

* Illustrated recipe

Tofu Steak

Why not try using tofu to replace meat? Broil it the Japanese way, with soy sauce. After all, vegetarian cuisine isn't only for vegetarians!

4 servings	
1 lb	(450 g) tofu
1/2 cup	(125 mL) soy sauce
	salt and pepper

■ Heat broiler.

■ Slice tofu into 1/2 to 1 inch (1 to 2 cm) thick pieces, baste in soy sauce and season with salt and pepper. Broil until browned on each side for a few minutes.

410

Roasted Tofu

Tofu has a very mild taste, and absorbs whatever flavors you choose to add to it.

4 servings

½ cup	(125 mL) cornmeal
2 cups	(500 mL) flour
¼ cup	(60 mL) wheat germ
1 tsp	(5 mL) curry
1 tsp	(5 mL) dry mustard
	pinch of thyme
1	garlic clove, finely sliced
	salt
1 lb	(450 g) tofu, cut into strips
½ cup	(125 mL) milk
2 tbsp	(30 mL) vegetable oil

■ In a bowl, mix all dry ingredients together. Dip tofu strips in milk and coat with dry ingredients.

■ In a skillet, heat oil and fry tofu until golden.

* Illustrated recipe

Tofu Shepherd's Pie

Not a trace of meat here, but this dish is full of proteins.

4 servings

¼ tsp	(1 mL) vegetable oil
1	small onion, chopped
2 cups	(500 mL) potatoes, mashed and seasoned
1 cup	(250 mL) tofu, crumbled
½ tsp	(2 mL) garlic powder
½ tsp	(2 mL) thyme
1 tbsp	(15 mL) yeast
2 tbsp	(30 mL) soy sauce
1 tbsp	(15 mL) sunflower seeds, ground
1 tbsp	(15 mL) sesame seeds, ground
14 oz	(398 mL) canned creamed corn
14 oz	(398 mL) canned corn niblets

■ Preheat oven to 350 °F (175 °C).

■ In a skillet, heat oil and sauté onion. Stir onions into seasoned mashed potatoes and set aside.

■ In a bowl, combine all other ingredients, except corn niblets.

■ Spread a layer of corn niblets in bottom of baking dish, cover with a layer of tofu mixture, followed by a layer of seasoned mashed potatoes. Bake for 30 minutes.

VARIATION

• **Sprinkle with grated cheese and broil until golden.**

411

Tofu Burgers

Garnish these tofu-burgers the traditional way, with slices of cheese and tomato, and the usual condiments. Hamburger-lovers will be pleasantly surprised.

4 servings

½	onion, chopped
½	green or sweet red pepper, very finely chopped
2 tsp	(10 mL) vegetable oil
1 lb	(450 g) tofu, crumbled
2	eggs, beaten
2 tbsp	(30 mL) whole-wheat flour
2 tbsp	(30 mL) soy sauce
¼ cup	(60 mL) Parmesan cheese
1 cup	(250 mL) breadcrumbs
2 tbsp	(30 mL) oil
4	sesame seed hamburger buns
2 tbsp	(30 mL) cottage cheese
	a selection of vegetables

■ In a bowl, combine all ingredients except breadcrumbs, oil, sesame seed buns, and cottage cheese.

■ Shape mixture into 4 patties, dredge with breadcrumbs and set aside.

■ In a skillet, heat oil, brown patties on both sides, serve on sesame seed hamburger buns, and garnish with vegetables and cottage cheese.

Tofu Omelet

Omelets are an excellent source of protein. This one is further enriched with the vegetable proteins in tofu.

4 servings

2	eggs, beaten
2 tsp	(10 mL) soy sauce
1	garlic clove, finely sliced
½	onion, chopped
	pinch of cayenne pepper
2 cups	(500 mL) tofu, diced
¼ cup	(60 mL) green bell pepper, chopped
	oil
1 tbsp	(15 mL) chopped parsley

■ In a bowl, beat together eggs and seasonings, add tofu and vegetables, and mix well.

■ In a skillet, heat oil, pour seasoned eggs into skillet and cover. Cook over low heat. Sprinkle with parsley and serve.

Spinach and Tofu Quiche

Tofu Loaf

Tofu gives this quiche a firmer consistency as well as increasing its nutritional value.

4 servings

2 tbsp	(30 mL) oil
2	medium-sized onions, finely sliced
1 cup	(250 mL) spinach, stemmed
2	eggs, beaten
1 lb	(450 g) tofu, crumbled
1 tsp	(5 mL) salt
½ tsp	(2 mL) pepper
½ tsp	(2 mL) nutmeg
¾ cup	(180 mL) grated Cheddar cheese
1	9-inch (22-cm) pie crust, uncooked

■ Preheat oven to 350 °F (175 °C).

■ In a skillet, heat oil, sauté onions and set aside.

■ Blanch spinach for 1 minute in boiling water, drain and set aside.

■ In a blender, mix together eggs, tofu and seasonings until mixture is smooth and creamy. Add onions, spinach and cheese and stir well. Pour into pie crust and bake for 45 minutes.

Cheese and tomatoes make this vegetarian meat loaf moist and tender. Cut it in slices to serve.

4 servings

2 tsp	(10 mL) oil
½ cup	(125 mL) water
¼ cup	(60 mL) millet seeds
12 oz	(350 g) tofu
1	egg
1 cup	(250 mL) tomato juice
1 cup	(250 mL) rolled oats
2 tbsp	(30 mL) sunflower seeds, ground
1 cup	(250 mL) grated cheese
¼ cup	(60 mL) soy sauce
2 tsp	(10 mL) garlic powder
½ tsp	(2 mL) basil
½ tsp	(2 mL) thyme
1	carrot, grated
½	green or sweet red pepper, chopped
1	onion, chopped

■ Preheat oven to 350 °F (175 °C).

■ Lightly oil a loaf pan and set aside.

■ In a saucepan, bring water to a boil, add millet seeds, cover and cook for 15 minutes.

■ Purée tofu in a blender. Add the egg and tomato juice. Pour mixture into a bowl, fold in all other ingredients and stir. Spread mixture in loaf pan and bake for 45 minutes.

* *Illustrated recipe*

413

Tofu Rice

To store tofu for any length of time, cover it with cool water. Refrigerate it and change the water every day.

4 servings

1 tbsp	(15 mL) oil
1	garlic clove, finely sliced
½	onion, chopped
½	carrot, grated
½ cup	(125 mL) tofu, diced
1 cup	(250 mL) rice, cooked
1 tbsp	(15 mL) sunflower seeds
2 tbsp	(30 mL) soy sauce
	pinch of curry powder
	pinch of cayenne
¼ cup	(60 mL) snow peas, diagonally sliced

■ In a skillet, heat oil and sauté the garlic, onion and carrot. Add tofu and cook a few minutes. Fold in all other ingredients, stir and serve.

Tofu Macaroni

Use macaroni made of whole-wheat or soya flour.

4 servings

5 tsp	(25 mL) vegetable oil
1 cup	(250 g) tofu, diced
2 tbsp	(30 mL) soy sauce
½ cup	(125 mL) carrot, grated
½ cup	(125 mL) cauliflower, in flowerets, blanched
¼ cup	(60 mL) broccoli, in flowerets, blanched
4 cups	(1 L) cooked macaroni
	salt and pepper

■ In a skillet, heat 3 tsp (15 mL) of oil, sauté diced tofu, and sprinkle generously with soy sauce.

■ In a separate skillet, heat the rest of the oil and sauté vegetables for a few minutes. Fold into tofu mixture, add cooked macaroni, heat through and adjust seasoning to taste.

414

Tofu Croquettes

Vary this dish with herb-flavored tofu.

4 servings

1	small onion, finely chopped
¼ cup	(60 mL) celery, finely sliced
1 cup	(250 mL) mashed potatoes
1 cup	(250 mL) tofu, crumbled
4 oz	(113 g) canned salmon, drained
1 cup	(250 mL) bread-crumbs
	salt and pepper
¼ cup	(60 mL) vegetable oil
	mayonnaise
	parsley

■ In a bowl, combine all ingredients except oil and mayonnaise, and shape into croquettes; set aside.

■ In a skillet, heat oil and fry croquettes on both sides until nice and golden. Sprinkle with parsley and serve with mayonnaise.

* Illustrated recipe

Tofu Spread

Serve this tofu appetizer with whole-cereal crackers, and avoid the animal fat of a cream cheese dip.

4 servings

½ lb	(225 g) tofu, drained and crumbled
1	small carrot, grated
1	French (dry) shallot, finely chopped
3 tbsp	(45 mL) mayonnaise
	salt and pepper
	pinch of turmeric

■ In a bowl, combine all ingredients and stir until smooth.

Tofu and Fines Herbes Butter

Tofu Dressing

Spread tofu butter thinly on bread slices, seal them in aluminum foil, heat, and serve with a piping-hot soup.

about 1 ¼ cups (300 mL)

1 cup	(250 mL) butter, softened
2 oz	(60 g) tofu, crumbled
3 tbsp	(45 mL) milk
1 tsp	(5 mL) mixed fines herbes
¼ cup	(60 mL) chopped parsley
2	green onions, finely chopped

■ Run all ingredients through blender until mixture is smooth and creamy.

■ Shape into rolls and refrigerate. Wait 2 hours. Cut into rounds.

GARLIC BUTTER

• **Add 2 finely sliced garlic cloves to basic recipe.**

An eggless mayonnaise for cholesterol counters!

about 2 cups (500 mL)

12 oz	(350 g) tofu, crumbled
¼ cup	(60 mL) sunflower oil
¼ cup	(60 mL) lemon juice
1 tsp	(5 mL) salt
2 tsp	(10 mL) honey
1 tbsp	(15 mL) onion powder
¼ cup	(60 mL) water
	pinch of dry mustard
1 tsp	(5 mL) celery seeds
2 or 3	green onions, finely sliced

■ Mix all ingredients (except last two) in blender, until mixture is smooth and creamy. Pour into a jar and add celery seeds and green onions. Keep in refrigerator.

Tofu Pudding

A delightful way to use up stale bread.

4 servings	
1 lb	(450 g) tofu, crumbled
6 or 7	whole-wheat bread slices
1 cup	(250 mL) milk
1 ½ cups	(375 mL) maple syrup
½ cup	(125 mL) raisins
	pinch of cinnamon
	pinch of nutmeg
2	eggs, lightly beaten

■ Preheat oven to 325 °F (160 °C).

■ In a bowl, combine all ingredients and mix well. Pour into an oven-proof dish and bake 30 to 40 minutes.

* Illustrated recipe

VARIATION

• Serve with maple syrup.

Tofu and Chocolate Pie

Keep this recipe a secret. Chocolate aficionados will never understand how a pie could be so light, yet so creamy.

4 servings	
Garnish	
1 lb	(450 g) tofu, crumbled
⅓ cup	(80 mL) sunflower oil
⅓ cup	(80 mL) honey
2 tsp	(10 mL) cornstarch
1 tsp	(5 mL) vanilla extract
1 tsp	(5 mL) cocoa
	pinch of salt
	graham cracker pie crust

■ Preheat oven to 350 °F (175 °C).

■ Combine all garnish ingredients in blender and mix well. Fold into graham cracker crust.

■ Bake for about 30 minutes or until filling no longer sticks to fingers when touched.

NUTS AND SEEDS

Health Snack

Homemade snack bars contain less sugar than the store-bought variety. They're wonderful energy-raisers, but don't forget that they contain lots of calories too.

about 25 squares

4 cups	(1 L) fast-cooking rolled oats
1 cup	(250 mL) coconut, grated
1 cup	(250 mL) nuts, finely chopped
1 cup	(250 mL) wheat germ
1 cup	(250 mL) sunflower seeds
1 cup	(250 mL) honey
½ cup	(125 mL) vegetable oil
½ tsp	(2 mL) vanilla extract

■ Preheat oven to 350 °F (175 °C).

■ Oil a cookie sheet and set aside.

■ In a large bowl, combine first 5 ingredients and set aside.

■ Heat honey in a saucepan and pour it over dry ingredients. Add oil and vanilla and stir.

■ Press into a large square on oiled cookie sheet and bake about 30 minutes. Remove from oven and refrigerate before cutting into squares.

* Illustrated recipe

Snacking Squares

Replace the raisins with carob chips, a natural substitute for chocolate.

about 12 squares

½ cup	(125 mL) powdered milk
½ cup	(125 mL) coconut, grated
⅔ cup	(180 mL) sesame seeds
¼ cup	(60 mL) raisins or chocolate chips
⅓ cup	(80 mL) peanut butter
2 tbsp	(30 mL) honey
1 tbsp	(15 mL) water

■ In a bowl, mix together powdered milk, coconut, sesame seeds, raisins or chocolate chips and set aside.

■ Melt peanut butter with honey and water in a small saucepan. Pour mixture over dry ingredients and stir. Spread in a pyrex dish, press firmly to pack, and refrigerate at least 1 hour before cutting.

Peanut Butter

If you use salted peanuts, add less salt to the recipe.

about 2 ¼ cups (560 mL)

2 cups	(500 mL) peanuts
¼ cup	(60 mL) butter
1 tbsp	(15 mL) honey
¼ tsp	(1 mL) nutmeg
½ tsp	(2 mL) salt

■ Blend all ingredients in a food processor until mixture is smooth and creamy.

■ For crunchy peanut butter, add ¼ cup (60 mL) peanuts to creamed mixture and blend for a few seconds.

VARIATION

• **Replace peanuts with cashews, pecans, hazelnuts, etc.**

Banana Nut Butter

Keep this homemade banana nut butter in the refrigerator to prevent it from turning rancid.

about 2 ½ cups (625 mL)

1 cup	(250 mL) hazelnuts
1 cup	(250 mL) sunflower seeds
1 tbsp	(15 mL) butter
½ cup	(125 mL) almonds
2	bananas, very ripe
½ tsp	(2 mL) salt
1 tbsp	(15 mL) honey

■ Whip all ingredients in blender until mixture is smooth. Add one of the following ingredients to enhance the flavor:

1 tbsp (15 mL) chopped mint leaves,

1 tsp (5 mL) chopped citronnella leaves

or

2 tsp (10 mL) julienned orange peel.

· Illustrated recipe

Soup's on! Although it's often a metaphor for "Dinner's ready," this common expression shows just how much we appreciate soup, and what an image of hospitality it conjures up for us.

Originally, soup was a hot liquid such as stock, wine, or sauce, poured over a slice of bread. In modern cooking, soup has become a stock thickened by bread, pasta, or rice, incorporating meat, fish, or vegetables. A really thick soup can be a meal in itself, as you can blend in all the ingredients you would normally serve on a dinner plate.

There's nothing like steaming hot soup, but there's a lot to be said for cold soups, too, especially on a warm summer day. Anyone who has tasted a smooth vichyssoise or a spicy gazpacho will agree that cold soups can be delicious.

Soups are often served at the beginning of a meal, and usually in the evening, although soup and salad is a good lunch menu. They are classified into two major groups: clear soups such as consommés, and thick soups such as cream soups, white or brown veloutés (with a flour thickener), soups with cut up meat or vegetables in them, and many others.

SOUPS

If you'd like more consommé ideas, consult pages 70-71.

Beef Consommé Brunoise

"Brunoise" refers to vegetables cut up or chopped very finely. They take very little time to cook, and look pretty in the bowl.

about 2 ½ cups (625 mL)	
10 oz	(284 mL) canned beef consommé
1 cup	(250 mL) water
2 tbsp	(30 mL) port, sherry or red wine
2 tbsp	(30 mL) carrots, finely chopped
2 tbsp	(30 mL) turnip, finely chopped
2 tbsp	(30 mL) leek white, finely chopped
2 tbsp	(30 mL) leek stalk, finely chopped
¼ cup	(60 mL) cooked beef, very finely diced
	salt and pepper

■ In a saucepan, bring consommé, water and wine to a boil. Add other ingredients, cover and simmer for 1 minute. Turn off heat, adjust seasoning and serve.

The consommé will have a slightly velvety texture if you use milk instead of water.

Pink Chicken Consommé

about 2 ½ cups (625 mL)	
10 oz	(284 mL) canned chicken consommé
1 cup	(250 mL) water
2 tbsp	(30 mL) tomato juice
1 tbsp	(15 mL) vodka
¼ cup	(60 mL) tomato, finely chopped
2 tsp	(10 mL) chopped chives
	salt and pepper

■ In a saucepan, bring consommé, water, tomato juice and vodka to a boil. Add other ingredients, cover and simmer for 1 minute. Turn off heat, adjust seasoning and serve.

* Illustrated recipe

Egg Consommé

Consommé is basically a meat stock. Human ingenuity has resulted in an endless variety of additions to consommés, from simple vermicelli pasta to profiteroles stuffed with purée de foie gras!

■ Simmer a piece of meat or poultry, with bone, along with a sprinkling of herbs for 3 to 4 hours. Pour through sieve and degrease. A delicious consommé!

Consommé with Profiteroles

24 profiteroles	
5 oz	(140 mL) milk
¼ cup	(60 mL) butter
	pinch of salt
¼ cup	(60 mL) flour
1	egg

■ Preheat oven to 375 °F (190 °C).

■ In a small stove-top casserole, heat milk, butter and salt and bring to a boil. Add flour and mix until dough no longer adheres to sides. Add egg and stir quickly. Remove from heat and refrigerate for 5 minutes.

■ On a buttered cookie sheet, using a pastry bag and small nozzle, shape small dough balls. Bake for 5 minutes until nice and golden.

■ In each bowl, place 6 to 8 profiteroles. Pour hot consommé over pastry and serve.

Nest Egg Consommé

1 serving	
1	egg
¼ tsp	(1 mL) flour

■ Mix egg and flour. In a small saucepan, bring consommé to a simmer. Add egg and flour mixture through a sieve or a small-holed colander. Mixture will form thin strands and cook in less than a minute. Garnish with chopped parsley.

* Illustrated recipe

Poached Egg Consommé

1 serving	
4 cups	(1 L) boiling water
¼ cup	(60 mL) tomato juice
¼ cup	(60 mL) beef stock
2 tbsp	(30 mL) vinegar
1	egg

■ In a small saucepan, boil water, tomato juice, beef stock and vinegar. Poach egg in liquid for 1 minute.

■ Place 1 poached egg in each bowl of hot consommé.

Parsleyed Crêpe Consommé

1 serving	
Dough	
3 tbsp	(45 mL) flour
¼ cup	(60 mL) milk
1	egg
2 tsp	(10 mL) chopped parsley
	salt and pepper
2 tsp	(10 mL) butter

■ In a bowl, combine all dough ingredients.

■ In a skillet, melt butter and cook 2 crêpes. Slice into julienne strips and put a little in the bottom of each bowl. Pour in hot consommé.

GARNISHED SOUPS

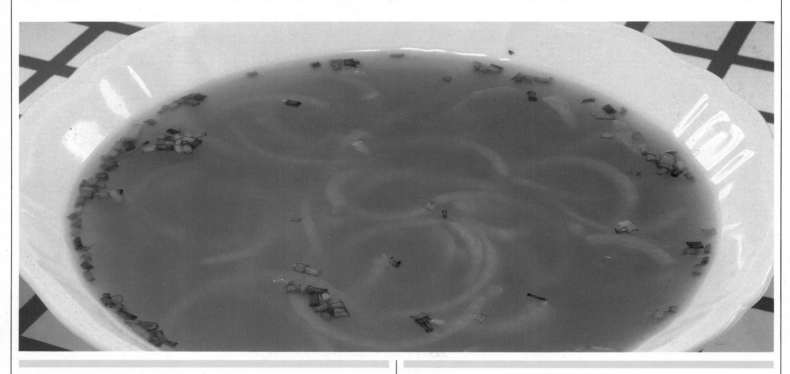

Spring Soup

The flecks of green vegetables give this soup a touch of spring freshness.

about 3 cups (750 mL)	
2 cups	(500 mL) chicken stock
1/2 cup	(125 mL) leek whites, finely sliced
1/4 cup	(60 mL) broccoli, broken into flowerets
1/4 cup	(60 mL) snow peas, cut into small pieces
2	leek leaves, julienned
	salt and pepper

■ In a saucepan, bring chicken stock to a boil. Add leek whites and broccoli and cook for 3 minutes.

■ Add snow peas and cook for 1 minute. Add leek leaves. Season with salt and pepper. Adjust seasoning and serve.

Onion and French Shallot Soup

In a clear soup served piping hot, the flavor of the stock is enhanced by adding onions and French (dry) shallots.

about 3 cups (750 mL)	
2 tbsp	(30 mL) butter
3	onions, cut into half slices
2	French (dry) shallots, chopped
1	garlic clove, finely sliced
1 cup	(250 mL) water
1/4 cup	(60 mL) dry white wine (optional)
1 1/2 cups	(375 mL) beef stock
	salt and pepper
1/4 tsp	(1 mL) ground nutmeg
1/2 tsp	(2 mL) chopped chives

■ In a stove-top casserole, melt butter and sauté onions, shallots and garlic. Add water, wine and beef stock. Cover and bring to a boil. Cook over low heat for 30 minutes. Season with salt, pepper and nutmeg. Sprinkle with chives.

• Illustrated recipe

424

Belmont Soup

Don't hesitate to use fresh sauerkraut if you have it on hand, otherwise get the canned variety.

about 3 cups (750 mL)	
3 tbsp	(45 mL) butter
¾ cup	(180 mL) sauerkraut, drained
2	green onions, finely sliced
½ cup	(125 mL) beer
2 cups	(500 mL) beef stock
	salt and pepper
½ tsp	(2 mL) cumin
½ tsp	(2 mL) nutmeg

■ In a stove-top casserole, melt butter and sauté sauerkraut and green onions. Pour beer and beef stock over mixture and bring to a boil. Cover and simmer over low heat for 15 minutes.

■ Season with salt, pepper, cumin and nutmeg.

Farmer's Soup

To give this soup a genuine homestead touch, add a few cooked white beans.

about 4 cups (1 L)	
1 cup	(250 mL) chicken stock
1 cup	(250 mL) beef stock
1 cup	(250 mL) tomato juice
¼ cup	(60 mL) carrots, diced
¼ cup	(60 mL) turnips, diced
¼ cup	(60 mL) tomato, diced
¼ cup	(60 mL) spinach, slivered
	salt and pepper
1 tsp	(5 mL) chopped basil

■ In a saucepan, bring chicken and beef stock along with tomato juice to a boil. Add carrots and turnips and simmer for 15 minutes. Add tomato and spinach. Season with salt and pepper and simmer for 1 minute.

■ Adjust seasoning. Sprinkle with basil and serve.

* Illustrated recipe

Brussels Sprout Soup

Be sure to wash the Brussels sprouts well. Let them soak for about ten minutes in water with a little vinegar added.

about 4 cups (1 L)	
2 ¹/₂ cups	(625 mL) chicken stock
	salt and pepper
¹/₂ cup	(125 mL) bacon, cut into pieces
1 cup	(250 mL) Brussels sprouts, blanched, quartered
1	garlic clove, finely sliced

■ In a saucepan, bring chicken stock to a boil and simmer for 20 minutes. Season with salt and pepper.

■ In a skillet, melt bacon and partially cook. Add Brussels sprouts and garlic and cook for 4 minutes. Degrease skillet. Pour bacon and Brussels sprouts into stock. Stir and simmer for 5 minutes. Degrease and serve.

Symphony Soup

This light but fragrant soup is a perfect appetizer.

about 3 cups (750 mL)	
1 ¹/₂ cups	(375 mL) chicken stock
1 cup	(250 mL) beef stock
³/₄ cup	(180 mL) fiddle-head greens
2	green onions finely sliced
	or
1	small red onion, finely sliced
	salt and pepper
1 tbsp	(15 mL) chopped parsley

■ In a saucepan, bring chicken stock and beef stock to a boil. Add fiddlehead greens and green onions (or red onion). Season with salt and pepper and simmer for 10 minutes.

■ Adjust seasoning and sprinkle with parsley.

Country Soup

There's plenty of room in country soup for all kinds of vegetables. This is a good chance to use up leftovers.

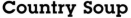

about 3 ½ cups (875 mL)	
1 cup	(250 mL) chicken stock
1 cup	(250 mL) beef stock
½ cup	(125 mL) vegetable juice
3 tbsp	(45 mL) butter
¼ cup	(60 mL) zucchini, thinly sliced and quartered
¼ cup	(60 mL) eggplant, diced
¼ cup	(60 mL) sweet red pepper, diced
¼ cup	(60 mL) yellow pepper, diced
	salt and pepper

■ In a saucepan, bring chicken stock, beef stock and vegetable juice to a boil.

■ Meanwhile, in a skillet, melt butter and cook vegetables for 2 minutes. Season with salt and pepper. Add vegetables to stock and simmer for 10 minutes. Adjust seasoning and serve.

Fisherman's Soup

Wash the mussels carefully before adding them to the soup.

about 3 cups (750 mL)	
1 cup	(250 mL) chicken stock
1 ½ cups	(375 mL) seafood bisque
20	mussels, well washed
½ cup	(125 mL) baby shrimp
	pinch of saffron
½ tsp	(2 mL) ground nutmeg
	salt and pepper

■ In a saucepan, bring chicken stock and seafood bisque to a boil. Add mussels and cook for 4 minutes or until mussels open. Remove mussels from stock and remove shells. Set aside.

■ Simmer stock for 10 minutes. Add shrimp and mussels. Season with saffron, nutmeg, salt and pepper. Stir and serve.

Hearty soups

Sunday's Oyster Soup

You can use fresh or canned oysters in preparing this recipe.

about 4 cups (1 L)

2 tbsp	(30 mL) butter
1	onion, chopped
1/2	carrot, julienned
1/2	green bell pepper, julienned
1	zucchini, julienned
1/4 cup	(60 mL) flour
2 cups	(500 mL) milk
1 cup	(250 mL) oysters, drained (keep juice)
	salt and pepper
	pinch of cayenne pepper
2 tbsp	(30 mL) chives, finely chopped

■ In a saucepan, melt butter and cook vegetables over low heat for 4 minutes. Add flour and cook over low heat for 2 minutes, stirring constantly. Add milk and oyster juice. Let mixture thicken while stirring.

■ Add oysters. Season with salt, pepper, and cayenne pepper. Cook 5 minutes longer. Sprinkle with chives and serve.

Clam Chowder

Only soups prepared with seafood deserve the name chowder.

about 4 cups (1 L)

7 oz	(200 g) canned clams
2	bacon slices, finely sliced
1	green bell pepper, diced
1	onion, chopped
1/4 cup	(60 mL) leek, finely sliced
1/2 cup	(125 mL) potatoes, diced
	salt and pepper
	pinch of thyme
2 cups	(500 mL) cream of mushroom soup
2 tbsp	(30 mL) chopped parsley
1/4 cup	(60 mL) lobster meat, diced

■ Drain clams and set juice aside.

■ In a saucepan, melt bacon, add clams, green bell pepper, onion, leek and potatoes. Cook for 4 minutes, stirring constantly. Season with salt, pepper, and thyme. Add cream of mushroom soup and clam juice. Cook mixture until potatoes are tender.

■ Add parsley and cubed lobster meat, and reheat.

• Illustrated recipe

Autumn Soup

This is a good soup to come home to on a chilly day.

about 4 cups (1 L)		
1 tbsp	(15 mL) vegetable oil	
8 oz	(225 g) ground beef	
½ cup	(125 mL) onion, chopped	
2 cups	(500 mL) béchamel sauce	
½ cup	(125 mL) carrot, sliced	
½ cup	(125 mL) celery, cut into chunks	
½ cup	(125 mL) potatoes, diced	
	salt and pepper	
	bay leaf	
3	tomatoes, fresh or canned	

■ In a stove-top casserole, heat oil and sauté ground beef over low heat.

■ Add onion and cook for 5 minutes, stirring constantly.

■ Add béchamel sauce and vegetables and bring to a boil. Cover and simmer for 20 minutes.

■ Add tomatoes, bay leaf, salt and pepper, and simmer for 10 minutes.

VARIATIONS

• **Replace ground beef with any leftover meat.**

• **Top soup with croûtons before serving.**

Corn Soup

A nourishing soup, perfect for taking to school or on the job.

about 5 cups (1,25 L)		
1 tbsp	(15 mL) butter	
1	onion, chopped	
1	medium-size potato, sliced	
1 ½ cups	(375 mL) chicken stock	
2 cups	(500 mL) corn niblets	
	salt	
1 ½ cups	(375 mL) milk	
	a few corn niblets to decorate	
	paprika	

■ In a stove-top casserole, melt butter and cook onion and potato. Add chicken stock and corn niblets. Season with salt and bring to a boil. Cover and simmer until potato is tender.

■ Remove from heat and let stand to cool for a few minutes.

■ Run through blender for 30 seconds.

■ Return mixture to stove-top casserole and add milk. Heat without boiling for 8 to 10 minutes.

■ Drop a few corn niblets on top of the soup, sprinkle with paprika, and serve.

* Illustrated recipe

Bean Medley Soup

*Sprinkle the soup with a
little grated cheese.*

about 4 cups (1 L)	
1 tbsp	(15 mL) butter
2	onions, finely sliced
1	garlic clove, finely sliced
14 oz	(398 mL) canned lima beans
14 oz	(398 mL) canned chick peas
19 oz	(540 mL) canned tomatoes
2 tbsp	(30 mL) tomato paste
½ tsp	(2 mL) oregano
½ tsp	(2 mL) salt
½ tsp	(2 mL) pepper

■ In a stove-top casserole, heat butter and cook onions and garlic. Add beans and chick peas and stir. Add tomatoes and tomato paste. Season with oregano, salt and pepper. Simmer for 20 minutes.

■ Adjust seasoning and serve.

Favorite Soup

*If you'd like to try a
different cereal, use
millet instead of rice.*

about 4 cups (1 L)	
1 tbsp	(15 mL) butter
1	garlic clove, finely sliced
2 tsp	(10 mL) chopped basil
19 oz	(540 mL) canned tomatoes
1 cup	(250 mL) chicken stock
	salt and pepper
	vermicelli
	rice
1 cup	(250 mL) spinach, coarsely chopped

■ In a stove-top casserole, melt butter and cook garlic and basil. Add tomatoes and chicken stock. Season with salt and pepper and bring to a boil. Add vermicelli and rice. Cover and simmer for 20 minutes.

■ Adjust seasoning. Add spinach and simmer a few minutes longer.

* Illustrated recipe

Potage Saint-Germain

Green Pea Soup

A pea soup that is a little lighter than the traditional French potage.

about 5 cups (1,25 L)

1 cup	(250 mL) split peas
2 tbsp	(30 mL) butter
1	leek, finely sliced
1	onion, finely sliced
2 cups	(500 mL) water
2 cups	(500 mL) chicken stock
½ cup	(125 mL) bacon, cut into pieces
1	bay leaf
	salt and pepper
¼ cup	(60 mL) 35% cream

■ Wash split peas and drain. Set aside.

■ In a stove-top casserole, melt butter and lightly cook leek and onion. Add split peas. Pour in water and chicken stock and bring to a boil. Add bacon and bay leaf. Season with salt and pepper. Cover and simmer for at least 1 hour.

■ Run mixture through blender, then add cream. Adjust seasoning and serve.

If you're using frozen peas, reduce the quantity of water to 4 cups (1 L) and shorten the cooking time to 30 minutes.

Garnish the soup with julienned ham.

about 8 cups (2 L)

8 oz	(225 g) dried green peas
¼ cup	(60 mL) salted pork back fat
7 cups	(1,75 L) water
1	onion, finely sliced
1	carrot, diced
	bay leaf
2 tsp	(10 mL) celery leaves, finely sliced
5	parsley sprigs
½ tsp	(2 mL) chopped savory
	salt and pepper

■ In a stove-top casserole, combine all ingredients and bring to a boil. Boil for 2 minutes. Reduce heat, cover and simmer for about 1 ½ hours, stirring from time to time.

■ Remove pork fat. Run soup through blender. Adjust seasoning. Decorate with a few small chunks of pork fat and serve.

431

Chicken Velouté

To lighten the velouté, use whole milk rather than cream.

about 8 cups (2 L)

2	carrots, diced
1	onion, chopped
4 cups	(1 L) chicken stock
3 tbsp	(45 mL) butter
3 tbsp	(45 mL) flour
8 oz	(226 g) chicken (or leftover cooked chicken)
¼ cup	(60 mL) fast-cooking rice
	salt and pepper
	pinch of chopped chives
	pinch of basil
¾ cup	(180 mL) 35% cream

■ In a microwave-safe dish, place vegetables and 1 cup (250 mL) chicken stock. Cook at HIGH for 6 minutes. Set aside.

■ In a large pyrex cup, cook butter and flour at HIGH for 1 minute. Pour rest of chicken stock into mixture and stir gently.

■ Add chicken, rice and cooked vegetables. Season with salt, pepper, chives and basil, and stir well. Cook at HIGH for 10 minutes and stir. Cook at LOW for 10 minutes.

■ Add cream and stir gently. Serve with croûtons.

Pepper and Tomato Velouté

When you're serving the soup, trickle a little cream on top for decoration.

about 6 cups (1,5 L)

3 tbsp	(15 mL) butter
1	sweet red pepper, cut into strips
1	green bell pepper, cut into strips
4 cups	(1 L) chicken stock
2 tbsp	(30 mL) flour
10 oz	(284 mL) cream of tomato soup
	salt and pepper
	green and red sweet peppers, julienned
	chopped chives

■ In a skillet, melt 2 tsp (10 mL) butter and cook peppers for 5 minutes. Pour 1 cup (250 mL) chicken stock into skillet and boil for 4 minutes. Run mixture through blender and set aside.

■ In a stove-top casserole, melt rest of butter. Add flour and stir. Add pepper mixture and rest of chicken stock, and bring to a boil, stirring constantly.

■ Add cream of tomato soup and simmer for 5 minutes. Season with salt and pepper. Garnish with julienned peppers and chopped chives.

* Illustrated recipe

Velouté of Asparagus

Using pre-cooked ingredients saves time.

about 6 cups (1,5 L)	
3 tbsp	(45 mL) butter
3 tbsp	(45 mL) flour
3 cups	(750 mL) chicken stock
20 oz	(568 mL) canned asparagus
	salt and pepper
1 tsp	(5 mL) chopped chives
	35% cream
	a few asparagus tips

■ In a skillet, melt butter and add flour. Cook for 2 minutes. Pour chicken stock over mixture and stir well. Add asparagus, season with salt, pepper, and chives. Simmer for 20 minutes. Run mixture through blender and pour into individual bowls. Add a thin strand of cream on top. Garnish with asparagus tips and serve.

* *Illustrated recipe*

FAST METHOD

• Heat 20 oz (568 mL) canned cream of asparagus soup according to directions on can. Add 10 oz (284 mL) canned asparagus and 1 tsp (5 mL) chopped chives, and simmer for 5 minutes. Run mixture through blender. Add 1 tbsp (15 mL) butter and ¼ cup (60 mL) 35% cream.

Endive Velouté with Fresh Herbs

If you use dried herbs, cut the amounts given in half.

about 6 cups (1,5 L)	
2 cups	(500 mL) chicken stock
2 cups	(500 mL) beef stock
3	endives, finely sliced
1 tsp	(5 mL) chopped chervil
½ tsp	(2 mL) chopped tarragon
¾ tsp	(3 mL) chopped basil
2 tsp	(10 mL) chopped parsley
½ tsp	(2 mL) ground nutmeg
3	egg yolks
1 cup	(250 mL) 15% cream

■ In a saucepan, heat chicken and beef stocks. Add endives and herbs. Season with nutmeg and simmer for 20 minutes. Cool and run through blender.

■ Stir together egg yolks and cream. Blend with stock. Return mixture to saucepan and heat without boiling. Adjust seasoning and serve.

Cream of Lettuce

Canadian Cream of Vegetable

Cream of Lettuce

Use the outer leaves of several lettuce heads, and keep the hearts for salads.

about 8 cups (2 L)

4 cups	(1 L) chicken stock
2 cups	(500 mL) potatoes, cut into pieces
1	Boston lettuce, washed, cut into pieces
	salt and pepper
	pinch of cayenne pepper
½ cup	(125 mL) plain yogurt
1 cup	(250 mL) partially skimmed milk
	shredded lettuce leaves

■ In a saucepan, bring chicken stock to a boil. Add potatoes and cook for 20 minutes.

■ Add lettuce and simmer for 1 minute. Season with salt, pepper and cayenne pepper. Run mixture through blender.

■ Meanwhile, in a bowl, mix together yogurt and milk and pour into blender and mix. Pour into soup tureen and garnish with shredded lettuce leaves. Serve very hot.

Canadian Cream of Vegetable

Add a few croûtons just before serving.

about 8 cups (2 L)

2 tbsp	(30 mL) butter
½ cup	(125 mL) carrot, diced
½ cup	(125 mL) turnip, diced
¼ cup	(60 mL) potato, diced
½ cup	(125 mL) leek, cut into chunks
½ cup	(125 mL) celery, cut into chunks
½ cup	(125 mL) onion, diced
1 cup	(250 mL) tomatoes, diced
3 cups	(750 mL) beef stock
	salt and pepper
½ cup	(125 mL) 35% cream
2 tsp	(10 mL) chopped parsley

■ In a stove-top casserole, melt butter and cook vegetables and diced tomatoes without browning for 5 minutes.

■ Add beef stock and season with salt and pepper. Bring mixture to a boil and simmer over low heat for 30 minutes. Run mixture through blender. Pour cream into mixture. Garnish with chopped parsley.

Cream of Leek

If you're preparing this soup a day ahead, don't add the milk until the last minute.

about 8 cups (2 L)	
3 tbsp	(45 mL) oil
4	leeks, washed, sliced
3	potatoes, diced
3 tbsp	(45 mL) flour
	salt and pepper
½ tsp	(2 mL) basil
½ tsp	(2 mL) tarragon
½ tsp	(2 mL) savory
5 cups	(1,25 L) stock
1 cup	(250 mL) milk or
½ cup	(125 mL) 35% cream
	fresh fines herbes

■ In a stove-top casserole, heat oil and sauté leeks for 3 minutes. Add potatoes and cook 5 minutes longer.

■ Add flour and stir. Season with salt, pepper, basil, tarragon and savory. Pour stock into mixture and cook for 40 minutes.

■ Run mixture through blender. Add milk or cream, garnish with fines herbes and serve.

* Illustrated recipe

VARIATION

• **Sprinkle grated cheese over soup and broil for a few minutes, then serve.**

Cream of Tomato with Bread

Here's an ingenious way of using up stale bread!

about 8 cups (2 L)	
2 cups	(1 L) milk
3	slices bread, crusts removed
2 tbsp	(30 mL) butter
3 or 4	onions, chopped
	salt and pepper
½ tsp	(2 mL) baking soda
28 oz	(796 mL) canned tomatoes

■ Pour milk into a stove-top casserole and place bread in milk. Soak and set aside.

■ In a skillet, melt butter and sauté onions. Add onions to bread mixture and bring to a boil. Reduce heat and season with salt and pepper. Add baking soda and tomatoes. Heat and serve.

Cream of Celery Medley

If you want to make the cauliflower and broccoli flowerets tender, cook them beforehand in the microwave on HIGH for 1 minute.

about 8 cups (2 L)	
20 oz	(568 mL) canned cream of celery soup
10 oz	(284 mL) milk
10 oz	(284 mL) water
¼ cup	(60 mL) broccoli, broken into flowerets
¼ cup	(60 mL) cauliflower, broken into flowerets
½ cup	(125 mL) broccoli stems
½ cup	(125 mL) cauliflower stems
¾ tsp	(3 mL) onion salt
½ tsp	(2 mL) celery pepper
¼ cup	(60 mL) 35% cream

■ In a saucepan, heat cream of celery soup with milk and water, and set aside.

■ In another saucepan, filled with lightly salted boiling water, blanch broccoli and cauliflower, then drain. Set broccoli and cauliflower flowerets aside for garnish.

■ Add broccoli and cauliflower stems to cream of celery soup. Season with onion salt and celery pepper and simmer for 10 minutes.

■ Run mixture through blender and gently pour in cream. Adjust seasoning and pour into serving bowls. Decorate with broccoli and cauliflower flowerets.

Cream of Mushroom

Using the simplest ingredients, you can easily add a personal touch to any canned soup.

about 6 cups (1,5 L)	
20 oz	(568 mL) cream of mushroom soup
10 oz	(284 mL) milk
10 oz	(284 mL) water
2 tbsp	(30 mL) butter
1 cup	(250 mL) mushrooms, sliced
1 tbsp	(15 mL) onion, chopped
1	garlic clove, finely sliced
1 tbsp	(15 mL) brandy (optional)
	salt and pepper
¼ tsp	(1 mL) nutmeg

■ In a saucepan, heat cream of mushroom soup with milk and water.

■ Meanwhile, in a skillet, melt butter and sauté mushrooms, onion and garlic. Add brandy and heat for 1 minute. Add mixture to cream of mushroom soup. Season with salt, pepper and nutmeg. Simmer for 5 minutes and serve.

* Illustrated recipe

436

Cream of Spinach and Watercress

Don't throw away the watercress stalks. They can be used to flavor a stock.

about 4 cups (1 L)

2 tbsp	(30 mL) butter
1	garlic clove, finely sliced
2 tbsp	(30 mL) onion, chopped
1 cup	(250 mL) spinach, stems removed
¼ cup	(60 mL) watercress, stems removed
10 oz	(284 mL) cream of celery soup
10 oz	(284 mL) milk
1 cup	(250 mL) chicken stock
	salt and pepper
1 tsp	(5 mL) chopped fennel
½ cup	(125 mL) 35% cream

■ In a stove-top casserole, melt butter and sauté garlic and onion. Cook spinach and watercress until limp.

■ Add cream of celery soup, milk and chicken stock, and bring to a boil. Simmer for 10 minutes.

■ Season with salt, pepper and fennel. Run mixture through blender and return to stove-top casserole. Add cream and heat mixture without boiling, stirring constantly, then serve.

Cream of Zucchini with Garlic

The soup will have more flavor and color if you don't peel the zucchini.

about 6 cups (1,5 L)

6	zucchini
2 tsp	(10 mL) salt
3 tbsp	(45 mL) butter
2	onions, sliced
2	garlic cloves, finely sliced
4 cups	(1 L) chicken stock
1	large tomato, peeled, cut into pieces
1 tsp	(5 mL) thyme
½ tsp	(2 mL) sugar
½ tsp	(2 mL) oregano
½ tsp	(2 mL) basil
¼ tsp	(1 mL) nutmeg
¼ tsp	(1 mL) pepper
½ cup	(125 mL) 35% cream

■ Slice zucchini finely and season with salt. Put in a sieve and let drain for thirty minutes.

■ In a stove-top casserole, melt butter, then add onions, zucchini and garlic. Cover and cook over low heat for 10 minutes.

■ Add chicken stock, tomato and seasonings. Run mixture through blender, then return to casserole. Add cream and heat for 5 minutes.

COLD SOUPS

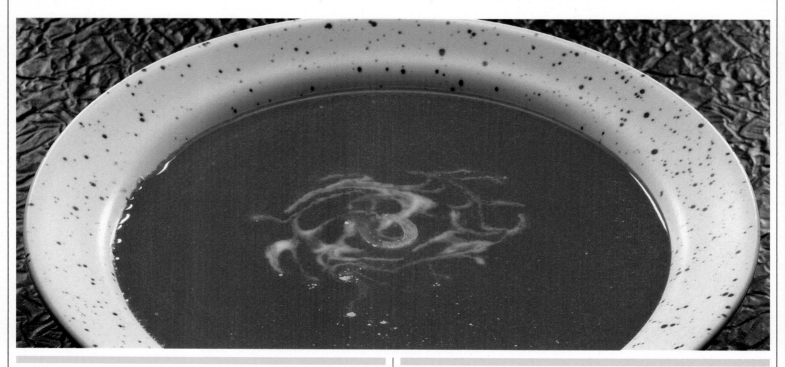

Vichyssoise

This soup is far better when served cold. Some people consider it the best cream soup of all.

about 8 cups (2 L)	
3 tbsp	(45 mL) butter
3 cups	(750 g) leek whites, finely sliced
1 cup	(250 mL) potatoes, sliced
2 ½ cups	(675 mL) chicken stock
1 cup	(250 mL) 15% cream
	salt and pepper
	chopped chives

■ In a stove-top casserole, melt butter and cook leek whites and potatoes without browning. Pour chicken stock into mixture and bring to a boil. Simmer until vegetables are tender.

■ Run mixture through blender and pour into soup tureen. Gently add cream. Season with salt and pepper. Refrigerate. Sprinkle with chopped chives before serving.

VARIATIONS

• **Replace potatoes with turnip or carrots.**

• **Sprinkle soup with nutmeg.**

• **Garnish with 1 tbsp (15 mL) red or black caviar.**

Borscht

When you're talking beet soup, you're talking borscht. This Russian soup is equally good hot or cold.

about 4 cups (1 L)	
7	small beets, cooked
1	large potato, cooked
2 cups	(500 mL) chicken stock
1 tbsp	(15 mL) wine vinegar
1 tsp	(5 mL) chopped tarragon
1 cup	(250 mL) sour cream
1	green onion, finely sliced

■ Run all ingredients through blender except for 1 beet, sour cream and green onion. Pour into soup tureen. Gently pour cream into mixture and refrigerate.

■ Meanwhile, grate remaining beet.

■ Pour soup into individual bowls and garnish with grated beet. Pour a thin sliver of sour cream over top and sprinkle with green onion.

* Illustrated recipe

VARIATIONS

• **Replace tarragon with ½ tsp (2 mL) chopped fennel and 1 tsp (5 mL) dried dill leaves.**

• **Replace 1 cup (250 mL) chicken stock with 1 cup (250 mL) light beer.**

Gazpacho

This Spanish soup is traditionally served with croûtons, chopped olives, and sliced hard-boiled eggs.

about 6 cups (1,5 L)

1	medium-size cucumber, peeled, chopped
2 to 3	medium-size tomatoes, coarsely chopped
1	small onion, finely sliced
1 tsp	(5 mL) garlic, finely sliced
2 cups	(500 mL) fresh breadcrumbs
2 cups	(500 mL) cold water
2 tbsp	(30 mL) wine vinegar
2 tsp	(10 mL) salt
2 tsp	(10 mL) olive or corn oil
	garlic croûtons
	green bell pepper, julienned

■ In a soup tureen, mix together vegetables, garlic and breadcrumbs. Add water, vinegar and salt. Run mixture through blender. Return to soup tureen. Pour oil into soup and stir with a wire whisk. Cover and refrigerate for at least 2 hours.

■ When ready to serve, garnish with croûtons and julienned peppers.

VARIATIONS

• **Replace cucumber with zucchini.**

• **Garnish with chives or finely sliced green onion.**

Cold Cucumber Soup

Garnish the cold soup with crunchy, julienned vegetables or croûtons.

about 4 cups (1 L)

2 to 4	medium-size cucumbers, peeled, seeded and quartered
2 cups	(500 mL) plain yogurt
1 cup	(250 mL) sour cream
1 or 2	small onions or green onions
½ tsp	(2 mL) salt
	pinch of black pepper
½ tsp	(2 mL) Worcestershire sauce
1 tsp	(5 mL) dill
2 tbsp	(30 mL) chopped fresh parsley
4	thin slices of cucumber

■ Run all ingredients through blender except dill, parsley and cucumber slices. Refrigerate mixture for at least 4 hours.

■ When ready to serve, pour into individual serving bowls, sprinkle with dill and parsley. Garnish with cucumber slices.

* Illustrated recipe

439

Cold Avocado and Watercress Soup

Sprinkle the avocado pulp with lemon juice to keep it from discoloring.

about 4 cups (1 L)	
2	avocados, peeled, cut into pieces
1	bunch of watercress, stems removed
	juice of ½ lime
	juice of ½ lemon
3 cups	(750 mL) chicken stock
	salt and pepper
	garlic salt
	oregano
2	slices white bread, crusts removed
¼ cup	(60 mL) vegetable oil
¼ cup	(60 mL) 15% cream
12	pitted black olives, finely sliced

■ In the blender or food processor, purée avocado, watercress, juices, chicken stock and seasonings.

■ Meanwhile, pour cold water over bread and drain. Add to avocado mixture and blend for a few seconds until smooth.

■ Add oil in trickles. Pour mixture into a soup tureen. Gently fold in cream and olives. Refrigerate until just before serving.

Quick Lobster Bisque

Break the rule that says one shouldn't serve wine with soup, and offer your guests a dry white or rosé wine.

about 6 cups (1,5 L)	
10 oz	(284 mL) canned cream of celery soup
10 oz	(284 mL) canned cream of tomato soup
3 ½ oz	(100 mL) lobster paste
	pinch of curry powder
2 cups	(500 mL) milk
1 cup	(250 mL) 15% cream

■ In a bowl, mix together all ingredients, then run through blender for 30 seconds. Pour into soup tureen and refrigerate.

VARIATION

• Replace lobster paste with canned baby shrimp.

Cold Asparagus Soup

If you use fresh aspara-gus, you can save time by cooking it for about 6 minutes in the micro-wave in a covered dish containing 1 tbsp (15 mL) of water.

about 4 cups (1 L)

12	fresh asparagus, cooked
	or
10 oz	(284 mL) canned asparagus
10 oz	(284 mL) cream of asparagus soup
1 ½ cups	(375 mL) milk
	salt and pepper
	tarragon
¼ cup	(60 mL) sour cream
	chopped parsley

■ In a bowl, mix together all ingredients except 4 tsp (20 mL) sour cream and parsley. Run mixture through blender. Refrigerate to cool.

■ When ready to serve, pour soup into individual bowls and garnish each serving with 1 tsp (5 mL) sour cream and chopped parsley.

Cantaloup Soup

Grate the ginger very finely to keep its subtle flavor.

about 3 cups (750 mL)

1	medium-size ripe cantaloup peeled, seeded, chopped
¼ cup	(60 mL) plain yogurt
¼ cup	(60 mL) orange juice
1 cup	(250 mL) sour cream
1 tsp	(5 mL) fresh chopped basil
1 tsp	(5 mL) grated orange peel
½ tsp	(2 mL) fresh, peeled, grated ginger
1 tbsp	(15 mL) Cognac or brandy

■ Blend all ingredients in food processor until smooth. Pour mixture through sieve into a soup tureen. Cover and refrigerate for at least 3 hours. Serve in cold bowls.

* Illustrated recipe

VARIATION

• Replace cantaloup with honeydew melon or 1 ½ cups (375 mL) straw-berries.

Sauces are an excellent way of giving certain dishes a lift or heating up leftovers.

The delicate aroma of a smooth, creamy béchamel sauce is always appreciated. Add a few ingredients just before serving (cheese, egg, mustard, shrimp, tarragon, etc.) and your food will take on a new dimension in a few seconds.

Butter sauces such as hollandaise or béarnaise are also easily varied. They delicately enhance the flavor of food and transform the most modest dish into a gastronomic treat.

Mayonnaise is surely the most versatile of all sauces. There is no reason why you can't blend in fines herbes, spices, capers, pickles, vegetables, or even fruit.

Don't forget about white and brown stocks, the vegetable stocks knows as "coulis," or the many fruit sauces.

Don't be afraid to play around with basic sauces. You'll discover completely new flavors that would be the envy of any connoisseur!

SAUCES

BÉCHAMEL SAUCES

Béchamel Sauce

about 2 cups (500 mL)	
½	onion
1	bay leaf
3	cloves
3 tbsp	(45 mL) butter
3 tbsp	(45 mL) flour
2 cups	(500 mL) milk
	salt and pepper
¼ tsp	(1 mL) ground nutmeg

■ Place bay leaf on sliced part of onion half. Prick with clove.

■ In a saucepan, melt butter and add flour and stir. Cook for 2 minutes, stirring constantly. Add milk and onion. Cook for 6 minutes, stirring constantly.

■ Remove onion. Season sauce with salt, pepper and nutmeg.

VARIATIONS

Egg Sauce

• To 1 cup (250 mL) béchamel sauce, add 3 chopped hard-boiled egg yolks along with 1 tsp (5 mL) Dijon mustard.

Parsley Sauce

• To 1 cup (250 mL) béchamel sauce, add 2 finely sliced garlic cloves along with 2 tsp (10 mL) chopped parsley.

Crab Sauce

• To 1 cup (250 mL) béchamel sauce, add ¼ cup (60 mL) lobster bisque along with 2 tbsp (30 mL) shredded crabmeat.

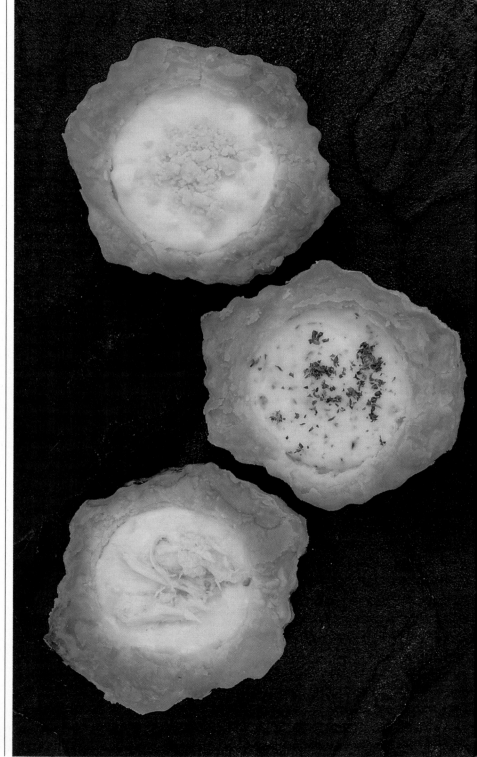

Top to bottom:
Egg Sauce ▪ Parsley Sauce ▪
Crab Sauce

Making a good béchamel sauce isn't perhaps as difficult as you think. The secret is to add the liquid all at once and to keep stirring. Once you've got the knack, you can thank the Marquis de Béchamiel (yes, with an "i") for having contributed to your reputation as a cordon bleu cook.

Mushroom Sauce

- To 1 cup (250 mL) béchamel sauce, add ¼ cup (60 mL) mushroom caps sautéed in 2 tsp (10 mL) butter.

Celery Sauce

- To 1 cup (250 mL) béchamel sauce, add ¼ cup (60 mL) undiluted cream of celery soup along with 1 tbsp (15 mL) diced celery, blanched for 1 minute.

Mornay Sauce

- To 1 cup (250 mL) béchamel sauce, add ¼ cup (60 mL) grated Parmesan cheese.

Soubise Sauce

- To 1 cup (250 mL) béchamel sauce, add 2 tbsp (30 mL) chopped onion, blanched for 1 minute, along with a pinch of chopped coriander and 2 tbsp (30 mL) 35% cream.

Cucumber Sauce

- To 1 cup (250 mL) béchamel sauce, add ⅓ cup (80 mL) cucumbers, julienned and blanched for 1 minute, along with 1 tsp (5 mL) chopped dill.

Top to bottom:
Mushroom Sauce ▪ Celery Sauce
▪ Mornay Sauce

HOLLANDAISE SAUCES

Hollandaise Sauce

about 1 cup (250 mL)

2	egg yolks
1 tbsp	(15 mL) white wine
½ lb	(225 g) clarified butter
	pinch of salt
	pinch of cayenne pepper
1 tsp	(5 mL) lemon juice

■ In a small saucepan, over low heat, whip egg yolks and white wine until lightly thickened.

■ Remove from heat. With a wire whisk, beat in clarified butter in small amounts. Add seasonings and lemon juice. Stir until mixture is smooth and creamy.

Mock Hollandaise Sauce

about 1 cup (250 mL)

2 tbsp	(30 mL) butter
2 tbsp	(30 mL) flour
1 cup	(250 mL) milk
	salt and pepper
1	egg yolk
1 tbsp	(15 mL) butter
2 tbsp	(30 mL) lemon juice

■ In a saucepan, melt butter and add flour. Stir and cook for 1 minute. Add milk, stir and cook for 4 minutes. Season with salt and pepper.

■ In a small bowl, beat egg yolk, then add small amount of hot sauce and stir. Add mixture to sauce and cook for 2 minutes. Remove from heat and add butter and lemon juice.

Top to bottom:
Béarnaise Sauce ▪ Shrimp Sauce
▪ Asparagus Sauce

Rich hollandaise or mock hollandaise sauces go well with broiled food, poached fish, and steamed vegetables, as well as with rice, noodles, and hard-boiled eggs. If you're not confident about making a succesful hollandaise sauce, try our mock-hollandaise. The result is pretty much the same, but it's far more likely to succeed.

VARIATIONS

Béarnaise Sauce

- To 1 cup (250 mL) hollandaise sauce, add 1 tsp (5 mL) chopped tarragon in vinegar, 1 chopped green onion, 2 tsp (10 mL) chopped parsley and a few drops of tarragon vinegar.

Shrimp Sauce

- To 1 cup (250 mL) hollandaise sauce, add 1 tbsp (15 mL) cold shrimp bisque and ¼ cup (60 mL) cooked and chopped shrimp.

Asparagus Sauce

- To 1 cup (250 mL) hollandaise sauce, add 2 tbsp (30 mL) asparagus blended in food processor, and 2 or 3 asparagus tips.

Choron Sauce

- To 1 cup (250 mL) hollandaise sauce, add 3 tbsp (45 mL) tomato paste along with 1 tsp (5 mL) chopped tarragon.

Mousseline Sauce

- To 1 cup (250 mL) hollandaise sauce, add ¼ cup (60 mL) stiffly whipped 35% cream.

Mint Sauce

- To 1 cup (250 mL) hollandaise sauce, add 2 tsp (10 mL) fresh, chopped mint leaves.

Maltese Sauce

- To 1 cup (250 mL) hollandaise sauce, add juice and julienned blood orange peel.

Horseradish Sauce

- To 1 cup (250 mL) hollandaise sauce, add 2 tsp (10 mL) horseradish in vinegar.

Top to bottom: Choron Sauce ▪ Mousseline Sauce ▪ Maltese Sauce

MAYONNAISES

Mayonnaise, Basic Recipe

about 2 cups (500 mL)

2	egg yolks
2 tsp	(10 mL) Dijon mustard
½ tsp	(2 mL) salt
2 cups	(500 mL) vegetable oil
2 tbsp	(30 mL) wine vinegar
¼ tsp	(1 mL) pepper
1 tbsp	(15 mL) boiling water
1 tsp	(5 mL) honey (optional)

■ In a bowl, with a wire whisk, mix egg yolks, mustard and salt. Pour oil in thin trickles, beating constantly. Whenever the mixture appears too thick, add 1 tsp (5 mL) vinegar.

■ Finally, add pepper and boiling water and stir. Adjust seasoning and serve.

N.B.: Add honey at the same time as the water for a sweeter taste.

Fines Herbes Mayonnaise

about 1 cup (250 mL)

1 cup	(250 mL) mayonnaise
½ tsp	(2 mL) chopped tarragon
½ tsp	(2 mL) chopped chives
½ tsp	(2 mL) chopped fennel
½ tsp	(2 mL) chopped basil

■ Mix together all ingredients.

Curry Mayonnaise

about 1 cup (250 mL)

1 cup	(250 mL) mayonnaise
¾ tsp	(3 mL) curry powder
¼ tsp	(1 mL) ground nutmeg

■ Mix together all ingredients.

Tartare Sauce

about 1 cup (250 mL)

1 cup	(250 mL) mayonnaise
1 tsp	(5 mL) chopped parsley
1 tbsp	(15 mL) chopped marinated pickles
1 tbsp	(15 mL) chopped capers
1 tbsp	(15 mL) old-fashioned mustard
2 tbsp	(30 mL) lemon juice

■ Mix together all ingredients.

Rémoulade

about 1 cup (250 mL)

1 cup	(250 mL) mayonnaise
½ tsp	(2 mL) chopped chervil
½ tsp	(2 mL) chopped tarragon
1 tsp	(5 mL) chopped parsley
1 tbsp	(15 mL) chopped marinated pickles
1 tbsp	(15 mL) chopped capers
1 tbsp	(15 mL) old-fashioned mustard
2 tbsp	(30 mL) lemon juice

■ Mix together all ingredients.

Top to bottom:
Fines Herbes ▪ Curry ▪ Tartare

Mayonnaise is an indispensable item in the kitchen because of its versatility. It makes an excellent accompaniment for cold meats (chicken, turkey, ham, or beef), poached fish, lobster, salmon, crab, vegetables and appetizers.

Sorrel Mayonnaise

about 1 cup (250 mL)

1 cup	(250 mL) mayonnaise
2 tsp	(10 mL) sorrel purée
1 tbsp	(15 mL) sorrel leaves, finely shredded

■ Mix together all ingredients.

Roquefort Mayonnaise

about 1 cup (250 mL)

1 cup	(250 mL) mayonnaise
1 tbsp	(15 mL) crumbled Roquefort cheese
1 tsp	(5 mL) Worcestershire sauce

■ Mix together all ingredients.

Chantilly

about 1 cup (250 mL)

1 cup	(250 mL) mayonnaise
1/2 cup	(125 mL) whipped cream

■ Mix together all ingredients.

Mikado

about 2 cups (500 mL)

1 cup	(250 mL) mayonnaise
1/2 cup	(125 mL) whipped cream
1/4 cup	(60 mL) mandarin oranges, coarsely chopped

■ Mix together all ingredients.

Aioli

about 1 cup (250 mL)

1 cup	(250 mL) mayonnaise
2	garlic cloves, finely sliced
2 tsp	(10 mL) lemon juice

■ Mix together all ingredients.

Russian Dressing

about 1 cup (250 mL)

1 cup	(250 mL) mayonnaise
2 tsp	(10 mL) horseradish in vinegar
2 tbsp	(30 mL) ketchup
1 tsp	(5 mL) chopped green onion
2 tbsp	(30 mL) caviar
1/4 cup	(60 mL) firmly whipped 35% cream

■ Mix together first 5 ingredients. Fold in whipped cream.

Top to Bottom: Roquefort ■ Mikado ■ Russian Dressing

BROWN STOCKS

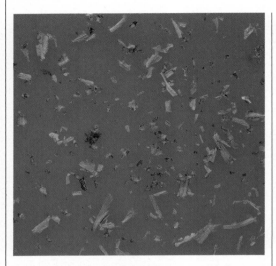

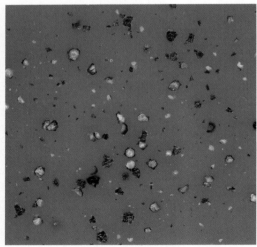

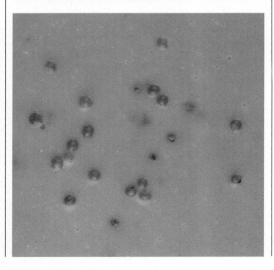

Bordelaise Sauce

about 3 cups (750 mL)

2 tsp	(10 mL) butter
3	green onions, chopped
¾ cup	(180 mL) red wine
2 cups	(500 mL) beef stock
	pinch of thyme
	pinch of tarragon
	salt and pepper
2 tbsp	(30 mL) kneaded butter (beurre manié)
1 tbsp	(15 mL) lemon juice
1 tbsp	(15 mL) chopped parsley
1 tsp	(5 mL) chopped tarragon

▪ In a saucepan, melt butter and sauté green onions without browning. Add wine and reduce liquid by half.

▪ Add beef stock and fines herbes and simmer for 5 minutes. Season with salt and pepper. Add kneaded butter and stir with wire whisk or beater until smooth. Pour mixture through sieve.

▪ When ready to serve, add lemon juice, parsley and tarragon.

Pepper Sauce

about 3 cups (750 mL)

½ cup	(125 mL) wine vinegar
3	green onions, chopped
⅓ cup	(80 mL) red wine
2 cups	(500 mL) beef stock
2 tbsp	(30 mL) kneaded butter (beurre manié)
½ tsp	(2 mL) crushed peppercorns

▪ In a saucepan, bring wine vinegar to a boil with green onions and wine. Reduce liquid by half.

▪ Pour beef stock into mixture and simmer for 15 minutes.

▪ Add kneaded butter and mix with wire whisk or beater. Add pepper and simmer until mixture thickens.

▪ Pour sauce through sieve and serve.

Sauce Diane

about 3 cups (750 mL)

2 cups	(500 mL) Pepper Sauce
¾ cup	(180 mL) 35% cream

▪ Pour sauce through sieve. Fold in whipped cream and pour into a saucepan. Heat without boiling.

VARIATION

• Replace black peppercorns with green or pink peppercorns in the Pepper Sauce.

Brown stocks owe their name to the fact that the dry ingredients have been lightly browned in butter before the liquid is added. They are mainly used with red meats and kidneys, and are added to certain soups to enhance the aroma.

Sauce Robert

about 3 cups (750 mL)

2 tsp	(10 mL) butter
1	onion, chopped
3 tbsp	(45 mL) wine vinegar
½ cup	(125 mL) red wine
2 cups	(500 mL) beef stock
2 tbsp	(30 mL) kneaded butter (beurre manié)
	salt and pepper
1 tbsp	(15 mL) old-fashioned mustard
1 tsp	(5 mL) honey
1 tsp	(5 mL) chopped parsley

■ In a saucepan, melt butter and sauté onion. Add vinegar and wine and let mixture reduce by half. Pour beef stock into mixture and simmer for 15 minutes.

■ Add kneaded butter. Season with salt and pepper. Stir with wire whisk or beater and simmer until mixture thickens.

■ Add mustard and honey. Pour through sieve. Sprinkle with parsley and serve.

Lyonnaise Sauce

about 2 cups (500 mL)

2 cups	(500 mL) beef stock
2 tbsp	(30 mL) kneaded butter (beurre manié)
1 tbsp	(15 mL) butter
1	onion, finely sliced
1	garlic clove, finely sliced
	salt and pepper

■ In a saucepan, heat beef stock, then add kneaded butter and mix with wire whisk or beater. Simmer for 15 minutes.

■ Meanwhile, in a skillet, melt butter and sauté onion and garlic. Add mixture to stock, season with salt and pepper, and simmer for 15 minutes.

Spanish Sauce

about 3 cups (750 mL)

2 tsp	(10 mL) butter
1	small carrot, chopped
1	small onion, chopped
1	celery stalk, chopped
1	bacon slice, cut into pieces
2 cups	(500 mL) beef stock
1 tbsp	(15 mL) puréed tomatoes
½ cup	(125 mL) mushrooms, quartered
1	bay leaf
3	parsley sprigs
	salt and pepper
2 tbsp	(30 mL) kneaded butter (beurre manié)

■ In a saucepan, melt butter and sauté carrot, onion, celery and bacon without browning.

■ Pour beef stock over vegetables and simmer for 15 minutes.

■ Add puréed tomatoes, mushroom quarters and herbs. Season with salt and pepper and simmer for 15 minutes.

■ Add kneaded butter and mix with wire whisk or beater. Return to saucepan and simmer until sauce thickens. Pour mixture through sieve. Garnish with finely chopped mushrooms and serve.

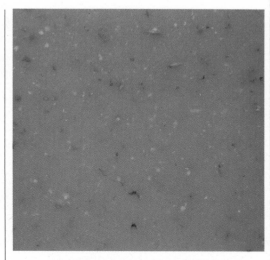

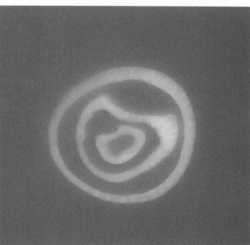

Top to Bottom: Sauce Robert ▪ Lyonnaise Sauce ▪ Spanish Sauce

WHITE STOCKS AND AROMATIC SAUCES

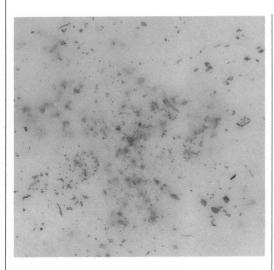

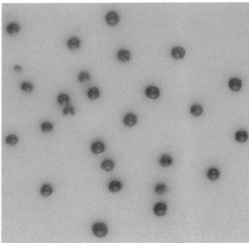

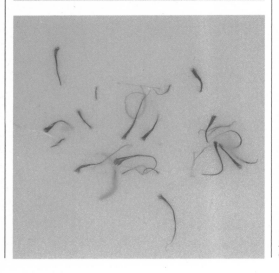

Top to Bottom:
Mustard Sauce ▪ Pink Pepper-
corn Sauce ▪ Saffron Sauce

Mustard Sauce

---

about 2 cups (500 mL)

1 tbsp	(15 mL)	butter
1 tbsp	(15 mL)	flour
2 cups	(500 mL)	chicken stock
		salt and pepper
2 tsp	(10 mL)	chopped parsley
1 tbsp	(15 mL)	old-fashioned mustard
¼ cup	(60 mL)	35% cream

▪ In a saucepan, melt butter, add flour and stir well. Pour stock in thin trickles, stirring constantly. Season with salt, pepper and parsley, and simmer for 10 minutes.

▪ Stir in mustard and cream and cook for 5 minutes without boiling.

Pink Peppercorn Sauce

---

about 2 cups (500 mL)

1 tbsp	(15 mL)	butter
1 tbsp	(15 mL)	flour
2 cups	(500 mL)	chicken stock
		salt
1 tsp	(5 mL)	pink peppercorns
¼ cup	(60 mL)	35% cream

▪ In a saucepan, melt butter, add flour and stir. Pour chicken stock into mixture in thin trickles, stirring constantly. Season with salt, then add pink peppercorns and simmer for 15 minutes. Fold in cream and heat without boiling.

Saffron Sauce

---

about 2 ½ cups (625 mL)

2 cups	(500 mL)	chicken stock
2 tbsp	(30 mL)	kneaded butter (beurre manié)
1		garlic clove, finely sliced
¼ tsp	(1 mL)	chopped coriander leaves
½ tsp	(2 mL)	saffron
		salt and pepper
½ cup	(125 mL)	35% cream

▪ In a saucepan, heat chicken stock. Stir kneaded butter into stock with wire whisk or beater. Add garlic, coriander leaves and saffron, and season with salt and pepper. Simmer until mixture thickens.

▪ Pour mixture through sieve. Fold in cream and return to saucepan. Cook for 5 minutes without boiling.

White stocks have a more delicate flavor than the more robust brown stocks. They are most often used with white meats such as veal, chicken and turkey, and are the basis of certain white sauces.

Aromatic Fish Sauce with Fines Herbes

about 2 cups (500 mL)	
4 tsp	(20 mL) butter
4 tsp	(20 mL) flour
2 cups	(500 mL) fish stock
½	garlic clove, finely sliced
	pinch of chopped tarragon
	pinch of chopped chives
	pinch of chopped chervil
	pinch of chopped thyme
1 tsp	(5 mL) chopped parsley
	salt and pepper
¼ cup	(60 mL) 35% cream

■ In a saucepan, melt butter, add flour and mix well. Pour fish stock into mixture in thin trickles, stirring constantly. Add garlic and fines herbes. Season with salt and pepper, and simmer for 10 minutes.

■ Fold in cream and heat without boiling.

Escargot Sauce

about 2 cups (500 mL)	
1 cup	(250 mL) clam and tomato juice
1 cup	(250 mL) seafood stock
3 tbsp	(45 mL) kneaded butter (beurre manié)
2 tsp	(10 mL) butter
12	canned escargots, sliced in half
½	garlic clove, finely sliced
1 tbsp	(15 mL) onion, chopped
	salt and pepper
2 tsp	(10 mL) chopped parsley

■ In a saucepan, heat clam and tomato juice and seafood stock. Stir in kneaded butter with wire whisk or beater and simmer for 10 minutes.

■ Meanwhile, melt butter in a skillet and brown escargots, garlic and onion. Add to stock and season with salt and pepper. Sprinkle with parsley and simmer for 5 minutes.

Aurora Sauce

about 2 cups (500 mL)	
4 tsp	(20 mL) butter
4 tsp	(20 mL) flour
2 cups	(500 mL) fish stock
¼ cup	(60 mL) puréed tomatoes
½	garlic clove, finely sliced
½ tsp	(2 mL) honey
1 tbsp	(15 mL) butter, in 6 tiny knobs

■ In a saucepan, melt the 4 tsp (20 mL) butter, add flour and stir well. Pour fish stock into mixture in thin trickles, stirring constantly. Stir in puréed tomatoes, garlic and honey, and simmer for 10 minutes.

■ When ready to serve, drop knobs of butter into mixture.

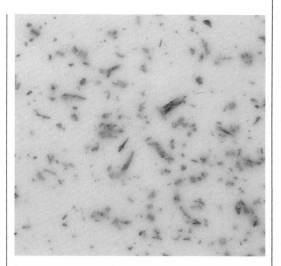

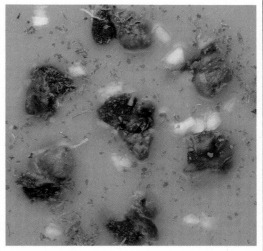

Top to Bottom:
Aromatic Fish Sauce with Fines Herbes ▪ Escargot Sauce ▪ Aurora Sauce

VEGETABLE COULIS

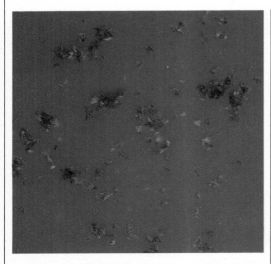

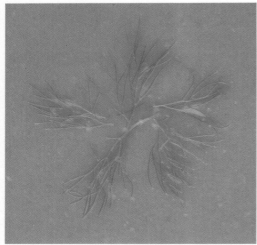

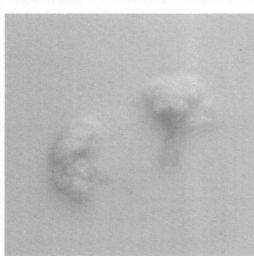

Top to Bottom:
Tomato Coulis • Asparagus
Coulis • Cauliflower Coulis

Tomato Coulis

about 4 cups (1 L)

2 tbsp	(30 mL) butter
¼ cup	(60 mL) carrots, finely sliced
¼ cup	(60 mL) celery, finely sliced
¼ cup	(60 mL) green bell peppers, finely sliced
¼ cup	(60 mL) potatoes, diced
¼ cup	(60 mL) onions, finely sliced
1	garlic clove, finely sliced
28 oz	(796 mL) canned tomatoes
¼ tsp	(1 mL) tarragon
¼ tsp	(1 mL) oregano
¼ tsp	(1 mL) thyme
2 tsp	(10 mL) chopped parsley
	salt and pepper

■ In a saucepan, melt butter and sauté vegetables and garlic without browning . Add tomatoes and fines herbes, and season with salt and pepper. Bring mixture to a boil, then simmer for 20 minutes.

■ Run mixture through blender. Return to saucepan and cook for 5 minutes.

■ Adjust seasoning, then pour through sieve and serve.

Asparagus Coulis

about 2 cups (500 mL)

2 tbsp	(30 mL) butter
10 oz	(284 mL) canned asparagus
2 tbsp	(30 mL) onion, chopped
1	garlic clove, finely sliced
¾ cup	(180 mL) chicken stock
¼ tsp	(1 mL) chopped chervil
¼ tsp	(1 mL) chopped fennel
	salt and pepper

■ In a saucepan, melt butter and sauté asparagus, onion and garlic without browning. Pour chicken stock and fines herbes into mixture, and season with salt and pepper. Simmer for 20 minutes.

■ Run mixture through blender, then return to saucepan and cook for 5 minutes.

■ Adjust seasoning, then pour through sieve and serve.

Cauliflower Coulis

about 3 cups (750 mL)

1 ½ cups	(375 mL) cauliflower (mainly stems)
1 tbsp	(15 mL) butter
1	green onion, chopped
¼ cup	(60 mL) potatoes, sliced
1 cup	(250 mL) milk
	salt and pepper

■ In a saucepan filled with lightly salted boiling water, cook cauliflower. Rinse under cold water and drain.

■ In a separate saucepan, melt butter and sauté green onion and potatoes for 5 minutes, then add cauliflower. Pour milk into mixture and season with salt and pepper. Heat over low heat for 20 minutes without boiling.

■ Run mixture through blender, then return to saucepan and heat for 5 minutes.

■ Adjust seasoning, then pour through sieve and serve.

Colorful, delicious and healthy, coulis are a wonderful new way of replacing rich sauces. The French term "coulis" may be unfamiliar to many readers. A coulis (pronounced "coolie") is a thick vegetable or fruit sauce made of one principal ingredient, with a variety of flavorings and thickenings and a minimum amount of fat.

Broccoli Coulis

about 3 cups (750 mL)	
1 tbsp	(15 mL) butter
1 ½ cups	(375 mL) broccoli (mainly stems), cut into pieces
2	green onions, chopped
1	garlic clove, finely sliced
¼ cup	(60 mL) potatoes, diced
1 cup	(250 mL) chicken stock
	salt and pepper
½ tsp	(2 mL) chopped tarragon

■ In a saucepan, melt butter and sauté broccoli, green onions, garlic and potatoes without browning. Pour chicken stock into mixture and season with salt, pepper and tarragon. Simmer for 20 minutes.

■ Run mixture through blender, then return to saucepan and cook for 5 minutes.

■ Adjust seasoning, then pour through sieve and serve.

Turnip Coulis

about 3 cups (750 mL)	
1 tbsp	(15 mL) butter
1 ½ cups	(375 mL) turnip, cut into pieces
2 tbsp	(30 mL) onion, chopped
1	garlic clove, finely sliced
1 cup	(250 mL) chicken stock
	salt and pepper
1 tsp	(5 mL) chopped parsley

■ In a saucepan, melt butter and sauté turnip, onion and garlic without browning. Pour chicken stock into mixture, and season with salt and pepper. Sprinkle with parsley and simmer for 20 minutes.

■ Run mixture through blender, then return to saucepan and cook for 5 minutes.

■ Adjust seasoning, then pour through sieve and serve.

Sweet Pepper Coulis

about 2 cups (500 mL)	
2 tbsp	(30 mL) butter
1	green bell pepper, cut into strips
1	sweet red pepper, cut into strips
1	onion, chopped
¼ cup	(60 mL) potatoes, diced
1	garlic clove, finely sliced
⅓ cup	(80 mL) vegetable juice
⅔ cup	(160 mL) chicken stock
	salt and pepper
1 tsp	(5 mL) paprika

■ In a saucepan, melt butter and sauté peppers, garlic, onion and potatoes without browning. Pour vegetable juice into mixture along with chicken stock. Season with salt, pepper and paprika, and simmer for 20 minutes.

■ Run mixture through blender, then return to saucepan and cook for 5 minutes.

■ Adjust seasoning, then pour through sieve and serve.

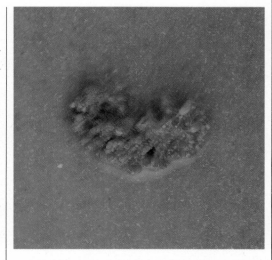

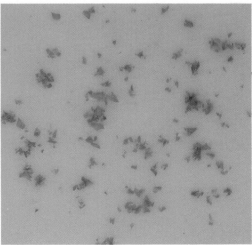

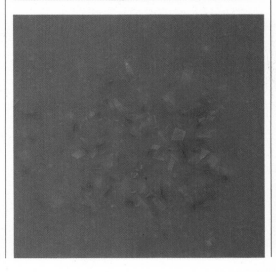

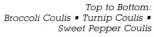

Top to Bottom:
Broccoli Coulis • Turnip Coulis •
Sweet Pepper Coulis

455

FRUIT SAUCES

Apricot Sauce

about 1 cup (250 mL)	
2 tbsp	(30 mL) butter
¼ cup	(60 mL) carrots, finely sliced
¼ cup	(60 mL) leek, finely sliced
¼ cup	(60 mL) celery, finely sliced
12 oz	(340 mL) canned apricots, drained, juice set aside
2 tbsp	(30 mL) champagne vinegar
1 tbsp	(15 mL) apricot liqueur
2 cups	(500 mL) chicken stock
	salt and pepper
2	mint leaves
1	chopped citronnella leaf
2 tbsp	(30 mL) wine vinegar
1 tsp	(5 mL) honey
¼ cup	(60 mL) kneaded butter (beurre manié)

■ In a saucepan, melt butter and sauté vegetables without browning.

■ Add half the apricots to mixture and stir. Deglaze with champagne vinegar, then add apricot liqueur and let liquid reduce by half.

■ Pour chicken stock into mixture, add rest of apricots, and bring to a boil. Season with salt and pepper. Add mint leaves, citronnella leaf and honey, and simmer for 20 minutes.

■ Meanwhile, in a small saucepan, boil reserved apricot juice and wine vinegar, and let liquid reduce by half.

■ Pour juice mixture into sauce and stir. Stir kneaded butter into sauce with wire whisk or beater and cook over low heat for 5 minutes.

These two fruit sauce recipes make use of a white and brown sauce respectively. They make a marvellous accompaniment for meats. Don't hesitate to vary the fruit content or even to blend several at once.

about 4 cups (1 L)	
2 tbsp	(30 mL) butter
¼ cup	(60 mL) carrots, finely sliced
¼ cup	(60 mL) leek, finely sliced
¼ cup	(60 mL) celery, finely sliced
12 oz	(345 g) frozen raspberries, thawed, undrained
¼ cup	(60 mL) raspberry vinegar
¼ cup	(60 mL) red wine
2 cups	(500 mL) beef stock
3	parsley sprigs
3	mint leaves
1 tsp	(5 mL) honey
¼ cup	(60 mL) kneaded butter (beurre manié)
	salt and pepper

■ In a saucepan, melt butter and sauté vegetables without browning. Add half the raspberries and stir well. Add vinegar and wine, and let liquid reduce by half. Pour beef stock into mixture, then add rest of raspberries. Bring to a boil. Add parsley, mint and honey, and simmer for 20 minutes.

■ Stir kneaded butter into mixture with wire whisk or beater. Season with salt and pepper, and cook over low heat for 10 minutes.

■ Adjust seasoning and serve.

* Illustrated recipe

WHITE AND RED BUTTER SAUCES

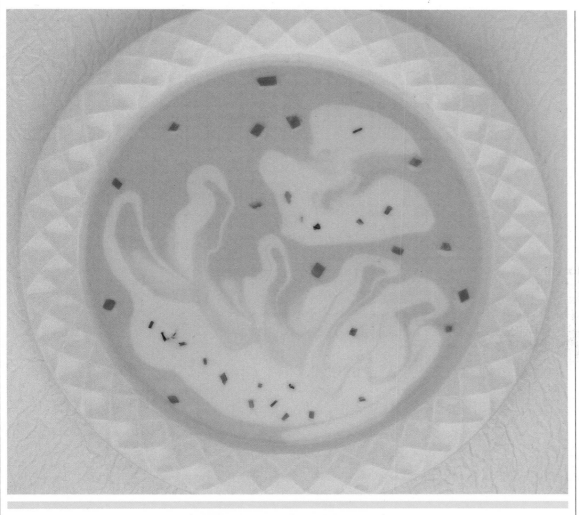

Red Butter Sauce

about 1 cup (250 mL)

¹/₂ cup	(125 mL) dry red wine
5	green onions, chopped
¹/₂ cup	(125 mL) 35% cream
8 oz	(225 g) butter, at room temperature
	salt and pepper
1 tsp	(5 mL) sweet red pepper, very finely chopped

■ In a small saucepan, bring wine and green onions to a boil, and let liquid reduce by half.

■ Add cream, stir well and let mixture reduce by half.

■ Over very low heat, beat in butter with a wire whisk and keep beating vigorously until the sauce is thick and creamy. Season with salt and pepper. Garnish with sweet red pepper.

N.B.: Don't let mixture come to a boil after adding butter.

VARIATION

• Add 1 tbsp (15 mL) finely sliced asparagus, or diced celery, tomato or orange.

The secret of butter sauces is to prevent them from turning oily. Keep beating as you add the butter, and don't let it sit around before serving.

White Butter Sauce

about 1 cup (250 mL)

¹/₂ cup	(125 mL) dry white wine
5	green onions, chopped
¹/₂ cup	(125 mL) 35% cream
8 oz	(225 g) butter, at room temperature
	salt and pepper
1 tsp	(5 mL) chopped fines herbes

■ In a small saucepan, bring wine and green onions to a boil, and let liquid reduce by half.

■ Add cream, stir well, and let mixture reduce by half.

■ Over very low heat, beat in butter with a wire whisk and keep beating vigorously until the sauce is thick and creamy. Garnish with fines herbes.

N.B.: Don't let sauce come to a boil after adding the butter.

Marinades

Sorrel Marinade

For fish

about 1 cup (250 mL)	
½ cup	(125 mL) olive oil
⅓ cup	(80 mL) champagne vinegar
1 tbsp	(15 mL) puréed sorrel
2 tbsp	(30 mL) chopped sorrel
½ tsp	(2 mL) chopped coriander
	juice of 1 lime

■ In a bowl, mix all ingredients. Add fish to mixture and marinate for 1 to 6 hours.

Citrus Fruit Marinade

For meat and fish

about 2 cups (500 mL)	
1 cup	(250 mL) grapefruit juice
½ cup	(125 mL) lemon juice
½ cup	(125 mL) orange juice
⅓ cup	(80 mL) vegetable oil
2 tsp	(10 mL) Worcestershire sauce
2 tsp	(10 mL) sugar
	salt and pepper
2 tbsp	(30 mL) julienned citrus peel

■ In a bowl, mix all ingredients. Let meat or fish marinate for 1 to 24 hours.

Beer Marinade

For chicken and pork

about 2 cups (500 mL)	
12 oz	(340 mL) beer
¼ cup	(60 mL) olive oil
2 tbsp	(30 mL) soy sauce
	juice of 1 lemon

■ In a bowl, mix all ingredients. Add meat and marinate for 1 to 24 hours.

Top to Bottom:
Sorrel Marinade ▪ Citrus Fruit Marinade ▪ Beer Marinade

Fragrant marinades are easy to make and extremely useful in flavoring and tenderizing food such as meat and fish.

Sweet and Sour Marinade

For meat

about 1 ½ cups (375 mL)

½ cup	(125 mL) Teriyaki sauce
½ cup	(125 mL) peanut oil
¼ cup	(60 mL) soy sauce
2	garlic cloves, finely sliced
1	green onion, chopped
2 tbsp	(30 mL) ketchup
¼ cup	(60 mL) wine vinegar
2 tsp	(10 mL) liquid honey
	salt and pepper

■ In a bowl, mix all ingredients. Add meat and marinate for 1 to 4 hours.

Cucumber Relish

about 3 cups (750 mL)

1 ½ cups	(375 mL) cucumber, peeled, seeded, sliced
½ cup	(125 mL) onion, sliced
1	green bell pepper, cut into strips
1 tbsp	(15 mL) salt
4 oz	(115 g) brown sugar
1 tbsp	(15 mL) horseradish in vinegar
1 tsp	(5 mL) old-fashioned mustard
¼ tsp	(1 mL) celery salt
1 cup	(250 mL) tarragon or champagne vinegar

■ Mix together cucumber, onions and green bell pepper. Season with salt and drain in a colander for 12 hours. Rinse.

■ Chop vegetables in the food processor, then add other ingredients except vinegar and stir.

■ Spoon mixture into jars. Add a thin layer of vinegar and refrigerate for 12 hours before serving.

Green Tomato Chutney

about 5 cups (1,25 L)

2 cups	(500 mL) miniature green tomatoes, cut into 8 pieces
½ cup	(125 mL) green apple, peeled, chopped
⅓ cup	(80 mL) green onions, chopped
½ tsp	(2 mL) celery salt
1 tsp	(5 mL) hot pepper, chopped
½ cup	(125 mL) brown sugar
1 cup	(250 mL) cider vinegar
½ cup	(125 mL) red tomato, diced
½ cup	(125 mL) sweet red pepper, diced
2 tsp	(10 mL) salt
½ tsp	(2 mL) ground nutmeg

■ Sprinkle green tomatoes with salt and drain in a colander for 12 hours. Rinse.

■ In a large saucepan, bring all ingredients except nutmeg to a boil. Simmer for 40 minutes or until vinegar is completely reduced. Add nutmeg and cook a few minutes longer. Let mixture stand to cool, then pour into jars.

Top to Bottom: Sweet and Sour Marinade ▪ Cucumber Relish ▪ Green Tomato Chutney

DESSERTS

Cakes, pies, flans and sweet treats of all kinds are the traditional finale of North American meals. They often appear at tea-time or at coffee breaks, and there's no doubt that family and friends find them a tempting addition.

Most of our sweet food is made of sugar, cream, chocolate and other tempting ingredients. Desserts can be a healthy component of our everyday eating, if you consider what goes into them. Some fruit desserts are light while being rich in Vitamin D, for example. Cookies and biscuits can be an excellent source of carbohydrates. Admittedly, the high fat content in many pastries is what makes them taste so good, and it's difficult to imagine giving them up entirely!

Indulging in the occasional wedge of lemon meringue pie, or a mousse topped with generous curls of dark chocolate is not really bad for you. Use a little moderation, and enjoy preparing and eating the good things in the pages that follow.

CAKES

Cakes often mean a party, but you can serve them at any time of day. Whether it's a tea-time treat or a lunch-time dessert, cake is always much appreciated.

Maple Syrup Bombe

Put a folded paper napkin under the bombe on the platter. This prevents any melting ice cream from spoiling the look of your dessert. Decorate it with whipped cream, nuts, fresh fruit, or caramel straws.

- In top of double-boiler, at low heat, simmer maple syrup and egg yolks; stir constantly until mixture thickens.
- Remove from heat; stir until mixture cools; add nuts.
- In a bowl, whip cream and vanilla extract until firm, and set aside.
- In a separate bowl, beat egg whites until stiff peaks form; add sugar when beating is three-quarters done.
- With a spatula, fold whipped cream into egg yolks and maple syrup, then gently fold in egg whites.
- Pour mixture into a 4-cup (1 L) plastic container. Freeze 8 hours.
- Place plastic container in hot water to unmold. Garnish with fruit and caramel straws (see p. 503).

6 servings	
²/₃ cup	(160 mL) maple syrup
3	egg yolks
½ cup	(125 mL) nuts
½ cup	(125 mL) 35% cream
½ tsp	(2 mL) vanilla extract
3	egg whites
3	tbsp (45 mL) sugar

Chocolate Mousse Cake

You can make these gourmet chocolate curls with a potato peeler. Decorate your cake after the chocolate icing has set.

8 servings

1 cup	(250 mL) all-purpose flour
1 tsp	(5 mL) baking powder
1/4 tsp	(1 mL) salt
3	eggs, beaten
1 cup	(250 mL) sugar
2 tsp	(10 mL) lemon juice
6 tbsp	(90 mL) milk

Mousse Icing

1/2 lb	(250 g) sweet chocolate squares
3 tbsp	(45 mL) cold water
1/4 cup	(60 mL) sugar
4	egg yolks
1 1/2 cups	(375 mL) 35% cream
4	egg whites

■ Preheat oven to 375 °F (190 °C).

■ In a bowl, combine flour, baking powder, and salt; set aside.

■ In a separate bowl, beat eggs and gradually add sugar. Blend well after each addition. Add lemon juice.

■ Heat milk without boiling.

■ Add dry ingredients to beaten eggs in 4 stages.

■ Pour heated milk directly into batter; stir well.

■ Pour batter into a round 8-inch (20 cm) unbuttered cake pan. Bake 25 minutes.

■ Remove from oven and let stand to cool on wire rack.

■ Turn it out of the pan and slice into 3 layers.

Mousse Icing

■ Melt chocolate squares with water in top of double-boiler. Add sugar and stir. Remove from heat and let stand to cool. Add unbeaten egg yolks and stir well.

■ Whip cream.

■ Beat egg whites until stiff peaks form.

■ Add whipped cream to chocolate mixture, then fold in egg whites.

Icing the Cake

■ Put the first layer in an 8-inch spring pan (or one that allows you to remove the sides later). Cover this layer with 1/4 cup (60 mL) icing. Repeat until all three layers are iced, and set aside the remaining icing.

■ Put the cake in the freezer. Take it out 10 minutes before serving, remove the sides of the pan, and ice around the edges. Decorate the cake with piping and chocolate curls, sprinkled with a little icing sugar.

Fruit Cake

12 servings	
1 1/2 cups	(375 mL) all-purpose flour
8 oz	(225 g) dates, pitted
4 oz	(115 g) raisins
4 oz	(115 g) chopped nuts
1/4 cup	(60 mL) red and green candied cherries
2	large eggs
3/4 cup	(180 mL) sugar
1/3 cup	(80 mL) shortening
1/2 tsp	(2 mL) baking soda
1/4 tsp	(1 mL) powdered cloves
3/4 tsp	(3 mL) powdered ginger
3/4 tsp	(3 mL) powdered cinnamon
3/4 tsp	(3 mL) powdered nutmeg
3/4 tsp	(3 mL) baking powder
1/2 cup	(125 mL) milk
	rum or Cognac

■ Preheat oven to 300 °F (150 °C).

■ Line a loaf pan with buttered brown paper.

■ Dredge dates, raisins, nuts, and cherries with 1/2 cup (125 mL) flour.

■ In a mixer bowl, combine eggs, sugar and shortening, and beat 4 minutes.

■ In a separate bowl, sift dry ingredients and add them to first mixture, alternating with milk. Gradually add fruit mixture.

■ Fill the pan half way and bake 1 1/2 hours.

■ Remove from oven; spoon rum or cognac over the cake, and let stand to cool.

■ Cover with clean cloth; put in a plastic bag and store in a cool place 2 weeks. This allows the cake's flavor to develop fully. You can serve it immediately if you wish, however.

Yesterday's Cake

Birthday cakes may be great at the party, but tend to lose their freshness the day after. Freeze what's left and use it to make a completely different cake.

8 servings	
4 cups	(1 L) leftover cake, diced
2	egg yolks
1 1/2 cups	(375 mL) sugar
1 cup	(250 mL) all-purpose flour
1 tsp	(5 mL) baking powder
1 1/2 cups	(375 mL) milk
2 tbsp	(30 mL) melted butter
1/4 tsp	(1 mL) vanilla extract

Meringue

2	egg whites
2 cups	(500 mL) brown sugar

■ Preheat oven to 350 °F (175 °C).

■ Butter a 9 x 12 inch (22 x 32 cm) baking dish.

■ Place leftover cake cubes in the dish and set aside.

■ In a bowl, combine egg yolks and sugar. Beat 3 minutes. Add flour and baking powder, and pour milk and butter into mixture. Stir well, and add vanilla extract.

■ Pour batter over cake cubes and bake 30 minutes.

■ Heat the broiler.

■ In a bowl, beat egg whites and brown sugar until stiff peaks form and spread the meringue on the cake or pipe it as shown.

■ Broil until meringue turns golden. Serve with a peach sauce.

Field Berry Cake

Wild fruit is available for only a few precious weeks each year. Here's a recipe that takes full advantage of the berry crop.

8 servings

½ cup	(125 mL) butter
1 cup	(250 mL) sugar
2	eggs
1 ¾ cups	(430 mL) all-purpose flour
1 tbsp	(15 mL) baking powder
	pinch of salt
¾ cup	(180 mL) milk
1 tsp	(5 mL) vanilla extract
1 cup	(250 mL) 35 % cream
¼ cup	(60 mL) sugar
2 cups	(500 mL) field berries: raspberries, strawberries, blue-berries

■ Preheat oven to 350 °F (175 °C).

■ Butter a 9 x 13 inch (22 x 34 cm) cake pan.

■ In a bowl, cream butter and gradually add sugar and eggs.

■ In a separate bowl, sift dry ingredients. Add to first mixture, alternating with milk and vanilla extract.

■ Pour batter into the pan and bake 30 to 40 minutes. Let stand to cool on wire rack.

■ Whip cream and sugar, and cover the cake. Garnish with berries or serve with a berry fruit salad.

Farmer's Honey Cake

Use up some of that leftover crystallized honey for your icing.

8 servings

½ cup	(125 mL) butter
1 tsp	(5 mL) vanilla extract
½ tsp	(2 mL) salt
1 cup	(250 mL) sugar
3	egg yolks
2 cups	(500 mL) all-purpose flour, sifted
1 tbsp	(15 mL) baking powder
½ cup	(125 mL) cocoa
	pinch of baking soda
1 tsp	(5 mL) cinnamon
1 cup	(250 mL) milk
3	egg whites
½ cup	(125 mL) sugar

Honey Icing

1	egg white
1 cup	(250 mL) honey
	pinch of salt

■ Preheat oven to 350 °F (175 °C).

■ Butter a cake pan.

■ In a mixer bowl, combine first 5 ingredients and mix until smooth.

■ In a separate bowl, sift dry ingredients and add to first ingredients, alternating with milk.

■ Beat egg whites and sugar until stiff peaks form.

■ With a spatula, fold egg white mixture into cake batter and turn it into the cake pan. Bake 60 minutes.

■ Let stand to cool, then spread the honey icing.

Honey Icing

■ In the top of double-boiler, heat all ingredients, beating with a wire whisk until icing thickens.

* Illustrated recipe

VARIATION

• Garnish cake with favorite fruit such as sliced kiwi and apricots or substitute Chantilly cream for the icing.

465

Upside-down Pineapple Cake

Replace pineapple slices with canned peach halves. The cake will taste just as delicious.

8 to 10 servings

3 tbsp	(45 mL) butter
19 oz	(540 mL) canned, sliced pineapple
¼ cup	(60 mL) cherries
½ cup	(125 mL) almonds
½ cup	(125 mL) grated coconut
½ cup	(125 mL) brown sugar
3 tbsp	(45 mL) milk
¼ tsp	(1 mL) ground ginger
⅓ cup	(80 mL) butter
1 cup	(250 mL) sugar
2	eggs
2 cups	(500 mL) all-purpose flour
1 tbsp	(15 mL) baking powder
	pinch of salt
¾ cup	(180 mL) milk

■ Preheat oven to 350 °F (175 °C).

■ Melt 3 tbsp (45 mL) of butter in a cake pan in the oven, and spread the pineapple, cherries and almonds over the butter.

■ In a bowl, mix the coconut, brown sugar, milk and ginger, and pour this over the fruit. Set aside.

■ Cream ⅓ cup (80 mL) butter and gradually add 1 cup (250 mL) sugar. Blend in the eggs one by one, then add the milk in a thin stream while stirring. Add flour, baking powder and salt, and stir well.

■ Cover the fruit with the batter. Bake for about 50 minutes.

Applesauce Cake

You can use home-made or commercial applesauce in this recipe.

8 to 10 servings

¾ cup	(180 mL) applesauce
1 tsp	(5 mL) baking soda
⅓ cup	(80 mL) shortening
½ cup	(125 mL) sugar
½ cup	(125 mL) raisins
½ cup	(125 mL) nuts
1 cup	(250 mL) all-purpose flour
¼ tsp	(1 mL) ground cloves
¼ tsp	(1 mL) ground cinnamon
	salt
1 cup	(250 mL) hot apricot jam

Apple Cream

2 tbsp	(30 mL) butter
1 cup	(250 mL) apples, sliced
¼ cup	(60 mL) sugar
½ cup	(125 mL) 35% cream

■ Preheat oven to 375 °F (190 °C).

■ Butter an 8-inch (20-cm) round cake pan.

■ In a saucepan, heat applesauce, add baking soda, and remove from heat. Set aside.

■ In a large bowl, cream shortening, add sugar, then raisins, nuts, flour, cloves, cinnamon, and salt, one ingredient at a time.

■ Pour applesauce into mixture and stir well.

■ Pour batter into the cake pan and bake 35 to 45 minutes.

■ Coat with Apple Cream.

Apple Cream

■ In a skillet, melt butter and sauté the apple slices. Add sugar, and cream, and stir well.

■ Garnish cake with mixture.

Beet and Carrot Cake

This cake will be even more nutritious if you use a mixture of white and whole-wheat flour.

8 to 10 servings

³/₄ cup	(180 mL) oil
1 ¹/₂ cups	(375 mL) sugar
3	egg yolks
1 tsp	(5 mL) vanilla extract
3 tbsp	(45 mL) hot water
2 cups	(500 mL) all-purpose flour
1 tbsp	(15 mL) baking powder
¹/₄ tsp	(1 mL) salt
1 tsp	(5 mL) cinnamon
2 cups	(500 mL) raw carrots, finely chopped
1 cup	(250 mL) raw beets, finely chopped
¹/₂ cup	(125 mL) chopped nuts
3	egg whites

- Preheat oven to 350 °F (175 °C).

- Butter an 8-inch (20-cm) round pan.

- In a bowl, combine oil, sugar, egg yolks, vanilla extract and water.

- In a separate bowl, sift dry ingredients and fold them into first mixture.

- Add carrots, beets, and chopped nuts. Stir well.

- Beat egg whites until stiff peaks form. Gently add to batter.

- Pour batter into cake pan and bake about 50 minutes.

- Ice the cake with a vanilla icing, and decorate it with cherries and chocolate sprinkles.

Green Tomato Cake

Let your family and friends guess the contents of this cake!

8 to 10 servings

1 cup	(250 mL) oil
2 cups	(500 mL) sugar
3	eggs
3 cups	(750 mL) all-purpose flour
2 tsp	(10 mL) baking powder
1 ¹/₄ tsp	(6 mL) baking soda
2 cups	(500 mL) green tomatoes, seeded, cut into small pieces
¹/₂ cup	(125 mL) maraschino cherries, drained, cut in half
¹/₂ cup	(125 mL) raisins, dredged with flour
1 tbsp	(15 mL) vanilla extract

Fudge Icing

¹/₄ cup	(60 mL) milk
1 cup	(250 mL) brown sugar
¹/₂ cup	(125 mL) butter
1 cup	(250 mL) icing sugar

- Preheat oven to 350 °F (175 °C).

- Butter a cake pan.

- In a bowl, beat oil, sugar and eggs.

- In a separate bowl, sift flour, baking powder, and soda.

- Add tomatoes and cherries. Stir and then blend with oil and egg mixture, alternating with dry ingredients.

- Add vanilla extract and stir.

- Pour batter into the pan and bake 1 ¹/₄ hours.

- Remove from oven; let stand on wire rack to cool.

Fudge Icing

- In a small saucepan, boil milk, brown sugar and butter for 5 minutes. Remove from heat; add icing sugar all at once. Beat until shiny and ice the cake. Decorate it with fresh fruit and nuts.

467

Coconut Velouté Cake

- Preheat oven to 375 °F (190 °C).

- Butter two, 9-inch (22-cm) square cake pans.

- Cream shortening, add sugar, a little at a time, add eggs, one at a time.

- In a bowl sift dry ingredients and add them to first mixture, alternating with milk. Add almond and vanilla extracts.

- Pour batter into cake pans and bake 25 minutes. Remove from oven and let stand on wire rack to cool.

Icing

- In a saucepan, boil water, sugar, and vinegar until candy thermometer registers 250 °F (120 °C). Set aside to cool.

- Pour syrup into egg whites, beating constantly until icing becomes firm. Add vanilla extract.

- Ice the cake and decorate with grated coconut and fruit.

Save time by making the syrup first, since it takes a good hour to cool.

6 to 8 servings	
¾ cup	(180 mL) shortening
1 ½ cups	(375 mL) sugar
3	eggs
3 cups	(750 mL) pastry flour
4 tsp	(20 mL) baking powder
¾ tsp	(3 mL) salt
1 cup	(250 mL) milk
½ tsp	(2 mL) almond extract
1 tsp	(5 mL) vanilla extract

Icing

⅓ cup	(80 mL) water
1 cup	(250 mL) sugar
1 tsp	(5 mL) vinegar
2	egg whites, beaten into stiff peaks
¾ tsp	(3 mL) vanilla extract
	grated coconut

Swiss Chocolate Roll

Once the cake is baked, turn it out onto a napkin sprinkled with cocoa. Cut off a narrow surround of crust, and you'll find it much easier to roll.

6 to 8 servings

1 cup	(250 mL) all-purpose flour
¼ cup	(60 mL) cocoa
1 tsp	(5 mL) baking powder
¼ tsp	(1 mL) salt
3	eggs
1 cup	(250 mL) sugar
⅓ cup	(80 mL) water
1 tsp	(5 mL) vanilla extract

Cocoa Cream

2 cups	(500 mL) 35% cream
½ cup	(125 mL) cocoa
½ cup	(125 mL) sugar
¼ cup	(60 mL) coffee liqueur

■ Preheat oven to 375 °F (190 °C).

■ Butter a 15 x 10 x ¾ inch (36 x 25 x 2 cm) cookie sheet, and line with wax paper.

■ In a bowl, sift flour, cocoa, baking powder and salt.

■ In a mixer bowl, beat eggs and gradually add sugar. Continue beating, then add water and vanilla extract.

■ Reduce beater speed and add dry ingredients.

■ Spread batter onto the cookie sheet, and bake 12 minutes.

■ Lift the cake onto a towel dusted with cocoa. Remove wax paper and roll cake with the towel, starting from the 10-inch end. Cool on a rack.

Cocoa Cream

■ In a bowl, combine all ingredients, cover and refrigerate.

■ After 1 hour, remove from refrigerator and beat with wire whisk until soft peaks form.

■ Unroll the cake and spread half the cocoa cream on it. Roll it again and ice it with the rest of the icing.

■ Garnish with slivered almonds, grated coconut, and chocolate chips. Serve with fruit.

PIES

Chocolate Pie

Chocolate pie reigns supreme as a family dessert. You can replace the corn flake crust with a graham cracker crust.

6 to 8 servings

Pie Crust

1 ¹/₂ cups	(375 mL) corn flakes, crumbled
¹/₄ cup	(60 mL) melted butter
2 tbsp	(30 mL) sugar

Filling

¹/₂ lb	(225 g) Philadelphia cream cheese
¹/₃ cup	(80 mL) chocolate syrup
1 cup	(250 mL) 35% cream

■ Preheat oven to 350 °F (175 °C).

■ In a bowl, combine pie crust ingredients. Press into a 9-inch (22 cm) pie plate and bake 10 minutes. Remove and let stand to cool.

■ In a separate bowl, whip cream cheese until light, then add chocolate syrup.

■ In a separate bowl, whip cream and fold it gently into the chocolate and cheese mixture.

■ Pour filling into the pie crust and refrigerate for a few hours.

Shimmer Jelly Pie

A wonderful, wobbly, gloppy dessert for hungry youngsters.

6 to 8 servings

3	packages of jelly powder, 3 oz (85 g) each, assorted flavors
1 cup	(250 mL) pineapple juice
1	package of lemon jelly powder, 3 oz (85 g)
2	packages of commercial whipped cream
1	graham wafer pie crust, baked

■ Prepare jelly mixes in 3 separate, large bowls, using only 1 ¹/₂ cups (375 mL) water instead of 2 cups (500 mL) as indicated on package directions. Jelly will fill ¹/₄ inch (1,25 cm) at the bottom of each bowl. Refrigerate. When jelly is firm, cut into cubes.

■ Meanwhile, in a saucepan, boil pineapple juice, add lemon-flavored jelly powder and dissolve completely. Add ¹/₂ cup (125 mL) cold water, stir and refrigerate until mixture becomes a thick syrup.

■ In a bowl, prepare whipped cream according to package directions. Add pineapple-lemon mixture and jelly cubes to whipped cream.

■ Pour entire mixture into pie crust.

■ Cover with whipped cream. Refrigerate 3 hours, then serve.

■ Reserve some jelly cubes of all colors to garnish, as shown here.

* Illustrated recipe

Sure Sugar Pie

Wait until the filling is cold before lifting this pie onto a serving platter.

8 servings

Filling

2 cups	(500 mL) brown sugar
1	egg, beaten
1 tbsp	(15 mL) all-purpose flour
½ cup	(125 mL) evaporated milk or 15% cream
1 tbsp	(15 mL) melted butter
	pie dough for 2 crusts

- Preheat oven to 400 °F (205 °C).

- In a bowl, combine all filling ingredients.

- Line a pie plate with 1 crust and add the filling. Cover with second crust. Pinch sides and cut a slit in the middle to let steam escape. Bake 25 to 30 minutes.

Strawberry Pie

A spectacular dessert, with whole strawberries lining the bottom, and halved strawberries decorating the whipped cream topping.

6 to 8 servings

2 cups	(500 mL) hot water
1 cup	(250 mL) sugar
3 tbsp	(45 mL) cornstarch
1	package of strawberry jelly powder
2 cups	(500 mL) strawberries, whole
1	pie crust, baked
1 cup	(250 mL) whipped cream
¼ cup	(60 mL) nuts
	strawberries, sliced in half

- In a small saucepan, heat water, sugar, and cornstarch at low heat until thick. Remove from heat.

- Dissolve strawberry jelly in the sauce thoroughly, and cool.

- Place whole strawberries in the bottom of pie crust and cover them with the strawberry jelly.

- Garnish with whipped cream, nuts and strawberry halves. Refrigerate until ready to serve.

Custard Pie

When it's sugaring-off time, serve the pie still warm and pour maple syrup over each serving.

6 to 8 servings

1 ⅓ cups	(330 mL) milk
3	eggs
⅔ cup	(240 mL) sugar
	pinch of salt
½ tsp	(2 mL) vanilla extract
	pinch of nutmeg (optional)
1	pie crust, uncooked

■ Preheat oven to 450 °F (230 °C).

■ In a small saucepan, heat milk until warm.

■ In a bowl, beat eggs, sugar, and salt until smooth.

■ Pour warm milk over egg mixture and stir constantly. Add vanilla extract and nutmeg.

■ Line a 9-inch (22-cm) pie plate with crust. Pour in filling and bake 10 minutes.

■ Reduce heat to 350 °F (175 °C) and bake 35 minutes. Check after 20 minutes. If the pie appears to be browning too quickly, cover it with aluminum foil and finish the baking.

Maple Syrup Pie

Test for doneness by inserting a knife tip. If it comes out clean, the pie is ready.

6 to 8 servings

1	pie crust, uncooked
2	eggs
1 cup	(250 mL) brown sugar
2 tbsp	(30 mL) all-purpose flour
1 cup	(250 mL) maple syrup
2 tbsp	(30 mL) melted butter
½ cup	(125 mL) nuts or pecans, chopped
1 tsp	(5 mL) vanilla extract
	pinch of salt

■ Preheat oven to 400 °F (205 °C).

■ Line a 9-inch (22-cm) pie plate with crust. Flute the edges.

■ In a large bowl, beat eggs lightly.

■ In a separate bowl, combine brown sugar and flour and add to the eggs.

■ Add other ingredients and stir, then pour into pie crust.

■ Bake 35 to 40 minutes until filling becomes firm, and serve with caramel sauce and chopped nuts.

Delicious Rhubarb Pie

Rhubarb grows faithfully in a corner of a garden, year in, year out, with very little trouble. Here's a memorable way to feature it, and a refreshing change from rhubarb compote.

6 to 8 servings

2	puff pastry crusts, uncooked
1 ½ cups	(375 mL) sugar
3 tbsp	(45 mL) all-purpose flour
½ tsp	(2 mL) nutmeg
1 tbsp	(15 mL) butter
2	eggs, beaten
3 cups	(750 mL) rhubarb cut into ½ inch (1,25 cm) pieces

■ Preheat oven to 450 °F (230 °C).

■ Line a 9-inch (22-cm) pie plate with 1 puff pastry crust.

■ In a bowl, combine all other ingredients and fill pie crust. Cover with the second crust, pinch edges, and make a slit in the middle to let steam escape.

■ Bake 15 minutes, then reduce heat to 350 °F (175 °C). Bake 40 to 45 minutes.

Special Blueberry Pie

Blueberries are a northern specialty. Here's a quick way of serving the results of a morning's picking.

6 to 8 servings

2 tbsp	(30 mL) cornstarch
2 tbsp	(30 mL) water
1 cup	(250 mL) blueberries
¼ cup	(60 mL) water
¾ cup	(180 mL) sugar
4 cups	(1 L) blueberries
1	pie crust, baked

■ In a bowl, dissolve cornstarch in 2 tbsp (30 mL) water and set aside.

■ In a saucepan, boil 1 cup (250 mL) blueberries with 1 cup (250 mL) water, pressing fruit to make a purée.

■ Add sugar and dissolved cornstarch, and boil 5 minutes or until mixture becomes clear syrup. Remove from heat and add blueberries.

■ Fold mixture into pie crust and refrigerate 2 hours before serving.

■ Garnish with whipped cream or ice cream.

Apple and Caramel Pie

Give this pie a little something extra by serving a cheese slice with each wedge.

6 to 8 servings	
3 tbsp	(45 mL) butter
¼ cup	(60 mL) all-purpose flour
¼ tsp	(1 mL) salt
1 cup	(250 mL) water
1 cup	(250 mL) sugar or brown sugar, well packed
6 cups	(1,5 L) apples, peeled, diced
1 tsp	(5 mL) vanilla extract
2	pie crusts, uncooked

■ Preheat oven to 400 °F (205 °C).

■ In a saucepan, melt butter, add flour and salt and boil 1 minute.

■ Remove from heat, continue to stir and add water and sugar.

■ Continue cooking at medium heat, stirring until the sauce boils or becomes thick and creamy.

■ Add apples, cover and cook at low heat 15 minutes, stirring often.

■ Remove from heat, add vanilla extract, let stand to cool.

■ Line a 9-inch (22-cm) pie plate with crust and fill with apple mixture. Cover with second crust and pinch sides. Make a slit in the middle to let the steam escape, and bake 30 to 35 minutes.

Lemon Meringue Pie

Sprinkle the meringue with powdered sugar before putting it in the oven, to give it an appetizing caramel color.

6 to 8 servings	
⅔ cup	(160 mL) sugar
¼ cup	(60 mL) cornstarch
¼ tsp	(1 mL) salt
1 ½ cups	(330 mL) water
2	egg yolks, beaten
2 tbsp	(30 mL) butter
2 tsp	(10 mL) julienned lemon peel
¼ cup	(60 mL) lemon juice
1	pie crust, baked

Meringue

2	egg whites
⅛ tsp	(0,5 mL) salt
¼ tsp	(1 mL) sugar

■ Preheat oven to 325 °F (160 °C).

■ In a bowl, combine sugar, cornstarch and salt. Add water and cook in double-boiler, stirring constantly until mixture thickens.

■ Gradually add egg yolks. Cook and stir 2 minutes.

■ Remove from heat and add butter, lemon peel, and lemon juice. Let stand to cool.

■ Pour lemon filling into pie crust.

■ In a separate bowl, whip egg whites, salt, and sugar until stiff peaks form. Spread meringue over the lemon filling and bake 15 minutes until golden. Garnish with lemon peel and fresh fruit.

* Illustrated recipe

Chiffon Pie with Fresh Peaches

Use different fruits, in season.

6 to 8 servings

³/₄ cup	(180 mL) sugar
1 ¹/₂ cups	(375 mL) peaches, diced
1	package unflavored gelatin
¹/₄ cup	(60 mL) cold water
¹/₂ cup	(125 mL) hot water
1 tbsp	(15 mL) lemon juice
	pinch of salt
¹/₂ cup	(125 mL) whipped cream
1	9-inch (22-cm) pie crust, baked

■ In a bowl, combine sugar and peaches, and let stand 30 minutes.

■ In a separate bowl, let the unflavored gelatin swell in cold water, then dissolve it in hot water. Cool.

■ Pour gelatin over peaches, add lemon juice and salt, and stir. Refrigerate until mixture is half-set.

■ Delicately fold whipped cream into the gelatin mixture, and pour the filling into the pie crust. Refrigerate.

VARIATIONS

Replace peaches with fresh or canned pineapple.

Replace peaches with fresh or canned plums.

Raspberry Surprise Pie

A pastry cook's specialty. The rich whipped cream covers a hidden treasure of brilliant ruby raspberries.

8 servings	
1½ cups	(375 mL) raspberries
½ cup	(125 mL) sugar
1	package raspberry jelly powder
¾ cup	(80 mL) boiling water
1	9-inch (22-cm) pie crust, baked

Pastry cream with gelatin

1 ½ tsp	(7 mL) gelatin
2 tbsp	(30 mL) cold water
3 tbsp	(45 mL) all-purpose flour
⅓ cup	(80 mL) sugar
1	whole egg
1	egg yolk
1½ cups	(375 mL) milk
½ tsp	(2 mL) vanilla extract
½ cup	(125 mL) 35% cream
3 tbsp	(45 mL) sugar
½ cup	(125 mL) raspberries

■ In a bowl, delicately mix raspberries and sugar and steep for 2 hours.

■ To prepare pasty cream, dissolve gelatin in cold water for 5 minutes, let stand.

■ In a saucepan, combine flour and sugar. Add egg and egg yolk. Stir in milk and continue to stir until custard thickens and begins to boil.

■ Remove from heat; dissolve gelatin in the custard and add vanilla extract. Cool and pour into pie crust.

■ In a saucepan, bring raspberries to boil, cook 30 seconds, and remove from heat.

■ In a separate bowl, dissolve the raspberry powder in boiling water, pour into raspberry mixture and refrigerate until it begins to set.

■ Stir gently to blend fruit, pour into pie crust on top of pastry cream, and refrigerate 30 minutes.

■ A few minutes before serving, whip cream and sugar until firm, and garnish the pie. Decorate with whole raspberries.

Apple Pie Amandine with Vanilla Milk

Serve this down-home pie while still warm, and garnish it with vanilla ice cream or lemon sherbet.

8 servings	
2 cups	(500 mL) apples, peeled, diced
¼ cup	(60 mL) powdered almonds
¼ cup	(60 mL) sugar
¼ tsp	(1 mL) vanilla extract
2 tsp	(10 mL) lemon juice
2 tbsp	(30 mL) raisins
3 tbsp	(45 mL) unsalted butter
¾ tsp	(3 mL) ground cinnamon
1	pie crust, unbaked

■ Preheat oven to 350 °F (175 °C).

■ In a bowl, combine apples, powdered almonds, sugar, vanilla extract, lemon juice, raisins, butter, and cinnamon.

■ Fill the pie crust, bake 30 minutes. Remove and let stand to cool. Garnish with vanilla milk.

VANILLA MILK

• In a heavy saucepan, boil 1 cup (250 mL) milk, ¾ cup (180 mL) sugar, and 1 fresh vanilla pod, or a few drops vanilla extract. Boil until mixture thickens a little. Serve hot or cold.

477

FLANS

Small Marshmallow Flan

If you want to make a large flan, use six eggs instead of four.

6 servings

½ cup	(125 mL) sugar
2 tsp	(10 mL) water
⅓ cup	(80 mL) sugar
¼ tsp	(1 mL) salt
4	eggs, lightly beaten
3 cups	(750 mL) hot milk
½ tsp	(2 mL) vanilla extract
½ tsp	(2 mL) cinnamon
12	marshmallows

■ Preheat oven to 325 °F (160 °C).

■ In a small saucepan, dissolve the first amount of sugar in the water and cook until caramelized. Pour a thin layer in the bottom of each of six ramekins, and set aside.

■ In a saucepan, blend the second amount of sugar with salt and eggs, adding the milk while stirring. Heat without boiling.

■ Put 2 marshmallow halves in the bottom of each ramekin.

■ Pour the custard through a sieve into ramekins, and sprinkle with cinnamon.

■ Stand the ramekins in a baking dish with 1 inch (2,5 cm) hot water, and cook in the oven for 25 to 35 minutes.

■ Cool and turn out onto individual plates. Garnish with marshmallow slices and fresh fruit.

ORANGE FLAN

• Add 2 tsp (10 mL) grated orange peel and 1 tsp (5 mL) grated lemon peel to the liquid. Replace the cinnamon garnish with nutmeg, and omit the marshmallows. Garnish with orange sections and kiwi slices, as shown opposite.

BREAD FLAN

• Substitute 1 cup (250 mL) breadcrumbs for 2 of the 4 eggs in the basic recipe, and omit the marshmallows.

GINGER FLAN

• Use the basic recipe. Put 1 ½ cups (375 mL) crumbled ginger snaps in the bottom of the six ramekins.

Crème Brûlée with Grated Coconut

Cool the crème completely before sprinkling brown sugar on it. Watch carefully when caramelizing the sugar, as it can easily burn.

6 to 8 servings

2 cups	(500 mL)	milk
¼ tsp	(1 mL)	vanilla extract
½ cup	(125 mL)	coconut, grated
3		eggs
½ cup	(125 mL)	sugar
1 tbsp	(15 mL)	cornstarch
2 tbsp	(30 mL)	brown sugar

■ Preheat oven to 325 °F (160 °C).

■ In a saucepan, boil milk, vanilla extract and grated coconut.

■ In a mixer bowl, beat eggs, sugar, and cornstarch 2 minutes.

■ Stir boiled milk into egg mixture.

■ Pour into casserole and boil 30 seconds, stirring constantly.

■ Pour mixture evenly into small ramekins; place in baking pan containing 1 inch (2,5 cm) hot water; bake 30 minutes.

■ Heat broiler.

■ Dust ramekins with brown sugar and caramelize under the broiler.

Fruit Flan

Garnish the bottom of the ramekins with a small amount of grated nuts.

8 servings

4		eggs, lightly beaten
½ cup	(125 mL)	sugar
¼ tsp	(1 mL)	salt
¼ tsp	(1 mL)	vanilla extract
2 cups	(500 mL)	milk
		fresh fruit

■ Preheat oven to 300 °F (150 °C).

■ In a bowl, combine eggs, sugar, salt, and vanilla extract.

■ In a small saucepan, allow milk to barely simmer. Pour into egg mixture and stir.

■ Pour mixture into 8 small ramekins and put them in a baking pan with 1 inch (2,5 cm) hot water. Bake 50 to 60 minutes. Test for doneness by inserting a knife blade in middle of flan. The blade should come out clean.

■ Unmold the flans and serve with fresh fruit (strawberries, raspberries, blueberries, or blackberries).

MOUSSES

If you want mousses done to perfection, make sure the ingredients used are finely grated or puréed. For Bavarian mousse, the mixture should be thoroughly lukewarm before you add the milk, to prevent curdling.

Apple Mousse

4 servings	
1 lb	(450 g) cooking apples
5 tbsp	(75 mL) honey
3 tbsp	(45 mL) water
	juice of 1 lemon
¼ tsp	(1 mL) cinnamon
3	egg whites, beaten

■ Peel, core and cut apples into pieces.

■ In a saucepan, cook apples with honey and water until mixture thickens to a compote. Cool.

■ Add lemon juice and cinnamon. Stir.

■ In a bowl, beat egg whites until stiff peaks form, and fold into apple compote.

■ Pour into serving cups. Garnish with maraschino cherries.

Bavarian Fruit Mousses

4 servings	
3 oz	(85 g) commercial flavored jelly powder of your choice
1 cup	(250 mL) boiling water
1 cup	(250 mL) milk
¼ cup	(60 mL) whipped cream

Garnishes

fresh fruits, maraschino cherries, chocolate scrapings or chips, nut slivers.

■ Boil the water in a saucepan and dissolve the jelly powder. Cool.

■ Add the milk and stir.

■ Pour the mixture into four dessert cups and refrigerate until the jelly is thoroughly set.

■ Garnish with whipped cream and a choice of fresh fruits, maraschino cherries, chocolate chips or scrapings, or slivered nuts.

WITH GRAPES

• Use Burgundy grape jelly powder. Garnish with red grapes and nuts.

WITH ORANGE

• Use orange jelly powder, and garnish with orange segments, maraschino cherries, and chocolate chips or scrapings.

WITH BANANA

• Use banana jelly powder and garnish with banana slices.

Chocolate Mousse

Chocolate lovers can't resist this treat!

4 to 6 servings

3	egg yolks
½ cup	(125 mL) sugar
8 oz	(225 g) semi-sweet chocolate squares
1 cup	(250 mL) 35% cream
6	egg whites

■ In mixer bowl, beat egg whites and ¼ cup (60 mL) sugar until foamy.

■ In top of double-boiler, at low heat, melt chocolate.

■ Gradually add melted chocolate to egg mixture; beat constantly; let stand.

■ In a bowl, whip cream with ¼ cup (60 mL) sugar until mixture is firm.

■ In a separate bowl, beat egg whites until stiff peaks form.

■ Set aside a portion of whipped cream.

■ With a spatula, fold rest of whipped cream into egg and chocolate mixture; add stiffenened egg whites.

■ Gently pour chocolate mousse into a deep serving dish or into individual cups.

■ Put remaining whipped cream into pastry bag with fluted nozzle attachment; decorate chocolate mousse with whipped cream; sprinkle chocolate curls over cream; refrigerate 4 hours.

Mousse-filled Oranges

Decorate each mousse with slender strips of blanched orange peel.

4 servings

4	oranges
1 tbsp	(15 mL) lemon juice
¼ tsp	(1 mL) vanilla extract
½ cup	(125 mL) sugar
½ cup	(125 mL) 35% cream
2	egg whites
3 tbsp	(45 mL) sugar

■ Slice tops from oranges and scoop out flesh with a spoon without breaking skin.

■ In blender, purée orange pulp.

■ In a stove-top casserole, combine orange pulp, lemon juice, vanilla extract and sugar; boil and stir until mixture thickens to the consistency of jam; cool.

■ In a bowl, whip cream until firm.

■ In a separate bowl, beat egg whites and sugar into stiff peaks.

■ With a spatula, fold whipped cream into orange mixture; add beaten egg whites.

■ Fill orange shells with orange mousse; decorate with blanched, julienned orange peel. Keep the shells from tipping by propping them up with arranged orange slices or some other device.

FRUITS

Pineapple Delight

Replace the maraschino cherries with segments of mandarin or another fruit.

4 servings

1 cup	(250 mL) water
1/4 cup	(60 mL) sugar
2 tbsp	(30 mL) cornstarch
1 cup	(250 mL) pineapple, crushed
1 tsp	(5 mL) lemon juice
	maraschino cherries

■ In a saucepan, heat water.

■ In a bowl, combine sugar and cornstarch; gradually add water; stir.

■ Add pineapple pulp and lemon juice; cook until mixture becomes smooth and creamy.

■ Remove from heat; refrigerate.

■ Pour into dessert cups; garnish with maraschino cherries. Serve with biscuits.

This brightly-colored dessert will be a hit at a party or picnic.

8 servings

Dough

1/4 cup	(60 mL) margarine
1/4 cup	(60 mL) sugar
2	eggs, unbeaten
1 cup	(250 mL) flour
2 tsp	(10 mL) baking powder
2 tsp	(10 mL) almond extract

Garnish

12 oz	(341 mL) pineapple
12 oz	(341 mL) sliced peaches
12 oz	(341 mL) sliced pears
	maraschino cherries

Icing

1 cup	(250 mL) orange juice
1 cup	(250 mL) sugar
3 tbsp	(45 mL) cornstarch

■ Preheat oven to 350 °F (175 °C).

■ Butter a 13-inch (34-cm) pizza pan.

■ In a bowl, using a fork, blend all dough ingredients.

■ Spread dough evenly by hand in pizza pan.

■ Bake 15 to 20 minutes, remove from oven, and let stand to cool.

Garnish

■ Place fruit on cooked pizza dough, beginning in the middle with pineapple, followed by peach slices, then pear slices. Top with cherries and set aside.

Icing

■ In a saucepan, heat orange juice and sugar.

■ In a bowl, dissolve cornstarch in 1 tbsp (15 mL) orange juice.

■ Add dissolved cornstarch and simmer a few minutes. Pour hot liquid over fruit.

■ Refrigerate a few hours before serving.

* *Illustrated recipe*

VARIATION

• **Vary fruit combinations: pears and strawberries or raspberries, for example, or pears, strawberries and kiwi.**

482

Chocolate Delights

Sweet treats and sur-prises that children love.

4 servings

8 oz	(225 g) semi-sweet chocolate
2 tsp	(10 mL) honey
2	bananas
5	large marshmallows
12	maraschino cherries, with stems

■ In a double-boiler, melt the chocolate and honey. Peel the bananas and cut them into four sections each.

■ Dip the banana sections and marshmallows half-way up in the chocolate. Set them on a piece of waxed paper to cool for 5 minutes.

■ Dip the cherries in the chocolate.

■ Serve them as they are, or with a cinnamon sauce.

Broiled Grapefruit with Honey

Since Vitamin C helps the body absorb iron, serve this dessert after a meal rich in this min-eral. Replace the honey with maple syrup.

4 servings

2	grapefruit
¼ cup	(60 mL) liquid honey
2 tsp	(10 mL) icing sugar

■ Heat the broiler.

■ Halve the grapefruit and loosen each segment from the white fiber with a small knife.

■ Pour the honey on top of the four halves, and sprinkle with icing sugar.

■ Broil for 4 minutes, and serve with other fruit garnish.

Strawberry Crêpes

You can use other fruit in these crêpes. Just let your imagination go to work …

6 to 8 servings

Garnish

1 ½ cups	(375 mL)	strawberries, sliced
¼ cup	(60 mL)	maple syrup

Crêpe Batter

1 cup	(250 mL)	all-purpose flour
1 tsp	(5 mL)	baking powder
½ tsp	(2 mL)	salt
1 cup	(250 mL)	milk
2 tbsp	(30 mL)	melted butter
2		eggs

■ Put the strawberries in a bowl and pour maple syrup over them. Soak for a few hours.

■ In a separate bowl, sift flour, baking powder and salt. Gradually pour in the milk and stir with a whisk until the batter is smooth.

■ Pour the batter through a sieve to get rid of the lumps. Add butter, then eggs, one by one, beating after each addition.

■ Heat a crêpe pan. Coat it lightly with butter and pour in a small amount of batter. Spread it evenly over the whole pan and cook on both sides until golden. Repeat this step until you have 6 or 8 crêpes. Keep warm in a heated serving dish.

■ Drain the strawberries and reserve the syrup.

■ Divide the strawberries among the crêpes and roll the crêpes. Arrange the rolls in a serving dish and pour the syrup over them. Garnish with whole strawberries.

Puff Shells with Strawberries and Cream

Pick your own strawberries in the garden or on a strawberry farm, and freeze them. You'll be able to offer your guests a summer treat in the depths of winter.

24 puff shells

1 cup	(250 mL)	water
½ cup	(125 mL)	butter or margarine
1 cup	(250 mL)	all-purpose flour
4		eggs
1 ½ cups	(375 mL)	fresh strawberries, cut in half
½ cup	(125 mL)	35% cream, whipped
3 tbsp	(45 mL)	icing sugar

■ Preheat oven to 325 °F (160 °C).

■ Bring water and butter to a boil, then reduce heat to low and add flour, stirring gently for 1 minute until the batter forms a ball. Remove from heat.

■ Add eggs, one by one, beating each time until the mixture softens.

■ On an ungreased cookie sheet, drop large spoonfuls of batter measuring ¼ cup (60 mL), keeping them 3 inches (7 cm) apart.

■ Bake 35 to 40 minutes or until puff shells are golden. Cool, keeping the shells out of drafts.

■ Cut the top off each shell and scoop out the center. Just before serving, stir half the strawberries into the whipped cream, and stuff the shells. Put back the tops, sprinkle with icing sugar, and garnish with the remaining strawberries.

Peach Melba

The great chef Escoffier created Peach Melba in honor of the famous Australian opera star, Nellie Melba.

4 servings

4	canned peach halves
	peach juice
1	cinnamon stick
1 cup	(250 mL) frozen raspberries, thawed, drained
¼ cup	(60 mL) Triple Sec or orange liqueur
1 cup	(250 mL) vanilla ice cream

■ Drain peaches and reserve juice.

■ In a saucepan, bring peach juice and cinnamon to a boil, then simmer 10 minutes.

■ Pour liquid over peach halves and cool.

■ In a blender, purée raspberries. Add Triple Sec or orange liqueur and refrigerate.

■ Place peach halves in dessert cups, garnish with a scoop of ice cream and coat with sauce.

VARIATION

• **Garnish with sweetened whipped cream.**

Fruit Salad

Chopped, unpeeled Granny Smith and Red Delicious apples will give this fruit salad added color.

4 servings

1 or 2	oranges
½ cup	(125 mL) water
¼ cup	(60 mL) sugar
1 or 2	apples
2	pears
2	bananas
	grapes
	cherries

■ Peel the oranges and remove the white membrane. Keep the peel.

■ In a saucepan, boil water, orange peel and sugar for 5 minutes.

■ In a large bowl, combine all fruit, whole or in pieces, and pour the syrup over it. Refrigerate for 2 hours.

Baked Apples

Perhaps you haven't had time to prepare dessert, or simply forgot ... This cheap and easy dessert will save the day.

4 servings

4	apples
½ cup	(125 mL) brown sugar
1 tsp	(5 mL) cinnamon
3 tbsp	(45 mL) butter
4	bread chunks, 2 x 2 x ½-in (5 x 5 x 1 cm)
	sugared water

■ Preheat oven to 350 °F (175 °C).

■ Butter a cookie sheet.

■ Wash apples and scoop out the center without piercing the peel.

■ Make a thin 2-in (5 cm) slit on the side of the apple to avoid bursting during baking process.

■ Fill apples with brown sugar, cinnamon and a little butter.

■ Place bread squares on a buttered cookie sheet with an apple on each, and baste with sugared water.

■ Bake 30 to 50 minutes, depending on size of apples. Baste with sugared water from time to time so that the bread doesn't stick to the pan.

■ Serve with caramel sauce.

Pear Daisy au Gratin

Pour a luscious raspberry coulis over this dessert, or serve it on the side in a sauceboat.

6 servings

6	fresh pears
4 cups	(1 L) water
¾ cup	(180 mL) sugar
¼ tsp	(1 mL) vanilla extract
2 tsp	(10 mL) lemon juice
½ cup	(125 mL) frozen raspberries
3 tbsp	(45 mL) sugar
3	egg yolks
2 tbsp	(30 mL) water or white wine
3 tbsp	(45 mL) sugar

■ Peel pears, slice in half and scoop out pulp.

■ In a saucepan, boil water, sugar, vanilla extract, and lemon juice for 5 minutes.

■ Add pears and cook over medium heat for 10 minutes.

■ In a separate saucepan, boil raspberries and sugar for 1 minute. Cool slightly then purée in the blender. Pass through a sieve and set aside.

■ Slice pear halves in 3 segments and arrange in a daisy shape in oven-proof dessert bowls.

■ In a double-boiler, beat egg yolks vigorously with sugar and water or wine. Stir over heat until the sauce is thick and foamy.

■ Coat each daisy with mixture and broil until slightly golden. Serve with a garnish of raspberry coulis.

* Illustrated recipe

Cantaloup Fruit Medley

Peanut Butter Banana Split

Replace the cantaloup with a honeydew melon.

4 servings

1	kiwi, sliced
¼ cup	(60 mL) blueberries
1	banana, sliced
1	orange, cut into segments
1 tbsp	(15 mL) lemon juice
2 tbsp	(30 mL) orange juice
1	cantaloup
1 cup	(250 mL) frozen raspberries, sweetened
	15 % cream
	crushed ice

■ In a bowl, combine kiwi, blueberries, banana, orange, lemon juice, and orange juice. Soak for 2 hours.

■ Cut top off cantaloup; spoon out seeds and scoop out pulp.

■ In a blender, purée pulp and raspberries and stir in cream.

■ Pour fruit salad into the cantaloup shell, followed by the purée.

■ Arrange on a bed of crushed ice.

Try a chocolate sauce or a fruit coulis instead of the peanut butter sauce given here.

4 servings

½ cup	(125 mL) brown sugar
⅓ cup	(80 mL) milk
¼ cup	(60 mL) honey
1 tbsp	(15 mL) butter
⅓ cup	(80 mL) peanut butter
2	bananas, sliced lengthwise
2 tbsp	(30 mL) chopped nuts

■ In a saucepan, at medium heat, combine brown sugar, milk, honey and butter. Stir to melt butter and dissolve brown sugar.

■ Remove from heat and add peanut butter. Beat with mixer until smooth and creamy. Cool.

■ Place a banana half in a dessert cup, top it with a scoop of ice cream and the sauce, sprinkle with nuts and serve.

Snacks

Blueberry Bran Muffins

Toss the blueberries in flour and they'll spread evenly through the dough.

12 large muffins

1 cup	(250 mL) plain yogurt
1 tsp	(5 mL) baking soda
1 cup	(250 mL) all-purpose flour
2 tsp	(10 mL) baking powder
½ tsp	(2 mL) salt
¾ cup	(180 mL) brown sugar
1	egg
½ cup	(125 mL) oil
1 tsp	(5 mL) vanilla extract
1 cup	(250 mL) blueberries, dredged in flour
1 cup	(250 mL) bran flakes

- Preheat oven to 350 °F (175 °F).
- Butter muffin pan.
- In a first bowl, mix yogurt and baking soda.
- In a second bowl, sift flour, baking powder and salt.
- In a third bowl, mix brown sugar, egg and oil. Add this to dry ingredients in small amounts, alternating with yogurt.
- Add vanilla extract, blueberries and bran flakes. Stir. Pour into muffin pan and bake for 35 minutes.

Surprise Muffins

Garnish muffins with a spoonful of jam.

12 muffins

1 ¾ cups	(430 mL) all-purpose flour
½ cup	(125 mL) sugar
1 tsp	(5 mL) baking powder
½ tsp	(2 mL) salt
1 tsp	(5 mL) grated lemon peel
2	eggs
⅔ cup	(160 mL) milk
⅓ cup	(80 mL) melted butter
⅔ cup	(160 mL) jam

- Preheat oven to 400 °F (205 °C).
- Butter a muffin pan.
- In a bowl, sift flour, sugar, baking powder, and salt. Add lemon peel, eggs, milk, and butter. Stir.
- Fill muffin pan (1 tbsp or 15 mL per cup) with a first layer of batter, top with 1 tsp (5 mL) jam, and cover with a further 1 tbsp (15 mL) of batter. Bake 12 to 15 minutes.

VARIATIONS

- **Add grated coconut, chopped nuts or raisins.**
- **Replace jam with your favorite jelly.**

* Illustrated recipe:
Top: Surprise Muffins
Bottom: Blueberry Bran Muffins

Nut Squares

Nuts are an excellent source of carbohydrates.

25 squares

1 cup	(250 mL) all-purpose flour
2 tbsp	(30 mL) icing sugar
½ cup	(125 mL) butter or margarine

Garnish

2	eggs
1 cup	(250 mL) brown sugar
1 tsp	(30 mL) all-purpose flour
1 tsp	(5 mL) baking powder
⅛ tsp	(0,5 mL) salt
1 tsp	(5 mL) vanilla extract
1 cup	(250 mL) chopped nuts
1 cup	(250 mL) grated coconut

■ Preheat oven to 325 °F (160 °C).

■ In a bowl, combine flour and icing sugar.

■ Cream in the butter until mixture becomes light and granulated.

■ Press shortbread mixture into a square 8-inch (20 cm) unbuttered baking pan and bake 20 minutes.

Garnish

■ In a bowl, beat eggs until foamy. Add brown sugar.

■ In a separate bowl, combine flour, baking powder, and salt. Add to the sugar mixture.

■ Add vanilla extract, chopped nuts and grated coconut.

■ Spread mixture over the shortbread and return to the oven for 30 to 35 minutes.

■ Cool completely before slicing.

Date Squares

Here is a variation of the traditional date squares. If you wish, sprinkle the bottom of the baking pan with oatmeal.

25 squares

1 cup	(250 mL) chopped dates
½ cup	(125 mL) water
½ cup	(125 mL) brown sugar
6 tbsp	(90 mL) butter
½ cup	(125 mL) sugar
2	egg yolks
1 tsp	(5 mL) vanilla extract
1 ½ cups	(375 mL) all-purpose flour, sifted
1 tsp	(5 mL) baking powder
2	egg whites
1 cup	(250 mL) brown sugar

■ Preheat oven to 350 °F (175 °C).

■ Butter a square 8-inch (20 cm) baking pan.

■ In a saucepan, boil dates with water and brown sugar until mixture thickens. Remove from heat and cool.

■ In a bowl, combine butter, sugar, and egg yolks. Add vanilla extract, then dry ingredients.

■ Pour batter into mold and top with dates.

■ In a separate bowl, beat egg whites into stiff peaks, add brown sugar and stir.

■ Pour egg whites over dates and bake 45 minutes. Cut into squares.

Cookies

Raspberry Jelly Cookies

Chocolate cookies with a delicious raspberry jelly filling are energy-raisers for healthy youngsters.

36 cookies

¼ cup	(60 mL) margarine
¾ cup	(180 mL) brown sugar
1	egg
⅓ cup	(80 mL) melted butter
1 tsp	(5 mL) vanilla extract
1 ½ cups	(375 mL) flour
½ tsp	(2 mL) baking soda
¼ tsp	(1 mL) salt
½ tsp	(2 mL) cream of tartar
	raspberry jelly

■ Preheat oven to 375 °F (190 °C).

■ In a bowl, combine margarine, brown sugar, egg, melted butter, and vanilla extract. Stir well.

■ In a separate bowl, stir all dry ingredients. Add to first mixture.

■ Shape into small pastry balls and place on ungreased cookie sheet. Bake 10 to 15 minutes. Cool, then join two cookies with raspberry jelly.

A different kind of brownie with a smooth butter-icing filling. To sour the milk, add 1 tsp (5 mL) white vinegar.

18 brownies

½ cup	(125 mL) shortening
1 cup	(250 mL) sugar
2	eggs
2 cups	(500 mL) all-purpose flour
2 tsp	(10 mL) baking powder
½ tsp	(2 mL) salt
½ tsp	(2 mL) baking soda
½ cup	(125 mL) cocoa
1 cup	(250 mL) sour milk
1 tsp	(5 mL) vanilla extract

■ Preheat oven to 350 °F (175 °C).

■ Butter cookie sheet.

■ In a bowl, cream butter and sugar.

■ Add eggs, one by one, stirring after each addition.

■ Mix dry ingredients and add them to the batter, alternating with milk and vanilla extract.

■ Spoon mixture onto cookie sheet. Bake 12 to 15 minutes.

Icing

■ Mix ½ cup (125 mL) butter, 2 cups (500 mL) icing sugar, 2 egg whites, 1 tsp (5 mL) vanilla extract.

* Illustrated recipe

Butter Thins

You can shape these melt-in-the-mouth cookies to suit the occasion, with leaves for summer picnics, hearts for St. Valentine's, fir trees for Christmas, and so on.

48 cookies

1 tsp	(5 mL)	baking soda
4 tsp	(20 mL)	hot water
1 cup	(250 mL)	butter
1 cup	(250 mL)	brown sugar
1		egg, beaten
3 cups	(750 mL)	all-purpose flour
		pinch of salt
1/2 tsp	(2 mL)	vanilla extract

Fudge Icing

1 cup	(250 mL)	brown sugar
1/4 cup	(60 mL)	butter
1/4 cup	(60 mL)	condensed milk
		icing sugar

■ Preheat oven to 375 °F (190 °C).

■ Dissolve baking soda in water.

■ In a bowl, cream butter and add brown sugar, egg, and dissolved soda. Stir.

■ One by one, add flour, salt, and vanilla extract and refrigerate at least 1 hour.

■ Roll dough into thin layer and cut with leaf-shaped cookie cutter.

■ Place on cookie sheet. Bake 8 minutes.

■ Meanwhile, in a saucepan, boil brown sugar, butter, and milk for 2 minutes.

■ Add icing sugar until mixture is creamy.

■ Make sandwich biscuits with fudge icing.

Carrot Cookies

Ice the cookies with a mixture of orange juice, icing sugar and a little butter.

36 cookies

1/2 cup	(125 mL)	butter
1/2 cup	(125 mL)	sugar
1		egg, beaten
1 cup	(250 mL)	carrot purée
1 tsp	(5 mL)	vanilla extract
1 cup	(250 mL)	brown sugar
2 cups	(500 mL)	all-purpose flour
1 1/2 tsp	(7 mL)	baking soda
1/2 tsp	(2 mL)	salt
3/4 cup	(180 mL)	raisins

■ Preheat oven to 350 °F (175 °C).

■ Butter a cookie sheet.

■ In a bowl, cream butter and add egg, carrot purée, and vanilla extract. Stir.

■ In separate bowl, sift all dry ingredients. Add to first mixture and stir until smooth.

■ Add raisins.

■ Spoon batter onto cookie sheet and bake 15 minutes.

Molasses Cookies

Prepare dough the night before and put it in the refrigerator. It rolls more easily, and can be cut with a cookie-cutter without sticking.

48 cookies

2 ½ cups	(625 mL) all-purpose flour
1 ½ tsp	(7 mL) baking soda
¼ cup	(60 mL) butter
1 tbsp	(15 mL) shortening
½ cup	(125 mL) brown sugar
1	egg
½ cup	(125 mL) molasses
¼ cup	(60 mL) water
	sugar

■ Preheat oven to 250 °F (120 °C).

■ Butter a cookie sheet.

■ In a bowl, sift dry ingredients and set aside.

■ In a separate bowl, cream butter, shortening, brown sugar, and eggs. Add molasses, water, and dry ingredients.

■ Spoon batter onto cookie sheet, dust with sugar and bake 15 minutes.

Raisin Cookies

These Christmas stand-bys are a good bet all year long.

36 cookies

½ tsp	(2 mL) baking soda
2 tbsp	(30 mL) milk
1 cup	(250 mL) brown sugar
1	egg
½ cup	(125 mL) butter
1 cup	(250 mL) raisins
1 ¾ cups	(430 mL) all-purpose flour

■ Preheat oven to 350 °F (175 °C).

■ Butter a cookie sheet.

■ Dissolve baking soda in milk and set aside.

■ In a bowl, combine brown sugar, egg and butter.

■ Add raisins and dissolved baking soda. Stir.

■ Add flour until mixture thickens into firm batter.

■ Spoon batter onto cookie sheet and bake for about 5 minutes.

Oatmeal and Raisin Cookies

Always keep wheat germ in the refrigerator.

48 cookies

1 cup	(250 mL) all-purpose flour or whole wheat flour
1 tsp	(5 mL) baking soda
½ tsp	(2 mL) salt
2 cups	(500 mL) rolled oats
¼ cup	(60 mL) wheat germ
¾ cup	(180 mL) butter
1½ cups	(375 mL) brown sugar
2	eggs
1 tsp	(5 mL) vanilla extract
¾ cup	(180 mL) grated coconut
¾ cup	(180 mL) raisins

- Preheat oven to 350 °F (175 °C).

- Lightly butter cookie sheets.

- In a bowl, combine flour, baking soda, salt, rolled oats, and wheat germ. Set aside.

- In a separate bowl, cream butter and add brown sugar, eggs, and vanilla extract.

- Add to first mixture and stir well.

- Add coconut and raisins.

- Spoon mixture onto cookie sheets and bake 12 to 15 minutes or until lightly golden.

VARIATION

- **Replace raisins with chocolate chips; add ½ cup (125 mL) chopped nuts.**

Refrigerator Cookies

Keep this cookie dough in the refrigerator. Ten minutes in the oven, and you have a plate of fresh cookies!

36 cookies

¾ cup	(180 mL) butter
½ cup	(125 mL) sugar
½ cup	(125 mL) brown sugar
2	eggs
¼ cup	(60 mL) corn syrup
1 tbsp	(15 mL) vanilla extract
2 cups	(500 mL) pastry flour
½ tsp	(2 mL) baking soda
½ tsp	(2 mL) baking powder
½ cup	(125 mL) candied fruit
½ cup	(125 mL) chopped nuts

- Preheat oven to 375 °F (190 °C).

- Cream butter. Add sugar, brown sugar, eggs, corn syrup, and vanilla extract. Stir until foamy, and set aside.

- In a separate bowl, combine dry ingredients and add them to the first mixture.

- Divide cookie dough in half. Add candied fruit to the first half, and chopped nuts to the second.

- Shape into 2-inch (5-cm) thick rolls. Wrap in plastic wrap and refrigerate.

- When needed, slice the rolls, put the cookie rounds on a buttered cookie sheet, and bake 8 to 10 minutes.

Sweet treats

Marshmallow Candies

These are a great hit at children's parties.

48 candies

24	large marshmallows, quartered
1 tbsp	(15 mL) 15% cream
½ cup	(125 mL) chopped nuts
½ cup	(125 mL) chopped dates
24	cherries, cut into pieces
1 cup	(250 mL) grated coconut

■ In top of double-boiler, melt marshmallows in cream.

■ Stir in the other ingredients, omitting coconut.

■ Refrigerate 1 hour.

■ Shape into small balls and roll in grated coconut. Keep in refrigerator.

Chocolatines—chocolates amandine—are the answer to a sweet tooth's prayer.

8 servings

½ cup	(125 mL) butter
½ cup	(125 mL) brown sugar, lightly packed
½ tsp	(2 mL) almond extract
1	egg yolk
½ cup	(125 mL) all-purpose flour
½ cup	(125 mL) rolled oats
1 cup	(250 mL) chocolate chips
¼ cup	(60 mL) toasted almonds, finely chopped
¼ cup	(60 mL) crushed nuts

■ Preheat oven to 350 °F (175 °C).

■ Butter an 8-inch (20-cm) square cake pan.

■ Cream butter and stir in brown sugar, almond extract and egg yolk.

■ Add flour and rolled oats.

■ Spread batter evenly in the pan and bake 25 minutes.

■ In top of double-boiler, melt chocolate chips and pour over cake. Sprinkle with chopped nuts.

■ Cool until chocolate hardens. Slice.

* Illustrated recipe

494

Rum Balls

If you've no time to grate the chocolate, use commercial chocolate sprinkles.

12 balls

5 oz	(142 mL) condensed milk
¼ cup	(60 mL) butter
¼ cup	(60 mL) grated coconut
¼ cup	(60 mL) cocoa
2 tbsp	(30 mL) sugar
15 to 20	digestive biscuits, crumbled
1 tsp	(5 mL) rum extract
1 cup	(250 mL) grated chocolate

■ In a saucepan, heat milk, add butter and stir.

■ Stir in grated coconut, cocoa, and sugar.

■ Add crumbled biscuits and stir until mixture thickens.

■ Stir in rum extract.

■ Refrigerate 1 hour.

■ Shape into small balls and roll in grated chocolate.

Caramel Fudge

This modern, quicker version of an old-fashioned American candy has lost none of its smoothness.

25 squares

1 cup	(250 mL) brown sugar
1 cup	(250 mL) sugar
1 cup	(250 mL) 35% cream
1 tsp	(5 mL) vanilla extract
1 tbsp	(15 mL) butter
½ cup	(125 mL) chopped nuts (optional)

■ In a deep microwave dish, combine brown sugar, sugar and cream. Cook at HIGH for 11 minutes.

■ Stir twice during cooking.

■ Add vanilla extract and butter, and beat until mixture thickens. Add nuts and spread mixture in buttered pan. Cut into squares and cool.

■ For creamier fudge, add 4 or 5 large marshmallows before beating.

Mocha Fudge

Marshmallows give candies a smooth consistency. You can also use 1 ½ cups (375 mL) commercial marshmallow sauce.

25 treats	
2 tbsp	(30 mL) butter
⅔ cup	(160 mL) evaporated milk
1 ⅔ cups	(410 mL) sugar
1 tbsp	(15 mL) instant coffee
2 cups	(500 mL) miniature marshmallows
5 ½ oz	(175 g) semi-sweet chocolate chips
1 tsp	(5 mL) vanilla extract
½ cup	(125 mL) chopped nuts

■ In a saucepan, combine butter, milk, sugar, and instant coffee. Bring to a boil over medium heat, stirring constantly. Continue to stir and boil 4 to 5 minutes.

■ Remove from heat and add marshmallows, chocolate chips, vanilla extract, and nuts. Stir vigorously 1 minute.

■ Pour into an 8-inch (20 cm) buttered square mold. Cool and keep in refrigerator.

■ Cut with a pastry cutter.

Coconut Cherries

These coated cherries contrast beautifully with a vanilla icing.

40 treats	
½ cup	(125 mL) soft butter
1 ½ cups	(375 mL) icing sugar
1 tsp	(5 mL) vanilla extract
1 tbsp	(15 mL) 35% cream
1 ½ cups	(375 mL) grated coconut
40	maraschino cherries, drained
1 cup	(250 mL) graham cracker crumbs

■ Mix together first 5 ingredients.

■ Roll cherries in mixture then roll in graham cracker crumbs.

■ Refrigerate in airtight container.

Date Pinwheels

If you have time, let the dough chill for 24 hours before rolling it.

24 cookies

Garnish

1 ⅓ cups	(330 mL) dates, cut into small pieces
⅔ cup	(160 mL) sugar
⅔ cup	(160 mL) water
1 tsp	(5 mL) vanilla extract

Pastry dough

1 ½ cups	(375 mL) brown sugar
⅔ cup	(160 mL) shortening
2	eggs, lightly beaten
2 ½ cups	(625 mL) all-purpose flour
¼ tsp	(1 mL) baking soda

- Preheat oven to 350 °F (175 °C).

- Cook dates with sugar and water.

- Add vanilla extract, stir and cool.

- Meanwhile, sift the dry pastry ingredients.

- Cut the shortening into small pieces and blend into the dry ingredients. Knead the dough gently, then stir in the eggs. Let the dough stand for 30 minutes.

- Roll out dough to ½-inch (1,25 cm) thickness.

- Bake on buttered cookie sheet for about 10 minutes.

Date and Cherry Bites

Use red and green candied cherries for a pleasant contrast.

24 bites

1 cup	(250 mL) almonds, slivered
½ cup	(125 mL) butter
1 ½ cups	(375 mL) dates, cut into small pieces
¾ cup	(180 mL) sugar
⅓ cup	(80 mL) candied cherries, cut up
½ cup	(125 mL) nuts, chopped
3 cups	(750 mL) corn flakes

- Grill almonds in oven and set aside.

- Melt butter in a saucepan over low heat. Add dates, sugar and cherries and stir until a soft paste forms.

- Stir in nuts and corn flakes.

- Shape into small balls, cool, and roll in the grilled almonds.

497

COULIS AND SAUCES

Pineapple Coulis

about 2 ¹/₂ cups (625 mL)

2 tbsp	(30 mL)	cornstarch
¹/₂ cup	(125 mL)	water
¹/₄ cup	(60 mL)	sugar
2 cups	(500 mL)	pineapple

■ Blend cornstarch with a little water and set aside.

■ In a saucepan, boil the water, sugar and pineapple for about 5 minutes.

■ Add the cornstarch and boil for 1 minute.

■ Run through the blender, then a sieve, to get a smoother coulis.

Blueberry Coulis

about 2 ¹/₂ cups (625 mL)

2 tbsp	(30 mL)	cornstarch
¹/₂ cup	(125 mL)	water
¹/₄ cup	(60 mL)	sugar
2 cups	(500 mL)	blueberries

■ Blend cornstarch with a little water and set aside.

■ In a saucepan, boil the water, sugar and blueberries for about 5 minutes.

■ Add the cornstarch and boil for 1 minute.

■ Run through the blender, then a sieve, to get a smoother coulis.

Apricot Coulis

about 2 ¹/₂ cups (625 mL)

2 tbsp	(30 mL)	cornstarch
¹/₂ cup	(125 mL)	water
¹/₄ cup	(60 mL)	sugar
2 cups	(500 mL)	apricots

■ Blend cornstarch with a little water and set aside.

■ In a saucepan, boil the water, sugar and apricots for about 5 minutes.

■ Add the cornstarch and boil for 1 minute.

■ Run through the blender, then a sieve, to get a smoother coulis.

Raspberry Coulis

about 2 ¹/₂ cups (625 mL)

2 tbsp	(30 mL)	cornstarch
¹/₂ cup	(125 mL)	water
¹/₄ cup	(60 mL)	sugar
2 cups	(500 mL)	raspberries

■ Blend cornstarch with a little water and set aside.

■ In a saucepan, boil the water, sugar and raspberries for about 5 minutes.

■ Add the cornstarch and boil for 1 minute.

■ Run through the blender, then a sieve, to get a smoother coulis.

Kiwi Coulis

about 2 ½ cups (625 mL)

2 tbsp	(30 mL)	cornstarch
½ cup	(125 mL)	water
¼ cup	(60 mL)	sugar
2 cups	(500 mL)	kiwis

■ Blend cornstarch with a little water and set aside.

■ In a saucepan, boil the water, sugar and kiwis for about 5 minutes.

■ Add the cornstarch and boil for 1 minute.

■ Run through the blender, then a sieve, to get a smoother coulis.

Pear Coulis

about 2 ½ cups (625 mL)

2 tbsp	(30 mL)	cornstarch
½ cup	(125 mL)	water
¼ cup	(60 mL)	sugar
2 cups	(500 mL)	pears

■ Blend cornstarch with a little water and set aside.

■ In a saucepan, boil the water, sugar and pears for about 5 minutes.

■ Add the cornstarch and boil for 1 minute.

■ Run through the blender, then a sieve, to get a smoother coulis.

Strawberry Coulis

about 2 ½ cups (625 mL)

2 tbsp	(30 mL)	cornstarch
½ cup	(125 mL)	water
¼ cup	(60 mL)	sugar
2 cups	(500 mL)	strawberries

■ Blend cornstarch with a little water and set aside.

■ In a saucepan, boil the water, sugar and strawberries for about 5 minutes.

■ Add the cornstarch and boil for 1 minute.

■ Run through the blender, then a sieve, to get a smoother coulis.

Peach Coulis

about 2 ½ cups (625 mL)

2 tbsp	(30 mL)	cornstarch
½ cup	(125 mL)	water
¼ cup	(60 mL)	sugar
2 cups	(500 mL)	peaches

■ Blend cornstarch with a little water and set aside.

■ In a saucepan, boil the water, sugar and peaches for about 5 minutes.

■ Add the cornstarch and boil for 1 minute.

■ Run through the blender, then a sieve, to get a smoother coulis.

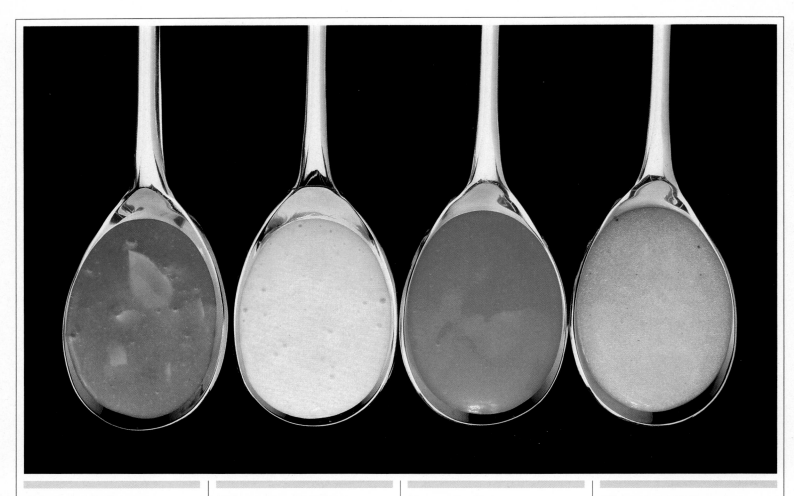

Almond Sauce

	about 2 cups (500 mL)
1	package of caramel pudding and pie filling
½ cup	(125 mL) sugar
1 cup	(250 mL) water
2 tbsp	(30 mL) butter
2 tbsp	(30 mL) toasted almonds

■ In a saucepan, combine pudding mix, sugar, and water. Bring to boil at low heat, stirring constantly.

■ Remove from heat. Add butter and almonds, and stir.

Cinnamon Sauce

	about 3 cups (750 mL)
3 cups	(750 mL) sugar
⅓ cup	(80 mL) condensed milk
1 tbsp	(15 mL) corn syrup
3 tbsp	(45 g) butter
1 tbsp	(15 mL) cinnamon

■ In a saucepan, at low heat, simmer sugar, milk and corn syrup until sugar has melted.

■ Remove from heat. Add butter and cinnamon and stir.

Peach Sauce

	about 2 cups (500 mL)
14 oz	(398 mL) canned peaches
	cottage cheese, to taste

■ Drain peaches and keep syrup.

■ In blender, purée peaches.

■ Add cottage cheese and reserved syrup and blend until smooth.

Caramel Sauce

	about 4 cups (1 L)
3 cups	(750 mL) brown sugar
1 cup	(250 mL) corn syrup
¼ cup	(60 mL) butter, softened
5 oz	(142 mL) condensed milk

■ In a saucepan combine the first 3 ingredients and boil 3 minutes. Remove from heat, add milk and beat with mixer until smooth.

Chocolate Sauce

about 2 cups (500 mL)

1 cup	(250 mL) sugar
2 tbsp	(30 mL) cocoa
1 tsp	(5 mL) vanilla extract
1 cup	(250 mL) boiling water
¼ cup	(60 mL) butter
¼ cup	(60 mL) 35% cream

■ In a saucepan, combine sugar, cocoa, vanilla extract, and water. Boil 5 minutes.

■ Remove from heat and add butter and cream. Stir until sauce cools.

Coffee Sauce

about 2 cups (500 mL)

2 cups	(500 mL) milk
¼ tsp	(1 mL) vanilla extract
	pinch of salt
6	egg yolks
½ cup	(125 mL) sugar
2 tbsp	(30 mL) instant coffee

■ Follow the recipe for Vanilla Sauce, adding the coffee to the milk mixture.

Rum Sauce

about 2 cups (500 mL)

½ cup	(125 mL) butter
1 cup	(250 mL) sugar
½ cup	(125 mL) 35% cream
1 tsp	(5 mL) vanilla extract
2 tbsp	(30 mL) rum

■ In a saucepan, over low heat, simmer butter, sugar, and cream 8 to 12 minutes.

■ Remove from heat. Add vanilla extract and rum.

Vanilla Sauce

about 3 cups (750 mL)

2 cups	(500 mL) milk
½ tsp	(2 mL) vanilla extract
	pinch of salt
6	egg yolks
¼ cup	(60 mL) sugar

■ In a saucepan, boil milk, vanilla extract, and salt.

■ In a bowl, beat egg yolks with sugar. Keep stirring while pouring boiling milk into mixture.

■ Return mixture to stove. Cook, stirring constantly until creamy.

■ Remove from heat and cool.

ICINGS AND SWEET TRIMMINGS

Cream Cheese Icing

about 2 cups (500 mL)		
½ lb	(225 g)	cream cheese
1 tbsp	(15 mL)	butter
½ cup	(125 mL)	apple-sauce
1 ¼ cups	(310 mL)	icing sugar

■ Soften and stir cream cheese and butter together.

■ Add the applesauce, then gradually blend in the sugar until icing reaches desired thickness.

Jiffy Chocolate Icing

about 2 cups (500 mL)		
¼ cup	(60 mL)	milk
2 tbsp	(30 mL)	cocoa
2 cups	(500 mL)	icing sugar, sifted
½ cup	(125 mL)	milk

■ Heat but do not boil ¼ cup (60 mL) milk, add the cocoa and blend.

■ Stir in the sifted icing sugar, then the rest of the milk.

■ Chill 1 hour in the refrigerator.

Brown Sugar Icing

about 2 cups (500 mL)		
⅓ cup	(80 mL)	butter
1 cup	(250 mL)	brown sugar
¼ cup	(60 mL)	milk
1 cup	(250 mL)	icing sugar, sifted

■ In a saucepan, combine butter, brown sugar, and milk. Boil for 2 minutes.

■ Remove from heat, add icing sugar and stir.

Vanilla Icing

about 2 cups (500 mL)		
3		eggs whites
1 ½ cups	(375 mL)	icing sugar, sifted
¼ tsp	(1 mL)	vanilla extract
2 tbsp	(30 mL)	orange juice

■ Blend and beat all the ingredients until the icing is firm.

■ If the icing isn't firm enough, add 3 tbsp (45 mL) icing sugar.

How to make caramel straws

- Melt ½ cup (125 mL) of sugar and 2 tsp (10 mL) water. Simmer until the liquid turns golden-brown.

- Dip a fork into the caramel.

- Wave the fork back and forth over the saucepan, letting viscous strings form, supported by the sides of the saucepan. These will harden in 2 minutes. Break them off and use them to decorate your favorite desserts.

How to make chocolate curls

- Choose a bar of chocolate with at least one flat surface.

- Use a potato peeler to peel curls of chocolate off the bar.

- The curls will vary in thickness according to the pressure with which you peel them off the chocolate bar.

Whipped cream garnish for cakes or pies

- Beat whipped cream and icing sugar into firm peaks.

- Use a pastry bag with a fluted nozzle.

- Giving a slight twist as you go, pipe rosettes of varying sizes until you have covered the whole cake or pie.

How to draw patterns on a coulis

- Pour the coulis onto a dinner plate or flat soup bowl. Draw a spiral with cream.

- With a toothpick or wooden skewer, work as shown from the outside in, then from the inside out. Alternate until you have created a pattern for the whole spiral.

503

GLOSSARY

Almonds, grilled or toasted: slivered almonds lightly browned in the oven.

Bain-marie: a double-boiler or a small pan of some sort placed in or above a larger pan containing water. Delicate foods are cooked or warmed by the heat of the water.

Baste: spoon or pour a liquid (pan juice, wine, oil, etc.) over meat or other food to prevent it from drying out while cooking.

Beater: a mechanical or electric utensil that performs the same function as the still-popular whisk or wooden spoon: blending a variety of ingredients together to form a smooth liquid of varying thickness.

Blanch: a food is placed in lightly salted, boiling water for a few minutes to tenderize it, remove the bitter taste, or make it easier to remove the skin.

Blend: stir, beat or otherwise combine ingredients to produce a homogenous mixture.

Blender: an electric utensil designed to chop food in liquid, from chunky to smooth, depending on the desired result. Some blenders will chop dry food such as breadcrumbs. (See *food processor*.)

Bouquet garni or herb bouquet: a combination of parsley, thyme, and bay leaf used in flavoring soups, stews, and other dishes. When fresh, the herbs are tied together with string and taken out when the cooking is done. A dried bouquet is wrapped in cheesecloth for easy removal.

Cubed: cut into cubes of about 1 in (2,5 cm) to get chunks (usually of meat) for casseroles and skewer cooking.

Deglaze: a liquid is poured into a pan used for frying meat or vegetables. The liquid absorbs the pan juices and can then be used to make a sauce.

Degreasing: the fat on the surface of a liquid is removed, either by skimming it off, or with a paper towel. This expression also refers to wiping or pouring off the fat from a frying pan before using the pan in a further cooking step.

Diced: cut into cubes or squares of about $1/2$ in (1,25 cm) or smaller. This is usually done with vegetables.

Drain: remove all liquid from a food, and if necessary pat the food dry.

Dredge: cover a food with a dry ingredient such as seasoned flour. This can be done by tossing the food in a bowl or a bag.

Fines herbes: in general, unless otherwise stated, this refers to the standard French mixture of chervil, parsley, tarragon, and chives. Other standbys are thyme and bay leaf, as well as fennel, basil, oregano, sage and saffron. Sometimes certain herbs are sold in a convenient bouquet or sachet, called a *bouquet garni*.

Food processor: a multi-purpose electric utensil with a variety of attachments that can chop or slice vegetables, mix a pie dough, mince meat, and so on.

Gratin: a covering of grated cheese or breadcrumbs that is added before putting certain dishes under the broiler to produce an attractive golden or browned effect.

Green onions: these are young or spring onions, commonly available in food markets. Although sometimes

called shallots or scallions, these terms are more correctly used for other forms of small onions (i.e., bulbs) used in flavoring foods.

Kneaded butter (beurre manié): equal parts of cold butter and flour creamed together and rolled into small balls, which can be conveniently added as a thickening agent in soups and stews.

Lardons: small chunks cut from a piece of pork back fat or a section of lean bacon, used to bring out the flavor in certain dishes, or to supply fat to lean meats in cooking.

Ramekin: a small, oven-proof dish, sometimes called a custard cup, in which individual servings can be cooked.

Reduce: to boil off part of a liquid in order to thicken it and concentrate the flavor.

Sauté: brown a food in oil or butter to seal in the juices. Although used almost interchangeably with *fry*, it implies a gentler heat unless otherwise mentioned.

Shallots: to avoid confusion in varying terminology, we use *shallots* to refer to French (dry) shallots, small dried onions with reddish-brown skins that have a slightly garlic taste, much valued for sauces and flavorings. (See *green onions* for comparison.)

Simmer: keep a liquid at a point just below boiling, so that the surface trembles but doesn't bubble.

Thicken: give a liquid more body by blending in beaten egg or knobs of kneaded butter, stirring constantly to keep it smooth.

INDEX

● : Technique
■ : Microwave Recipe